RECONSTRUCTION IN MISSISSIPPI, 1862-1877

JERE NASH

University Press of Mississippi / Jackson

*Publication of this book was made possible
through a grant from the Phil Hardin Foundation.*

The University Press of Mississippi is the scholarly publishing agency
of the Mississippi Institutions of Higher Learning: Alcorn State University,
Delta State University, Jackson State University, Mississippi State University,
Mississippi University for Women, Mississippi Valley State University,
University of Mississippi, and University of Southern Mississippi.

www.upress.state.ms.us

The University Press of Mississippi is a member of the Association of University Presses.

Publisher: University Press of Mississippi, Jackson, USA
Authorised GPSR Safety Representative: Easy Access System Europe - Mustamäe tee 50,
10621 Tallinn, Estonia, *gpsr.requests@easproject.com*

Library of Congress Control Number: 2025940342

Hardback ISBN 978-1-4968-5853-5
Epub single ISBN 978-1-4968-5852-8
Epub institutional ISBN 978-1-4968-5854-2
PDF single ISBN 978-1-4968-5855-9
PDF institutional ISBN 978-1-4968-5856-6

British Library Cataloging-in-Publication Data available

Grey F. Ferris
1946–2008

W. Charles Sallis
1934–2024

Contents

Preface and Acknowledgments

Since Reconstruction ended 150 years ago, only one fair and comprehensive account of the history of that period in Mississippi has been published, and that was the two-volume, 1039-page narrative by William C. Harris.[1] His last volume appeared in 1979.

While any new account of Reconstruction in our state must certainly start with Harris, the good news for contemporary readers is that the field of Reconstruction history, and the era it encompasses, has exploded since 1979.[2] Historians, economists, political scientists, and other scholars have explored the dozen years following the Civil War from all perspectives and in great depth. This short book is offered to readers as an introduction to that period of time in Mississippi. It benefits from much of the new research over the last forty years, especially the experiences of the 430,000 Black Mississippians whose lives were transformed by the abolition of slavery, the decisions that led to a state economy based almost exclusively on agriculture and growing cotton, and the role of the federal government in shaping the rebuilding of the state following the devastation of the War. The bibliography and endnotes provide a number of sources for those who want to dig deeper into a particular topic.

For example, located at the United States National Archives in Washington are virtually all the records generated by the Freedmen's Bureau throughout its nearly four-year tenure, millions of documents that provide a wonderfully rich and contemporaneous picture of formerly enslaved people experiencing freedom. The most comprehensive analysis of those documents has come from the Freedmen and Southern Society Project. To date, that collection of scholars has published six volumes, totaling more than 5,600 pages, and reproducing about 50,000 documents from the millions they have reviewed, transcribed, organized, and annotated. Reading through the published selections from Mississippi gives one an almost firsthand view of what is perhaps the most pivotal moment in our state's history. The editors of that series wrote in their introduction that "no event in American history matches the drama of emancipation. In the United States, emancipation accompanied the military defeat of the world's most powerful slaveholding class. It freed a larger number of slaves than did the end of slavery in all other New World societies combined."[3] A number of accounts from those collections are included in this narrative history.

Two other sources that proved invaluable were DeeDee Baldwin's website at Mississippi State University, Against All Odds: The First Black Legislators in Mississippi, and Eric Foner's *Freedom's Lawmakers: A Directory of Black Officeholders During Reconstruction*.[4] As a result of their extraordinary research, I was able to identify each of the Black legislators who served during Reconstruction.

Scholars are continuing to mine other archives of the period to explore a variety of relevant topics, including the effectiveness of the Union military occupation, the Freedman's Bureau, and the Southern Homestead Act; the Compromise of 1877; family relationships after the War; agricultural and farming practices; the realization among some Confederates that the War had been lost long before the surrender; and the rise of the Ku Klux Klan. References for those sources are also included in the bibliography.

For the reader, descriptive terms for groups of people that were prevalent during Reconstruction and into the early twentieth century, such as Bourbon, yeoman, Whig, Scalawag, Carpetbagger, Redeemer, and New Departure, are largely avoided. In the end, only three classifications mattered in Mississippi: white Republican, white Democrat, and Black Republican. Those are the ones used in this book. On the other hand, quotations by whites that employ ugly and derogatory terms for Blacks or graphic descriptions of white-on-Black violence are not avoided. Understanding what life was like in Mississippi during this time, especially for African Americans, requires the full picture. Finally, a more recent shift among scholars of the Civil War and Reconstruction era has been to recognize the humanity of Black men, women, and children by using terms other than "slave" or "contraband" to describe their status or terms other than "owner" to describe their relationship. I have adopted that approach in this narrative history, except for direct quotes from others of the time and where the use of a term is critical for historical context.

To the extent readers might want to explore a topic in more detail, the endnotes were used to provide not just one source but oftentimes several sources. Few of the findings and conclusions in this book are unique to me; they represent a consensus of the professionals working in the field today, and the endnotes were the appropriate place to demonstrate that consensus.

Speaking of other authors, that brings us to the acknowledgments. One of the great joys of writing a book of history is reading what others have written about that topic. This book was made possible by the work of many scholars who devoted years to research and writing about Reconstruction and the larger Civil War era. That makes it easy for someone like me to come behind them and deliver to you a relatively short synthesis of the best of that writing as it applies to Mississippi. A full list of all the works I used as references for this book is provided in the Bibliography. There are many worthy of your time.

First to be acknowledged is William Harris and the comprehensive research he compiled for his two books. I drove over to North Carolina several years ago to visit with Dr. Harris to get his take on the field some forty years after his second volume had been published. As we were ending our conversation, I asked for his advice in writing the book you are reading now. He offered two recommendations: say something new and do some original research. The first one was easy, thanks to the vast amount of new literature on Reconstruction. The second one was more difficult, as the existing primary sources of that time—newspapers and magazines, transcribed speeches, manuscript holdings, memoirs, congressional reports, and other government documents—have been thoroughly reviewed and analyzed by many others. It was only after I examined the returns from the 1868 and 1875 elections through the prism of a modern campaign consultant that I realized some fresh research would offer a different verdict of those critical elections.

This volume is one of nine that make up the Heritage of Mississippi Series and that cover the history of the state from a variety of perspectives. It is published jointly by the Mississippi Department of Archives and History, the Mississippi Historical Society, and the University Press of Mississippi, with funding assistance from the Phil Hardin Foundation. The Heritage of Mississippi Series is aimed at a broad audience of teachers, students, historians, and interested general readers. Consequently, I owe enormous gratitude to the Board of Editors of this series, and especially John Marszalek and the late Elbert Hilliard, for their decision to let me write this contribution to that series, and for their endless patience in waiting for me to deliver the manuscript. A big tip of the hat goes to Brother Rogers at the Mississippi Department of Archives and History and Craig Gill, Katie Turner, Shane Gong Stewart, Jennifer Mixon, and Courtney McCreary at the University Press of Mississippi for shepherding my writing and turning a rough manuscript into a published book. It was Shane who connected me with Kerri Jordan, copy editor *extraordinaire*. Thank you, all.

My research has taken me to the Department of Archives and Special Collections of the University of Mississippi Libraries, the Archives and Special Collections and the Ulysses S. Grant Presidential Collection at the Mississippi State University Libraries, the Civil War Interpretative Center in Corinth, and, in Jackson, the Mississippi Library Commission, the State Law Library of Mississippi, and the Mississippi Department of Archives and History. These institutions have extraordinary resources and deeply committed staffs. They were all a pleasure to work with and learn from. A special note of appreciation to Ally Mellon at Archives and History for devoting hours to finding the photographs and other images you will see in this book.

For reading through parts or all of the manuscript and catching mistakes, offering smart edits, and improving my writing, I am very grateful to Chuck Bolton, Tracy Carr, Danny Cupit, Kane Ditto, Michael Morris, Luther Munford, Tim Smith, and Ryan Semmes.

Heartfelt thanks and appreciation go to the twelve men and women who follow. Over the years, at one time or another, they proofed chapters of the manuscript; dug through files at the National Archives or the Library of Congress in Washington; tracked down old books, graduate research papers, or court cases; transcribed handwritten letters from 150 years ago; spent hours in front of microfilm readers looking for a specific newspaper article or government report; searched for some obscure article on the internet; or read through hundreds of pages of government reports from the years after the Civil War looking for just the right piece of information needed to satisfy a paragraph or complete a footnote. Thank you to: Mattie Abraham, Susanna Blount, Nancy Brown, Schuyler Dickson, Jessi McClain, Jana McNair, Tara Pawley, Nicole Roussell, Leslie Scott, Tyler Sellers, David Warrington, and Garrett Wilkerson.

Finally, this book would not have been possible without the constant patience, support, and encouragement of Holly and Oliver. This is your book, too.

Introduction

What secessionists set out to build was something entirely new in the history of nations: a modern proslavery and antidemocratic state, dedicated to the proposition that all men were not created equal.
—Stephanie McCurry[1]

To describe the significance of freedom to four million black slaves of the South is to test severely our historical imagination.
—Leon F. Litwack[2]

There are no battlefields in Reconstruction, at least none that cover vast acres of land. The sites of the famous Civil War battles—Gettysburg, Fredericksburg, Shiloh, Vicksburg, Chancellorsville, and Antietam—have attracted tens of millions of visitors since becoming national park sites. You can walk the field where Major General George Pickett made his charge at Gettysburg and visualize troop locations and the strategy behind movements and placements.

The battlefields of Reconstruction were much different. They were defined not by military campaigns but by election campaigns. The battles took place at hundreds of precincts throughout an entire state, especially in 1868 and again in 1875 in Mississippi. Moreover, a different kind of battle occurred at thousands of farms, plantations, schools, shops, and homesteads as formerly enslaved men, women, and children negotiated the meaning of their newly acquired freedom. You can't visit any of those battlefields. You can't visualize political strategy like you can military strategy. All that you can see is the state in which you live.

It was in reaction to the decade following the end of the Civil War that the Mississippi of the twentieth century was largely created: the continued emphasis on agriculture, and especially the growing of cotton, as the economic engine; a grueling system of labor associated with agriculture that ultimately became known as sharecropping; the imposition of segregation and Jim Crow to ensure political, social, and economic inequality for a majority of the state's population; and the unwillingness to invest in education. Not until the late 1960s did any of this change. Mississippi has been trying to recover and reinvent itself ever since.

Reconstruction is the period of American history that is traditionally assigned the dates from 1865 to 1877 to coincide with the end of the War, the process of readmitting to representation in Congress the eleven Southern states that had seceded, and the ultimate withdrawal of federal troops from the South. In short, the issues associated with restoring the Union.

Nevertheless, it was the end of slavery—and the embrace of freedom by four million men, women, and children who had been enslaved their entire lives—that ultimately distinguished the era. Many historians now date the beginning of Reconstruction to January 1, 1863, when President Lincoln issued the Emancipation Proclamation, followed by the early debates in Congress over the role of the federal government in dismantling slavery, and the adoption of the Thirteenth Amendment. This narrative takes that approach, though for Mississippi, Reconstruction began even earlier when Union forces moved into Mississippi to take Corinth in the late spring and early summer of 1862.

As the Union Army advanced through northeast Mississippi, enslaved men and women abandoned farms and plantations by the hundreds and followed the soldiers to Corinth. It was a phenomenon inconceivable to whites, who believed Blacks had no understanding of freedom and were not capable of living as free men and women. Over the following months, though, Blacks created a new community in the Union encampment, were paid for their labor, and established schools for their children. These expressions of freedom were replicated throughout the South as the War progressed into Confederate territory and would ultimately have a profound effect on Union military strategy. What we know from contemporaneous accounts found in letters, reports, and memoirs from Union soldiers, missionaries, government officials, and reporters is that the vast majority of those who emerged from slavery embraced their freedom and knew instinctively that freedom in the early years of Reconstruction would be primarily sustained by the right to vote, the right to an education, and the right to own land. How Black Mississippians sought to realize all three is central to this Reconstruction narrative.

Reconstruction then, or at least this slice of that history, is an exploration of the meaning of freedom—the practice of freedom by those who had been enslaved and the response of white Mississippians—and how one group welcomed it and how the other would not.

At the end of the War, and over the ensuing ten years, those two population groups that occupied Mississippi would engage life in ways that are simply unimaginable to us today.[3] The 430,000 Black men, women, and children who had been enslaved would gain their freedom, would become citizens of the United States, would be paid for their work, and would begin to enjoy activities whites in Mississippi took for granted: attending the church of their choice, marrying whom they wanted to marry, taking a walk to a pond to fish, reading a book, attending school, and owning property. The men would exercise the right to vote, serve on juries, and stand for public office. These and other pleasures had been denied to them. For their entire lives—not just their adult lives—their entire lives, they had been held in captivity, against their will. They were not citizens of America. They had no legal rights that courts were bound to respect. They were not even considered full human beings for purposes of the United States Constitution. They were assigned a monetary value and recorded as such by the Census Bureau, akin to horses, cattle, mules, and other animals. They were bought, sold, and traded just like other property.

For the 350,000 white Mississippians, this was all they knew. For their entire lives, as with their parents and grandparents, they were taught Black people could not function as human beings on par with whites, and, in fact, enjoyed their bondage—their absence of freedom—because they were not equal to whites. As such, slavery was the backbone of the state's successful cotton economy and the foundation of the Southern "way of life." And that "way of life," otherwise known as white supremacy, provided an explanation for the ordering of human lives because white supremacy was said to be part of God's plan. This white Mississippians believed to their collective core. Anything else was not thinkable. To preserve that part of God's plan, Southerners went so far as to launch a war that ultimately lasted four years, cost the lives of more than 620,000 Americans, and left their section of the country ravaged.

Historian Erik Mathisen captured what was at stake for white Mississippians when the state seceded: "By 1860, Mississippi's plantations alone produced the lion's share of the nation's cotton crop, with only 11 percent of the nation's slave population. Unsparing, ruthlessly efficient, and profoundly powerful, slavery in Mississippi was the institution that secessionists dreamed of when they closed their eyes: a system of black bondage guaranteed by white supremacy and a system of local, state, and federal governance that protected the institution and insulated slaveholders."[4] While the Civil War and Reconstruction shattered the mythology of slavery—that Blacks enjoyed their subjugation, were incapable of understanding freedom, and would never abandon their plantation or farm—both failed to upend, or even undermine, white supremacy. For the ninety years following the fateful election of 1875 that ended Reconstruction in our state, white supremacy continued to serve as the foundation for the political, economic, social, and cultural landscape in Mississippi. Not until the 1964 Civil Rights Act, the 1965 Voting Rights Act, and the 1969 federal enforcement of school desegregation lawsuits did official state government recognition of and support for white supremacy finally end.

Throughout Reconstruction, Mississippians responded to broader movements in the country, to changes in the national and international economy, and to congressional and presidential initiatives as they worked to recover from the devastation of the War and embark on new applications of freedom. Events in the political life of a state rarely happen in a vacuum. There is almost always a reason, a connection, or a motive. One aim of this book was to uncover the genesis of actions or achievements or tragedies and to demonstrate how the interrelatedness of the people and events of the time led to success or failure. Reconstruction in Mississippi cannot be understood without realizing that what happened in our state was connected to and, in many ways, dependent on forces beyond our boundaries.

In some cases, Mississippi instigated congressional action, as when it adopted the Black Code in the fall of 1865—which is covered in Chapter 4— or failed to approve the new state constitution in the summer of 1868—as explained in Chapter 7. In other instances, Mississippi was on the receiving end, as when it was placed under military occupation from 1867–1870—covered in Chapter 5—or when the Ku Klux Klan and other paramilitary terrorist groups tried to impose their own version of law and order throughout the state in 1870 and 1871—as described in Chapter 8. President Andrew Johnson was chiefly responsible for the tragic decisions that prevented formerly enslaved families from acquiring land of their own, as explained in Chapter 3. President Ulysses S. Grant made the disastrous choice in the spring of 1869 to allow a second vote on a new state constitution, covered also in Chapter 7, and the fateful resolution in the fall of 1875 to withhold federal troops during the election that year, which is reviewed in detail in Chapter 11. Apart from the give and take coming from Washington, the newly formed political party of white and Black Mississippi Republicans achieved two singular accomplishments: drafting the state's most inclusive constitution and enacting the state's first-ever comprehensive system of public education. The 1868 Constitutional Convention is described in Chapter 6 while the legislative struggle to create a system of public schools is detailed in Chapter 8.

In the end, though, it was economics that wrecked any chance the new Black citizens of the state might have of translating their economic freedom into economic power. The international economy set the price of cotton and that price remained stubbornly low to sustain anything other than a subsistence standard of living, as explained in Chapter 9, while the financial crisis that engulfed the nation in 1873—described in Chapter 10—created the dynamic in Washington and Mississippi that gave white Democrats in the state the political leverage they needed to retake control of state government in the fall of 1875 and end Reconstruction.

On March 31, 1876, when the United States Senate was debating a resolution offered by Indiana Senator Oliver Morton to establish a special congressional committee to investigate the allegations of fraud, intimidation, and violence associated with the Mississippi election the previous year, Blanche K. Bruce was on the floor. Bruce, a Black man from Bolivar County, was one of Mississippi's two senators. The term he would serve from 1875 to 1881 would represent the only time an African American would serve a full term in the United States Senate until Edward Brooke was elected as a Republican by the voters of Massachusetts in 1966.

In the course of the debate, Bruce made his case for the adoption of the resolution by citing examples of the various ways white Democrats had undermined the integrity of the election. Close to the end of his speech, when he was done with the evidence, he spoke from his heart about freedom and the meaning of that freedom:

> The close of the war found four millions of freedmen, without homes or property, charged with the duty of self-support and with the oversight of their personal freedom, yet without civil and political rights! The problem presented by this condition of things was one of the gravest that has ever been submitted to the American people.
>
> We want peace and good order in the South, but it can only come by the fullest recognition of the rights of all classes. The opposition must concede the necessity of change, not only in temper but in the philosophy of their party organization and management.
>
> We simply demand the practical recognition of the rights given us in the constitution and laws, and ask from our white fellow citizens only the consideration and fairness that we so willingly extend to them. Let them generally realize and concede that citizenship imports to us what it does to them, no more and no less.[5]

The plea helped move the Senate to adopt the resolution, though while the investigation took place, its findings made little difference among the newly elected white Democrats in Mississippi.

Back up, though, to 1862, and the beginning of this book's narrative. Just fourteen years earlier to the month that he was standing on the floor of the United States Senate, Blanche Bruce was an enslaved man attached to a family of farmers in Brunswick, Missouri. Later that summer and fall, as Black men, women, and children in northeast Mississippi were discovering freedom for the first time in their lives, Bruce, then living in Lawrence, Kansas, had likewise become a free man and would begin his journey to Mississippi.

Much of the history you will read in the pages that follow was withheld from school textbooks in Mississippi for more than a hundred years. As described in the Epilogue, white politicians, aided and abetted by professional historians and educators across the country, purposefully distorted the history of the Reconstruction. By omitting facts and recreating events to suit their ideology, they crafted a fictionalized account of Reconstruction as an excuse for building a stark, racially segregated society.[6]

These politicians, historians, and educators portrayed Black men and women emerging from slavery during Reconstruction as incapable of governing, managing a business, owning land, or contributing to the culture of the state. Reconstruction in Mississippi textbooks became a demonstration of Black incompetence and corruption to justify segregation and Jim Crow. The successful careers of John R. Lynch, Hiram Revels, Benjamin Montgomery, James Lynch, and Blanche Bruce, among others described in this book, would have undermined the account of dishonest and inept Black men; hence, they were ignored. Their public policy contributions, such as the state's first public school system, were distorted and minimized.

In a history of Mississippi they wrote in 1891, Robert Lowry and William H. McCardle did their part in fabricating memories of Reconstruction that went unchallenged for decades: "In selecting delegates to [the 1868 Constitutional] Convention a large number of the most intelligent white citizens in the State were excluded from participation . . . while the negroes, ignorant and unscrupulous, [knew] nothing of the responsibility attaching to the elective franchise."[7]

Nearly sixty years later, Merton Coulter, a nationally recognized historian at the University of Georgia, defended the "Old South" when he wrote, "Slavery had not been an unmixed evil for the Negroes; it had brought them from barbarism and sometimes slavery in Africa to America and subjected them to the white man's civilization, the product of a thousand years of freedom."[8] For decades, textbooks in our state incorporated the Lowry, McCardle, and Coulter distortions and misrepresentations, among many others.

Even as late as 1964, the pivotal year of the Civil Rights Movement, the Mississippi history textbook used in public schools throughout the state opened the chapter on Reconstruction with this preface: "The war was over, but the fighting was not; reconstruction was a worse battle than the war had ever been. Yet, by 1875, the old political order had returned, and white and black people set about the task of getting along together in the New South as they had in the Old."[9]

"... *as they had in the Old.*"

A full century after the end of the War, and the same year that Congress passed and President Lyndon Johnson signed the Civil Rights Act of 1964, public school textbooks used in classrooms throughout the state endorsed the white mythology of slavery and Reconstruction. Blanche Bruce and other Black public officials, educators, farmers, and craftspeople would refute and undermine the myths, though their accomplishments and achievements were never officially told to Mississippians, white or Black, for more than a century. Their story begins in Corinth in the summer of 1862.

RECONSTRUCTION IN
MISSISSIPPI, 1862–1877

MAP OF MISSISSIPPI, 1870

Source: County population data from the 1870 United States Census. The sixty-five counties shown on the map are early 1870, matching the counties recorded by the Census. The remaining seventeen counties were created after July 1, 1870. **Credit:** Map by Ben Pease.

CHAPTER 1

1862–1864
The Beginning of Freedom

Where the army of the Union goes, there slavery ceases forever.
—UNION CAPTAIN FROM WISCONSIN[1]

The Negro is the key to the situation—the pivot upon which the whole rebellion turns.
—FREDERICK DOUGLASS[2]

Reconstruction took hold in Mississippi long before the Civil War ended. For more than half the War's duration, formerly enslaved men, women, and children abandoned farms and plantations to serve in the Union Army, attend school, receive payment in exchange for their labor, negotiate contracts, and worship in their own churches—in short, they experienced freedom.[3]

The phenomenon was one white Mississippians could scarcely comprehend. Virtually all of them believed Blacks were inferior human beings incapable of understanding freedom. The Confederate States of America Vice President Alexander Stephens captured the sentiment when he declared the Confederacy "rests upon the great truth that the Negro is not equal to the white man; that slavery, subordination to the superior race, is his natural and normal condition."[4]

These whites began the War convinced enslaved men and women would never leave the certainty of work, housing, and food to pursue freedom. One confident planter remarked that his "niggers knew nothing about the war and cared less." A newly enrolled Confederate soldier felt little concern leaving his family "to the care of the niggers" because "they're ignorant poor creatures, to be sure, but as yet they're faithful."[5] Nevertheless, as the Union Army moved through the South, overrunning towns, farms, and plantations, Blacks deserted by the thousands. Their ability to secure freedom so early in the War rested on a legal loophole.

That account began in Virginia, near the James River, in May of 1861. It was there that General Benjamin F. Butler established a Union encampment at Fort Monroe. Not long thereafter, Butler and his troops were confronted by runaway slaves seeking safety. Almost a year and a half in advance of the Emancipation Proclamation, these Black men and women were forcing Butler to make a decision, not only about their personal future but also about the connection between slavery and the War. While Butler had no legal authority to free them, he had little interest in complying with the Fugitive Slave Law and returning them. Butler solved this dilemma by declaring them "contraband of war"; consequently, they would be treated as any other property seized during combat. He would keep them.[6]

Like any military conflict, field officers were the first to contend with circumstances their superiors had yet to anticipate. In 1861, the federal government was prosecuting the War to preserve the Union, not to liberate those who were enslaved. On the other hand, President Lincoln, Republican Members of Congress, and other Union generals soon concluded, after Butler's initiative, that putting formerly enslaved individuals to work for the army accomplished two complementary goals: they could provide much-needed labor as well as intelligence about Confederate locations and movements, while, at the same time, their employment would undermine the stability of the Confederacy by undermining the institution of slavery. As General Ulysses S. Grant observed early on, "I don't know what is to become of these poor people in the end but it [is] weakening the enemy to take them." Less than two months into the War, enslaved men and women had made their status an issue that Union military and political leaders had to address.[7]

Congress responded by adopting the First Confiscation Act, authorizing Union troops in combat situations to seize property, including enslaved men and women who had abandoned their homes. Six months later, Congress amended the articles of war to prohibit soldiers from returning fugitive slaves.[8]

Thanks to Butler's ingenuity, the stage was set for many of the 22,000 enslaved men, women, and children in and around Corinth, Mississippi, to begin their journey to freedom. Slavery was still legal and in force, which meant they were not official citizens nor were they vested with any legal rights. But in northeast Mississippi, in the summer and fall of 1862, thousands of those who had been enslaved experienced freedom for the first time in their lives.[9]

For one significant reason was Corinth first on the Union Army's target list for Mississippi: located in the middle of the town was the intersection of two of the most important railroads in the western region of the Confederacy—the Memphis & Charleston, the only direct line from the Mississippi River to the Atlantic Coast, and the Mobile & Ohio, from northern Kentucky to the Gulf of Mexico. Take Corinth, Union leaders knew, and their army would deprive the Confederacy of a major link in the transportation system it needed for logistical and communications support. Just as important, it could serve as the staging area for the federal drive to Vicksburg.[10]

After defeating Confederate troops at the Battle of Shiloh in West Tennessee on April 7, 1862, Union soldiers began a march to Corinth with more than twice the number of Southern troops stationed there. Recognizing they were outnumbered, the Confederates abandoned the town at the end of May.[11]

On July 17, 1862, Congress passed the Second Confiscation Act—which vested field officers with more authority to seize Confederate land and fugitive slaves. General Ulysses S. Grant, now in command of Union troops in the area, under pressure from hundreds of formerly enslaved individuals and families streaming into Corinth, sought guidance from Washington and a few weeks later received the kind of instructions he had been waiting for: "The administration has come up to what the people have long demanded—a vigorous prosecution of the war by all the means known to civilized warfare. The Negroes must now be made our auxiliaries in every possible way they can be, whether by working or fighting." On August 11, Grant issued military guidelines to enforce the new confiscation legislation: fugitive slaves would no longer be turned away; instead, the "contrabands," as they were now being called throughout the army, would be put to work.[12]

By the middle of September, more than 2,000 had arrived, looking for work, food, shelter, and medical care. General Grenville M. Dodge, commander of the garrison at Corinth, responded by authorizing a chaplain assigned to his troop, James M. Alexander, to create a separate camp for the refugees.[13]

Grant shared these new developments with his sister: "Their *institutions* are beginning to have ideas of their own, and every time an expedition goes out more or less of them follow in the wake of the army and come to camp." Grant needed workers and Black men and women were demanding their freedom. As one historian wrote, "The combined demands of Union soldiers and runaway slaves soon proved irresistible." Grant put the fugitives to work as cooks, teamsters, hospital attendants, laborers, personal servants, and laundresses.

They constructed fortifications, farmed nearby land, and provided valuable information on local terrain and Confederate encampments.[14]

LINCOLN'S EMANCIPATION PROCLAMATION

On September 19, 1862, Grant's Army took Iuka and surrounding territory in Tishomingo County. Three days later, President Lincoln dramatically altered the nature of the War. Up to that point, he had been waging combat solely to preserve the Union, a position he laid out in his first Inaugural Address: "I have no purpose, directly or indirectly, to interfere with the institution of slavery in the States where it exists. I believe I have no lawful right to do so, and I have no inclination to do so." That was soon followed, though, by his opinion on secession: "no State upon its own mere motion can lawfully get out of the Union; resolves and ordinances to that effect are legally void, and acts of violence within any State or States against the authority of the United States are insurrectionary."[15]

At the outset of hostilities, Lincoln was willing to concede on slavery to preserve the Union. But the first eighteen months of the War had demonstrated not only that the Confederacy was in the fight for the long haul, but that it was becoming increasingly impractical to return the refugees freed by the advancing federal armies. The time had ripened for Lincoln to threaten the Confederate states with something far more radical than merely losing the War: losing their slaves. On September 22, 1862, Lincoln signaled the South: unless they halted the conflict by the end of the year, he would free all the enslaved individuals in the states "still in rebellion" on January 1. It would become known as the Emancipation Proclamation. Lincoln hoped the threat embedded in the unprecedented proclamation would force Southerners to the bargaining table.[16] It had taken eighteen months, but Lincoln had bided his time as Northern public opinion coalesced on the side of abolition while he was able to navigate his conflicting constituencies: the Northerners who feared a massive immigration of newly freed Blacks, the border state residents who still engaged in slavery, and the Union soldiers who might be unwilling to fight if they were asked to risk their lives to liberate millions of Black men, women, and children.[17]

Two weeks later, the Confederates sought to regain Corinth, a battle they lost on October 4, 1862. Suffering yet another loss and retreating to points further south in Mississippi, the Southern army ceded Grant control of north Mississippi from Memphis to Corinth. He was now in a strategic position to make plans to take Vicksburg.[18]

John Eaton Jr., circa 1860–1875. Brady-Handy photograph collection, Library of Congress, Prints and Photographs Division.

But the demands and challenges of the care for the runaway fugitives were formidable. With Corinth and its surroundings coming under the control of Grant's army at the same time as the public release of Lincoln's September proclamation, more and more enslaved people deserted their farms and made their way to Corinth. An officer described the scene as "the oncoming of cities" producing "a veritable moral chaos."[19]

Grant took charge in early November by appointing John Eaton Jr., a chaplain from Ohio, to "oversee the Contrabands" in the area and put them "to work picking, ginning, and baling all cotton now outstanding in the fields." Grant instructed doctors to help care for the sick and provided a regiment for protection. Alexander's unofficial work in Corinth became official: those who had been enslaved could be paid for their work and the army would provide medical care, food, clothing, and blankets.[20]

A month later, Grant had captured additional north Mississippi targets while Union forces on the Arkansas side of the Mississippi River moved toward Vicksburg.[21] As more farms and plantations were abandoned and more fugitives left, Union Army camps quickly became Union refugee camps. By December, Grant, recognizing he had a burgeoning problem on his hands, promoted Eaton to the general superintendent of contrabands for the entire army waging combat in the Mississippi Valley. This official rank vested Eaton with the authority to appoint assistant superintendents, require troops to guard refugee camps, and solicit donated goods.[22]

The same day Eaton's orders were released, Mississippi Governor John Pettus convened a special session of the Legislature, declaring "the struggle is now for her existence as a state." Pettus recommended that the "entire white male population of the State from sixteen to sixty years of age be enrolled in the militia" to counter "the vast armies sent by our enemies for our subjugation."[23]

On the day after Christmas, 1862, all was not well in Confederate Mississippi. Sherman and his forces arrived on the western bank of the Mississippi River north of Vicksburg about the same time Jefferson Davis defined the stakes in an address to the Mississippi Legislature in Jackson: "even life itself should be willingly laid down on the altar of their country." Meanwhile, in Washington, Abraham Lincoln was preparing to formally release his proclamation.[24]

On New Year's Day, 1863, President Lincoln followed through on his September threat and issued the Emancipation Proclamation. While the declaration excluded the 450,000 enslaved men, women, and children in the border states of Delaware, Kentucky, Maryland, and Missouri and more than 300,000 in Union-occupied Tennessee, Louisiana, and Virginia, the executive order freed the remainder of the country's enslaved population wherever it could be enforced. As one historian observed, "As the Union army moved deeper into the South, they became essentially an army of liberation."[25]

By the spring of 1863, close to 23,000 Black refugees were under Eaton's jurisdiction throughout the Mississippi Valley, including nearly 3,700 in Corinth, 1,400 in Memphis, 2,400 in Lake Providence, Louisiana, and 5,000 in Cairo, Illinois. But the numbers fluctuated daily—Eaton once wrote they "circulated much like water"—and they were growing: by the summer of 1864, Eaton had more than 114,000 under his purview.[26]

The typical refugee showed up at a camp with nothing more than the clothes he or she was wearing, once described by Eaton as "not enough to cover their nakedness." Some came with horses, mules, or oxen, some with wagons, but most came on foot. In nearly all of the refugee camps, they lived in old army tents; were provided with food and clothing but almost always less than the rations allocated for the soldiers; and, if they were lucky, had access to medicine to treat various diseases, such as pneumonia, typhoid fever, measles, and smallpox. Nevertheless, by late spring, the camp at Corinth was becoming an independent community. Refugees had built cabins to replace the tents, along with a school, church, hospital, and commissary. Each cabin had its own subsistence garden. Children cultivated a small cotton field near the school. Men and women worked as blacksmiths, shoemakers, carpenters, and seamstresses; purchased all of their clothing; and paid a tax of a dollar a month. Eaton's March report showed a total of 3,657 contrabands; among them were 658 fieldhands, 36 blacksmiths, 48 carpenters, 180 teamsters, 200 cooks, 80 seamstresses, and 150 laundresses. Altogether 1,260 of the women had children; 120 of the men and 40 of the women could read; and there were 1,559 children. By the fall more than seventy new buildings had been constructed. The able-bodied men were working for the army—building fortifications, running sawmills, digging canals, serving as scouts—while the women and children were picking cotton at area farms.[27]

As the War progressed, officers, soldiers, reporters, and missionaries writing home made clear that Corinth was an exception and that while the refugee camps represented the chief way station for freedom for the runaway slaves, life for them was anything but easy. Eaton once described the scene at Vicksburg soon after the siege as thousands of "refugees were crowded together, sickly, disheartened, dying on the streets. Not a family of them was well-sheltered, clothed, or fed; no physician, no medicines, no hospitals; many of the persons who had been charged with feeding them either sick or dead." A resident writing in a journal in Natchez remembered the contrabands "were gathered near the city by the thousands in [camps] without food or shelter. . . . The odors were disgusting at the distance of half a mile."

Neither Grant nor Sherman nor other Union officers cared much for the fugitives other than what they represented—a tool to help win the War. To protect the health and morale of their own men, the Union leaders needed "contraband camps" to separate the refugees from the army troops. Moreover, Grant had no choice but to build the camps near his troops since he had been prevented from moving them to Northern locations because politicians, editors, and activists there raised the "specter of black inundation" in the North. To make things worse, Union troops were not above stealing the possessions the refugees brought with them or the paychecks some began to earn for work in the camps or with the army. One Union soldier wrote to his wife, "The Southern people are rebels to the government but they are White and God never intended a Nigger to put white people down." One of the worst examples of Union soldier prejudice occurred in the spring of 1863, near Vicksburg, when some cavalrymen of the Tenth Illinois regiment "stomped on the face of a black child, permanently blinding him in one eye."[28]

But it was the pervasive paternalism among Union officers, even among men like Eaton, who cared genuinely about the future of the fugitives, that characterized white attitudes in the governance of the camps. The officers believed the refugees needed white guidance and control to guide them through the early days of freedom. As one historian wrote, the widely held opinion in the North was that slavery weakened its victims by "placing them in a childlike dependency upon slaveholders." Eaton believed slavery had left them severely damaged, leaving him to constantly wonder, "How was the slave to be transformed into a freeman . . . to make the Negro a consciously self-supporting unit in the society in which he found himself, and start him on the way to self-respecting citizenship."[29]

It was this tension that would influence the decisions made in Washington toward the formerly enslaved for the remainder of the War and the years following. How much government oversight should be exercised over the lives of the refugees? And what form should that oversight take? Would the formerly enslaved men and women be influenced more by wages or by ownership of land? How the federal government ultimately resolved these issues is at the heart of how Reconstruction evolved in the years following the Civil War.

Despite the hardships prevalent in the camps, Eaton wrote in his own memoir published a few years after the War what freedom meant to the men and women who had abandoned the plantations:

> One fact in connection with the Negro must ever be borne in mind. The testimony alike of my officers and of the visitors to the Valley is all but unanimously to the effect that despite the suffering to which the freedmen were subjected in their desperate passage from slavery to freedom—suffering which in many cases must have far exceeded that which they had experienced in bondage—scarcely a single instance could be quoted in which a Negro voluntarily returned as a slave to his master. Discouraged, panic-stricken, and suspicious they were, but ready to exchange their hard-won and unhappy freedom for the sometimes easier conditions of slavery they were not.[30]

BLACK MEN JOIN THE UNION ARMY

In early spring 1863, the Lincoln administration raised the stakes in Mississippi when the Army's Adjutant General, Lorenzo Thomas, was sent to do what would have been unthinkable two years earlier—recruit former slaves for service in the Union Army. Once again, Corinth was ahead of Washington. With the backing of General Dodge, Alexander had created an unofficial company

Corinth Ceremony with Army Adjutant General Lorenzo Thomas, May 1863. Courtesy of the Corinth Civil War Interpretive Center.

of Black men to guard the refugee camp nearly nine months before the War Department authorized such action in the Mississippi Valley. In a stirring letter sent to Washington, Eaton fully endorsed the move: "Yes, arm him! It will do him worlds of good. He will know then he has rights, and dare maintain them. . . . These men will make good soldiers. Arm him and let the world see the black man on a vast scale returning good for evil, helping with blood and life the cause of the race that hated, oppressed, and scorned him. We can hurt the rebels more by the use of the negro than by any other means in our power."[31]

Thomas made it to Corinth in May, 1863, and visitors to the city today can stand in the very place where he stood to address the refugees and the Union soldiers 150 years ago. The site is the Verandah-Curlee House, one of four houses remaining today from the antebellum period. Eaton described the scene as a "day of speeches and parades. At the appointed hour, and after the children had sung some songs, Thomas stood on the steps of the house looking out over more than 2,400 contrabands and hundreds of Union troops that Alexander had assembled in order around the house."

Thomas's speech was recalled by Eaton in his memoir:

Thomas told these former slaves that he lived where their great friend President Lincoln lived and saw him daily, that the president had sent him out here so far to tell them they were free and to tell all the soldiers they must receive them, treat them kindly, provide work for them and pay them, feed them if hungry, clothe them if naked and to make soldiers of the strong and healthy men so that they might fight for the liberty of their wives and children and against the rebellion, which has raised great armies to overthrow our great and good Government upon them as slaves.

The President had made them free to overthrow that rebellion by taking away the laborers who furnished it food and clothing and now he was going to use them further for the overthrow of the rebellion by putting arms in their hands to fight against it. Will you fight soldiers? I tell you these things not only because I am commanded to do so by the President, but because I feel them. I was raised by slaves. I once owned slaves. I know what all the prejudices are upon this Subject but I have overcome them. I expect the whole Army as good soldiers and officers to overcome them.

Eaton recalled the response was "vociferous" and that "the cheers rolled up from the depths of their hearts for the President, for the good news, for the General, cheer following cheer, their echoes flying along the defenses erected by the [Confederates] and over the field red with the blood of friends and foes of liberty and union."

Thomas and his party then toured the refugee camp "through the acres upon acres of garden so free from weeds . . . and took a look at the hundreds of acres of cotton cultivated by their free hands, then at the hospitals in excellent condition." James Alexander, the Union chaplain, was so moved by the day's events that he turned to Eaton and said, "Now I am prepared to die." He resigned his post as chaplain and organized a Black regiment from the Corinth refugees. One historian estimated that 16,000 to 18,000 formerly enslaved men from Mississippi fought for the Union Army. Another using pension records filed by troops and their widows suggested it could be much higher. And they became Union soldiers at great peril, for a former slave becoming a prisoner of Confederate troops meant something far different than a white Union soldier getting captured. The most publicized incident occurred at Fort Pillow, Tennessee, in the spring of 1864 when troops attached to a regiment commanded by Confederate General Nathan B. Forrest accepted the surrender of several hundred Black soldiers and then proceeded to murder them. Even back at the army camps, many white physicians refused to treat the contraband troops. Regardless, by the War's end, some 180,000 Black men had volunteered for service in the Union Army.[32]

THE UNION PRESENCE IN MISSISSIPPI

The other major development that year affecting the refugee camps was the influx of volunteers from numerous charitable organizations throughout the

North. The American Missionary Association (AMA) was the first to establish a significant presence throughout Mississippi and was the first to Corinth. By summer, the AMA had close to a dozen dedicated missionaries working in the refugee camp there. They reported that more than 1,000 refugees had learned to read and 500 students were attending their makeshift schools. The "blacks' thirst for knowledge amazed" one missionary who wrote, "You will find them every hour of daylight, at their books." Distraught that there had been "no administration of the Lord's Supper or Baptism since the war broke out," the AMA volunteers established the Union Christian Church of Corinth. By the fall more than 2,000 were attending Sunday services, and more than 400 were enrolled in Sunday school. One missionary reported that "the prayers offered were intelligent and pertinent. Each one prayed for the Union army and very appropriately. I saw an earnestness in reference to the Christian life that I have seldom seen." Much like the Black refugees, who followed the tracks of the Union Army through Mississippi, so did the AMA and other charitable organizations. By early 1864, for example, the AMA school in Vicksburg was teaching more than 1,500 formerly enslaved children.[33]

In the meantime, Grant's forces were headed to Vicksburg and through the region of Mississippi with the highest concentration of large plantations. Of the more than 430,000 enslaved men, women, and children in the state in 1860, two-thirds lived in the western half of the state.[34] In May 1863, the Union Army captured Port Gibson, Raymond, and Jackson, and on July 4, the Confederate garrison at Vicksburg surrendered. Black refugees by the thousands were by now a regular feature of Union movements through this part of Mississippi. One Bolivar County resident noted, "The county is left almost alone and negroes are going where they please." A Port Gibson resident complained to the governor, "The negroes are under no restraint at night." Noting the arrival of the Union Army and the disappearance of the slaves, one plantation supervisor near Vicksburg wrote in his diary, "The Yankees came and set the Negros All Free and the Work All Stopped." The next day, his entry read, "Negros All Free no work dun." A plantation owner in Washington County watched all 200 of the men, women, and children he had enslaved leave when Union troops informed them of their new status as free people. Former slaves were not only serving in the Union Army but working as guides, scouts, and sources of intelligence about geography and encampments. They built fortifications, bridges, and roads, and repaired railroads. They grew cotton on nearby plantations for the Union Army, generated money for the federal treasury, and raised vegetables and corn for the troops. And many of them were paid for their work, a historic first. Their skills in carpentry, ironworking, weaving, and manufacture of shoes, shingles, and bricks were now being used against the slaveholders. As one historian noted, "These skilled Negro artisans, with a practical monopoly of their trades in many neighborhoods and with experience in dealing with the whites who hired them, found little difficulty in making the transition to freedom."[35]

After the capture of Vicksburg, and for the remaining two years of the War, life in Mississippi was defined by the ebb and flow of federal troops in and out of the state. The boundaries of occupation changed constantly. Union forces assumed control of Jackson in May 1863, ceded the city back later that month, retook it again in July, gave it up yet one more time, and then regained it early in 1864. Grant took Holly Springs, lost it, and took it again. At the end of 1863 and beginning of 1864, in preparation for the Meridian campaign, Union soldiers gave up Corinth. Movements like this occurred throughout the state. Whenever Grant or Sherman secured a region of the state, landowners would retreat to the interior. When the federals left, landowners would return, as would slavery. The same held for the seat of state government. The capital was mobile, moving from Jackson to Meridian back to Jackson then to Columbus and Macon. As one historian described it, "Freedom seldom advanced steadily or uniformly. The tide of federal military success carried freedom forward; military failure saw freedom in retreat and slavery given new life. The promise embodied in the Emancipation Proclamation counted for little unless the Union armies enjoyed military success."[36]

The constantly changing boundaries between towns and regions of the state controlled by Union forces and those controlled by Confederate forces created vexing problems for the enslaved population. As one scholar noted, the fugitive slaves "inhabited a no man's land between hostile armies." Many ended up in refugee camps; some men signed up for service in the Army; others "fled to the woods to make out as best they could." Some stayed on farms and negotiated new labor arrangements. In a process called "running the Negroes," the unlucky ones were forced to travel to other parts of the state as whites fled the Union Army.

All who escaped were under constant threat from slaveholders and rebel guerrillas. A Confederate bounty hunter captured four runaways, for example, and instead of returning all of them, he returned three and hanged one to send a message. There were reports from refugee camps of women showing up "bloodied for having had their ears carved off as lessons to other potential runaways." A group of farmers petitioned the governor to spare a white man drafted by the Confederate Army and instead put him to use in tracking down fugitive slaves because he had a "pack of Negro dogs" especially suitable for the task. Paramilitary organizations were formed under such titles as "local guards" and "home guards" to capture runaway slaves. Ads were placed in local newspapers, such as one looking for a "negro boy named Patrick. He may have fallen into some military camp, and any person who may find him will be suitably rewarded." As one farmer wrote in his journal, "With the appearance of the Yankees, the restlessness and reluctance to work" he had observed during the past several months suddenly flared into "wild confusion" and "a general stampede." In less than six weeks, more than twenty left him and those who remained might as well have gone, "they being totally demoralized and ungovernable."[37]

Attempting to respond to the deteriorating circumstances, Governor Pettus summoned the Legislature into a special session in November 1863 and urged the members to seek solutions, declaring, "Every able-bodied Negro man that falls in the hands of the enemy is not only a laborer lost to the country in the production of supplies for the support of our armies in the field, but he is under the present policy of the U.S. government a soldier going into its army." The Legislature agreed and authorized criminal prosecution for slaveholders who allowed their slaves to leave the premises or gave them access to horses or mules.[38]

A NEW FORM OF LABOR

After recruiting formerly enslaved men for the army, General Thomas set his sights on the remaining refugees. Like Eaton and his contemporaries, he believed they needed guidance and assistance to make the transition to freedom. Unwilling to wait for Congress and the civilian government to catch up with developments in the field, Thomas set about devising that transition plan. His inspiration was to assume control of the abandoned farms and plantations (i.e., a different kind of contraband, but property nevertheless) and lease them to Northern businessmen and investors, who would then hire refugees to work the fields. Doing this would accomplish the twin goals of removing the remaining fugitives from the camps, where disease and unhealthy living conditions were becoming acute, and placing them into situations where they were working. The added advantage would be to generate revenue for the federal government once the crops were sold. Although the plan looked good on paper, Thomas's scheme was largely unsuccessful. While many of the Northerners chosen for the task possessed general business skills and necessary startup capital, they had very little agricultural experience. Moreover, the fugitive slaves wanted their own land to farm. They had little interest in

returning to a system that reminded them of slavery, even if there was payment involved. Competing with Thomas's initiative were plantation owners
who recognized the world had changed and began to negotiate labor contracts with these newly freed workers.[39]

Perhaps most damaging to Thomas's plan were the constant Confederate
guerilla raids. Farms and plantations were remote from Union encampments, and unless there was an active Union military presence, contrabands
working the fields were easy targets for soldiers. As one historian concluded,
"While the Yankees struggled to reorganize plantation agriculture based on
wage labor, the rebels set out to destroy it." In a series of attacks on plantations managed by the federal government during the summer of 1863, for
example, "Confederate soldiers torched buildings, commandeered tools, and
livestock, killed dozens of slaves and kidnapped hundreds more." Similar
raids continued for the rest of the War. Throughout the remainder of 1863
and through 1864, there were intense and very public debates among and
between army and civilian officials about how to manage the abandoned
plantations, how to transition from a slave to a wage labor system, and what
to do with all the refugees who had deserted the plantations. No one system
ever won out.[40]

By the end of the War, neither the Army nor the federal government had
developed anything approaching a workable program. However, at the end
of 1863, the degree to which the future of the refugee camps was subordi-
nated to the future of the Union Army was made clear: General Sherman
finally got approval to take troops on a campaign of destruction from Jackson
to Meridian and back, along an important railroad line and where Meridian
served as a key railroad junction. Sherman gave up the garrison at Corinth
in order to obtain troops to travel across central Mississippi. That meant the
camp at Corinth was closed and the refugees moved to Memphis. Sherman's
march to Meridian took place in February 1864.

In north Mississippi, meanwhile, Sherman's order to close the Corinth
camp "fell like a bombshell among our contented people," remarked one
of the chaplains working at the camp, "but military orders are preemptory
and without a reason why, and must be obeyed." Going from well-built
wooden houses in Corinth to used army tents in Memphis was how the
contraband families spent the winter of 1863–1864. Later in 1864, a Union
calvary detachment, under General Grierson, made a similar sweep back
through north Mississippi, destroying plantations and freeing hundreds of
Black men, women, and children. But neither Sherman nor Grierson left
forces to occupy the lands they covered. The former slaves instead followed

the Union Army to their camps. A relief worker in Vicksburg reported to his superior that Sherman was returning to Vicksburg "with no less than eight thousand coloured people just released from slavery." Sherman himself wrote that behind his army were "10 miles of negroes . . . a string of ox wagons, negro women and children behind each brigade that equaled in length the brigade itself."[41]

EARLY RECONSTRUCTION DEBATES IN WASHINGTON

Meanwhile, back in Washington, Congress began debating Lincoln's proposal for Reconstruction, which he submitted in December 1863. To the consternation of many Congressional Republicans, the president was willing to offer a full pardon and the restoration of property rights to any person who took an oath of future loyalty to the Union and pledged to accept the abolition of slavery. Lincoln would then allow a minority of those pardoned voters, consisting of 10 percent of the votes cast in the 1860 election, to form a government, establish a new state constitution, and elect representatives to Congress. Known as the "10 percent plan," it failed to include provisions on voting rights or property rights for the freed slaves. Fearing that Lincoln's plan would restore the same white leaders to power who had urged secession, the abolitionists in Congress proposed their own plan, which made readmittance to the Union contingent on a majority—as opposed to Lincoln's ten percent—in each Southern state taking an oath to the effect they had never in the past supported the Confederacy. Known as the "ironclad oath," this feature of the congressional plan would have effectively eliminated most of the white population from participating in any future election. Nevertheless, it passed both houses in 1864. Believing that an overly harsh response from the federal government would make it difficult to repair the Union while also jeopardizing his reelection campaign that year, Lincoln vetoed the bill.[42]

Lincoln went on to handily win another term, though the year ended without any formal plan or agreement on how Reconstruction should proceed. The War, on the other hand, had settled two issues: secession and slavery. Regarding slavery, one historian observed that its "legal destruction" was the "product of presidential proclamation, congressional action, state legislation, and constitutional amendment, but the practical destruction of slavery was the product of war."[43] For Mississippi, the debate was just beginning: How would its future be transformed in the absence of slavery?

CHAPTER 2

1865
Mississippi at the End of the War

The battles launched to preserve plantation slavery had instead opened the door to its destruction.
—Historian Gregory Downs[1]

The Confederacy is dead. . . . Thus ends a war in which the South has gained nothing and lost millions of property and thousands of precious lives.
—Mississippi farmer[2]

At about two in the morning, a few days before Christmas 1865, J. T. Trowbridge arrived at the Corinth railroad depot, hoping to find a place to spend the night. Trowbridge, an author and journalist from Massachusetts, was one of many writers and reporters to tour the South in the months following the end of the War, using newspaper columns, magazine articles, and books to describe and chronicle for Northern and international readers the devastation in that part of the country.[3]

Three and a half years earlier, the same depot and town had been a significant wartime asset targeted and acquired by the Union Army. Until it was abandoned a year earlier, it was one of the major Union garrisons in that region of the country. Now, Trowbridge had stopped over to see how the town had recovered. He found a room in a boarding house and wrote of the bullet holes in the walls, the broken windows, and the Union graffiti on the walls: "The Union, it must be preserved!" He described the inability of the fire in the room to generate much heat as it "couldn't get a purchase on the cold." "Corinth," observed Trowbridge, "is a bruised and battered village surrounded by stumpy fields, forts, earthworks, and graves. The stumpy fields are the sites of woods and groves cut away by the great armies. The graves are those of soldiers slain upon those hills. Beautiful woody boundaries sweep round all."[4]

"Bruised and battered" indeed! In 1860, Mississippi was the seventh wealthiest state in America. On a per capita basis, it was the wealthiest. Ten years later, when the new census data were released, the state had dropped to number twenty-six.[5] In the fall of 1860, Mississippi produced the largest cotton crop of any state in the Union, more than 1.2 million bales. In the fall of 1867, the cotton crop barely totaled 300,000 bales. Not for another thirty years would the 1860 output be surpassed.[6]

All the major towns, except for Natchez and Columbus, were partially or totally destroyed, including Jackson, Vicksburg, Corinth, Holly Springs, Oxford, Port Gibson, Raymond, and Yazoo City. While towns in the northern part of the state largely escaped battle action toward the end of the War, which gave them a head start on recovery, those hit especially hard toward the end fell along the path of General Sherman's march in February 1864 from Vicksburg to Meridian. Sherman had two goals: not only destroy infrastructure but also morale, a campaign he described as "a swath of desolation 50 miles broad across the state of Mississippi, which the present generation will not forget."[7] By the time his troops had left Meridian, Sherman reported that "for five days, 10,000 men worked hard and with a will in the work of destruction, with axes, crowbars, sledges, claw bars, and with fire, I have no hesitation in pronouncing the work as well done. Meridian, with its depots, storehouses, arsenal, hospitals, offices, hotels, and cantonments, no longer exists."[8]

A traveler through Meridian some fifteen months later described what little growth had occurred: "A frame one-story shanty labeled 'Liquors for Sale'; two straight railway tracks in the midst of a wide expanse of mud; a crowd of yelling Negro porters; half a dozen houses that may have been used for storing cotton and whiskey; [several] hotels, some disconsolate looking negro huts; a few shabby residences. . . . There may have been other things in Meridian, but, if so, they were buried in the mud."[9]

As for the capital city, a little more than a year later, the *New York Times* reprinted a famous letter to the editor from a writer in Jackson that depicted a town hollowed out from the 1863 and 1864 battles:

Once a beautiful city, [Jackson] is now a mass of ruins. Piles of brick and mortar cover the once famous retreats of wealth and fashion. Numerous columns, shattered and charred, have suggested the name of 'Chimneyville.' The State House, the Governor's Mansion, the City Hall, and the Asylum are the only public buildings remaining. Great scarcity

Old State Capitol Building, Jackson, Mississippi, circa 1865. Courtesy of the Archives and Records Services Division, Mississippi Department of Archives and History.

prevails in this region. Paralysis has possessed the people. They have planted nothing and extreme poverty prevails in almost every household. The Confederate authority is not recognized—the Federal has not been established—and thus the country is suffering all the grief of an interregnum, or, more properly, of anarchy.[10]

Connecting many of the towns had been railroads, and as one historian wrote, "At the end of the war, the railroad companies were all broke, with their lines heavily damaged. Rapid movement about the state was difficult if not impossible. . . . By 1865, Mississippi's infrastructure was so beaten down that it was impossible to even obtain the simplest of such items as paper, cotton cards, or medicines. The legislature did not have enough paper to conduct its sessions, and the state treasurer could not even obtain a ledger book to keep up with his office's disbursements."[11]

Rail lines also linked farmers to the buyers of their cotton. The growth of railroads in the state corresponded to the record production of cotton. The destruction of those rails was a critical part of the Union Army's plan to weaken the Confederacy by upending its economy. The vital role transportation played in successful farming operations was underscored in Thomas Cockrell's exhaustive study of the Meadow Woods Plantation in Oktibbeha County covering the years from 1839 to 1889. He came to the following conclusion about the operations of the farm as the War came to an end: "The failure of Mississippi agriculture in the war was not due to ineffective conversion and productivity. . . . The failure was in distribution."[12]

The anecdotal data from the dispatches of traveling journalists, memoirs written by soldiers returning home, and government surveys all describe a state whose physical resources had been largely obliterated, including railroads, fences and the fields they lined, roads and bridges, farm buildings, levees along important waterways, and telegraph lines.[13]

For people to manage and overcome a crisis, information about news and events was critical. Even that was nearly impossible in 1865. At the start of the War, Mississippi had more than seventy newspapers, a number that had dwindled to less than a dozen by the end, with a publication schedule that was irregular at best. A former soldier who had returned to his farm in central Mississippi wrote in his journals of a large blackboard that had been erected in the village square for people to post news and that served the community as its sole source of news.[14] Without credible and timely news, people relied on word of mouth and small group meetings. Consequently, rumors and false stories took on exaggerated importance.

Newspapers largely depended on the mail for their delivery, and given the disruption of roads, rail lines, and inland waterways, full restoration of reliable postal operation would take several years. A frustrated newspaper editor complained, "The mails through the state of Mississippi since the surrender of General Taylor have been completely suspended and inoperative, and the people a few miles from the railroad lines, on which the conductors and expressmen have been very kind in circulating needed information, are kept as entirely ignorant of the daily or weekly news and the acts and wishes of the government as the inhabitants of Timbuctoo or the wild men of the Rocky Mountains."[15]

And then there were the basics, like food and health. One historian wrote, "The term destitution may well be used to describe the condition of many of the people of Mississippi following the war. In fact, during the entire period, thousands of people lived in dilapidated huts, wore shabby, inadequate clothing, and were often unable to secure sufficient food to maintain their health." Moreover, parts of the state faced epidemics of cholera, smallpox, and yellow fever.[16] At one point, the US Army requested more than 100,000 rations a month to provide necessary food to people.[17]

All of the features of a modern society—transportation, currency and banking, mail, security, functioning local governments, ready access to food, utilities, and health care—were absent in Mississippi in 1865. That getting them back up and running was so difficult—yet so essential to

rebuilding the economy—was in large part a product of the overwhelmingly rural nature of the state.

At the time of secession, Mississippi's sixty counties contained only twenty-
nine incorporated municipalities, with only five having a population over
2,500: the largest being Natchez at 6,612 and Vicksburg at 4,591. The other three
were Columbus at 3,308, Jackson at 3,191, and Holly Springs at 2,987. Everyone
else lived in small villages or on farms.[18] Mississippians also lived in different geographical patterns than they do now. Two regions, in particular, looked
at the time nothing like they do today. First, the Delta before and after the
War was largely bottomland hardwood forests and swamps. The farming areas
were almost all found along the high ground adjacent to the riverbeds surrounding the Mississippi, Yazoo, Sunflower, and Big Black rivers. The massive
clearing, cleaning, and leveling that we now recognize as the flat Mississippi
Delta would not be realized for several decades. Second, the entire southeast
region of the state was largely populated by towering pine trees and a water-
front overlooking the Gulf of Mexico. Only 33,000 people, or just 4 percent of
the state's population, lived south of the northern boundaries of Clarke, Smith,
and Jasper Counties. It was a frontier in the purest sense of the word.[19]

Half of the state's 780,000 people lived on the west side, largely along the
Mississippi, Yazoo, and Pearl Rivers, and half lived on the east side, though
almost all of them north of Meridian. The racial breakdown varied significantly by region, with 61 percent of newly freed Black families living in the
western region, while just 39 percent lived on the east side. Only the Black
Prairie area in the east, containing what is now Lowndes, Noxubee, Oktibbeha,
Clay, and Monroe Counties, with farmland nearly equal to the Delta, was
majority Black.

Rebuilding Mississippi's economy after the War presented challenges that
were both daunting and unprecedented. When a major disaster hits the state,
like Hurricane Katrina in 2005, there are at least functioning local governments to organize and manage a rebuilding program; the federal government with its resources; banks and insurance companies to cover losses; a
postal service to deliver mail; utility companies to restore power, gas, and
water; and law enforcement and judicial systems to preserve order. In 1865,
Mississippians had no currency and no mail delivery. By leaving the Union,
the state was forced to create its own monetary and postal systems as part
of the Confederacy, both of which collapsed with the surrender. And while
federal money had begun to circulate along the Mississippi River towns,
where the Union Army had continued to control commerce after the siege of
Vicksburg, federal greenbacks, as they were called, were rare in the rest of the

state. Moreover, the banking system had fallen apart and most individuals and families had little to no assets to use as collateral for loans when they were available. Most local governments and criminal justice systems had ceased to function, and many of the rural areas, cut off from each other and from town centers, were dominated by vigilante justice and a "lawlessness amounting almost to anarchy." Observers complained about "robbing and plundering that was going on with perfect impunity" and "roads that were infested with bands of highwaymen."[20]

The loss of what passed for transportation infrastructure in 1865, in an overwhelmingly rural state, meant that many of the populated areas of the state were cut off from each other at the same time they were without functioning civil governments, reliable sources of news, and adequate food and shelter.

The agricultural economy of Mississippi consisted almost entirely of growing cotton and shipping it out of state. Notwithstanding the need to repair farmland, acquire implements and field animals, and rebuild the transportation infrastructure necessary to deliver a crop to a buyer, a successful crop depended on people to work the fields. Without people to cultivate the land and plant, weed, and harvest the crop, it wouldn't matter if Mississippi had the best distribution network in the country. And it was here that the War upended the farming business, for labor from the formerly enslaved would no longer be free nor compulsory.

THE END OF SLAVERY TRANSFORMS MISSISSIPPI

With only a handful of garment manufacturing plants scattered around the state, plus other small mills, foundries, and gins attached to farms or logging operations, Mississippi's antebellum economy was driven almost completely by agriculture.[21]

Given that outlook, an observer described the task at hand: "The War left Mississippi almost nothing except the soil, and that very much burdened."[22] Making the prospects even bleaker, by the time General Taylor surrendered the Mississippi troops in May of 1865, the planting season had largely come and gone. It was, in part, due to this timing that one observer in the fall of 1865 wrote, "Of the male population of the county, I would estimate that not more than one-tenth of the whites and one-fourth of the blacks seem to have any employment or business of any kind."[23]

In the middle of the nineteenth century, a critical component of a successful farming operation was animals that could help work the fields. Most of what livestock remained in Mississippi at the outset of the War was either stolen or killed as Union soldiers worked their way through the state. The value of livestock in the state was calculated to be almost $42 million in 1860. Eight years later, that figure had plummeted to less than $17 million.[24] A soldier returning to his home in rural Hinds County found "only four old mules remained of the eighty-five that counted on the plantation when the Yankees arrived. These four poorly fed and decrepit animals connected to worn and rusty plows by old patched gear did what little plowing was done in 1865."[25]

The soldier who wrote those words in his journal was one of the lucky ones. Over the four years of the war, Mississippi contributed 96,414 white men to the Confederate cause, of which 22,843 became casualties, including 15,265 who either were killed on the battlefield or by diseases. When the 1860 Census counts were made public a few months before Mississippi seceded, the report showed 99,838 white males between fifteen and sixty years of age.[26] In other words, there was hardly a white family in the state that was untouched by the War. As for the 436,631 enslaved men, women, and children counted by the 1860 Census, or 55.3 percent of the Mississippi population, the War and the Emancipation Proclamation bestowed on them the right to their freedom and transformed their lives.

Contrary to what many have imagined over the years—that antebellum Mississippi was the land of huge plantations, worked by thousands of enslaved Black men and women—more than 93 percent of the state's 37,000 farms were less than 100 acres and 63 percent were less than 50 acres. Only half of Mississippi's 62,878 white families were slaveholders before the War, and a mere 316 had more than 100.[27] In other words, the farm economy was connected to virtually all of the white residents in the state, and these small farms were everywhere except for the interior of the Delta and southwest Mississippi.

The contemporaneous literature of the times is filled with examples of Blacks exercising their freedom and seeking land to call their own, whites recoiling and rebelling at the changes, and clashes between the two groups. In Natchez, for example, returning Confederate soldiers patrolled the streets and "forcibly carried former slaves out of town and left them to starve or return to the former owners." Military officers reported to their superiors that "in parts of Alabama, Mississippi, and Texas, former Rebel soldiers killed an average of one Black man per day during the summer of 1865."[28]

The opposing sides of that conflict were described by historian John Willis: "Many former slave owners recoiled at the prospect that destitute, semiskilled, agricultural laborers, individuals who until very recently had been held and treated as human chattel, must be regarded as free people with civil rights.

More than just a prized labor supply to be fought over by white elites, freed people proved eager to determine their own fates and unwilling to accept conditions that smacked of slavery."[29]

The observations of a Union admiral during the War were not only ignored but willfully pushed aside by whites: "I have scarcely ever yet met with a Negro who has not been able to support himself, they are naturally astute at making money, and when they are not it is an exception to the rule. . . . Quite a number of them have good trades, and we have now in the fleet contrabands who are considered our best mechanics. . . . The servants are all intelligent and could make more money out of the service than in it."[30] Through his journey from Corinth to Memphis, down the Mississippi River to Vicksburg and Natchez, Trowbridge would encounter the usual response from whites, "That's freedom! That's what the Yankees have done for 'em! They'll be dead before spring. Niggers can't take care of themselves. The Southern people were always their best friends. How I pity them. How much better off they were when they were slaves."[31]

A reporter for the newly established *Nation* magazine found the same attitude among whites gathered around a stove in the lobby of a Vicksburg hotel: "Then the talk went on about the injustice and folly of emancipation; how miserable the lot of the freedman must necessarily be; slave labor, and how the United States undoubtedly ought to pay the value of every emancipated slave."[32]

A congressional committee charged with assessing conditions in the South took testimony from people throughout Mississippi in the months following the surrender. One businessman who worked for an association of New England manufacturers, traveling the South looking for cotton to purchase, was asked about the sentiments of the people in the South toward the Union:

> When they speak of the Union, it is usually either with unmitigated severity and denunciation or else with indifference, as of something they do not appreciate, to say the least. Nowhere did I find Southern feeling so intense as in Alabama and Mississippi. If a Negro man is able-bodied, strong, and willing to work, he can generally make a living. But if he refuses to work in the cotton field, and is not a mechanic, and tries to set up for himself, he has not much of a chance given him. He is sure to be marked and is not very safe there.[33]

White farmers and landowners, who had backed a losing war and lost almost everything, who had lived in the belief that Blacks were inferior to whites, were now confronted with those same Blacks demanding wages for their work or land to own themselves. Marry that situation with a nineteenth century federal government that had just begun to experiment with intervening in the day-to-day affairs of states and localities and had neither the resources nor the political will to impose the kind of rebuilding program on the South that could actually make a difference, and Mississippi was left with a set of social, political, and economic challenges that would not be resolved for another 90 years.

THE BEGINNING OF A RECOVERY

The May 1865 surrender served neither as a clean demarcation between the War and Reconstruction nor between the prosecution of the War and the rebuilding effort. During the War, the Union Army never "occupied" Mississippi and never operated a government that sought to supersede the Confederate government that Mississippi established following secession. Instead, Union forces moved through the state to wage specific campaigns, the major ones being Corinth in the fall of 1862; Vicksburg, and the greater Jackson area, in the spring and summer of 1863; and Sherman's march from Vicksburg to Meridian in the winter of 1864. While there were minor skirmishes at other times, this sporadic movement of Union soldiers in and out of the state allowed the Confederate government to continue to function, though not always operating out of the State Capitol building in Jackson, and gave residents time to rebuild.

Whitelaw Reid, a British journalist touring Mississippi in the summer of 1865, found Vicksburg had "already lost most of the traces of the siege. . . . Cotton already dotted every little spot of arable land within the Rebel lines and beyond them many a broad field." After visiting Natchez, he wrote, "Buildings in Natchez, which the Government had seized, were being restored to the former owners. Business had revived. Northern men had established themselves as commission merchants and dealers in plantation supplies, and were infusing new energy into the town."[34]

In some places, Northern investors showed up with capital to rebuild the rail lines, knowing that their competitor, the steamboat industry, had long been operating along the Mississippi River during the War under federal protection. Moreover, cotton buyers in New Orleans and Memphis began to offer some farmers credit towards equipment and supplies for a new crop of cotton.[35]

More fascinating is that historians have accumulated evidence to indicate that many white Mississippians had grown tired of the War before the actual surrender, had come to believe defeat was imminent, and were ready to move on. As one scholar described it, "The desire for peace, the opportunity to restore the means of livelihood, and, for many, simply survival, were by late 1864 the critical factors in the state of mind of a great many Mississippians. Loyalty to the Confederacy or the Union was of secondary importance to a people who were tired of bloodshed, disillusioned, almost destitute, and anxious for a government that would protect their lives and remaining possessions and give them a chance to produce and market their crops."[36] Historian David Sansing wrote of a May 10, 1865, public meeting in Jefferson County where prominent citizens adopted resolutions repudiating secession and expressing a desire for the restoration of civil government and the prompt return to status quo ante bellum.[37]

Likewise, for many serving in the Confederate Army, reality was beginning to take hold. A local Mississippi official wrote to Jefferson Davis in 1864 that "Mississippi is in a most deplorable condition. . . . Very many of the middle class, a large number of the more intelligent, and nearly all of the lower class of her people are drifting to the Yankees. Desertion from the army, trading with the enemy, and the removal of deserters and their families into the lines and the supposed lines of the enemy is now the order of the day." At one point, so many men were leaving their positions with the Army that Confederate General Nathan Bedford Forrest condemned them as "roving bands of deserters, stragglers, horse-thieves, and robbers, who consume the substance, and appropriate the property of the citizens," and Mississippi's governor was authorized by the state Legislature to use the state militia to go after deserters.[38]

This tension between loyalty to the Confederacy and finding a way to survive and care for a family helped to kick-start the rebuilding program in the state. In more than just a few cases, individuals chose to reunite with their families and attempt a return to "normal" life.[39] Even someone as prominent as James Alcorn, a wealthy landowner in Coahoma County and a future governor and United States senator, retreated to his plantation, smuggled cotton to Northern investors, and invested the profits in more land and Union currency.[40]

As the War was heading into its third year, months before the Confederate disasters at Gettysburg and Vicksburg, one of the Jackson newspapers flexed its editorial muscles and dared the Union to persist in its attacks on Mississippi: "Our opinion is that the northern rump of a government has well-nigh spent its strength, and if it persists in urging the war upon the emancipation policy, it will find an enemy at home which will give it enough to do."[41] Notwithstanding the editor's bluster, in the months that followed, Vicksburg fell, formerly enslaved Black men were recruited to join the Union Army, Sherman marched through central Mississippi, destroying much of what he saw, Mississippi troops surrendered, and slavery was abolished. Freedom would now be tested in Mississippi.

CHAPTER 3

1865–1866
The Experience of Freedom

Verily the work does not end with the abolition of slavery, but only begins.
—FREDERICK DOUGLASS[1]

The United States Supreme Court issued its most infamous decision on March 6, 1857, when it ruled in *Dred Scott v. Sandford* that slaves and their descendants were not American citizens and thus were not entitled to "all the rights and privileges and immunities guaranteed" by the Constitution.[2]

The man who wrote that 7-2 opinion—Chief Justice Roger B. Taney—was still chief justice, and still had his majority on the court, in the summer of 1864 as the War was in the middle of its fourth year and the Emancipation Proclamation was less than seventeen months old. President Lincoln and Republicans in Congress knew the end of the War was no guarantee of freedom for Black Southerners. Confederate leaders talked openly about reinstituting slavery after the War, and others feared a Taney court would undermine any good done with emancipation. Amending the Constitution to prohibit slavery was the only answer. While the Senate approved the Thirteenth Amendment in April of that year, Republican leaders in the House failed to gain the two-thirds vote necessary to send the proposal to the states. That achievement was barely accomplished in a lame-duck session of Congress in January 1865, following the 1864 campaign in which President Lincoln was reelected and Republicans increased their number in both houses of Congress. Eleven months later, twenty-seven states—the required three-fourths number—had ratified the Thirteenth Amendment to the United States Constitution.[3]

The Union victory, the Emancipation Proclamation, and, finally, the adoption of the Thirteenth Amendment transformed Mississippi's majority

Black population into free people, a social, cultural, political, and economic upheaval that whites in the state, and across the South, could hardly fathom.

While most whites could, and would, continue to believe Blacks were inferior human beings, they could no longer legally enslave them. They would, however, spend the next 100 years working to deny Black Mississippians legal and voting rights; equal educational, social, and civic opportunities; and access to land ownership and other avenues that could lead to economic independence. The legal term for this practice was segregation, though this way of life in the South was more often referred to by its informal name: Jim Crow.

During the War, as enslaved men and women sought their freedom in Union camps, they became known as "contrabands," or refugees, as discussed in Chapter 1. After the War, during the early years of Reconstruction, before they were granted citizenship by Congress and the Fourteenth Amendment, they were referred to as "Freedmen." Today, the more inclusive terms Freedpeople and Freedpersons are used.

THE EXERCISE OF FREEDOM

During the months immediately following the Confederate surrender, Black men and women engaged in activities that were otherwise unremarkable to any free person, but which they had been denied all their lives: they traveled to destinations of their choosing, wore the clothes they wanted to wear, sang the songs they wanted to sing, took time off from work, went to the church of their choice, reunited with their families, walked to a store, drank whiskey when they wanted to drink whiskey, attended school. Later it meant getting a different job, negotiating for wages and working conditions, marrying the person they wanted to marry, retaining custody of their children, and demanding land of their own. These men and women were no longer anyone's property.[4]

In doing these things, Freedpeople were not only rebelling against bondage and exercising their freedom, they were communicating their right to enjoy their freedom and to choose how and when they wanted to enjoy it. That any person would want to do this seems beyond dispute. Historian Ralph Perman captured the phenomenon when he wrote, "Wherever they went and whatever they did, the newly freed did not respond aimlessly and in bewilderment. Freedom [meant] independence and autonomy, not just the absence of the most obvious features of enslavement."[5]

White Southerners, on the other hand, could hardly comprehend the phenomenon, much less sympathize with it. Rather than witnessing an expression of freedom, what they saw were ex-slaves being lazy, rude, intemperate, pushy, and insubordinate.[6] For their entire lives, whites had justified slavery on the grounds that Blacks were inferior human beings, incapable of understanding freedom, and whites' reaction to this extraordinary turn of events was captured by Perlman when he wrote, "They simply could not understand how their former charges had suddenly lost their servility. It was impossible for them to believe and even more difficult to explain how blacks whose supposed innate dependence and inability to fend for themselves that had justified enslavement in the first place could have discovered these new notions on their own."[7]

An emissary appointed by President Andrew Johnson to tour the South in 1865, Carl Schurz, had a similar reaction after talking with countless whites: "It is that the negro exists for the special object of raising cotton, rice, and sugar for the whites and that it is illegitimate for him to indulge, like other people, in the pursuit of his own happiness in his own way. Although it is admitted that he has ceased to be the property of a master, it is not admitted that he has a right to become his own master."[8]

Journalist Whitelaw Reid spent a year in the South, beginning in May 1865, sending dispatches to his home paper and subsequently publishing his observations in book form in 1866. Toward the end of his journey, he reported on conversations he had while on a railcar to Jackson that singled out the uniqueness of the Mississippi backlash:

There were, of course, many individual exceptions, but the prevailing sentiment with which the negro was regarded was one of blind, baffled, revengeful hatred. Hearing one person say, "The infernal sassy niggers had better look out, or they'll all get their throats cut yet" and another "Let a nigger dare to come into my office, without taking off his hat, and he'll get a club over it." Such were the voices I heard on every hand—in the hotels, on the cars, in steamboat cabins, among returned soldiers . . . from men of all ages and conditions. More or less, the same feeling had been apparent in Tennessee, Georgia, Alabama, and Louisiana; but it was in Mississippi that I found its fullest and freest expression. However these men may have regarded the negro slave, they hated the negro freeman. However kind they may have been to negro property, they were virulently vindictive against a property that escaped from their control.[9]

Not only had whites suffered the humiliation of losing a war contemporaneously with experiencing the financial despair of losing millions of dollars of property represented by the emancipation of the South's enslaved population, but they were also suddenly confronted with a social and political world they had never known. That dilemma was described by another historian when he wrote the destruction of slavery "confronted each planter with problems his most deeply held assumptions told him were insoluble. Not only did he believe that a decent Southern society required the labor and race controls that only slavery provided, but he was also still wedded to the notion that it was impossible to manage successfully a staple-producing plantation using free black labor." Despite the assertions by many white Mississippians that "men are rightful property, that emancipation is wholesale robbery, and that the U.S. government is the grandest thief in the world," planters nevertheless "saw no choice but to remain and go on planting; the search for a system to replace slavery became the central concern of their economic lives."[10]

This transformation in the social relationships between Blacks and whites was exacerbated by the overwhelming need for planters and farmers to have people work the fields and by the nearly universal belief among those same white planters that Black men and women would only work in the fields if they were forced to work in the fields. That fear was aptly characterized in a newspaper editorial: "The thriftless, thoughtless Negro would jingle his last month's wages to the planter's face and tell him to do the rest of the work."[11]

Freedpeople, however, pushed back against those assumptions, demanding control over their own lives. As they embraced their freedom, in ways large and small, white newspaper editors joined with their white readers in countless editorials and stories to express amazement at the impertinence of Black men and women and disgust at the choices they were making in reordering their lives. This outpouring of opinion led a group of Blacks in Mississippi to once observe, "Our faults are daily published by the editors, and not a statement will you ever see in our favor."[12] Historian Douglas Blackmon explained why: "Recognition of freed slaves as full humans appeared to most white Southerners not as an extension of liberty but as a violation of it, and as a challenge to the legitimacy of their definition of what it was to be white."[13]

THE FREEDMEN'S BUREAU

As the War became more about emancipation and less about preserving the Union, federal officials came to realize that in winning the War, the future of four million enslaved men, women, and children would be dim indeed without some form of federal assistance to both protect their freedom and to help with adjustment to the new social and economic order.

The debate and discussion about what this kind of program should look like took place in the nation's capital from early 1863 until March 3, 1865, when Congress passed, and President Lincoln approved, legislation creating the Bureau of Refugees, Freedmen, and Abandoned Lands. Located within the War Department and conceived as a temporary agency, it quickly became known as the Freedmen's Bureau. The agency remained in existence until December 1868 and was the "nation's first large-scale experiment in social welfare."[14]

Rather than provide it with an appropriation, Congress gave the Bureau responsibility for all of the abandoned property within the Confederacy, assuming that leasing land under its control for farming could provide the Bureau with sufficient funding. Moreover, it expected most of the Bureau officials would be commissioned officers in the Army (and thus on the Army's payroll) and that the Army would provide any supplies and materials needed for its operation. Beyond providing procedures for acquiring and leasing abandoned land and using Army supplies, the legislation provided little else in the way of detailed duties. "The lack of specificity," as one writer observed, "meant the Bureau's job would be as big as the problems its men encountered in the war-ravaged South." For the next three years, the Bureau would operate hospitals, courts, and schools; distribute food, clothing, and other necessities; provide emergency housing and medical aid; negotiate and supervise labor contracts; reunite families and find homes for orphans; operate special courts to mediate claims; and generally cushion the transition from slavery to freedom. For Massachusetts Senator Charles Sumner, the newly enacted Bureau was fundamental to ensuring that "the Freedman's rights shall be protected and his new-found liberty be made a blessing."[15]

Historian Paul Cimbala described the person chosen to head this new agency: "The task of organizing the agency to cope with this duty and all other matters related to the Freedpeople fell to a veteran soldier well known for his Christian ideals and the bravery proven by his empty right sleeve, but with little experience with ex-slaves, Major General Oliver Otis Howard."[16]

Howard realized the enormity of the job helping to make real the freedom of four million men, women, and children soon after he told Secretary of War Edwin Stanton he would accept the job as commissioner: "The Secretary sent for all the papers, correspondence, and reports dealing with the freedmen and refugees. They were brought in, heaped together in a large, oblong basket. Holding each end of the basket, Stanton smilingly presented it to Howard and said, 'Here, general, here's your Bureau!'" More to the point, another official warned him that he did not have the "power to fulfill one-tenth of the expectations of those who framed the Bureau."[17]

On June 20, 1865, Colonel Samuel Thomas arrived in Mississippi as the newly appointed assistant commissioner in charge of Freedmen's Bureau operations for the state. Thomas had served as a key aide to John Eaton in Mississippi as part of the contraband operation. More importantly, from his perspective as directing the Bureau's operations in the state, he had served as the commanding officer of a Black regiment during the War and thus had a front-row seat in working with and observing the life and times of Blacks and their interactions with whites.[18]

Confronting Thomas and his staff were more than 430,000 newly freed men, women, and children who, by definition of their previous servitude, had no land or other property such as horses, mules, wagons, or equipment; no money; few clothes; and little formal education. They were spread throughout 37,000 rural farms or plantations or living in the few incorporated towns or villages Mississippi had at the end of the War. Of that number, only about 25 percent had obtained their freedom during the War either as "contrabands," refugees, or as Union soldiers.[19] As one official remarked, "The emancipated slaves own nothing, because nothing but freedom has been given to them."[20]

Moreover, Thomas had the unenviable task of creating a new organization from scratch, recruiting staff, working out relationships with military officers, opening local offices, creating procedures and job duties, developing financing and budgets, and identifying ways to make contact with both the ex-slaves and white farmers and landowners. Specifically to reach out to Freedpeople, Thomas appointed assistants for the various geographical regions of the state who were officers in the United States Colored Infantry. And because he had worked in the state, Thomas knew people he could hire who would represent his wishes throughout the new organization. By July 29, 1865, Thomas reported to Howard that almost every county had a Bureau staff member working in it, complete with office space and procedures, and that his headquarters in Vicksburg was also fully staffed and operating. By the end of September, more than 50 officers from the military were on staff, plus 160 civilians. Staffing was made easier because of the close connection between the military force occupying the state and the Freedmen's Bureau reporting to the Secretary of War. And, by then, the roles had been worked out. The Bureau's responsibility was to aid the newly freed men, women, and children while the military was tasked to largely preserve security and law and order.[21]

Individual Bureau officials were empowered to provide assistance in any way they found necessary, within the resources available to them at the time. At its peak in the summer of 1865, for example, the Bureau in Mississippi was providing more than 110,000 rations per month. While that number declined to less than 13,000 by the end of the year, the number of hospitals operated by the Bureau had grown during that same time from three it assumed from the Army at the end of the War to ten, including hospitals in Corinth, Meridian, Natchez, and Jackson. Close to 19,000 patients were being treated for ailments and diseases ranging from fevers to syphilis, snake bites, tetanus, and intestinal worms. At the height of its involvement in education, the Bureau operated fifty schools with more than 90 teachers who served more than 5,800 students.[22]

To inform people about its policies and expectations, the Bureau issued what they called "circulars" or what today would be referred to as regulations. Bureau officials distributed the circulars by hand, printed them in local newspapers, and read them aloud in community meetings. One official in the northern part of the state reported that over two months in the fall of 1865, he had made twenty-five speeches in front of crowds ranging from 250 to 2,000, attended by Blacks as well as whites.[23] Early on, one of the most critical aspects of their work was simply informing both Black and white Mississippians what the end of the War meant: freedom for those who had been enslaved.[24]

Even though Bureau officials and employees took seriously their charge and sympathized with what it meant to leave slavery, they oftentimes adopted a paternalistic response to their role, believing that maintaining order meant putting Freedpeople back to work and instilling proper respect for authority. What comes across in many of the Bureau circulars and speeches is their need to inform the ex-slaves of the responsibilities they must assume as "free" people, the most important of which was the imperative to work. Idleness would not be condoned. Thomas and his team believed slavery had left Freedpersons ill prepared to live in a free world, that they were "cut adrift from those who not only fed, clothed, and housed them, but also advised, protected, and taught them all they knew." Without the guiding hand of their "masters," Thomas believed, Black men and women were like "sheep without a shepherd." Consequently, Freedpersons were not permitted to avoid work or travel the countryside without having a specific place to go. In one circular, Thomas claimed, "Freedom does not mean the right to live without work or at other people's expense, but means that each man shall enjoy the fair fruits of his labor."[25]

The white reaction in Mississippi to the work of the Freedmen's Bureau can be summed up by a small poem a Panola County newspaper ran on its masthead: "Breathes there the man, with soul so dead, Who never to himself hath said, G-d D--n the Freedmen's Bureau."[26]

One Bureau official noted in a report that when he attended religious services at a local Methodist church, "every woman within a radius of ten feet arose and either took a seat away or left the building." The editor of a local Hinds County newspaper denounced the Bureau by claiming, "It affords sinecures for worthless officials, who find in their salaries ample compensation for the dirty work in which they are engaged. . . . While they prey upon their black dupes . . . by keeping up a hostility between the races." The Vicksburg newspaper declared the Bureau "inimical to the true interests" of the state.[27]

In his dissertation describing Mississippi in the years following the War, historian Ross Moore concluded that "much of the criticism leveled at the Bureau was doubtless justified, but the fact remains that had it not been for this agency the Negro would have been at the mercy of his employers. The real foundation of the Southerners' hatred was the fact that white planters did not want any interference from anyone in handling their laborers. The planters were opposed to any organization of the Negroes, nor did they want the black man's interest looked after by the Bureau."[28]

WHITE MISSISSIPPIANS CONFRONT THE FREEDMEN'S BUREAU

While the creation of the Freedmen's Bureau was a rare and innovative move on the part of the federal government, neither Presidents Andrew Johnson nor Ulysses Grant—nor ultimately the majority of Congress—would be willing to engage in the kind of massive government spending and public policy intervention necessary to right the wrong of slavery in the years following the War. Not only were white politicians in Washington saddled with their prejudices, but asking mid-nineteenth-century politicians to create a "New Deal" or a "Great Society" program to aid the Freedpersons meant asking them to ignore all they believed about the limited role of the federal government.

Nevertheless, the missed opportunity for Mississippi comes across time after time in the letters and reports contained in the Freedmen's Bureau files—the willingness of Black men and women to work and the unwillingness of whites to accept Freedpersons as equal citizens.[29]

The relationships between whites and Blacks were certainly not defined by all whites failing to recognize the changes and by all Blacks recognizing the need to work. The compendium of Bureau documents includes instances of white planters adjusting fairly to the new system and ex-slaves engaging in random acts of violence and embezzlement. But the record is more often than not filled with reports that describe beatings and other forms of intimidation and that make abundantly clear that asking white Mississippians to change their perceptions of a Black person's role in society would constitute nearly an impossible request.

Despite Sam Thomas warning planters that "the old appliances of slavery must be abandoned entirely, and the fact [is] that the Negro is a man, and entitled to the common treatment due a human being," one Bureau official reported after traveling extensively throughout the northern and central parts of the state, "Most of the Planters whom I met professed to have relinquished all idea of forcible control, but a number insisted that for any impudence, they would 'knock down' or 'shoot a nigger.' They could not endure the thot [*sic*] of giving up the blessed privilege of 'licking a nigger.' I think however that the disposition to do this is quite as dangerous in the case of many who are not so outspoken, as of these, more violent in language."[30]

Another example comes from a letter sent by a Columbus, Mississippi, planter to the Northern District office of the Bureau:

> Some few weeks ago since for the grossest insolence, I struck a negro woman that formerly belonged to me when she in turn struck and fought me like a tiger. She went to the [local Bureau official] and I followed her and he told her and me both that I had done for her just right and that she would have to be punished and he ordered her back home to me and to stay here. She in the meantime goes off and rents her a room and prepares to leave. I the next morning before breakfast gave her a whipping. She goes again to the [local official] and makes complaint and he sends a guard and arrests me and fines me. Now this woman was not whipped severely.[31]

Beating was again the topic in this December 4, 1865, affidavit of an Okolona Freedwoman, who explained what had happened to her when she complained to her employer of backache after he had ordered her to get up and make a fire: "He replied he did not care anything about my Damned back and to come out there and he would make it ache." She described how she was whipped with a stake used to hold up the side boards of a wagon after being forced to take off her clothes. Then she was told that if she reported him to the Bureau he would kill her. In sending this letter to his superiors, the local Bureau official noted in his cover letter that the affidavit was typical of the "evidence which comes to us daily of abusive treatment."[32]

The journalist Whitelaw Reid noticed the same phenomenon during his travels, "Nothing could overcome this rooted idea that the negro was worthless, except under the lash. These people actually believe that, in submitting to the emancipation of the slaves, they have virtually saddled themselves with an equal number of idle paupers."[33] If whites failed to understand the end of slavery meant the end of beatings, they would surely fail to accept the right of Blacks to serve on juries, vote, receive an education, or own land.

Land was the key. The Freedmen and Southern Society editors set the stage for what could have created opportunities for Blacks to become equal partners in the rebuilding of Mississippi when they wrote: "Former slaves everywhere rejected the continuation of such detested features of bondage as corporal punishment, close supervision, sunup to sundown hours of work, and the hard-driving pace of gang labor. Southern employers, for their part, endeavored to reclaim as much as they could of the power they had enjoyed in the old order. Denied the right to own their workers or to compel labor by force, their predominance now rested on their ownership of land."[34]

THE PROMISE OF LAND[35]

Few slogans have remained a mainstay of Reconstruction literature more than "Forty Acres and a Mule." Black men and women understood it to mean they would be provided with land of their own to farm, or as a reporter found after touring the South in 1865, their "sole ambition was to become the owner of a little piece of land, and to dwell in peace and security at his own free will and pleasure." No promise held out more real hope for ensuring Black families would become both financially independent and economically competitive than the promise of land.

Whites knew this instinctively and fought it bitterly, not only because they had no interest in giving up any of their land but more because they recognized that creating a class of self-sufficient Black Mississippians would threaten the supply of labor they needed to work their farms and plantations, would threaten their hold on political power, and would undermine the very fabric of their social culture. While most whites masked this threat by claiming Blacks were mentally incapable of returning a profit from land of their own, it was the threat to their own way of life that animated their opposition to a land program.[36]

What ultimately happened was predicted by William Whiting, War Department solicitor, who was instrumental in drafting the Freedmen's Bureau legislation. Whiting, according to one historian, was "a Massachusetts man with a hatred of the Old South's aristocratic land pattern, and he fervently believed that unless the large estates were broken into small farms the South would develop a semi-feudal system based on the hired labor of Negroes and poor whites." James McKaye, an early abolitionist who helped craft one of the early reports that led to the Freedmen's Bureau legislation, echoed Whiting when he once wrote, "No such thing as a free, democratic society can exist in any country where all lands are owned by one class of men and cultivated by another."[37]

Providing Freedpeople with land of their own became part of conversations in Congress as government officials were suddenly and unexpectedly confronted with the challenge of responding to the demand for freedom by the former slaves. Reports from refugee camps, missionary associations, and the Army gave support to the idea that ownership of land was the way to "translate emancipation into substantive freedom" by effectively ruling out "any halfway station between freedom and slavery." Historian Vernon Lane Wharton echoed those conclusions when he wrote of the Black men and women emerging from slavery: "Their very lives were entwined with the land and its cultivation: they lived in a society where respectability was based on ownership of the soil; and to them to be free was to farm their own ground."[38]

The "forty acres" part of the slogan can be found in congressional speeches and reports from the South early in the War. It gained an official imprimatur on January 16, 1865, when General William Sherman, while moving along the southeast side of the country and, in turn, liberating thousands of enslaved families, issued Field Order 15. The order reserved several hundred thousand acres of land constituting a strip of coastline stretching from Charleston to northern Florida for the "exclusive use of ex-slaves" and provided for the allotment of "forty-acre homesteads." Its genesis was apparently a meeting that twenty Freedpeople had with Sherman and Secretary of War Stanton in Savannah, Georgia. According to the minutes of the meeting that were subsequently made public, the newly freed Black men were asked how they could best care for themselves and aid the government in maintaining their freedom. Their answer was simple: "The way we can best take care of ourselves is to have land, and turn it and till it by our own labor." Stanton was later quoted as saying this was the first time in the history of the nation that government officials had "gone to the Negroes and asked them what they wanted for themselves." By June, some 40,000 Black men, women, and children had settled on 400,000 acres of "Sherman" land. After Sherman allowed the Army to lend the new settlers mules for use in cultivating the land, the slogan "forty acres and a mule" took shape and grew.

The forty-acre provision then showed up at the last minute in the compromise legislation creating the Freedmen's Bureau a few weeks later. Section 4 of the bill contained the key provision: "That the [Freedmen's Bureau] commissioner, under the direction of the president, shall have authority to set apart, for the use of loyal refugees and freedmen, such tracts of land within the insurrectionary states as shall have been abandoned, or to which the United States shall have acquired title by confiscation or sale, or otherwise, and to every male citizen, whether refugee or freedman, as aforesaid, there shall be assigned not more than forty acres of such land."[39]

Naturally, the first conflicts took place in early 1865 when defeated Confederates began returning to the land they had left, only to find it in the hands of the federal government and being farmed by Freedpeople. To avoid any questions about title to land, Commissioner Howard worked through all of 1865 to transfer legal title to this land to the Freedmen's Bureau, a total that came to 858,000 acres throughout the South, with more than 80,000 acres in Mississippi.

Realizing this was not close to the acreage he needed to meet the demands of Freedpeople wanting their forty-acre plots, Howard, and his allies in Congress, openly began discussing ways to obtain more land. Pennsylvania Representative Thaddeus Stevens was one of several leaders in Congress who argued for taking land outright from the rebels: "Every inch of the guilty portion of the usurping power should be held responsible to reimburse all the cost of the war; to pay all the damage to private property of loyal men, and to create an ample fund to pay pensions to wounded soldiers and the bereaved friends of the slain." Stevens liked to exclaim that land should be seized to pay the expenses of the War, "to punish the Confederates, and to provide for 'loyalists' and for the blacks." "The white people of the South," he maintained, "were entitled to no rights of person or property and the United States should treat the former Southern States as conquered provinces."

President Johnson, on the other hand, was moving in the opposite direction. Beginning on May 29, 1865, and in subsequent executive proclamations, he spelled out the process by which states could rejoin the union. The provision that undermined Howard's land initiative allowed most ex-Confederates to regain their land once they had taken an oath of loyalty to the United States. As the claims began to spiral out of control in the summer and fall, Howard and his staff were desperate to avoid restoring so much land, not only because it deprived Freedpersons of the chance to have land of their own, but giving up the land would deprive the Bureau of the only source of money it could use to operate—rental or lease payments for land under its control.

Howard opted to confront the issue directly on July 28 by issuing Circular No. 13, which directed that abandoned and confiscated land under title with the Bureau be reserved for refugees and ex-slaves. Howard instructed his staff to, "with as little delay as possible," select eligible parcels within their respective jurisdictions and divide them into lots for rental or sale to Freedpeople. "The pardon of the President," he wrote, "will not be understood to extend to the surrender of abandoned or confiscated property thus reserved." Moreover, no land under the Bureau's control could be restored to its antebellum owners without Howard's personal authorization.

The proverbial line in the sand was therefore drawn by Howard. As complaints from landowners throughout the South found their way to the White House, Johnson overruled Howard and effectively nullified the promise of land ownership that was written into the Freedmen's Bureau legislation. On September 12, Johnson wrote and then forced Howard over his signature to issue Circular No. 15, overriding Circular No. 13 and easing the way for ex-Confederates to recover title to their land. Moreover, by narrowing the definition of confiscated and abandoned land available for the Freedmen, Circular No. 15 also shut down the Bureau's acquisition of additional land. Howard wrote in his autobiography years later that he thought of resigning at the time but decided to remain in hopes of doing what he could to alleviate suffering and help with the transition. White Southerners, seeing the handwriting on the wall, took little time to reclaim their land. Howard's director in Mississippi, Samuel Thomas, echoed the concerns of everyone who had advocated on behalf of the Bureau's land program when he wrote that "the Freedmen of the State are becoming alarmed at the large amount of property that is being turned over to owners, and say that it is a breach of faith on the part of the Government, as they have been promised land to work, but the present policy will leave them no lands, and drive them to work for low wages."

Later in the fall, he wrote Howard again, this time asking permission to set aside specific sections of land:

This land has already been set apart for the same purpose for which I ask it, by Department orders, and cultivated by Freedmen during the last two years successfully. The Freedmen have built houses, and expended money on the land, with the expectation that the Government would sustain their claim to it in preference to that of the rebel owners. The citizens of the state will not sell or rent land to Freedmen; they say, if Freedmen are allowed land to work, they will make money so easily that they will not hire out for wages. This I believe to be true; I believe a negro

need not work one half as hard now on ten acres of a group as he did in
the days of Slavery, yet he will get far better support, and have time to
educate himself and money to educate his children.[40]

Notwithstanding what Howard, Thomas, and others wanted to happen,
President Johnson repeatedly undercut their efforts and sided with the
Southern landowners.

By the early fall of 1865, Thomas was reporting that only 13,500 of the original 80,000 acres were leased to Black families. And that number would continue to decline.[41]

Early in 1866, after it became clear the promise of land would never be
fulfilled, Merrimon Howard, a Mississippi ex-slave, wrote to the Freedmen's
Bureau, making plain the disappointment that he and others were feeling: "we
are left with no land, no house, not so much as a place to lay our head . . .
despised by the world, hated by the country that gives us birth, denied all of
our writs as a people, we were friends on the march . . . brothers on the battlefield, but in the peaceful pursuits of life it seems that we are strangers."[42]

The demise of "forty acres and a mule" raises the kind of fundamental
questions about the Union response to the failed Confederate rebellion that
had repercussions for the decades that followed: Should people who took up
arms against the Union be able to keep their land? Should the newly freed
Black men and women have had access to some of the land they helped to
improve and farm during slavery? Should Blacks who fought for the Union
Army receive some special compensation? By shutting down the prospects for
land ownership among the Freedpeople so early in Reconstruction, President
Johnson effectively answered "no" to all these questions.

With the prospects for ownership of land disappearing through the fall
of 1865 and into the winter of 1866, Black men and women were left with
nothing but their labor, for the planters not only owned the land, but they
also owned the livestock, equipment, tools and all the other resources necessary for a profitable farming operation. Of the Freedpeople who had developed specific trade skills, many of them moved to towns seeking work. Others
sought domestic jobs or positions as hired hands on barges and steamboats
or in mills. But for the vast majority, who had neither the means to travel nor
the skills with which to bargain, agriculture remained their path to survival.

At the beginning of the year, John Eaton had made a similar observation:
"The Freedmen do best for themselves and the government as independent
cultivators of small farms. Those who worked for themselves, have raised
on average the most cotton per acre and have saved sums varying from one

hundred dollars to ten thousand, while those who have worked for hire, have rarely laid up anything."[43]

Even then, having to negotiate with Blacks for the right to use their labor was as foreign to whites as letting them vote, marry, read, or travel.

A NEW FORM OF LABOR

In the early postbellum South, the employment relationship in the fields or a shop, or even in a home between Freedpersons and their white employers was governed by a signed, written contract. Most of the 1865 and early 1866 contracts, to the extent one could call them fair and balanced, were that way because the Freedmen's Bureau spent a substantial share of their manpower and resources overseeing, approving, and enforcing the contractual process.[44]

Mississippi Bureau director Samuel Thomas was convinced that "fair wages for a day's work would eventually secure for black families the capital necessary to lease and then buy their own lands independently and freely." Knowing what he knew about the plantation culture from having lived and worked in Mississippi during the War, Thomas instructed his staff to be wary of the white planters and to represent the Freedpersons as best they could. Thomas was sure that the law of supply and demand would enable them to obtain the highest wages possible, though he warned planters that uncompensated labor was "beyond the pale."[45]

In a July 19, 1865, letter to a staff person in Washington County, Thomas enjoined him to think anew and placed the success of the endeavor squarely on him: "In the discharge of your new district, you must be governed by the orders and circulars furnished to you from this office. You must [rid] yourself as far as possible of old ideas, and look at this Free labor movement as something you are interested in, and think it depends on you whether it succeeds."[46] Thus began, in the summer of 1865, a grand experiment in applying free-market principles of supply and demand for labor in Mississippi and throughout the South. The process would take years to evolve and would ultimately settle on a form of labor remuneration known as sharecropping, which would not change until well into the twentieth century when the introduction of tractors and then mechanical cotton pickers dramatically reduced the need for labor in the fields.

Enunciating a free-market labor policy was, of course, relatively easy. Applying it in rural areas where it had never been practiced would have been a challenge in and of itself. But applying it in Mississippi in the wake of the destruction of its agricultural infrastructure, with a white population full of prejudice and anger and forced to embrace a concept completely foreign to their way of life, presented almost insurmountable hurdles.

Nevertheless, planters and farmers had little choice, though many of them could not abandon the belief that Freedpeople had to be treated as slaves to generate work. Carl Schurz reported that he heard from planters "hundreds of times" and "wherever I went" the observation that "you cannot make the negro work without physical compulsion." And when Blacks walked "away from the plantations, it was conclusive proof of the incorrigible instability of the negro, and the impracticability of free negro labor." And if some individual "negroes violated the terms of their contract, it proved unanswerably that no negro had, or ever would have, a just conception of the binding force of a contract, and that this system of free negro labor was bound to be a failure."[47]

All of these struggles were rooted in the need for landowners and farmers to control their labor. That was all they had known, and they were constantly pushing for a labor code that was "molded to their needs necessary to control black labor." As a Meridian planter remarked, "I do not care one cent for the niggers being free if they will only leave them here to work and let me manage [them]." [48]

As for Black workers, they were tasting freedom for the first time, and their responses were as varied as their number living in Mississippi. Many chose to remain, others sought better working conditions at other farms and plantations, some bargained with multiple planters, and still others took off looking for family members or excitement in the city or to try their luck at other jobs such as trades and domestic service. Planters, on the other hand, were forced to negotiate contracts, especially when it became clear Blacks would travel.[49]

In the more rural areas of the state, Carl Schurz found that "the colored people are kept in slavery still. The white people tell them that they were free during the war, but the war is now over, and they must go back to work again as before." In other areas, he found planters and farmers offering work only to the able-bodied and driving the "young and infirm" off the land.[50]

One of Thomas's first directives was issued on August 4, 1865, as Circular No. 9:

It is important that the Planters of Mississippi both understand the new relation which they sustain to the new labor of the State, and cheerfully accept the facts of the new situation. Abuses of the Freedmen of the gravest character are often reported to this office. These must be stopped. The Planters should learn that their interests and those of the Freedmen are co-incident. . . . Emancipation is a fact. The Government is pledged to maintain it. Yet many of the Planters are found going back, in thought, to re-argue the question of Freedom, and to dispute that fact; thus throwing obstacles in the way of the successful working of the free-labor system. . . . The interests of the Planters and the Freedmen lie parallel to each other. They cannot become hostile unless prejudice makes them so.[51]

Many of the first sets of contracts were reminiscent of slavery, with landowners believing nothing less would motivate the Freedpersons to do the work. The contracts called for working on all seven days, specifying the number of hours and the way the work would be organized, and designating who would supervise the work, as well as indicating penalties. From the perspective of the Freedmen's Bureau, the system of contract labor was created to "ensure a ready supply of labor and restore order and productivity to the agricultural economy" all the while "providing a transition to freedom and self-sufficiency for the former slaves."[52]

Black men and women, however, made clear they wanted nothing to do with contracts that reminded them of their days under bondage. Their only hope was that a Freedmen's Bureau official would fail to approve the contract and demand changes on their behalf. But there was never enough Bureau staff to represent the 430,000 Freedpeople in the state.

As Black men and women came to realize they could negotiate with competing planters, the market began to offer some protection against overly restrictive contacts. A planter near Vicksburg, for example, complained to the Bureau in July 1865 that some of his former slaves had contacted workers still remaining on his farm, telling them of the higher pay they were receiving on another farm and convincing them to leave. The planter's request was simple and breathtaking: use the power of the Bureau "to return the blacks" who had left him.[53]

On the one hand, a letter from a local Bureau official in Meridian on September 26, 1865, to the Jackson headquarters reported that he had "observed a marked improvement among the Freedmen under my charge, in becoming more settled and becoming convinced that to labor is the lot of all. Their desire to roam about seems to have, to some extent, been satisfied. They are rapidly earning money with which some of them express a determination to educate their children, to whom they seem much attached."[54]

On the other hand, others were attempting "to subsist off the land by fishing, cutting wood for sale to riverboats, herding a few hogs, or even squatting on unclaimed lands and raising enough corn to live." In early 1866, one of the Natchez newspapers complained: "Few persons are aware of the extent of the

Negro village situated on the river above the cotton press. There are probably not less than a thousand souls living there in small cabins, each surrounded by a little enclosure under cultivation. The cabins are equidistant and arranged with a degree of regularity which gives the place a very neat appearance. How these people live is a mystery to us, and yet the village seems to be in thriving condition."[55] And then there were, of course, those who, after years of slavery, wanted to do nothing and didn't want to work, while others were happy to enter "the underworld of petty larceny and even semi-organized plunder to survive without going back to the plantation."[56]

The first year of this experiment using a limited and highly compromised version of the free market to govern employee and employer relationships in Mississippi left most of the participants unhappy. Whites were unhappy that they even had to negotiate with Black men and women, not to mention having to have their contracts approved by the Freedmen's Bureau. Blacks were unhappy they had no land of their own and the contracts they had to sign had less than favorable provisions.

Contracts ended in December 1865, which favored the planters by giving them some assurance that labor would be available through the harvest season. Most of the contracts provided for payment at year-end, once the crop had been harvested and the owner had sold it. Consequently, the contracts were promises, and once again it fell to the Freedmen's Bureau to enforce the contracts when the plantation owners would summarily dismiss the workers without any payment. In effect, these contracts served as "interest-free loans equal to the amount of the deferred pay." The payment came either in individual wages or, more often, as a share of the crop. On the other hand, the Bureau forced employers to provide food and housing for all family members covered by the contract, even for those too young or too old, or too sick, to work.[57]

Even though Bureau officials tried to encourage workers to remain on farms and plantations and sign contracts, even under less-than-ideal conditions, many whites just couldn't absorb the changes or appreciate the work of the Bureau. As a Mississippi planter remarked, "The negro is a sacred animal. The Yankees are about negroes like the Egyptians are about cats."[58]

As 1865 turned into 1866, more and more Black men and women refused to sign contracts for the 1866 growing season, either because they were holding out hope for their "forty acres" or because they wanted to ensure fairer working conditions. The first full year after the surrender would test the willingness of Congress to confront President Johnson over the extent of the federal involvement in Reconstruction while testing the ability and the willingness of the Freedmen's Bureau to persuade whites to negotiate fair contracts and Blacks to enter into those contracts.

The end of 1865 also witnessed the ratification of the Thirteenth Amendment and the official end of slavery in America. While countless whites throughout Mississippi believed Freedpeople would be ruined by freedom, John Eaton knew better. He had probably spent more time with fugitive slaves throughout the War than any other white person, and he knew what course they wanted. Near the end of the War, Eaton was asked by a congressional committee, "What of the motives which induced those under your care to change their relations to their masters?" Eaton responded: "Can't answer short of 100 pages. Bad treatment, hard times, lack of the comforts of life . . . because they wished to be free . . . none wish to return; many would die first. All delighted with the prospect of freedom. Most have a tolerably well-developed idea of freedom and long to enjoy it."[59]

During one of the debates over Reconstruction legislation, a Member of Congress asked rhetorically, "What is freedom? Is it the bare privilege of not being chained? If this is all, then freedom is a bitter mockery, a cruel delusion." In other words, as one historian observed, "Did freedom mean simply the absence of slavery, or did it imply other rights for the emancipated blacks, and if so, which: civil equality, the suffrage, ownership of property?"[60] Answering that question would consume the next ten years in Mississippi.

CHAPTER 4

1865–1866
The Black Code

I think God intended the niggers to be slaves. Now since man has deranged God's plans, I think the best we can do is keep 'em as near a state of bondage as possible.
—Southern planter[1]

Given the outcome of the War, the only way to keep Mississippi's Black population in "as near a state of bondage as possible" would be for the white political leadership to curry favor with the federal government, restore the state's status in Congress, reorganize a state government, and adopt laws to reimpose as much control as possible over the lives of the Freedpersons. That job fell initially to William Sharkey and William Yerger once Mississippi Governor Charles Clark was arrested by Union soldiers on May 22, 1865.[2]

Charles Clark had succeeded John Pettus as Mississippi's governor two years earlier, and by the time of his arrest, the last session of the Mississippi Confederate Legislature had adjourned, Abraham Lincoln had been inaugurated for a second term and then assassinated, General Lee had surrendered his Virginia army at Appomattox, General Taylor and General Forrest had surrendered their Mississippi forces, CSA President Jefferson Davis had fled the Richmond capital and dissolved the Confederate government, and Vice President Andrew Johnson had taken the oath of office as the seventeenth president of the United States.

With Congress out of session in May, and having left no clear direction for unifying the country before it adjourned months earlier, the task of Reconstruction fell to President Johnson. A Tennessee Democrat and United States senator before the War, Johnson repudiated the decision of his home state to secede and unlike his Southern colleagues in the Senate refused to resign his seat. Mississippi's delegation—two senators and five representatives—gave up their seats in Congress soon after the state voted to secede in early 1861. In 1862, after Union forces had overtaken much of Tennessee, President Lincoln appointed Johnson as military governor of the state. Two years later, Lincoln asked him to join his reelection ticket as vice president in a show of bipartisanship.[3]

Johnson assumed a presidency confronted by events utterly unique in the country's history. Not only were the legal and political issues unprecedented to this time and place, the national government had never been challenged with reuniting state governments that had rebelled against the Union. In addition to the economic wreckage in which the South found itself, the social and civic upheavals associated with the abolition of slavery, and the uncertainty about the process by which the Confederate states would return members to Congress and resume participating in the political affairs of the country, there was a burgeoning political tug-of-war in Washington between Republicans in Congress and the president over who would manage Reconstruction.

With Congress out of town, its members watched helplessly as Johnson took charge. He began meeting with leaders from the Southern states, appointing provisional governors, and authorizing them to convene constitutional conventions to begin the process of disowning slavery and demonstrating loyalty to the Union. Johnson wanted to move quickly for Congress was scheduled to return to Washington in early December, and he wanted to present them with a set of reorganized state governments ready for a reunion.[4]

Given the confusion in Washington, Governor Clark convened what remained of the Legislature on May 18 to attempt a reorganization of state government. He and the assembled legislators were soon warned by federal forces that martial law was in force and that the former Confederate officials would be prevented from meeting in any official capacity. Four days later, Clarke surrendered the government to a Union general, was arrested and promptly imprisoned, and Mississippi fell under peacetime military rule.

Before his arrest, however, Governor Clark, with the Legislature's authorization, asked William Sharkey and William Yerger, both opponents of secession in 1861, to travel to Washington, meet with the president, and determine what steps would be "necessary to bring the state back to the Union." It was at that meeting, which took place on June 8, that President Johnson suggested that when a convention was held to draft a new constitution to govern the affairs of the state, it should adopt a provision abolishing slavery.[5]

A week later, Johnson issued a proclamation appointing William Sharkey as provisional governor, providing for the restoration of federal authority in the state and for Sharkey to prescribe rules and regulations for calling a convention to amend the constitution and to create a new Legislature.[6] The most controversial provision of the proclamation granted amnesty and pardons to virtually all of the people who had "participated in the existing rebellion" so long as they took an oath to support the United States Constitution and in particular all of the laws with regard to the emancipation of the enslaved.

In what was the earliest known record of Blacks in Mississippi coming together to stage a public protest, a mass meeting was held in Vicksburg soon after Johnson's proclamation in June. An appeal to Congress was drafted that opposed the amnesty provisions and supported voting rights for Black men. Nevertheless, Sharkey set an early August date for the election of convention delegates, with the convention itself called for later in the month. Any white man qualifying under the requirements of the president's proclamation could vote and serve as a convention delegate.[7]

1865 CONSTITUTIONAL CONVENTION

In the early months of Reconstruction, there was no consideration of allowing Black men to participate in elections. The delegates to the convention were all white men, though most of the leaders of the secessionist movement took no part in the process. William Yerger was elected from Hinds County and quickly became a leading voice on the convention floor.[8]

At this point in 1865, only a few months away from the surrender, there were more questions than answers: How would Mississippi regain its political standing in Washington? What concessions would the state have to make? Would the Union Army imprison any Confederate officials? Historian David Sansing has written about the large number of state newspapers and white citizens and officials who spoke out in the early summer, urging their fellow Mississippians to accept defeat. At a public meeting in Jefferson County, for example, a resolution was adopted repudiating secession and supporting the restoration of civil government. Sansing concluded from his research that most white Mississippians were hoping for "*status quo ante bellum*, minus slavery."[9]

When they were released in May, Johnson's terms for the return of the Confederate states were viewed by many as lenient and gave promise to many whites that the penalty for causing the War would be mild. A Friars Point newspaper that covered the Mississippi delegation meeting with President

Johnson reported: "Johnson assured a delegation from Mississippi that there was no disposition on the part of the federal government to deal harshly with the Southern people."[10]

While white Southerners may have been lulled into thinking that losing slavery may be the only cost of the War, a group of Republicans in Congress—who came to be known as "Radical Republicans"—were furious with Johnson's overtures to the South and began to work towards a plan far different from any proposed by Johnson.[11]

These Congressional Republicans envisioned a South where Black men and women would enjoy a political, economic, and social standing equal to that of the white population, a transformation that neither Johnson nor Southern whites had ever anticipated. Moreover, these Republicans had a partisan interest in prolonging Reconstruction: keeping Southerners out of Congress for as long as possible would enable them to consolidate their political strength in Washington. As a Democrat and a Southerner, Johnson would never share any of those goals. Historian Steven Hahn once explained that the president "might have despised the big slaveholders and land-holders, but he had no love for the slaves and freedpeople. He imagined a post-emancipation world run by and for white people with blacks as a sub-ordinate laboring class."[12]

DETERMINING WHAT FREEDOM MEANT
FOR BLACK SOUTHERNERS

Mississippi's constitutional convention, held August 14–22, 1865, at what is now the Old Capitol Museum on State Street in downtown Jackson, was the first to convene under Johnson's Reconstruction plan. Consequently, it was watched closely by the national media, the Johnson administration, and Republicans in Congress. Reporters from several national newspapers were in Jackson to cover it.[13]

While the convention was in session, Governor Sharkey received the following telegram from President Johnson: "I am gratified to see that you have organized your convention without difficulty. I hope that without delay your convention will amend your state constitution, abolishing slavery and denying to all future legislatures the power to legislate that there is property in man; also that they will adopt the amendment to the Constitution of the United States abolishing slavery." And then Johnson dropped the hammer: "If you could extend the elective franchise to all persons of color who can read the Constitution of the United States in English and write their names, and to all persons of color who own real estate valued at not less than two hundred and fifty dollars, and pay taxes thereon, you would completely disarm the adversary and set an example the other states will follow."[14] From Johnson's perspective, the "adversary" were the "Radical" Republicans in Congress. Placating them at this stage, Johnson was gently suggesting, might be the best way to secure an early end to Reconstruction. Nevertheless, Sharkey made clear in a message to Johnson that allowing any formerly enslaved man the right to vote "was impossible in Mississippi."[15]

Ignoring the suffrage issue, the convention delegates took four days to decide how best to convey to the rest of the nation that Mississippi was abolishing slavery. The debate centered on who was responsible and whether farmers and plantation owners would receive financial compensation for the loss of what they believed was their "property"—the 430,000 Black men, women, and children who were now free.

While all of these arguments seem foolhardy in light of the Thirteenth Amendment, at the time of Mississippi's convention, the ratification process had stalled at twenty-three states voting to approve the amendment; twenty-seven were needed and it wasn't clear in August if that number would be met.

Sizeable blocs within the convention maintained Mississippi should not accept the blame for abolishing slavery. Instead, they wanted to shift responsibility entirely to the federal government. Other factions wanted to draft language that would leave open the possibility that a court could order the United States government to provide compensation for their "losses."

Delegate Hugh Barr of Lafayette County argued it would be incorrect to allow the people of the state and future generations to think that the convention had voluntarily abolished slavery, when actually its abolition had been forced on them by a "conqueror." Delegate George Potter of Hinds County maintained, "If then it be true that slavery is dead here in the State of Mississippi, I think no man can deny, as a historical fact, that that extinction has been produced by the action of the Federal authorities."[16]

Delegate Robert Hudson of Yazoo County proposed to bar slavery but only after the newly elected representatives were seated in Congress and Congress had restored civil authority in the state without military intervention.

Still another delegate offered the defiant position: "I think it unwise and unbecoming for the people of Mississippi to make another concession until the federal government complies with its obligations. . . . [Mississippi] should have been recognized as a sovereign state in the federal union and left to deal with this question of testimony as a matter of state policy, over which the federal government should have no control. . . . It should have been so, and I am unwilling to move another inch until it is so."[17]

No doubt many of the delegates had heard from constituents during the election similar to one who wrote Sharkey in the summer, informing the governor that voters would not be supporting "any man in favor of freeing the Negroes." Another letter writer pointed out to Sharkey that people in his county were claiming that slavery was not dead. Yet another cited the Bill of Rights in arguing the federal government could not take away his slaves without compensation since "no man shall be deprived of life, liberty or property without due process of law."[18]

Ultimately it was a long William Yerger speech, focusing on his June meeting with Johnson, which held sway: "The course of argument of those who advocate [the Barr proposal] strikes me with astonishment. They seem actually to ignore the events of the past five years—to ignore the present condition of the people and of the State; and in some dreamy, abstract revery, to indulge in visions and fancies of Constitutional law and Constitutional government, which they think ought to prevail, but which men of practical commonsense, viewing facts—stubborn facts, as they are—well know are not attainable at this time by the people of this country."[19] Then describing his conversation with President Johnson, Yerger argued: "The President then stated there was one thing that the Southern people must understand: that they must accept the condition of things produced by the war—that they must look upon and consider the institution of slavery as ended forever— that this would be a sine quo non in the establishment of civil government."[20] Barr's proposal lost 41-51, and then by a vote of 87-11, the delegates approved the new language to Mississippi's constitution that Yerger supported: "The institution of slavery having been destroyed in the State of Mississippi, neither slavery nor involuntary servitude, otherwise than for the punishment of crime, whereof the party shall have been duly convicted, shall hereafter exist in this State."[21]

The convention then turned to the most gracious way to revoke the secession ordinance without undermining the "patriotism" of the white Mississippians who had followed the directives of the 1861 convention called to legalize the rebellion. The question was whether to use "null and void" or "repealed and abrogated" or "null and of no binding force." Supporters of "null and void" argued for sending the clearest and strongest signal to Washington that Mississippi was finished with slavery and secession.

Opponents countered that "null and void" was too drastic and could easily be interpreted as an admission that secession was wrong. "Repeal" they argued cast no aspersions on the motives of the delegates to the secession convention. The delegates ultimately opted for "null and void" but not before killing the softer version by a mere two-vote margin and thus, in the words of the author of the provision, "Mississippians had been engaged in revolution but had failed."[22]

On August 24, the delegates wrapped up the convention by adopting the new constitution, without submitting it to a vote of the people, in addition to calling for elections for state and local officials in October. Governor Sharkey received a telegram from President Johnson expressing congratulations on the work of the convention, "and paving the way to readmission into the Union and expressing an earnest hope that all obstacles to such readmission would soon be removed."[23]

Sharkey later defended the decision to avoid a popular vote on the constitution in testimony before a congressional committee: "I was so well satisfied with the temper, disposition, and wish of the people that I did not think it necessary to submit the amended constitution to them at all. I was perfectly sure that the people were fully and fair represented. The members of the convention were elected on the general proposition of reforming the constitution, and I have no doubt that they represented truly the sentiments of a large majority of the people of the state."[24]

Throughout the writings and speeches of the white leadership of the time, such as this statement by Sharkey, when he refers to "the people of the state" he unknowingly telegraphed that the newly freed Black men, women, and children did not qualify as "people of the state," certainly not in a way that would require their participation in the affairs of the state. The *Dred Scott* decision was only eight years old and the legal and moral reasoning that animated it was made clear by at least one legislator when he said, "The Negro would never become a citizen; that had been clearly demonstrated by the Dred Scott decision."[25]

Johnson's telegram notwithstanding, the failure of the convention to heed the president's earlier request and provide voting rights to some or all Black men gave Johnson's opponents sufficient ammunition to claim that "going easy" on the rebellious states would fail to change anything in the South. A Massachusetts newspaper editorialized that "the United States can be no party to your oppression. . . . One-half the people of your state cannot . . . exercise those rights which in a republic are the pride and the safety of a freeman; you have simply reorganized a government of privilege."[26]

1865 ELECTION, LEGISLATIVE SESSION, AND THE BLACK CODE

It was in Mississippi, in the early fall of 1865, that the promise of a "*status quo ante bellum*, minus slavery" plan for Reconstruction was lost. A variety of factors came to bear on the white men going to the polls in October that caused them to elect members of the Legislature of a style and temperament different from the earlier convention delegates. Those elected were instead predisposed to stand their collective ground and ignore the suggestions coming from Washington to ratify the Thirteenth Amendment and accept some degree of political equality for Freedpersons.

In addition to the unprecedented challenges of rebuilding the state, historian William Harris identified a variety of real and emotional pressures felt by white voters: planters were facing acute labor problems, rumors of insurrections among Freedpersons were sweeping the state, prospects for the forthcoming crop were becoming critical, the state remained under military occupation, Union soldiers stationed in Mississippi included Negro troops, and the Freedman's Bureau was interjecting itself on behalf of the former slaves.[27]

Another historian, Vernon Lane Wharton, added to the litany of anxieties when he observed, "All of the businessmen and planters of the state felt that everything depended on the large-scale production of cotton, and that for such production they believed disciplined Negro labor to be essential. They also felt that any large group of idle freedmen would immediately constitute a serious social problem and threaten the maintenance of order and the protection of property."[28]

And then there was, of course, the overarching sentiment expressed by a newspaper editorial writer, "The Legislature must insure that the Negro be kept in the position which God almighty intended him to occupy: a position inferior to the white man."[29]

The three candidates for governor had opposed secession, though the man who was elected, Benjamin G. Humphreys, a native of Claiborne County, and a Sunflower County planter when the War broke out, ultimately became a general with the Confederate forces. Voting was light on October 2, and Humphreys won with a plurality of the votes, most likely because veterans knew of his service and the other two candidates split the remaining votes. There were no runoff elections in 1865. As for the Legislature, only four members had served in the 1861 convention called to approve Mississippi's decision to secede, and less than a majority had served previously as legislators or in the constitutional convention.[30]

Also on the ballot were elections for the five members of the Mississippi congressional delegation. That they would never take their seats in the United States House of Representatives was partly a consequence of what the state Legislature did in the ensuing three months.

Following the elections, Humphreys was sworn in as governor and the Legislature convened in Jackson at the State Capitol on Monday, October 16, 1865. In his Inaugural Address that afternoon, Humphreys not only described the challenges but established the political boundaries for the work of the Legislature: "The highest degree of elevation in the scale of civilization to which [the Freedmen] are capable, morally, and intellectually, must be secured to them by their education and religious training, but they cannot be admitted to political or social equality with the white race. It is due to ourselves—to the white emigrant invited to our shores—and it should never be forgotten—to maintain the fact that ours is and shall ever be a government of white men. The purity and progress of both races require that caste must be maintained."[31]

It was another "first" for Mississippi when its Legislature became the first Southern legislature to convene under the guidelines established by President Johnson. Just like the constitutional convention earlier, reporters and observers from many national and regional newspapers were there to follow the business and determine if the state could reconcile itself to the abolition of slavery and the loss of the War. In other words, would the Legislature ratify the Thirteenth Amendment to the Constitution and what laws would they approve applicable to Black men and women?[32]

As it turned out, these newly elected white legislators ended up being their own worst enemies. While at least some of them had to know what was needed for the state to gain acceptance in Washington, for it was surely telegraphed by congressional leaders and national editors, in the end, it was not something they could bring themselves to do. Even the Speaker of the House, Monroe County representative S. J. Gholson, argued that "a conciliatory policy toward the North, to the exclusion of the practical interests of Mississippians, would not work."[33]

For forty-five days, from October 16 to December 6, 1865, the Legislature approved more than 270 bills and resolutions, responding to the demands of the time. Despite all they did, what they are remembered for today, and what they bequeathed to the Johnson administration as 1865 was coming to an end, was a series of bills that sought to regulate the conduct of Black Mississippians. The bills became known, infamously, as the Black Code. And they became a rallying cry for Johnson's congressional opponents and Northern newspaper editors anxious for a reason to punish the South.[34]

GOV. BENJAMIN GRUBB HUMPHREYS
Photographic copy of an oil portrait in the Mississippi Hall of Fame.

Governor Benjamin G. Humphreys, circa 1866. Courtesy
of the Archives and Records Services Division, Mississippi
Department of Archives and History.

By the middle of November, legislators had been in Jackson for a month, unable to produce any legislation regulating the activities of the newly freed Black men, women, and children. On November 17, Johnson telegraphed Governor Humphreys to tell him: "The troops will be withdrawn from Mississippi when, in the opinion of the government, peace and order and the civil authority have been restored and can be maintained without them. There is no concession required on the part of the people of Mississippi or the Legislature, other than a loyal compliance with the laws and Constitution of the United States, and the adoption of such measures giving protection to all freedmen or freemen, in person and property."[35]

Three days later, Governor Humphreys sent his own message to legislators: "By the sudden emancipation of over three hundred thousand slaves, Mississippi has imposed upon her a problem of vast magnitude. Under the pressure of Federal bayonets—urged on by the misdirected sympathy of the North on behalf of the enslaved Africans—the people of Mississippi have abolished the institution of slavery. The Negro is free. Whether we like it or not, we must realize that fact now and forever. To be free, however, does not make him a citizen, or entitle him to political and social equality with the white man."[36] Five days later, the governor had on his desk the most comprehensive measure among the Black Code set of bills, which carried the ironic title of "An Act to Confer Civil Rights on Freedman."[37]

Section 1 allowed Freedpersons to sue or be sued, though that right was narrowed considerably in that a Black person could appear in court as a witness only when another Black person was involved. Even more restrictions were imposed when a separate bill passed later in the session provided that if a Black person brought legal action against a white person, and a judge (who were all white at the time) found the Freedperson's charges were false, the judge could issue a fine and court costs against the Freedperson. The bill ended with a double dose of intimidation. If the Freedperson was unable to pay the fine, the judge could hire him or her out to the most available planter to "work off" the fine.

The most widely ridiculed provision allowed Black men to acquire personal property, though that right was limited to the renting or leasing of land within the corporate limits of municipalities. Unlike today, virtually all of the land in Mississippi at the time was outside the boundaries of towns and cities. While that section was defended on the grounds that private property in the county could provide rallying spaces for "the idle and disorderly of the race," it stood, as one historian observed, "as a direct discouragement to the most industrious and ambitious of the Negroes, and as an almost insurmountable obstacle to those who hoped to rise from the status of a common laborer."[38]

Another section granted Black men and women the right to marry each other, though if a Black person tried to marry a white person, the penalty prescribed for that crime was life imprisonment.

The focus of the bill, however, soon moved from creating a few rights to the real purpose: forcing Black men and women to work in a system that benefited the white farmer and planter. Not only were farmers concerned about having people available to work the crops, but they saw no reason for the Black man and woman to engage in any other work, as Governor Humphreys reminded them in his inaugural address: "The negro is peculiarly adapted to the cultivation of the great staples of the South. He should be encouraged to engage at once in their production by assurances of protection against the avarice, cupidity, and injustice of his employer."

The bulk of the "civil rights" bill enacted guidelines and requirements for work. In fact, the bill required a Black person to obtain written certification on an annual basis of employment. All employment contracts had to be approved by a local county official (all white) or "two disinterested white persons in the county." If a worker quit the contract before the end of the term, he would forfeit his wages for the entire year. The bill further authorized any local officer, or any other person, to arrest anyone who had quit his or her contract. And, with language that would bring smiles to an antitrust lawyer, the legislation prohibited any white person from recruiting from another planter any Black worker under a contract. Even 150 years ago, white legislators instinctively knew the pitfalls of allowing Freedpersons to offer their services in a competitive environment. For those without an annual contract on a farm or plantation, they were required to obtain a license for irregular work from the local governing authority.

A separate Black Code bill required local officials to identify all Black children under the age of eighteen who were orphans or whose parents did not have the means to support their children, a vague criterion left to the discretion of local white officials. Once those children were identified, local judges were authorized to assign the minors as apprentices to "some competent and suitable person"—called "masters" in the law—on the terms determined by the court. Separate provisions authorized the "master" or "mistress" "to inflict such moderate corporeal chastisement as a father or guardian is allowed to inflict on his or her child or ward at common law." Additional sections prohibited the apprentice from leaving without the "master's" consent and others from competing for the apprentice. There was, of course, no public school system in the state and there was no obligation under this new law for the "master" to provide an education.[39]

Consumed as they were with Blacks not working, legislators adopted a separate bill aimed at prohibiting vagrancy, a term in common use at the time and that encompassed a variety of activities, such as loitering or resting on a park bench, all of which represented the opposite of work. Governor Humphreys left no doubt regarding his position on vagrants in his November 20, 1865, message to the Legislature: "Vagrancy and pauperism, and their inevitable concomitants, crime, and misery, hang like a dark pall over our once prosperous and happy, but now desolated and ruined land. Our rich and productive fields have been deserted for the filthy garrets and sickly cellars of our towns and cities." This Black Code measure criminalized anyone who "neglected their calling or employment," misspent what they earned, or failed to provide for the support of themselves or their families. The language went further and prohibited Freedpeople from "unlawfully assembling, either with themselves or with white persons," and vested with local judges (all white) the power to enforce the new law. As with the civil rights bill, if a Freedperson could not pay a fine, then the local official or judge could "hire out" the worker to anyone in the county to pay off the fine.[40]

Perhaps the most egregious of all the Black Code bills was a provision requiring local officials to levy a per-person $1 annual tax on every Black man and woman between eighteen and sixty. Local officials (all white) were authorized to use the proceeds of the tax to create a county Pauper Fund to cover any payments made to help "with the maintenance of the poor of the freedmen." Failure to pay the tax would allow the local officials to arrest a Freedperson and hire him or her out to pay off the tax.[41]

While white officials in Mississippi never hid their belief that the Black race was inferior to the white race, nor their desire for Blacks to return to work on the plantations or farms, in many cases they clothed their motives in a paternalism that was prevalent throughout the South and that was articulated by the special committee established to develop the legislation: "Your committee has thought it best to deny to the freedmen some unbridled privileges for the present, not for any apprehension or sense of danger to the white population, but from the clear conviction that such denial and restrictions will be for their present and ultimate good."[42] Some fifty years later, in the heart of the Jim Crow years, a Mississippi writer defended the Black Code in the same way: "It cannot be denied that the [Black Code] legislation was, largely if not wholly, meant to preserve the negro from the evil tendencies already marked, of town settlements, the vices such as vagrancy and petty criminality incident to it; by keeping them on the farm to conserve their as yet unimpaired habits of industry, physical vigor, and freedom from the taints of certain diseases."[43]

Not content with what they had done, legislators passed still more laws to prohibit Black men and women from riding in the same railway cars as whites; from owning or possessing guns, ammunition, or bowie knives; and from engaging in any seditious speeches, insulting gestures, or disturbances of the peace.[44] Moreover, in one broad and sweeping enactment, the Legislature referenced "all the penal and criminal laws now in force in this State, defining offenses and prescribing the mode of punishment of crimes and misdemeanors committed by slaves" and declared them applicable to Freedpersons. The word "slave" was left in the bill.[45]

Because legislators were worried that the existing court system could become swamped with cases brought against the formerly enslaved Black men and women as a result of all the new laws, they enacted a new county court system, the one still used today.[46] As many historians have observed, the fundamental effect of the Black Code legislation was to shift the role and responsibility of the "master" to the state.[47]

On the other hand, the assembled legislators made sure to care for the Confederate veterans among them, passing legislation to identify all soldiers requiring artificial legs, forgiving all unpaid Confederate taxes, wiping the record clean for any Confederate veteran who entered the War with a misdemeanor on his record, and allocating 20 percent of the state's annual revenue for a special fund to care for disabled and destitute Confederate veterans and the families of deceased veterans.[48]

Finally, to ensure the social order crafted by the legislation could be enforced, the Legislature created a State Militia and limited it to white men between the ages of eighteen and forty-five.[49]

It was toward the end of the Session that legislators turned their attention to the proposed Thirteenth Amendment to the United States Constitution. By the time the Legislature convened, the amendment lacked four states to obtain the necessary three-fourths margin for ratification. Before the Mississippi House took up the debate on November 27, 1865, South Carolina ratified the amendment. On the same day debate took place in the Mississippi Senate—December 2—Alabama approved the amendment. Two more were needed.

President Johnson had written to Sharkey on November 1, expressing that it was "all important that the Legislature adopt the amendment to the constitution abolishing slavery. The action of the Legislature of Mississippi is looked to with great interest at this time, and a failure to adopt the amendment will create the belief that the action of the Convention, abolishing slavery, will hereafter be revoked. . . . I trust in God that the Legislature will adopt the Amendment, and thereby make the way clear for the admission of Senators and Representatives to their seats in the present Congress."[50]

With the eyes of the country focused on Jackson and the State Capitol, legislators proved unwilling to give Johnson what he needed. They ended up voting to adopt the conclusions of a report authored by a special committee charged with making a recommendation as to ratification. It wasn't the first section of the proposed amendment outlawing slavery that disturbed them so much—they agreed slavery had ended—it was the second section that proved too much to swallow: the twelve words that provided "Congress shall have the power to enforce this article by appropriate legislation." As the authors of the committee report explained, "The committee is apprehensive that if this second section is incorporated into the constitution, radicals, and extremists will further vex and harass the country on the pretension that the freedom of the colored race is not perfect and complete until it is elevated to a social and political equality with the white." The report urged a vote against ratification.[51]

South Carolina's governor had received nearly the same telegram as Sharkey, and after assurances from Johnson's Secretary of State William Seward that the second section did not expand on the existing powers of Congress, South Carolina's Legislature approved the ratification on November 13 with this stipulation: "Any attempt by Congress towards legislating upon the political status of former slaves, or their civil relations, would be contrary to the Constitution."[52]

Two weeks later, the Mississippi House took up the report. Before approving it by a vote of 45-25, the representatives added this paragraph to make clear its intent: "Resolved therefore, by the Legislature of the State of Mississippi, that it respectfully refuses to adopt and ratify the proposed amendment to the Constitution of the United States." The Mississippi Senate took up the House-passed report on December 2, the same day that Alabama approved ratification (using the South Carolina proviso). Not only did the Senate overwhelmingly support the report, by the margin of 20-4, but they approved an amendment removing the word "respectfully" from the ending paragraph.[53]

Two days later the state Legislature left town at the same time North Carolina's Legislature was approving ratification. On December 6, Georgia's vote met the three-fourths requirement and the Thirteenth Amendment became the law of the land.[54]

The reaction across the country to the work of Mississippi's Legislature was uniformly negative. The most descriptive editorial came from the *Chicago Tribune*: "We tell the white men in Mississippi that the men of the North will convert the State of Mississippi into a frog pond before they will allow such laws to disgrace one foot of soil in which the bones of our soldiers sleep and over which the flag of freedom waves."[55] A Pennsylvania newspaper editor wrote that Mississippi "withholds her assent to the ratification of the Constitutional amendment, has refused the freedmen the right to testify in the State courts, and appears determined to deny them the rights and privileges which the president demands for them and without which freedom is a name." Blacks in Mississippi likewise wrote letters to Washington protesting the Black Code, while one group traveled to Washington to hand deliver a petition to Members of Congress urging them to take action.[56]

With President Johnson's backing, General Howard, director of the Freedmen's Bureau, ordered the provision prohibiting Black men and women from leasing or renting lands in the county to be ignored. And General Wood announced the War Department, which continued to have Mississippi under military rule, would prohibit the "prosecution of Negroes charged with offenses for which whites were not prosecuted."[57] The Vicksburg newspaper, somewhat cynically, explained why the provision was unnecessary: "The Negroes of this State own no lands, and if they rent, lease or buy, they have to obtain the land from the white citizen."[58] Howard later observed that if the Black Codes were enforced, "slavery would be restored in far worse form than it was before."

Responding to the national outcry, a Jackson newspaper joined with a few others to criticize the Legislature's work: "It appears, therefore, that our legislature in its overtopping anxiety to feed the prejudices of a certain class of people . . . in its insane proclivity to strain at gnats, after having swallowed the camel, has succeeded in fastening upon us indefinitely the Negro bureau . . . and caused its own legislative authority to be treated with contempt."[59]

Historian David Sansing summed up the net effect of the session: "There were a variety of reactions to the Mississippi Legislature of 1865 and the body of law it produced. There was, however, agreement on one point. The Legislature ruined Mississippi's chance for readmission to the 39th Congress and jeopardized the presidential plan of reconstruction."[60] His assessment was echoed by an early twentieth-century historian, James Baine: "If the Southern men had intended as their one and desirable aim, to inflame the public opinion of the North against them, they would have proceeded precisely as they did."[61]

Legislators, on the other hand, sympathized with the sentiments of a letter writer to a Natchez newspaper, "If Congress wanted to punish the South further by bestowing Negro equality, let not Mississippi be a party to it. If we must die, politically and socially let them commit the murder, and not we commit suicide."[62]

White leaders in Mississippi were no doubt hoping for the political landscape to evolve in a way described by the authors of the legislative report urging opposition to the Thirteenth Amendment: "It is the anxious desire of the people of Mississippi to withdraw the negro race from National and State politics; to quiet forever all subjects and questions connected with it; and so far as forecast and precaution can do so, to forestall and prevent the outbreak of agitation hereafter."[63]

If that was their hope, they had given politicians in Washington plenty to consider as they began determining the state's future. The day the Legislature adjourned was the day the 39th Congress convened its first Session. Soon thereafter, a select committee was created to determine the status of Reconstruction in the states; the US senators and representatives from the Southern states were not invited to take their seats in Congress; Mississippi's bill "conferring civil rights on the freedmen" was read into the congressional record and called "an arbitrary and inhuman act that makes the freedmen the slaves of society"; and legislation was introduced to declare any state law null and void that sought to make a distinction of color, race, or previous servitude.[64] Republicans in control of Congress had concluded that the Southern states should be restored by the joint action of both houses of Congress and the president. Until that was done no legal governments existed in the South; the Johnson governments were provisional.[65]

As 1865 was drawing to a close, the only thing standing in the way of social and political life in the state returning to the prewar days was the presence of the Freedmen's Bureau and what remained of military officers and soldiers. US Senator Charles Sumner and US Representative Thaddeus Stevens and other "Radical" Republicans in Congress aimed to dramatically alter the balance of power between Blacks and whites in Mississippi.

CHAPTER 5

1866–1867
Congressional Republicans Take Charge

The whole fabric of Southern society must be changed. Never can it be done if this opportunity is lost.

—US Rep. Thaddeus Stevens[1]

Above all of the avengers who counseled and concerted together for the punishment and degradation of the South, Thaddeus Stevens towered like Lucifer in the Satanic Court.

—Mississippi historian J. S. McNeily[2]

In the way that *Dred Scott* remains the ugliest stain on the record of the Supreme Court, the three-fifths compromise represents the ugliest stain on the United States Constitution.

Found in Article I, Section 2, Paragraph 3, it was there the framers had to come to terms with slaves as human beings as they confronted the challenge of who to count for purposes of determining the apportionment of representatives among the various states. Including the enslaved as full persons would, Northerners knew, give the Southern states an unfair edge in the numbers of House members. Since they were not "free persons" and were not allowed to vote, these delegates argued, they should not be counted. The resulting "compromise" calculated the worth of an enslaved person as three-fifths of a white person for purposes of the apportionment.[3]

The end of slavery forced the authors of Reconstruction policy in Congress to revisit this provision of the Constitution, along with *Dred Scott*. Were the formerly enslaved worthy of citizenship and were Black men worthy of the vote?

It would take five years and two new amendments to the United States Constitution, but by the end of 1870, those two questions had been answered in the affirmative. Frederick Douglass once observed that "no political idea was more deeply rooted in the minds of men in all sections of the country than the right of each state to control its own affairs."[4] By adopting the Fourteenth and Fifteenth Amendments, Congress had begun to alter "the fabric of Southern society" and in so doing ventured deeper than any before in prescribing limits on the "right of each state to control its own affairs."

The two years covered by this chapter birthed what has become known as the era of "Radical Reconstruction."[5] The term "radical" applied to a group of Republican leaders in Congress who opposed President Johnson's lenient approach to the former Confederate states and instead proposed sweeping reforms of Southern society and politics, including immediate enfranchisement of Black men and confiscation of plantation land for distribution among Black families. The two most familiar to us today are Senator Charles Sumner of Massachusetts and Representative Thaddeus Stevens of Pennsylvania. One hundred and sixty years ago, though, the Radical leadership consisted not only of Sumner and Stevens but also a dozen others, including Senators Benjamin Wade (Ohio), Henry Wilson (Massachusetts), Zachariah Chandler (Michigan), and Roscoe Conkling (New York) and Representatives George Boutwell (Massachusetts), James Ashley (Ohio), George Julian (Indiana), James Wilson (Iowa), and William Kelley and John Broomall (both Pennsylvania).[6]

A typical speech from a "Radical" member—this one by Stevens—could articulate their vision for the South while taunting Confederate whites: "This is not a white man's government. To say so is political blasphemy, for it violates the fundamental principles of our gospel of liberty." The goal of Reconstruction, Stevens then argued, was "to overcome the prejudice and ignorance and wickedness which resisted such reform."[7]

A Natchez newspaper editorial spoke for many when it offered this rebuttal to Stevens and his fellow Radicals: "We have no objections to negroes voting in Massachusetts or Ohio, or to carrying out in those states the doctrine of miscegenation to all its practical consequences; but when Mississippi shall be willing to place whites and blacks upon a social and political level, to escape the degradation we will become a voluntary exile from the home of our birth and seek asylum in some more congenial time."[8] Even sixty years later, the memory of Thaddeus Stevens could inflame the white Mississippi historian, as in this example from Dunbar Rowland, who served as the first director of the Mississippi Department of Archives and History: "After the death of Lincoln, and the accession of Andrew Johnson to the presidency, the radical, or bitter and vindictive element of the Republican Party, represented by Thaddeus Stevens, gradually gained the upper hand, and at his death in 1868 Stevens bequeathed his hatred of the South to others."[9]

Through laws adopted by the 1865 Legislature, positions made clear in newspaper editorials, and the numerous reports that accumulated in the offices of the Freedmen's Bureau, whites in Mississippi actively opposed any intervention on the part of the federal government to assist Black men, women, and children, and, instead, intended to construct a society that, in the words of historian Kenneth Stampp, "would replace slavery with a caste system that would keep Negroes perpetually subordinate to the whites, where Negroes were to remain a dependent laboring class, governed by a separate code of laws, play no active part in the South's political life, and [remain] segregated socially."[10]

The Radical Republican membership in Congress, however, upended this plan, enforced military rule on the South, turned formerly enslaved Black men into voters and officeholders, and enacted the Fourteenth and Fifteenth Amendments to the US Constitution. That legacy would be remembered a century later when the media would report following the Mississippi election of 1986 that Mike Espy had become the first African American congressman since Reconstruction, or following the 1991 election, Kirk Fordice was referred to as the first Republican governor since Reconstruction, or in the aftermath of the 2011 election that Republicans would be in control of both houses of the Mississippi Legislature for the first time since Reconstruction.

It was also this "Radical Republican" legacy that provoked white Mississippi voters to withhold their state's electoral votes from the Republican nominee for president from 1876 to 1964.

One of the poignant ironies of the Reconstruction era is that "Radical" Republicans had no congressional majority following Appomattox. They would have been unable to gain control of the agenda in Washington and impose their will on the South but for the uncompromising tactics of President Andrew Johnson and the intransigence of Southern white leaders that moved moderate Republicans to their side. This shortsightedness on the part of Southern white politicians was captured by historian Michael Perman: "Southern politicians focused their attention on defending their region's autonomy and strengthening its defenses. In the process, they overlooked the danger that . . . Johnson's ability to defend his policy, and therefore the South, from the most radical element in the Republican Party was bound to be seriously undermined."[11] Though Secretary of Navy Gideon Welles was a supporter of President Johnson, he once noted in his diary that "the entire south seem to be stupid and vindictive, know not their friends, and are pursuing just the course which their opponents, the Radicals, desire."[12]

In that sense, white Mississippi leaders played a leadership role in empowering Radical Republicans by adopting the harsh Black Code, refusing to acknowledge that secession was illegal, and rejecting the Thirteenth Amendment, all in the most vituperative way possible.

LIFE ON THE GROUND IN MISSISSIPPI

While Congress was returning to Washington in December 1865 to engage with President Johnson, Mississippi was consumed with rebuilding its transportation and municipal infrastructure, organizing agricultural land and operations for the new crop season, continuing to sort out the relationships between Freedpeople and whites, and waiting to see what more would be required of the state to rejoin the Union.[13]

Getting ready for a new crop meant renegotiating contracts between Black workers and planters. Many of the formerly enslaved were waiting to sign contracts until the new year, leaving many planters nearly "desperate in their efforts to secure dependable laborers." In many cases, the workers had not been paid at the end of 1865 while in other cases they were seeking better contracts by letting planters bid on their services or were holding out because of rumors that forty-acre plots might materialize for them at the end of the year. Connected to all of these individual transactions was the role of the Freedman's Bureau in regulating and approving the contracts while the Legislature was busy enforcing the Black Codes on terms favorable to the planters.[14]

Sam Thomas kicked off 1866 on behalf of the Freedman's Bureau with this unusually paternalistic message addressed "to the Colored People of Mississippi."

The time has arrived for you to contract for another year's labor. I wish to impress upon you the importance of doing this at once. If you do not contract with the men who wish to employ you, what do you propose to do? You cannot live without work of some kind. Your houses and lands belong to the white people, and you cannot expect that they will allow you to live on them in idleness. . . . Some of you have the absurd notion, that if you put your hands to a contract, you will somehow be made slaves. This is all nonsense, made up by some foolish or wicked person. Any white man treating you so would be punished. I hope that a sense of justice, benevolence, and enlightened self-interest will lead the white people to set you a good example of faithfulness and honor in observing contracts.[15]

A few weeks later, though, Thomas received this letter from a Black man in Fayette, expressing an opposing viewpoint:

I have just read your advice to the freedmen in which you urge the freedmen to enter into Contrack which is all right and good enough as far as it gos. . . . The Steat law is in force and the offercer has told me that it was against the laws of the Steat for freedmen or free men to rent or lese land. . . . It was and is my wishes to show the world that we the free people and freed people was willing to except the new order of things and show to the world that we would work . . . but they say the law is a ganest them and now we to are forbid or denide the right of rent-ing, we are denide the right of Scholing our Children, we are shut . . . out from all the blessings of freedom. . . . What kind of free Country is this that one white man Can Get drink but the Black man Cant buy whiskey at all not Even for sickeness, if slavery is dune and the people of Culler is free why not be free indeed. . . . The people will work if they be let alone, evrything is dune to upset us. . . . The sooner the whit man reachees back and takes the black man by the hand the sooner he will buld up his Country. . . . The black man and white man must take each orther by the hand or the Country is lost forever. . . . I hope you will be able to read this Col. as you will see from this that I have ben a Slave and my Chance for writing is poor.[16]

According to the editors of the volume of the Freedmen's Bureau's papers in which this correspondence was reproduced, there is no record of a response from Thomas. Nevertheless, this writer articulated a set of grievances that ultimately were rarely met. Not being able to rent land or obtain education for their children or purchase commodities of their choosing were just some of the many challenges Freedpeople faced as Mississippi whites were coming to terms with the need to make a crop and the presence of free Blacks able to negotiate employment contracts.

In the meantime, there was an ongoing tug-o-war between white officials throughout the state wanting to enforce the Black Code and the Freedmen's Bureau that sought to override the provisions that were unduly harsh and discriminatory. The editors of the Freedmen's Bureau's papers captured one example in early 1866 with correspondence between a Bureau official in

Jackson and the mayor of Clinton. One of the Black Code laws targeted the ex-slaves by defining vagrants as "all freedmen, free negroes, and mulattoes" over the age of eighteen who were found on or after January 8, 1866, "with no lawful employment or business" and required any Freedperson living in a town who was not under a contract to obtain a license from the mayor "to do irregular and job work." On January 12, 1866, the Army issued a directive that federal officials in the former Confederate states were required to "protect from prosecution colored persons charged with offences for which white persons are not prosecuted in the same manner and degree." That led the Bureau official to complain to the Clinton mayor that he was "requiring the Colored people to pay money for certain papers issued by them, and are threatening and otherwise annoying these poor people." The mayor took issue with the directive of the federal government, though he did admit that "one of our Magistrates here did threaten to fine a freedwoman $20 for not keeping a reputable house." The mayor ended with this mild threat: "I shall continue until the term of office expires or until I shall be estopped by some power more potent than that which placed me in the position to do my duty."[17]

There was this August 31, 1866, memorandum from a Bureau official in Jackson reporting that planters were "running their hands off without settlements & treating them in such a manner that they would have to leave, losing all wages due them for their past 6 months labor. Tis true that this is not done by a majority, but it is done by many." A February 1, 1866, affidavit of three Washington County Freedmen who "once belonged to" Mr. W. F. Smith and who complained that even though they had worked for him through 1865, he refused to pay them at year's end until a Bureau official traveled to the plantation and "compelled him to agree to settle with us all." A long report of a Bureau official in April outlined his travel to farms in Coahoma County, finding some "generally at work and getting along smoothly" while at another stop, after making "due allowance for prejudice and former notions regarding the colored man," he found "in some cases, cause for complaint on the part of the planter in consequence of Freedmen failing to faithfully perform their obligations."[18]

A report of an official at Grenada in early 1866 disclosed that his office was crowded from "early morn to dewey eve" with complaints and he found that "there is no law for the darkie, that a white man is bound to respect." In the case of the Black Code legislation that allowed local judges to declare children orphans and "bind them over" to "plantation owners" as apprentices, the official wrote that "the avaricious Slaveholder of former days, in this apprentice law, sees a chance to effectively apply it in case of young and active children and stay not for the law to be carried out by proper officials, but run before they are sent, snatching all irrespective of orphanage, willingness or ability of parents or relatives to care of their children." That being said, he also reported that "the negroes are hiring rapidly and usually, (especially contracts made before me) for good wages from 8. to 15 pr month, & a third & fourth of the crop."[19]

The volume of Freedmen Bureau papers covering 1866 is full of reports and correspondence that give an on-the-ground view of life in Mississippi as Blacks and whites adjusted to an economic and labor world neither had ever experienced. The editors concluded "that while some white Southerners found reason to sell or rent land to freedpeople, most were steadfastly and even violently opposed to doing so. To employers, every ex-slave who cultivated land independently was one less hand available for hire, not to mention an example that fomented dissatisfaction among laborers working for wages or a share of the crop."[20]

The editors found Blacks and whites "clashed over the extent and character of supervision; the days, hours, and pace of labor; modes of discipline; the form and amount of compensation; access to garden plots and other productive resources; and myriad other matters" such as corporal punishment, failure to pay, and interference with their family lives. Planters and other employers complained that Freedpeople had "worked poorly, resisted supervision, behaved impudently, and deserved no more than they have received in year-end settlements." The editors also found that as 1866 gave way to 1867, the "former slaves and their employers became increasingly conversant with the ways of free labor. They negotiated new labor contracts and participated in end-of-the-year settlements. Some features of work under slavery—corporal punishment, minute and unremitting supervision, workdays that stretched from daybreak to dark—became less common, although they by no means disappeared."[21]

The opposing view, which the white-owned newspapers of the day broadcast frequently, can be found in this editorial: "The fact is, in many cases, the freedmen, instead of illustrating the principle that has been claimed by some 'philanthropists,' for all human beings, that freedom and wages are sufficient incentive to industry and application, have become so indolent, as to require admonition and even threats."[22] In the meantime, as Mississippi whites were coming to terms with free Blacks and free labor, their hopes for a "*status quo ante bellum*, minus slavery" would soon disappear.

IN WASHINGTON: RADICAL REPUBLICANS
VS. JOHNSON AND THE OLD SOUTH

The 39th Congress convened in Washington on December 4, 1865, and for the next fourteen months engaged in an epic battle with President Andrew Johnson over control of Reconstruction. Johnson, a prisoner of his own prejudices and ego as events unfolded in 1866 and 1867, and outmatched when it came to legislative strategy, watched Congress routinely override his vetoes; became the centerpiece of a losing campaign in the 1866 midterm elections; and avoided, by a one-vote margin, getting impeached, convicted, and removed by the Senate.

The first order of business when Congress returned, after refusing to seat the congressional delegations from the former Confederate states, was to create a Joint Committee on Reconstruction and authorize it to examine the state of the South, take testimony, and report back with findings and recommendations. Six senators and nine representatives—twelve Republicans and three Democrats—made up the committee's membership, with Senator William Fessenden of Maine, a moderate Republican, named as the chairman.[23] Writing about the committee some fifty years later, white Mississippi historian J. S. McNeily described it as a "germ of all our woes."[24]

After meeting for nearly six months, the committee published its 836-page report in June. The authors spent a significant part of the introduction reminding their audience of the consequences of the South's decision to secede, form their own government, and wage the "most determined and malignant" war against the "loyal people" of the United States. Moreover, the authors pointed out, white Southerners had failed to admit their wrong and offered no "repentance for their crime," giving up on the War simply because "they had no longer the power to continue the desperate struggle." They then got to the heart of the matter: "A large proportion of the population has become, instead of mere chattels, free men and citizens. Through all the past struggles these had remained true and loyal, and had, in large numbers, fought on the side of the Union. It was impossible to abandon them, without securing them their rights as free men and citizens."

After listening to all the testimony and examining all of the materials they had accumulated, and finding that those rights would remain unsecured if left to the discretion of Southern whites, the committee concluded: "There is no general disposition to place the colored race, constituting at least two-fifths of the population, upon terms even of civil equality" and, as a result, "your committee has been unable to find in the evidence submitted to Congress . . . any satisfactory proof that either of the insurrectionary states, except, perhaps, the State of Tennessee, has placed itself in a condition to resume its political relations to the Union. The language of all the provisions and ordinances of these States on the subject amounts to nothing more than an unwilling admission of an unwelcome truth."[25]

Moreover, the committee became convinced that the Black Codes, having now been approved in states besides Mississippi, were being used to force Freedpeople back "into agricultural labor under strict discipline," and that white officials were "working collectively to keep down wages" and to prevent Black Southerners from "receiving fair trials" in the civil courts.[26]

The pages of testimony about life in Mississippi were filled with reports like the following:

From a treasury agent stationed at Natchez—the general feeling had been one of submission, but since the Johnson Plan had been inaugurated, "the old bitterness" had returned. When asked his opinion if the people would prefer the establishment of the confederacy or the maintenance of the Union, he replied, "They would prefer the establishment of the Confederacy."[27]

From an Army major—the Freedmen were much worse in Mississippi than in any other Southern state he had been in. There was decided opposition to justice being done the Negro, and the Black Code definitely operated against the Negro. He had written a DeSoto County planter, asking him to surrender a young girl, a former slave he now had in his possession, to her mother. He declined, saying, "As to recognizing the rights of freedmen to their children, I will say there is not one man or woman in all the south who believes they are free, but we consider them as stolen property."[28]

From a captain with the Freedmen's Bureau in Pike County—the Freedmen had been run off the land at the end of the year without any payment; Freedmen were "flogged, murdered, and driven off plantations after crops had been gathered without being paid." He described one black man who had been hung and skinned for stealing a horse.[29]

In early March, former governor William Sharkey testified in front of the committee and offered a different perspective on the Freedpeople, whom he claimed were doing "remarkably well." However, after telling the members that the majority of whites "are all kindly disposed towards them" he admitted, "the poorer classes, who have always had an antipathy to them, still have that antipathy." He acknowledged some of the provisions of the Black Code had been "foolish," but claimed the greatest harm in Mississippi came from the Freedmen's Bureau and the remaining military officers. If "all the troops and the Freedmen's Bureau had been withdrawn," he told the members, "I verily believe that if at the time I was there . . . , I could have had a perfect state or order throughout the State in two weeks." Some 100 years later, attitudes of white elected officials had changed little when responding to questions about the role of the federal government in protecting the rights of Black Mississippians. In 1988, for example, then US Senator John Stennis told a reporter, "My idea was that the [1964 and 1965] so-called civil rights bills were too abrupt . . . went too far and were out of line. . . . It takes time to make adjustments."[30]

When asked if Freedpersons are "disposed to accumulate property," Sharkey responded, "In very few instances," and then he offered a remarkable observation about their future: "My expectation concerning them is that they are destined for extinction, beyond all doubt. . . . I think they will gradually die out. Some of them will become thrifty and prosperous; but, as a general rule, I think they are destined to extinction."[31] Apparently, no one on the committee had the presence of mind to ask a follow-up question.

As the testimony continued through the winter and into the early spring, the evidence, along with the continuing efforts in the South to defy the Freedmen's Bureau and adopt more Black Code legislation, provided all the evidence Radicals, and many of the moderates, needed to push for more oversight of the South. As one historian observed, "For the South to have gained almost immediate autonomy in its domestic affairs, as it would have under Johnson's program, it would have required of its leaders extraordinary restraint, a quality for which they had not been distinguished in recent years. The South obliged with its Black Codes."[32]

At the outset, though, the large moderate faction of Congressional Republicans was predisposed to support Johnson. Nevertheless, they had also concluded that additional efforts were needed in the South to protect Black Southerners and ensure the same rebels who had prosecuted the war would not end up serving as political leaders. It was a moderate then, Lyman Trumbull, a senator from Illinois and chairman of the Judiciary Committee, who opened the new year by having his committee send to the full Senate a bill to extend the life of the Freedmen's Bureau, to fund it with an appropriation, to strengthen its power to supervise labor contracts, and to vest it with new authority to create special courts to protect the civil rights of the Freedpeople.[33] Set to expire in early summer, the Bureau had gained significant support among the congressional moderates and was viewed as the major tool available to Congress to counter Johnson's laissez-faire approach to the South and to combat the mistreatment of the Freedpeople.[34]

With the moderates leading the way, and joined by the Radicals, the bill passed easily in February, made the Bureau permanent, allowed the military to establish their own judicial proceedings, authorized the construction of buildings for hospitals and schools, and provided for a system of support for indigent persons.

For the Radicals, who were in a minority in Congress and who wanted to use this opportunity to transform the political and economic life of the South, they needed the larger group of moderate Republicans to join their cause. The passage of the Black Codes helped. The findings of the Reconstruction Committee helped. But it was Johnson who pushed them over for good.[35]

A few days after passage, President Johnson surprised his moderate Republican allies by issuing a veto, complaining the bill was an overreach of the federal government: It provided for the construction of schools—"first time for the federal government to ever get involved in local education"—and when it came to the help for the indigent Freedpeople, Johnson wrote, "The idea on which the slaves were assisted to freedom was that, on becoming free, they would be a self-sustaining population. Any legislation that shall imply that they are not expected to attain a self-sustaining condition must have a tendency injurious alike to their character and their prospects."[36]

The Radical and moderate members spent the next five months developing compromises with the language and ultimately approved and then overrode a Johnson veto of a new bill that continued the Bureau through 1868. In the meantime, worried about the possible loss of the Freedmen's Bureau and the South's enforcement of the Black Codes—along with the message Johnson's veto was sending the Southern states—the Radicals teamed with the moderates, who were now becoming less eager to side with Johnson and his extreme views, to pass the nation's first civil rights act in March 1866.[37]

Like the Freedmen's Bureau legislation, the Civil Rights Act was authored by Senator Lyman Trumbull, who was becoming more and more disenchanted with Johnson. As Trumbull described the reason for the bill, "A law that does not allow a colored person to go from one county to another, and one that does not allow him to hold property, to teach, to preach, are certainly laws in violation of the rights of a freeman. . . . The purpose of this bill is to destroy all these discriminations." As one historian noted, "The shadow of the Black Codes hung over [the civil rights] debates."[38]

The act vested the former slaves with full United States citizenship and set out a list of basic rights available to them, and anyone else, in any state: to make and enforce contracts; to sue, be parties, and give testimony and evidence in trial proceedings; and to ensure the full and equal benefit of all laws and legal proceedings. The act was not only a direct rebuke to *Dred Scott* and the Black Codes, it likewise sent a political message that one historian described as "a warning that unless Southern states accepted a broader concept of black rights, there would be further intervention."[39]

Again, confounding his friends on Capitol Hill, Johnson vetoed the Civil Rights Act on March 27. It was with this veto that Johnson's prejudices and anger got the better of him, and left the moderates appalled and with all the excuses they needed to continue their political affiliation with the Radicals. In his veto message to Congress, Johnson asked rhetorically, is it "sound policy to make our entire colored population and all other excepted classes citizens of the United States? Four million of them have just emerged from slavery into freedom. Can it be reasonably supposed that they possess the requisite qualifications to entitle them to all the privileges and immunities of citizens of the United States?" By then he was losing control, moving quickly to argue the bill sought to create "a perfect equality of the white and black races" and leading him to predict, "In no one of these can any State ever exercise any power of discrimination between the difference races." Finally, he lost what moderate friends he might have had in Congress when he argued, "the details of the bill seem fraught with evil" and they establish "for the security of the colored race, safeguards which go infinitely beyond any that the General Government has ever provided to the white race." Congress had heard all it needed to hear. Thirteen days later, the veto was overridden, at the same time achieving a milestone: the first substantial piece of legislation enacted over a president's veto since the adoption of the Constitution.[40]

As testimony taken by the Joint Committee, along with letters and reports coming to individual members of Congress, continued to show a South determined to push back the gains made by Blacks as a result of emancipation, Radical and moderate leaders looked for ways to ensure that no Supreme Court could turn the newly enacted Civil Rights Act into another *Dred Scott* decision. The answer was a constitutional amendment, and it was here that the federal government ventured more deeply than ever in prescribing limits on the ability of state governments to undermine the civil rights of its people. While it would take decades for the Supreme Court to use the provisions of the amendment to address state-sanctioned discrimination, the fullest expression finally came in 1954 with *Brown v. Board of Education*.[41]

As one legal historian put it, "Until the 14th Amendment, the United States had no definitive statement about who could claim citizenship and by what means. The 14th Amendment's connection between citizenship and rights took the nation in an utterly new legal direction. Citizenship, granted by the federal government, had never before implied such broad claims to rights." Or, as Representative Thaddeus Stevens put it, the purpose of the amendment "allows Congress to correct the unjust legislation of the states [that is, the Black Codes], so far that the law which operates upon one man shall operate equally upon all." The citizenship provision was the congressional response to *Dred Scott*.[42]

Yet another irony of Reconstruction is that the words and phrases in Section 1 of the amendment, so important to contemporary litigation, were not the focus of the debate in 1868.

SECTION 1. All persons born or naturalized in the United States, and subject to the jurisdiction thereof, are citizens of the United States and of the state wherein they reside. No state shall make or enforce any law which shall abridge the privileges or immunities of citizens of the United States; nor shall any state deprive any person of life, liberty, or property, without due process of law; nor deny to any person within its jurisdiction the equal protection of the laws.

The legal safeguards built into the definition of citizenship, due process of law, and equal protection of the laws, had achieved a general consensus among congressional Republicans during the winter and spring of 1866. It was the implications of four million Black men, women, and children in the Southern states no longer defined by the three-fifths compromise that Republican congressmen needed the Fourteenth Amendment to resolve.[43]

Granted citizenship by Section 1, as well as by the Civil Rights Act, and their freedom by the Thirteenth Amendment, the Freedpeople would be on equal standing with whites when it came time for Census workers to count the population. Unless something was done, the South would be due more representatives in the House, at the expense of the North and Midwest, at the conclusion of the 1870 Census. As one historian described the thinking of Republicans, "Why should former Confederates be rewarded after seceding, forcing the nation into war, opposing abolition, and then denying civil and political rights to African Americans whose presence now enhanced their own political power?" Or as the Radical congressman from Massachusetts, George Boutwell, declared, "And who are these white men of the South? They are the men who have been in arms against the Republic . . . and they are of a race which through two centuries has been contaminated by the vilest crime, the crime of slavery, until the whole public sentiment of the South has become debauched."[44]

The obvious remedy would have been to vest voting rights with the Black men. But as historians have pointed out, the votes didn't exist in Congress in 1866 to get that done. So, Republican leaders in Congress had to craft language that would either provide an incentive for Southern leaders to enfranchise Black men on their own or punish them if they didn't. The language in Section 2 accomplished that goal and withheld seats in the House on a proportional basis to the number of "male inhabitants of a state" who were denied the right to vote. Moreover, they added a Section 3 to the amendment to prevent anyone who had "engaged in insurrection or rebellion against the same, or given aid or comfort to the enemies thereof" from holding office, though they allowed Congress, by a two-thirds vote of each House, to "remove such disability."[45]

It was in the Fourteenth Amendment that the word "vote" was first used in the United States Constitution. Before 1866, determining who would vote, and in what manner, was understood to be the exclusive province of state governments. There is no generalized right to vote in the original Constitution. Even though the federal government and, by application, the state governments are established as "republican governments" with officials elected to office by a vote of the people, the process by which elections were to be held and who would participate in those elections was left entirely to the states by the framers of the 1789 Constitution. That Congress was considering such a fundamental change by nationalizing a standard for voting was more than former governor William Sharkey could fathom when he told a Vicksburg newspaper that he was "utterly opposed to negro suffrage in any way it can be fixed, partial or impartial" and that he believed "Congress has nothing to do with the subject and cannot legally touch it." Sharkey and his fellow Southern politicians, as one legal scholar put it so succinctly, "did not realize how much the war had changed America."[46]

By the time summer arrived, the Radicals were on a roll. The final report of the Reconstruction Committee was released, and on June 13, 1866, Congress approved the Fourteenth Amendment and sent it to the states for ratification. Four weeks later, they overrode President Johnson's veto of the compromise bill to reauthorize the Freedmen's Bureau. On July 24, the application from the Republican leadership in Tennessee was approved, and it became the first Confederate state to be readmitted and granted voting privileges in Congress, adding to the Republican majority.

BACK ON THE GROUND IN MISSISSIPPI

For much of Mississippi's history, there have always been dissenting voices to the decisions white political leaders have made. These officials in positions of leadership have always known alternative paths were available; they just never took them. As there was white public opposition to secession in 1860 and to massive resistance in the late 1950s and early 1960s, some whites were urging moderation during the Reconstruction years.

One such example was James L. Alcorn, a Coahoma County planter. While he will be featured prominently in this narrative after 1869, in 1866 he was so well regarded by the politicians of his day that he was one of two white men appointed by the 1865 Legislature to serve as a United States senator. Even though he, along with the rest of the delegation, was never officially recognized by Congress, Alcorn spent enough time in Washington and was a savvy enough businessman and political observer that he could feel the direction the country was headed. In August 1866, he wrote a letter to the people of his state that was subsequently published in newspapers throughout Mississippi. His critical observation explained the political land-scape: "The Republicans have jumped to the conclusion that, if they con-sent to your political rights, they would be out-voted in the next contest for the Presidency. This consideration underlines the fact of your exclusion from representation."[47] Consider acceding to some of the Radical demands, Alcorn suggested, such as civil and voting rights, look at the Tennessee example, regain your voting rights in Congress, and then you can have a voice, and electoral votes. [48]

Governor Humphreys, the former Confederate officer, was more likely swayed by the letters he was receiving and editorials he was reading that condemned the Radicals for "pushing Negro suffrage simply to punish the South." After Johnson vetoed the legislation extending the Freedmen's Bureau, Humphreys presided over a meeting that called for citizens to sign resolutions in support of the President's actions.[49]

With the Civil Rights Act of 1866 threatening the legality of much of the Black Codes and the proposed Fourteenth Amendment granting citizenship to the Freedpeople, Humphreys responded by calling an October special

James Lusk Alcorn, circa 1850s. Courtesy of the Archives and Records Services Division, Mississippi Department of Archives and History.

session of the Legislature. Accordingly, a Vicksburg newspaper offered this advice to legislators:

> The South is now asked to adopt a constitutional amendment as a pledge of future loyalty, when it is unblushingly avowed that even then they do not intend to keep faith with us. One of the provisions of this amendment forever excludes from office, every man of the South who had taken an oath to the United States government, and then resigned his office to aid his state and section. The Democratic Party cannot live, except by giving up a right policy, which has been unsuccessful, and adopting a policy

that is wholly wrong, but which has been triumphant. Well, then, let the Democratic party die. Let it sink to the lowest depths of perdition.[50]

In his address to the joint session on October 16, Humphreys echoed the editors and pulled no punches in describing the choices before the all-white Legislature:

> The Radical Congress has enacted laws and proposed amendments to the Constitution, which if adopted will destroy the rights of the States and of the people, and centralize all the powers of government in the Federal Head.... This amendment is such an insulting outrage and denial of the equal rights of so many of our worthiest citizens who have shed lustre and glory upon our section and our race, both in the forum and in the field, such a gross usurpation of the rights of the State, and such a centralization of power in the Federal government, that I presume, a mere reading of it, will cause its rejection by you.[51]

Over the three-month session, the Legislature ultimately relaxed some of the Black Code provisions, especially following the outcome of the 1866 congressional elections, but not before voting unanimously to reject the ratification of the Fourteenth Amendment.[52]

Historian Charles Sallis explained the ramifications of their decisions: "Southern leaders did not perceive the significance of the situation from the Northern point of view. Nor did Southerners anticipate that, as a consequence of their refusal to ratify the amendment, they had contributed to their own doom. They showed that they had no intention of changing the status of the Negro beyond what was required by the Thirteenth Amendment."[53]

THE 1866 CONGRESSIONAL ELECTION

All of the political maneuvering in Congress was done knowing the 1866 midterm elections were right around the corner. As one historian described the political context for the campaign, "The Fourteenth Amendment was framed with the elections of 1866 very much in mind. . . . the Amendment supplied Republicans with a platform for the fall campaign, while leaving to the future the issue of black suffrage. The Report of the Joint Committee, released in June, provided an official explanation and defense of the Amendment upon which, as one widely read publication declared, 'A great party must take its stand.'"[54]

By the time the results were in, the anti-Johnson Republicans had achieved substantial victories. They won control of every Northern legislature, prevailed in every Northern gubernatorial contest, and gained more than two-thirds majorities in both houses of Congress.[55]

Like any campaign, success in 1866 would hinge on which side controlled the message being delivered to the voters. The Democrats, with Johnson's help, tried to carry the day by appealing to the racial prejudices of Northern and Midwestern voters (since only Tennessee among the Confederate states would be participating). The challenge for the Republicans was to maintain the focus on slavery, the cost of the War, and the arrogance of Southern leaders. Even though the Radicals knew universal suffrage for Blacks was next on their legislative agenda, they also knew they would lose if it became the campaign centerpiece. As one observer at the time said, "It was the issue of Union that would win votes, not that of Negro suffrage, the party cannot carry the elections on the universal negro suffrage issue, as there is much prejudice still in the Northern states." Or, as another one put it more bluntly, "Slavery was sectional but racism was national." Commented one Radical congressman: "It was unwise for abolitionists to talk of justice and humanity to the Negro as if these were decisive considerations. It was a question not of justice, but of political dynamics. It is a question of power, not of right." Democrats, of course, knew this, which is why, for example, a friendly newspaper declared, "Negro suffrage is the hinge of the whole Republican policy. It is what they most value in the Reconstruction laws; it is the vital breath of the party."

To combat that appeal, the campaign managers for the Radicals had to change the terms of the debate to the "well-grounded distrust" Northern voters had of the Southerners and hope that distrust "simply outweighed their prejudice against blacks." Voters had to be made "fearful that Johnson was going to lose the peace and allow unrepentant rebels to regain control of the South." In other words, with Johnson's plan of Reconstruction, the War would have been all for naught. As the campaign evolved, the Radicals were given a gift: Johnson personally joined the debate.[56]

Even though he was not on the ballot, Johnson campaigned throughout the country against the Radicals and their newest friends, the moderate Republicans. Johnson made the Fourteenth Amendment a key issue during the campaign, publicly declared Sumner and Stevens traitors, and used the most incendiary language possible on the hustings. Even Johnson's friend Gideon Welles described his speeches as "essentially but one speech often repeated, rambling, vulgar, vindictive, and loaded with self-pity." Like all campaigns built around an appeal to bigotry, they ultimately become consumed with the single issue driving the bigotry and thus leave themselves open to attack on a variety of other fronts. A classic example came from a headline from a Democratic newspaper following the Republican convention: "First Grand National Convention of Negro Worshipers, Free Lovers, Spiritualists, and Negro Equality Men." The Republicans, on the other hand, could appeal to Union patriotism—"Every unregenerate rebel . . . every deserter, every sneak who ran away from the draft calls himself a Democrat" or to the memory of the War—"Every man who labored for the rebellion in the field, who murdered Union prisoners by cruelty and starvation . . . calls himself a Democrat" or to the dangers of allowing Southern whites to regain power—"Every wolf in sheep's clothing who pretends to preach the gospel but proclaims the righteousness of man-selling and slavery . . . calls himself a Democrat."[57]

As it turned out, the prejudice of most voters was no match to their lingering anger for what the war had done to the North. Once Johnson joined the campaign, his plan for Reconstruction became a central issue. And when they became convinced his plan would extract no serious concessions from the South, the voters turned on him.

Historian Eric Foner also identified a byproduct of decisions by the white Southern political leadership to fight Congress at every turn: "Most of all, [it] reinforced blacks' identification with the federal authority. Only outside intervention could assure the freedmen a modicum of justice."[58]

MILITARY CONTROL

With the added margins in Congress, the Radicals took full advantage of their opportunity and pushed the boundaries of what had heretofore been an unacceptable reach into the states by the federal government. Congress alone would now decide the terms by which the Southern states—"conquered provinces" as one historian referred to them—would be readmitted as voting members at the nation's capital. The reasons for huge victories in November—Johnson's recalcitrance, the refusal of Southern states to accept the terms of the Fourteenth Amendment, and the continued mistreatment of Freedpeople—would continue to supply the Radicals with the ammunition they needed to stretch those boundaries. Even moderate leader Lyman Trumbull declared that Congress had the authority to "enter these states and hurl from power the disloyal element which controls and governs them."[59]

Beginning on March 2, 1867, Congress approved the first of four Reconstruction Acts that declared the "rebel states" no longer constituted legal state governments nor provided "adequate protection for life or property" in any of those states. With that as the basis for action, the Reconstruction Acts divided the former Confederate states, except for Tennessee, into five districts to be controlled by military officers. Mississippi was placed in the fourth district, along with Arkansas. The military was then required to register all male voters twenty-one and older, regardless of "race, color, or previous condition," and allow those men to vote in "fair elections" on delegates to a constitutional convention, on whether or not to approve a new constitution, and on the selection of statewide and legislative officials elected under the new constitution. Once a majority of voters had ratified the new constitution, once the state Legislature, duly elected pursuant to the new constitution, had ratified the Fourteenth Amendment, and once Congress had approved the new constitution, a state would be eligible to resume representation in Congress and to "rejoin the Union." Mandating universal male suffrage, congressional approval of state constitutions, and military control of elections were all unprecedented congressional forays into the operations of state governments.[60]

Even though Johnson vetoed the first three acts, they were all overridden the day Congress received the veto messages. By then, Johnson was reduced to comparing the military occupation to slavery:

> [The act] reduces the whole population of the ten States, all persons of every color, sex, and condition, and every stranger within their limits, to the most abject and degrading slavery. No master ever had a control so absolute over his slave as this bill gives to the military officers over both white and colored persons. The purpose and object of the bill, the general intent which pervades it from beginning to end, is to change the entire structure and character of the State governments and to compel them by force to the adoption of organic laws and regulations which they are unwilling to accept if left to themselves. The negroes have not asked for the privilege of voting; the vast majority of them have no idea what it means.[61]

With the first veto override, the overwhelming majority of Congressional Republicans had finally arrived at a consensus: military oversight and time were needed for "public opinion to sink deep roots and permit 'Northern capital and labor, Northern energy, and enterprise' to venture south to establish 'a Christian civilization and a living democracy.'" Notwithstanding the extraordinary ways in which Congress was willing to involve itself in the affairs of a state, the Reconstruction Acts represented a compromise between the Radicals and the moderates: military control was temporary, not permanent;

General E. O. C. Ord, circa 1870–1875. Library of Congress, Prints and Photographs Division, LC-USZ62-17480.

vesting Black men with the vote only applied to the South, not the rest of the country; while the military was given broad new powers to implement the law, no new federal agency was created to provide assistance; and the legislation contained nothing specifically designed to help Freedpeople overcome the economic barriers they were facing.[62]

By the end of March, General E. O. C. Ord opened a headquarters in Vicksburg and assumed control of military operations in the state.

While many white officials in the state, as well as planters and businessmen, recognized they had lost control of their fate with the new Congress and had no choice but to submit to the demands of the Reconstruction Acts if they ever wanted to rejoin Congress and lose the military presence in the state, there were the stubborn ones who couldn't move beyond the changes. One of those was former governor Sharkey, who led a legal fight against the Reconstruction Acts, regretting "the supineness exhibited by many of the Southern states and leaders, asserting that in case such weakness becomes general, the South is lost." The case came to be known as *Mississippi v. Johnson* and was the first suit to be brought against a president of the United States in the United States Supreme Court. Sharkey's lawsuit attempted to prevent President Andrew Johnson from enforcing the Reconstruction Acts. The court decided that the president has two kinds of tasks: ministerial and discretionary. Discretionary tasks are ones the president can choose to do or not to do. Ministerial tasks are ones required by his job. In fact, if he fails to do them, he could be violating the Constitution. The court ruled that by enforcing Reconstruction, Johnson was acting in an "executive and political" capacity—a discretionary rather than a ministerial one—and so he could not be sued.[63]

With the Reconstruction Acts written into law by Congress and approved by the Supreme Court, the action shifted to the ten states. There was no way around the requirements established by Congress for the former Confederate states to rejoin the Union. Two years after the War's end, the path toward reunification was finally clear, though it was nothing like white Mississippians envisioned they would be facing in the summer of 1865. Being lulled by President Johnson into thinking that little would be required, Mississippi politicians misread Congress and Northern attitudes about the War. Some even let their cockiness get the better of them as journalist Whitelaw Reid found on his trip to Mississippi: "We are the only ones that understand the nigger. Wait till Johnson gets things a-going here, and we'll make a contract that will make a nigger work."[64]

Washington would continue to serve up lots of political theater, culminating in the failure of the Senate by one vote to convict President Johnson of impeachment charges in 1868 and the election of Ulysses S. Grant as the eighteenth president of the United States later that year. But Mississippi would participate in none of it. Not until 1870 would the state have voting members in Congress and not until 1872 would Mississippians have a chance to cast a vote in a presidential election.[65]

Radicals would continue to push for confiscation of land from the wealthy Southern planters for distribution to the ex-slaves, though the move never gained support from a majority of Congress. Despite pleas from Sumner that the plantations were "so many nurseries of the Rebellion [that] must be broken up and the freedmen must have the pieces," and from Stevens that "the wicked enemy [must] pay the expenses of this unjust war," the proposal failed to generate any political momentum.[66]

Historians have identified three main reasons. First was the "sanctity" of private property, regardless of the owner, which had more permanence in the political world than expanding who could enjoy voting or civil rights.[67]

Second, the Radicals had most likely pushed a legislative program that had gone beyond what their Northern constituencies would accept politically.

This became evident when Ohio voters defeated a referendum to amend the state constitution to allow for Black voting at the end of 1867. As one historian wrote, "Clearly, they had gone too far too fast and had over reached the limits of northern sentiment."[68]

It was the third hurdle, though, that would prove timeless. It surfaced again 100 years later when Congress debated the Civil Rights Act of 1964 and the Voting Rights Act of 1965 and remains relevant today: Is the right to vote all that is needed to ensure economic prosperity? In the years after the War, the consensus answer was yes. As one Radical senator explained, "The ballot will finish the Negro question; it will settle everything. . . . We need no vast expenditures, we need no standing army. . . . The ballot is the freedman's Moses." "The majority of Northerners," explained a historian, "had not enthusiastically embraced emancipation before, nor did they embrace enfranchisement now, but they were convinced that Southern black enfranchisement could prevent a conservative comeback and would keep the Republicans in power throughout the South and in Washington." Moreover, many argued that giving land away, without the need to earn it, would "ruin the Freedmen" by leading them to believe they could acquire land without having to work for it.[69]

The most powerful response to the complaint that Black men and women shouldn't be "given" any land without paying for it is that they had paid for it—for their entire lives they were the ones who had given the land its value and they were the ones who had harvested the crops, all without any compensation. It was their slave labor that had created Mississippi's wealth.[70]

Ultimately, confiscation failed "because many of the radicals thought legal and political rights were enough, they didn't understand the need for economic support and how laws can be flouted when they alone support an economically dependent class, especially a minority group against whom is directed an intense racial prejudice." Looking back, historian Kenneth Stampp captured the consequences: the Reconstruction program "would have only the most limited economic content; the [ex-slaves'] civil and political rights would be in a precarious state for many years to come; and the radical influence in Southern politics would probably collapse as soon as federal troops were removed. . . . The failure of land reform probably made inevitable the ultimate failure of the whole radical program."[71]

Once the decision was made to force Freedpeople into labor contracts, the health of Mississippi's economy, along with the viability of the new labor arrangement, became dependent on the price of cotton and the success of the crop. And that news was anything but good. A combination of too much rain; too many insects and boll weevils; too much uncertainty associated with rebuilding the agricultural and transportation infrastructure after the War; too little stability with the new labor relationships; and, late in 1867, too low a price for a bale of cotton all together contributed to dismal economic returns. For 1866 and 1867, Mississippi was only able to produce about 300,000 bales of cotton each year, which was down from 860,000 bales in 1861 and 1.2 million bales in 1860. The 1867 crop generated about half the income of the 1866 crop because of the dramatic decline in the price per bale. These weak economic returns, in turn, made it much harder for the state to recover, for planters to accept their new relationship with Black workers, and for those workers to find a way to become economically independent.[72]

CHAPTER 6

1868–1869
A New Constitution
Black and White Republicans Assert Their Power

When the labors of this motley assembly came to an end, the instrument which they called a Constitution proved to be worthy of its parentage: a league with death and a covenant with hell.
—NEWSPAPER EDITOR ETHELBERT BARKSDALE[1]

This Constitution dodged nothing. Under its provisions the Negro was a man, and all men were to be equal in their right to life, liberty, and the pursuit of happiness.
—CONVENTION DELEGATE A. T. MORGAN[2]

Of the four constitutions that have governed Mississippi since statehood, only one was approved by the voters; only one provided for broad and inclusive voter participation; and only one prohibited discrimination in public transportation and appropriation of public funds. That constitution was the Constitution of 1869, drafted and ratified during Reconstruction and written by Black and white Republicans.

Moreover, it was this constitution that was the first to create Mississippi's statewide system of public education and required the Legislature to fund it with a newly established common school fund. Finally, unlike the Constitution of 1890, the Reconstruction constitution contained no requirement that schools be segregated and no restriction on the marriage of Blacks and whites.[3]

Adopting a new constitution that provided the franchise to Black men was a requirement of the federal 1867 Reconstruction Acts and a predicate for Mississippi to resume representation in Congress. Getting that done would take almost two and a half years, starting with a registration of all eligible male voters in the state. The man charged initially with conducting the registration and subsequent elections was General E. O. C. Ord, commanding general of the Fourth Military District, which comprised Arkansas and Mississippi.[4] Appointed to the post on March 10, 1867, Ord made it to Vicksburg on March 26, where he established his headquarters, assigned Major General A. C. Gillem with the responsibility for Mississippi, and issued orders that required all Freedmen's Bureau circulars to be approved by his office. Ord was a native of Maryland, a West Point graduate, and had seen military service in Mississippi with Grant and Sherman at Corinth, Jackson, and Vicksburg. He was returning to Mississippi on the appointment of President Johnson at the suggestion of Grant.[5]

A few days later, Ord exercised his military authority by promulgating orders referring to the Humphreys administration as "the provisional government," ending all elections until the new voter registration was completed, and instructing all civil officers in the state that he would fill any vacancy occurring in any elective position. By the fall, Ord had dispatched more than 2,000 troops to fifteen different posts throughout the state and increased the staff and resources of the Freedmen's Bureau. Despite these moves, Ord tried to "encourage the development of moderate white sentiment toward the reconstruction acts" by meeting with Governor Humphreys, allowing the current slate of elected officials to remain in office, and enforcing the existing laws of the state except where they conflicted with congressional legislation. This restrained approach was reflected in Ord's early published advice: "The most important duty devolving upon the freemen in their new condition is that of providing by their own labor for the support of themselves and families. They now have a common interest in the general prosperity. This prosperity does not depend so much on how men vote as upon how well each member of society labours and keeps his contracts."[6]

Ord was returning to a state with deep economic problems. Two years of mostly unprofitable farming had left the state's planters with more debt than profits. While Ord's chief task was to craft and oversee a process by which the state could meet congressional requirements to rejoin the Union, doing his part in helping to grow the economy would, he thought, more likely than not contribute to the peaceful end of military control. With this in mind, Ord worked with the Freedmen's Bureau to enforce labor contracts and to encourage farmers and other employers to negotiate fairly and honor their agreements. Throughout the spring and summer and into the fall, Ord issued general orders cracking down on horse stealing, seizing illegal whiskey distilleries, and prohibiting local officials from collecting poll taxes.[7]

"Nevertheless," as one historian wrote, "by the fall it had become clear to Ord that the real threat to the economic success of blacks was . . . the disposition of planters to deal unfairly with them in the yearly crop settlements. From throughout the state black complaints of mistreatment and outright fraud at the hands of planters and merchants flooded the headquarters of Ord and Gillem, even before the cotton-picking season had begun." Ord responded by ordering his staff to investigate every case where "landholders are without legal cause but upon frivolous pretexts driving off their laborers with a view to withhold their arrears of wages, or share in the growing crops" and later by establishing boards of arbitration to settle disputes between planters and laborers. These boards, along with agents of the Freedmen's Bureau, resolved "hundreds of disputes over cotton wages, with almost 500 being decided in October alone."[8]

In the meantime, during the spring and summer months, Ord and his staff created a system throughout the state to register every man twenty-one years of age and over, except for those whites disqualified by the Reconstruction Acts. In carrying out this responsibility in a very public way, creating election districts, hiring more than 180 local registrars, prescribing detailed policies on registration and voting, and planning for the special election, Ord was making real something that would have seemed unfathomable to white Mississippians at the end of the War—formerly enslaved Black men vested with the power to vote. In less than two years, slavery had been abolished, Black men and women were negotiating labor contracts, Black children were attending schools, and Black men would soon be voting and holding elective office. Ord himself drove the point home later in the summer after receiving complaints that local whites, by falsely linking registering to vote with paying taxes, were purposefully confusing the Freedmen. Ord's command issued a directive that registrars were to inform the Freedmen "that the registration where their names have to be entered and an oath taken, is not to impose any tax, or hold them to any military or other service, but simply to enable them to share equally with white men in the privilege of choosing who shall hold office in the County, State, and United States wherein they reside."[9]

For native whites, they responded to Ord, military control, Black voters, and the possibility of a new constitution through newspapers, letters, and journals.

For the Freedmen, the response was more dramatic and unprecedented, for they would be voting and running political campaigns for the first time in their collective history.

WHITE DEMOCRATS RESPOND

By the time Ord arrived in Mississippi, white political leaders who had assumed control of the state's affairs in the summer of 1865 had all the reason they needed to fear their social, economic, and political world would be different going forward.[10]

Since blaming themselves for military control was not an option—notwithstanding the adoption of the Black Codes, refusal to ratify the Thirteenth and Fourteenth Amendments, and mistreatment of Blacks—white Democrats in Mississippi developed a long list of others to blame, including abolitionists "working to cause a second war," Northern Radicals engaged in a mission to "punish the south," and Republicans seeking to gain political control of the South.[11]

Nevertheless, some whites were slowly reconciling themselves to a changed world if for no other reason than meeting the demands of Congress was the only way to rejoin the Union, elect Southern congressmen to office, and end military control. As one newspaper editor observed, "Until Mississippi's representatives were seated in Congress, it was useless to indulge in acrimonious censure of Northern Radicals."[12] Moreover, as a planter told the journalist Whitelaw Reid, "No harm would be done the South by Negro suffrage. The old owners would cast the votes of their people almost as absolutely and securely as their own." Or, as one prominent white leader remarked, "It is not the negroes we have to fear, but unprincipled white men who will seek to use them for selfish and wicked ends." And some whites were no doubt worn down by the fight and had resigned to wait for the outcome. As William Sharkey reported to Governor Humphreys in early 1867, "The aspect of public affairs is very gloomy; we are in a revolution, civil as yet, but very likely to become bloody, and in that count the South has nothing to hope for, nothing to expect but oppression and utter ruin."[13]

Others though just couldn't rise above their bitterness. The editor of the Brandon newspaper called the Reconstruction Acts an "inequitable enormity," while the Meridian newspaper exclaimed, "No master ever had a control as absolute over his slaves as this gives the military officers."[14]

As with most political and social transformations—in this case, from slavery to freedom to voting for Blacks—the reactions, adjustments, and effects are never very clear at the outset. There is rarely a linear or coordinated response. In the case of Mississippi, it took time for white Democratic leaders and their constituents to sort through all the changes, assess the impact, test options, and come to some overall consensus about how they wanted to respond.

Harris ably demonstrates this in his review of hundreds of newspaper articles, letters between private citizens and elected officials, memoirs, and reports in the months following the imposition of military control. What should be the response to the calling of the constitutional convention, Black suffrage, free labor, and the possibility of a new constitution? Harris found one group of white Mississippians who argued for a moderate approach, recognizing Blacks would soon have the vote, regardless of what happened in the state. As one editor said, "No sane or intelligent man can for a moment doubt that the question of negro suffrage has ceased to be an open one. . . . Neither can the question of reconstruction be an open one." Better to cooperate with the moderate factions in Congress than let the Radicals gain the upper hand was their way of thinking. Others went further and even launched attempts to build coalitions with the Freedmen, hoping in that way to control their votes before others gained control.

But ultimately none of those approaches appealed to the great mass of white Mississippi voters. As one scholar wrote, "Whites, after the initial shock of the military reconstruction acts had worn off, became increasingly hostile to the policy of cooperating with those whose object, they believed, was to rivet upon the south 'the vilest and most corrupt despotism which has disgraced the annals of history.'" It was probably more than the average white Democrat could withstand, seeing ex-slaves registering to vote and attending political rallies, not to mention negotiating for fair wages and having their children attend schools. Appearing to agree with the changes, rather than continuing to actively oppose them, would lend credibility to the changes and continue a process of the South bending to the will of the North.[15]

Not least among the reasons why a moderate approach to Black voters, including attempts to build coalitions with them, didn't work out were the Freedpeople themselves. They knew better. They had lived in Mississippi with these same whites. The real state of mind of these whites had been absorbed instinctively by Black men and women and was once articulated by historian Vernon Lane Wharton when he wrote, "In too many hundreds of instances in the past two years, most of the cooperationists, along with the white masses, had made entirely too clear their real attitude toward the [Freedman] and his hopes for a rise in status. The desires of a majority of the old citizens had been reflected in the Black Code."[16]

Not necessarily complicating these decisions but surely aggravating them was the continuing weakness in the state's economic recovery, the continued decline in the price of cotton, and the corresponding problems with finding enough money to finance state and local government operations.

BLACKS RESPOND

For Black men in Mississippi, participating in an election, both as a voter and, for some, also as a candidate, was a first-in-a-lifetime experience, or as historian Eric Foner described it: "The passage of the Reconstruction Act inspired blacks with a millennial sense of living at the dawn of a new era."[17]

The question then became how they would translate these new rights into effective political action. How would individuals who had heretofore never participated in any election or campaign mobilize themselves to successfully engage in a process that had been controlled by whites since "the dawn of the" new era?

Over the last several decades, historians have given us a picture of a people adjusting to the new system slowly and tentatively, with a "diverse and complex reaction," but gradually gaining confidence in their ability to make their votes count and even offer themselves as candidates. At first, they quite naturally focused on their individual lives, and those of their families—securing employment, reuniting family members, obtaining housing—before reaching out to and becoming involved with groups and the political process. The response varied from rural to urban areas and was dependent on the presence of federal troops or Freedmen Bureau agents. Gradually, though, they began to meet, share information and experiences, compare notes, learn about new opportunities, and make plans. Today, we would call this networking. Many early gatherings took place in churches, though other informal organizations emerged with meetings held in schools, homes, or in the woods or fields to ensure security and autonomy. For example, in one Mississippi town, Blacks formed a society to read newspapers aloud to those who were illiterate. Churches, though, quickly became a safe space for Freedpeople. Previously forced to worship with whites, one of their first acts of independence was to abandon those churches and form their own, with their own pastors and own traditions.

During the early stages of Reconstruction, ministers and pastors constituted the largest group of Black activists. "But," observed one scholar, "the number of preachers beaten and the many churches burned to the ground by irate whites testified to the fact that the black minister did not always play the role expected and demanded of him. If he viewed himself as the moral and religious caretaker of his people, he would be drawn inexorably into the political arena." James Lynch, a Maryland native who moved to the state in 1868 to organize on behalf of the Methodist Episcopal Church and would later become the first Black to hold statewide office, often said, "Where visions of the 'halter' rise up before me, I commence as a preacher and end as a political speaker."[18]

In the meantime, Northern Republicans seized the opportunity handed to them by the enfranchisement of Black men and mobilized the Union League.

Formed during the Civil War as a patriotic club to support Lincoln and his administration in the northern and border states, the Union League was controlled by the national Republican Party leadership. The organization required its members to take an oath of secrecy that bound them against divulging the proceedings of their meetings. Sensing a chance to support Congressional Republicans and undermine President Johnson, all the while building new Republican majorities in the Southern states by organizing newly enfranchised Blacks, Union League officials moved south with enough resources to fund a Southern organizing campaign, including paid organizers and printed materials. Black voters, in turn, were ready for this kind of mobilization, not only because of the vote but also because of continuing dissatisfaction with the lack of land and the way they were being treated on farms and plantations. The response was dramatic, with tens of thousands of Freedpeople joining local clubs throughout the South. Whites, of course, thought differently about more Northerners coming into the state, with one newspaper editor complaining that the clubs were "composed mostly of negroes and controlled by the refuse of Northern penitentiaries," were "instruments of Republican political control," and were "prolific breeders of social disorder." Blacks who participated in League activities put their employment at risk, as a typical report from a Freedmen's Bureau official in Wilkinson County remarked, "many contracts . . . annulled by planters since the organization of the Union Republican Club."[19]

Organizers arrived in Mississippi in early 1867, and a state council was established in June 1867. What researchers have found is that by tapping into nascent Black organizations, the Union League movement spread rapidly, creating a "strong sense of community," safe spaces for debates and planning, and the impetus for "the eventual politicization of the freedmen." The secret nature of the league helped to cover up what Blacks were doing and, in many cases, local leaders camouflaged the real purpose of the leagues, calling them aid societies. Moreover, the gatherings gave Freedpeople a sense of power, and the vow of secrecy meant they could talk freely. "Once persuaded they could speak their minds, they needed little urging to denounce the memory of slavery and those who continued to oppress them," as one league official wrote. Typically League meetings began with a prayer from a local minister. Usually, "a Bible, a copy of the Declaration of Independence, and an anvil or some other emblem of labor lay on the table" at the front, new members took an initiation oath, and pledges followed "to uphold the Republican Party and the principle of equal rights, and to 'stick to one another.'" The leagues and other organizations, such as churches and schools, transcended politics and gave Freedpeople unprecedented opportunities to share information, compare notes about employment contracts, teach reading, organize, and test leadership skills. There was also the psychological benefit of actively participating in organizations such as the league: they were engaging in activities that had been prohibited during slavery. As one historian remarked, they were doing "the opposite of slavery."[20]

A remarkable phenomenon gradually developed among some of the leagues that could only be called drilling—military-style marching, sometimes involving guns, sometimes not; sometimes in the practice of marching to the polls to lessen the impact of intimidation; sometimes just marching in an open field. While military officers received letters from whites complaining about the marching, League leaders knew the sight of Black men marching with arms would infuriate farmers and planters, or as the practice was described by one historian, "Brandishing of firearms became a crucial token of emancipation." The scene was once captured by the editor of a Hinds County newspaper: "Our usually quiet village was enlivened Monday by the presence from adjacent plantations of from three hundred to five hundred of the newly manufactured 'American citizens of African descent.'"[21]

The connection Blacks made with the Republican Party and with voting was explained once by a white leader who recounted a speech he had witnessed at a League gathering:

> [The speaker] stepped forward to the edge of the stage and looking around exclaimed: "Am I dreaming? Is this Charleston where I came ten years ago to see human beings sold at auction . . . Going! Going!" and then he suddenly stopped and looking up to the sky, pointed upward and went on: "Look yonder. Do you see what is bidding for you? The soul of Abraham Lincoln . . . Lincoln takes the whole lot—gone!" You could feel the effect of this speech all through the crowd. The old woman in front of me shouted: "Yes, you blessed old man, Hallelujah." What do you suppose we can say in reply to that?[22]

As the historian Eric Foner once wrote, "The Republican Party—the party of emancipation and black voting rights—became an institution as central to the black community as the church and the school. And voting was the central act of freedom."[23]

THE 1867 ELECTION

It was in the fall of 1867 that the reality of Reconstruction was made plain to white Mississippians. At the conclusion of Ord's voter registration process, he announced that 79,179 Blacks and 58,385 whites had registered to vote.[24] The Freedpeople were in the majority, and, as whites knew, they were getting organized.

Every man who signed up to register was required to take an oath of allegiance to the Union and be a resident citizen of the state for at least nine months and at least twenty-one years old. Whites who had served in an official capacity before or during the War in support of the Confederate government were disqualified, pursuant to the Reconstruction Acts. A constant source of confusion for the registrars was determining the real ages of younger Black men, many of whom had no proof of their birth dates (a matter of record keeping that slavery did not require). When, for example, Benjamin Courtney went to register in a south Mississippi county and was asked to prove his age, he replied, "I was a slave at the time and they would not allow us to know our own age." It was also a source of controversy with white editors who complained that Black voter rolls were inflated, as a Natchez newspaper once wrote, with "at least five hundred negroes under twenty-one years of age registered as voters after being urged to commit perjury by the white Radical leaders."[25]

To put those numbers in some perspective, the 1860 and 1870 Census data yield an estimate of 90,100 Black males, twenty-one years and older, living in the state at the time, while there were 84,700 white males twenty-one years and older. Given the overwhelmingly rural nature of the state and the lack of effective transportation and communication systems, the registration process would not have picked up all eligible Blacks while the Reconstruction Act restrictions on former Confederates played a role in reducing the white numbers.[26] With registration completed, Ord issued an order on September 26, 1867, prescribing election rules, apportioning the 100 delegates to a constitutional convention among the sixty-one counties, and setting November 5 as the date of the election to call the convention and elect delegates.[27]

The publication of these raw statistics not only "shocked the native whites," who had not anticipated such a large number of Black voters, but it also generated intense debate about whether to participate in the election or boycott it. In this particular election, not voting was a legitimate option for white Democrats since the Reconstruction Acts required a majority of all registered voters to determine the outcome in any election calling for a convention.

Staying at home could deprive Ord of that majority. In the absence of meeting that threshold, the election outcome would be invalid.[28]

Just as appalling to the whites, Ord declared Black men would be eligible to serve as election officials and as delegates to the convention. A typical response came from the editor of a Vicksburg newspaper: "We hoped that this shameful humiliation would have been spared our people, at least until the freemen of Mississippi decide whether they will submit to negro equality. . . . The order is injudicious, if not insulting to that race whom God has created the superior of the black man, and whom no monarch can make his equal."[29]

Debate among whites about whether or not to sit out the election continued all summer and into the fall. Some argued they had everything to lose and nothing to gain by a "do nothing" policy while others complained that participating in any process that endorsed Black suffrage was tantamount to becoming "traitors to their race." The former maintained that acceptance of Black suffrage and helping to write a new constitution was the only way to return Mississippi to the Union and resume her voice in Congress, while the latter group argued the power of Radicals was "waning" in Congress and whites in Mississippi should just wait it out. The former argued that unless whites participated and stayed involved, more radical measures might be implemented, such as confiscation of land and further white disfranchisement. Worse than Black suffrage, these white leaders argued, was Black domination at a constitutional convention.[30]

In the meantime, following on the heels of the Union League organizing, Republican clubs and county conventions were planting seeds and getting established. All of that activity naturally led to the first Republican party convention in the state, held in Jackson on September 10, 1867. About a third of the delegates were Black, while white delegates included former Union soldiers and other Northern immigrants, native-born white Mississippians, and officials associated with the Freedmen's Bureau. The convention called for universal free education and civil and political rights free of any distinction based on race or color in education.[31]

In the end, white Mississippians largely stayed home, refusing to endorse the process, and, of course, hoping that would translate into less than a majority turnout. On the other hand, the newly enfranchised Black men came out in full force to cast a vote for the first time in their lives, or to borrow a more descriptive phrase of election day from a historian: "the scene had no real precedents." The final tally came to 69,739 votes for and only 6,277 votes against, or 54 percent of the total number of registered voters, which yielded the required majority.[32]

The cover of an 1867 issue of *Harper's Weekly* magazine, celebrating Black men voting for the first time in the South. Library of Congress, Prints and Photographs Division, LC-DIG-ppmsca-31598.

The day before the vote, the *Natchez Democrat* declared: "If the colored men will meet in secret conclave with degraded white men, if they will not listen to our counsels, if they will consider us their enemies, and not their friends, let them suffer the consequences."[33] On the day of the vote, that same newspaper kept pounding away, "Today is negro day. They are to choose whether they will be friends of the white people of this country, and be by them befriended, or whether they will . . . draw a dividing line between themselves and the community by which they hope to be sustained."[34]

None of it mattered to the Freedpeople, while the "trauma of defeat for whites was heightened by the ominous fact that the freedmen had turned out in large numbers in most counties and had cast their ballots solidly for the convention and for Republican candidates." Moreover, the decision by whites to boycott the election allowed Republicans to win such an overwhelming majority of delegates to the convention that there would be no need to compromise with the few conservative Democrats who were elected as delegates.

In early December, Ord's office released the proclamation calling for the constitutional convention to be held in the Hall of the House of Representatives at 11:00 on Tuesday, January 7, 1868.[35]

The end of 1867 witnessed one of the worst crops in recent Mississippi history and represented a continuing economic challenge for whites seeking to make good use of their farmland and for Blacks seeking to make good on the employment contracts for 1867 and to negotiate reasonable contracts for the new year. The commanding general of Mississippi, General Alvan Gillem, reported the cotton crop "has not exceeded half of what was regarded as an average crop, and that has commanded but one-half of the previous year, thus reducing the proceeds to one-fourth of what was anticipated."[36]

No sooner had the convention convened than the state's dismal economy became a focal point for the delegates and a source of frustration between the Republicans and Gillem. A committee of the convention conducted its own investigation and promptly informed Gillem that only eleven counties were "free from distress and suffering" while finding that at least 30,000 people were "destitute and suffering" and another 40,000 were in "straightened and needy circumstances." The committee recommended that the county boards of supervisors retain the poll tax, rather than send the proceeds to the state, and use those proceeds to pay people who qualify to "work on the public roads, or some other public works, of said counties, simply supplying said destitute persons with sufficient food and clothing necessary to keep them warm and this to be continued only till they can get employment and wages elsewhere. By this means, the roads of the different counties might be put in good order, at very little expense."[37]

After surveying his staff, Gillem responded in late February to the committee with a series of "eyewitness" accounts from military officers and agents of the Freedmen's Bureau. In his transmittal, Gillem pronounced himself "satisfied that the estimate of the committee of 30,000 is much too great," though he announced that Bureau agents had been instructed "to procure labor for all such as are able and willing to earn a support, including providing transportation," and that the "aged and decrepit and orphan children will be cared for in hospitals and asylums." The reports also indicated the demand for labor exceeded the supply in parts of the state, and that the Bureau was constantly receiving requests to hire laborers. Moreover, the general declined to order the use of the poll tax as requested by the committee by calling attention to the fact that "there are no funds in the State Treasury and that the State Prison and Lunatic Asylum are now supported at the expense of the United States."[38]

Nevertheless, a report from Greenville found many destitute families, with the local Bureau agent urging the military to send troops to help. The report indicated Freedmen were worried about the planters "ejecting all" of them from their lands except those who could work. "I would state," wrote the agent, "that I believe there is a combination on the part of a great many planters to hold off in respect to hiring laborers, expecting the Government to compel them to work, and thereby be enabled to get them for their food and clothing alone." From an officer who examined the counties bordering along the Yazoo River: "Freemen are in a destitute condition mainly because they will not hire out to farmers and planters. Reasons: wages are too low. . . . Saw no destitution among the planters or people generally." The report from a soldier in the Grenada area was more hopeful: "Found most had entered into contracts. Found better results in Panola and DeSoto. The agent in those counties had obtained contracts for everyone and had one very flourishing school with plans for another to open."[39]

Gillem may have been hesitant to over-emphasize any economic problems as he had just assumed district-wide command from Ord. Believing that Ord had exaggerated the ramifications of the crop failures at the end of the year, President Johnson replaced Ord with Gillem on December 27. This move came after Ord had pleaded for supplies and food for the state. At the same time that Gillem was under siege from the convention delegates, he was receiving "almost daily petitions and memorials [from whites] asserting the existence of organized companies of freedmen and asking for the presence of troops." Gillem's quandary was that "planters were reluctant to employ freed-men for the new year and blacks were reciprocating by rejecting the contracts they were offered." As the new head of the military command, with control of the Freedmen's Bureau, Gillem instructed all agents at his disposal to "use every means in their power to procure situations for laborers on the best terms." Needing work, many of them had no choice but to settle for less than they had received the previous year.[40]

In the middle of all the reports and correspondence reprinted in the con-vention journal, there is a fascinating note from Gillem, in which he is frus-trated those farmers and planters ignored his advice earlier in 1867 that they devote a sufficient amount of acreage for grains: "In connection with this sub-ject, again urge those engaged in agricultural pursuits to devote more land and labor to the production of corn and wheat. Had this suggestion on this subject been heeded last year, instead of the threatened famine, there would have been a large amount of breadstuffs for export. The present destitution should serve as a warning."[41]

At the end of the year, a Mississippi planter wrote to a friend in Oregon, bemoaning the situation in his home state: "We are in a far worse condition than we were one year ago or even last spring. The overflow [of the rivers], army worm, failure of the cotton crop, its present ruinous prices, the demor-alization of the freedmen as the laboring class, and the attempts to elevate the Servile over the white race have brought universal ruin upon our people."[42] For this white Mississippian, and many others, they could do nothing but watch as the "servile" helped to frame a new constitution.

THE 1868 CONSTITUTIONAL CONVENTION

"Gentlemen of the Convention, the hour of our assembling has arrived." With those words, Alston Mygatt opened an extraordinary and unprecedented ses-sion on the floor of the House of Representatives in the State Capitol Building. For the twenty-seven years that the building had functioned as the seat of state government, no Black person had ever walked on the floor as a voting member. Now, at 11:00 o'clock on Tuesday morning, January 7, 1868, seventeen Black men joined seventy-three white men as voting delegates to a conven-tion that would write a state constitution.[43]

Even more poignant, it was on that same day, January 7, in 1861, that 100 white delegates, elected for a much different purpose, had met in the same building, walked on the same floor, and very soon thereafter voted to secede from the Union.[44]

Mygatt, a white delegate from Warren County who had settled there from New York in 1837 for health reasons and who had maintained his antislavery and pro-Union sentiments during the War, albeit discretely, and who ultimately became the state president of the Union League, was elected temporary president of the convention. He continued with his opening statement that Tuesday morning:

> And with that—the hour that our Registrars have so long toiled to bring out—the hour that all loyal men of this State have labored to hasten, and now rejoice to behold—the hour that all opponents of reconstruction, and a disloyal press, have striven hard to prevent, has come. This hour brings to an end that system that enriches the few at the expense of the many—that system that hindered the growth of towns and cities, and built up large landed aristocracies—that system that discouraged agricultural improvements, and mechanic arts—that destroyed free schools, and demoralized church and State, has come to an end. The last sand has fallen from the glass of old-time dispensations, and they have gone to return no more forever.[45]

Mygatt went on to highlight the significance of the 1861 and 1868 dates: "Two points of time are important in our history—the day this State seceded, and the day of our assembling to effect her return. It is a notable fact—a remarkable coincidence—that [seven] years ago, this day, in this hall, the sword of treason, by an act of secession, tore this State from its peaceful position, and sent it adrift on the dark and unknown sea of blood and ruin."[46]

In addition to the seventeen Black Republicans, the delegate total included twenty-one Northern white Republicans and fifty-four Southern whites. Of the Southern whites, the consensus is that between sixteen and eighteen of them called themselves either Democrats or Conservatives but were united in their votes against the Republican positions. The remaining thirty-five or so Southern whites were generally inclined to support reforms, though served as a moderating voice on many of the key votes. This faction of conservative whites was lower than their percentage of the state because of their decision to boycott the 1867 election. Half of the Black delegates were ministers while farmers and laborers made up the other half, with virtually all of them coming from counties in the Delta or Central regions of the state. As for the whites, they were, by and large, either lawyers, physicians, or planters. Almost half of Southern whites came from the northern part of the state while the majority of Northern whites came from the Delta region, which included all of the counties along the Mississippi River and home to most of the larger plantations. According to the most comprehensive scholarly study yet of the Reconstruction conventions, the delegates from the Delta, who were largely Northern whites and Blacks, had the highest voting percentage for the Republican agenda while the delegates from northern Mississippi, largely native-born whites and small farmers, had the lowest rate.[47]

A Hinds County newspaper had this less than enthusiastic observation about the delegates: "A Negro barber, a white Copiah County loafer, a Negro waiter, and an ex-Yankee soldier. . . . In former conventions Hinds has been represented by the Sharkeys, the Johnstons, the Yergers, etc., men of the first class of ability and eloquence in the South. . . . Now we have a team, not one of whom would be permitted (in any capacity other than a servant) to enter the residence of any gentlemen of Hinds County. The bottom of the hill has certainly been reached."[48]

At least fourteen of the white delegates were former Union soldiers, including General B. B. Eggleston, a native New Yorker. It was Eggleston's campaign for permanent president of the convention that set up the first bell-wether test. His opponent, the candidate of the Democratic Conservatives, was John W. C. Watson, a lawyer from Marshall County and a member of the 1865 Constitutional Convention. When Eggleston easily prevailed by a vote of 53-33, the tilt in favor of the Republicans was readily apparent.[49]

The presence of Black men walking the floor of the House chamber as official voting members of the convention was not the only indignity conservative whites across Mississippi had to endure. Consider just the physical presence of the delegates and the 1865 white political leadership in Jackson. The Reconstruction Convention was being held in the same building where the Legislature had met only ten months earlier and just four blocks from the Governor's Mansion where Benjamin Humphreys still lived and still served as "provisional governor." Moreover, the governor's official office was on the first floor of the same Capitol building where, on the second floor, the convention was being held. White legislators and other state officials, elected in 1865 and continuing to serve in their respective positions, watched helplessly as a group of men, elected under a system administered by military officers and over which they had no control, used the public facilities of the state to craft a constitution that would govern them and the affairs of the state. A historian once wrote that these officials had been "ushered into the limbo of forgotten men." Humphreys's exasperation at his predicament was evident in his response when he was once asked for information by a committee of the convention: "I presume you do not expect me to admit that the Convention now in session in this city, by virtue of the 'Military Bills' passed by Congress, has any constitutional right to require me to account to it for my administration of the civil government of the state of Mississippi."[50]

Yet one more cause for affront among the white political leaders who had assumed power in 1865 and the white opinion makers who had resumed publishing newspapers and giving speeches was the presence of whites at the convention who were voting with the Freedmen. The neutral terms used to identify them earlier in this chapter were Northern white immigrants and Southern white Republicans. For the ex-Confederates, they needed terms that would be short, memorable, and derisive: Northern whites became known as Carpetbaggers, a member of "the lowest class" of Northerner who was "able to pack all of his earthly belongings in his carpetbag" for the journey south to "fatten" on the South's misfortunes. Scalawag became the noun of choice for the Southern whites who aligned with the Republicans, "the local leper of the community." A newspaper in Yazoo City obviously thought something more descriptive was needed, so the editor referred to them as "white niggers." The line in the proverbial sand of public opinion was drawn by a Vicksburg newspaper editor when he wrote: "If there is a white man who refuses to affiliate with his own race, in maintaining the rightful supremacy of white men in the South, we have no use for that man. His face may be white, but his heart is blacker than night. . . . The dogs who are false to their own race and lineage must be so marked that all men will recognize and avoid them."[51]

Walter Stricklin, a white delegate from Tippah County, knew his audience when he once offered a tongue-in-cheek substitute for the preamble: "We, the carpetbaggers and scalawags from the states of Ohio, Vermont, Connecticut, Maine, and Africa, do ordain and proclaim this to be the document upon which we predicate all of our hopes for the success of the radical party." Four years later, the editor of the Hinds County newspaper was still seething when he wrote, "A Democrat had rather be called a horse thief than a scalawag." "Carpetbaggers" and "Scalawags" became ubiquitous terms throughout the Reconstruction era, showing up in newspapers and magazine articles whenever a writer needed to hurl an insult. Moreover, the white historians of Reconstruction continued to use the terms pejoratively forty and fifty years after the last "Carpetbagger" had left Mississippi.[52]

To capture for the reader the scene in early 1868, Jackson was still a small town and still rebuilding from the War. The 1870 census counted almost 4,200 municipal residents, about half white and half Black. The county, on the other hand, had 10,000 whites and 21,000 Blacks. Downtown Jackson consisted of two streets on either side of Capitol Street, which connected the Capitol building with the train depot about fifteen blocks directly west of the Capitol (near where it stands today). Most of the businesses were located on State Street to the south of the Capitol, with residential areas largely confined to streets surrounding the downtown. To the east of the Capitol building, off the bluff, was the flood plain of the Pearl River. Much of the business of the convention—the committee meetings, the late-night discussions, and the arguments—occurred in the "hotel and boardinghouse rooms" that had been built since the War and where the delegates were staying.[53]

The convention was covered by newspapers, with out-of-town reporters filing their stories via telegraph. Except for four or five newspapers friendly to the Republican Party, the print media was decidedly aligned with the white conservatives. In fact, as one historian pointed out, they ended up competing with one another for the most descriptive and inflammatory headlines to describe the convention. A few samples include the "great polecat reconstruction convention," the "chain-gang convention," "General Ord's bogus convention," "Ord's Nigger Convention," or the "collection of wild and imported animals." A few days after the convention convened, a Natchez newspaper described the delegates as the "illegitimate offspring of negro supremacy" that was "begotten of vindictive malevolence, conceived in treachery, . . . and upheld by military despotism."[54]

In addition to freely using "Carpetbagger" and "Scalawag" to identify the white delegates, newspapers would include the adjective "colored" beside the name of any of the Black delegates who were featured in their coverage. The effect, as one historian pointed out, was to undermine "the cause of moderation in the convention. In their hell-bent desire to denigrate the assemblage . . . editors seemed to compete with each other for first prize in an undeclared contest to determine who could describe the convention in the most ludicrous terms."[55] At one point, an editor coined the gathering as "the Black and Tan Convention." That label has persisted through the years.

These editors weren't the only obstacle faced by the delegates. Only four days into the work of the convention, the gas company in Jackson sent Eggleston a letter asking for a deposit "sufficient to cover the amount of gas that may be used by the Convention." Gas was used to heat and light the Capitol, both of which were needed in the cold, short days of the winter. While the letter didn't overtly threaten to turn off the gas to the Capitol unless a deposit was made, a similar letter had not been sent when the Legislature convened a year earlier.[56]

A public relations obstacle was created by Governor Humphreys himself when, a few days before the convention convened, he issued a proclamation claiming, without any evidence, that the Freedmen were conspiring to "seize the lands and establish farms, expecting and hoping that Congress will arrange a plan of division and distribution" and if that didn't happen, they were prepared to go to war. The governor then admonished the Freedmen to avoid any such activity and exclaimed: "What is not known of your plans and conspiracies will be discovered and anticipated, and the first outbreak against the quiet and peace of society, that assumes the form of insurrection, will signalize the destruction of your cherished hopes and the ruin of your race." The governor refused to give up the source of his information and ultimately a committee of the convention concluded the governor's claims "were so utterly without foundation."[57]

To add even more public pressure on the delegates, white conservatives met in Jackson on January 15, 1868, to protest. Styling themselves as the "Democratic White Men's Party of Mississippi," the the convention's purpose was to "place the white men of the Southern States under the governmental control of their late slaves, and degrade the Caucasian race as the inferiors of the African negro," and was thus "a crime against the civilization of the age." This was followed by the state assembly of the regular Democratic Party on February 19–20 in Jackson with 200 delegates from all but eighteen counties attending. Resolutions sanctioned the actions of the January convention and declared it to be the duty of all whites to defeat the proposed constitution: "Their ignorance and incapacity to exercise the privileges of suffrage and to discharge the responsibilities of making laws and holding office, forbid that we consent to invest them with these privileges or to consent to any legislation designed to establish the political or social equality of the white and black races."[58]

Finally, it was during the convention that Congress undertook the impeachment of President Andrew Johnson. The articles of impeachment were filed against Johnson on March 5 by the House, stemming from his attempt to dismiss Secretary of War Edwin M. Stanton, but culminating in his continuing efforts to use the presidency to thwart the effort on the part of the Republicans in Congress to manage Reconstruction. Johnson was acquitted in the Senate by one vote on May 16. All of this was followed closely by local newspapers and the delegates to the convention, who adopted a resolution endorsing the impeachment.[59]

Despite all the obstacles, the diversions, and the pressure, the delegates met for a little more than four months and approved a new constitution. In the years following the convention, white historians and officials complained about the length and cost of the convention. When they did so, they inflated the cost and failed to mention that the expense they calculated was the cost of publishing the convention proceedings in several newspapers and of conducting the ratification election, items that no other convention had incurred. While whites were outraged at Blacks voting and serving as delegates, at Northern whites who had only recently taken up residency, and at the cost, especially since they were being taxed to pay for the convention, it was the substantive matters of public policy that defined the document this convention produced. And it was those substantive issues that the framers of the 1890 Constitution undermined or rejected.[60]

For as long as whites and Blacks had lived in Mississippi, it was a given among whites that they were not merely members of different races; Blacks were inferior, and laws should be used to segregate the races and enforce that inferiority. More than any other theme of the Reconstruction convention, it was the repudiation of that tradition that defined the new Constitution: discrimination was prohibited in public transportation and appropriation of public funds, voting for men was expressly granted regardless of race, and the rights to receive education, serve on juries, and marry the person of one's choosing were memorialized with no racial restrictions.[61]

Only when you read the very first right enumerated in the Declaration of Rights article that opens the 1832 Constitution do you realize that the Constitution only applied to whites: "Section 1. That all freemen, when they form a social compact, are equal in rights."

Article III authorized the vote for "every free white male person" and specified that the census required by the Constitution only include "free white inhabitants" while it was in Article VII that the lives of "slaves" were regulated. Whenever the term "person" or "citizen" was used in the 1832 Constitution, it was understood to refer only to whites. *Dred Scott* only reinforced that view. The new Constitution would be the first in the state's history to apply its privileges, rights, and responsibilities to the state's residents regardless of race.

Throughout the South's history, miscegenation had been a word and a theory used constantly by white political leaders to undermine racial equality and provoke fear among the average white voter. In the absence of slavery and the associated state laws that authorized marriage only among whites, the issue of interracial marriage suddenly had contemporary relevance.[62] Consequently, a few weeks into the convention, George Stovall, a white delegate and farmer from Carroll County, raised the danger of leaving the issue unattended by offering a proposal to ban the marriage of Blacks and whites. His reasoning is worth reproducing in full: "Whereas, the fact has been demonstrated by physiologists, and long since settled as an axiom of science, that the progeny resulting from an intermarriage between the white and black races are very liable to produce a character of hereditary diseases; that the children of the pure white or black, are not subject to diseases incurable in their nature, and most destructive to human life; that the general intermarriage of the two races occupying the South, will inevitably result in the destruction of both."

The potency of the issue among whites was made plain when an effort to quickly kill the proposal died on a 10-55 vote. Stovall's resolution came up for debate again the following day, at which point Thomas Stringer, a Black delegate from Warren County, argued against it by declaring that no law should be enacted to limit "who a man should have as a partner for life." Stringer was born a free Black in Maryland and ultimately moved to Mississippi in 1866 to begin the organization of the Mississippi Conference of the African Methodist Church. At the time of the convention, he was serving as pastor of a church in Vicksburg. One historian described him as a "genius of organization" and that his "influence upon the constitution of 1869 was as great as that of any other man in the convention." Doctor Stites, a Black delegate from Washington County, apparently decided the convention needed some humility and perspective, so he introduced an amendment to Stovall's resolution that "white men living with and cohabiting with females of color, except under and by virtue of the rights of marriage, are guilty of a greater crime than that of adultery and that the Legislature under the forthcoming Constitution, be required, at its first session, to make such laws as will prevent the spread of such crime, and shall impose a fine and imprisonment on such white men, or disqualify them from the rights of citizenship." Once everyone caught their collective breath, recognizing the traditions that had been prevalent in the state during slavery, a procedural motion was made to kill all amendments and resolutions dealing with the issue and bring an end to its consideration. That move was approved by a narrow 36-34 margin.[63]

For whites, segregation in public transportation, such as train or ferry travel, was a particularly public way to demonstrate power over Blacks. It was part of the 1865 Black Code and was sure to come up in the convention. The report of the committee on the Bill of Rights contained a section that provided "the right of all citizens to travel shall not be infringed upon nor in any manner abridged in this State." An amendment was then offered to expand that right to include travel "on all public conveyances" and, more dramatically, to "be entertained in all public places." By a losing margin of only three votes, 35-38, a public accommodations law was almost enacted in Mississippi, a full

96 years ahead of the 1964 Civil Rights Act. After an amendment was passed to drop the entertainment provision, which was apparently too far ahead of its time, but retained the public conveyance language, the section was approved and made part of the constitution.[64]

For the Black delegates, though, they knew land and education were the paths to economic prosperity. The early reports from Union officers in charge of refugees, as well as the missionaries who had traveled south to work in the refugee camps, were full of observations about the hunger for education among the formerly enslaved. One federal official reported that Blacks "instinctively associated the absence of educational opportunities with bondage and the privilege of learning with freedom," while a Freedman promised to send his children to the new schools "because education was the next best thing to liberty." Denied land by President Johnson, Black delegates used the new constitution to prevent a similar denial of education. Led by Stringer, the convention began debate on March 9 of a new Article VIII that would create a statewide system of public education.[65]

While granting Freedpeople the rights of citizenship and voting was surely revolutionary, both were required by the Fourteenth Amendment and the Reconstruction Acts. Mandating a statewide system of education for all children and requiring the Legislature to pay for it was arguably the unexpected shock to any expectations white conservatives may have had for the convention.

From the perspective of white conservatives, the "shock" was understandable. They were less than three years away from a time when state law prohibited the existence of schools for enslaved children or even the small number of "free Negroes" who lived in Mississippi. Moreover, it was unlawful for any enslaved person to acquire books without "the consent of their owner." All these whites had known, for their entire lives, was captured by an infamous letter that once appeared in a Wilkinson County newspaper: "Knowledge and slavery are incompatible."[66]

That opposition to education was rooted in a variety of reasons, all summarized by the historian W. E. B. DuBois: "Property owners did not want to be taxed for school for laborers"; "laborers did not need education for it made their exploitation more difficult"; "Negroes could not and would not learn, and thus their education involved an unjustifiable waste" of resources; "education of the Negroes would be labor lost"; "schools encouraged social and racial equality"; and, finally, "schooling itself ruined niggers."

For the ex-slaves, having free access to formal education for themselves and their children represented the opposite of slavery; it represented freedom. Knowledge, they knew, was power. Education armed Blacks with tools to negotiate contracts, buy or rent land, borrow money, or learn a new skill or trade. It was for the very reasons that they wanted an education and that whites were opposed to them having it.[67]

All of that may explain why of the thirteen articles in the 1869 Constitution, only the article setting out the provisions for education begins with a preamble containing a statement of purpose:

> Section 1. As the stability of a Republican form of government depends mainly upon the intelligence and virtue of the people, it shall be the duty of the Legislature to encourage, by all suitable means, the promotion of intellectual, scientific, moral, and agricultural improvement, by establishing a uniform system of free public schools.

The remainder of the article provided for an elected statewide superintendent of education, a state Board of Education composed of the secretary of state, the attorney general, the superintendent, and a school superintendent in each county. The new constitution authorized the appointment of the county superintendent by the state Board of Education, with the advice and consent of the Senate, though it permitted the Legislature to make the office elective. The article went on to require schools to be open at least four months of the year and to create a common school fund of such taxes as the Legislature may choose to create to fund the schools so as "to properly support the system of free schools." To prevent the Legislature from using the appropriations to favor white students over Black students, the delegates required that "all school funds shall be divided pro rata among the children of school age."

Coming out of committee, the article was silent on the question of whether Black children could attend school with white children. The leader of the convention conservatives, William Compton, a white physician from Marshall County, a member of the 1865 Convention and infamous for referring to one of the Black delegates as that "saddle-colored individual from Hinds," offered an amendment to require segregated schools. That moved Stringer to argue there should be "no distinctions but those that God had made. The people were all descended from Adam and were of one blood." Compton's move failed on a 15-39 vote. After adding a new section authorizing the Legislature to establish a state agricultural college, the convention adopted the entire article, thus creating a constitutional right to a free education for every child in the state.[68]

After approving the education provisions, on March 19, the full convention took up the committee's recommendation of the franchise article, which Stringer had earlier introduced.[69]

Since the Reconstruction Acts required the enfranchisement of all Black males, adding that provision to the constitution was largely a foregone conclusion at the convention. Nevertheless, the conservative delegates forced a vote on a proposal to limit the vote to whites only, or as a friendly white historian would write some thirty years later, "to secure the adoption of a provision that would exclude from the franchise the great mass of ignorant blacks." The proposal failed on a 15-65 vote. Additional efforts were made to add educational qualifications and longer residency requirements but they likewise died on lopsided votes. "The bitterness became so great though," as one historian later wrote, "that personal altercations and fights were of common occurrence. The president of the convention was assaulted in front of the capitol building by a Democratic delegate. Other fights occurred. A majority of the members on both sides went armed."[70]

With that issue finalized, the question then became how far the delegates would go in preventing the former Confederates from voting and holding office. There were two sections in the Franchise article the Republicans wanted to use to disqualify the ex-Confederates.

First up was Section 3, which prescribed the registration oath. Unlike today, people who went to register to vote in the nineteenth and early twentieth centuries had to take an oath before completing the registration form. The delegates wanted to use the oath to embed in the constitution the voting restrictions of the Reconstruction Acts—legislators who supported secession and high-ranking Confederate military officers—but then they went further by adding the following phrase to the oath: "And I admit the political and civil equality of all men, so help me God." If the Republican delegates wanted to craft the hottest iron to stick in the collective eye of their enemies, making them swear to this was surely it. The Conservative attempt to remove these restrictions from the proposal died on a 17-49 vote.[71]

Then there was Section 5, which outlined limitations on the persons who could hold elective or appointive office. Here the delegates expanded the Reconstruction Acts umbrella restrictions and proposed to prohibit anyone who had been a member of the legislature voting to call the secession convention; a member of the secession convention; anyone who had served in any office, civil or military, in the secessionist government (or "pretended government authority" as the delegates referred to the Confederate States of America); or—and here was the kicker—"anyone who gave voluntary aid, countenance, counsel or encouragement to persons engaged in armed hostility." As whites would point out in countless speeches, advertisements, and flyers during the ratification campaign, these provisions would exclude almost all native-born Mississippi whites from holding any office in the recon-structed government. Various votes to weaken these restrictions took place on April 8, 10, and 16, all of which failed.[72]

After the last vote, and eighty-seven days into the convention, when it became clear there was no chance of defeating any of those limitations, twelve of the conservative delegates, led by Compton and Townsend, resigned from the convention. Two others joined them in the ensuing days.[73]

A week later, the convention adopted the full Article XII on the franchise, repudiating Section 1 of Article III of the 1832 Constitution that limited the right to vote to "every free white male person."[74] Three weeks later, the convention adjourned on May 18. Seventy of the 100 delegates signed the final document, including all seventeen Black members.

The Constitution of 1869 was full of other provisions that are still with us today, while others were changed by the 1890 Constitution, though later restored by court cases or subsequent amendments.

- The 1832 Constitution limited the governor's term to two years; the 1869 Constitution extended the term to four years and allowed for gubernatorial succession; the 1890 Constitution removed the succession provision, though it was later restored by an amendment in 1986.
- Before the 1869 Constitution, counties were governed by a board of police; the name was changed in 1869 to a board of supervisors.
- In a debate that is still alive today, the delegates provided for guber-natorial appointment of all judges, a feature retained by the 1890 Constitution. It wasn't until the "populist era" in the state that amend-ments were approved by the voters in 1910 (for chancery and circuit judges) and 1914 (for supreme court justices) to the 1890 Constitution, making the positions elective.
- The 1832 Constitution eliminated the position of lieutenant governor. The 1869 document restored the position as presiding officer of the Senate and second in command of the state should something hap-pen to the governor.

These were not the provisions targeted by the politicians who called for a con-vention in 1890 to draft a new constitution. While the delegates to the 1890 convention retained the article on education, they added a new section requir-ing segregated schools. And while the Fourteenth and Fifteenth Amendments forced them to maintain the Franchise article granting the vote to all men twenty-one years and older, they added five impediments to the exercise of

that right: a $2 poll tax, an increase in the state residence requirement from
six months to two years, an increase in the district residence requirement
from one month to one year, a list of crimes that would disqualify someone
from voting (crimes that were identified by the delegates as most likely to be
committed by Blacks), and a requirement to explain to the registrar any provision of the constitution. Moreover, they removed the prohibitions on racial
discrimination on public transportation and appropriations while adding a
specific limitation on interracial marriage.

But all of that was in the future. In May of 1868, the delegates produced
a constitution that applied to all Black and white citizens, guaranteed free
education to all Black and white children, and vested the right to vote with
all Black and white men. It would take two elections and another eighteen
months to get it adopted. When it finally happened in November 1869,
Mississippi had the only constitution in its history that was free of racial discrimination and that had been approved by the voters. That may explain why
the conservative white historian J. S. McNeily, writing some forty-seven years
later for the Mississippi Historical Society, described the 1868 convention as
having "brought forth an abortion of government so perverted and putrid
that it would not have survived birth pangs, but for the incubation and prop
of a national congress and the bayonets of the army."[75]

CHAPTER 7

1868–1869
A New Constitution
White Democrats Assert Their Power

> The uprising of the people of Mississippi against Negro rule was a most
> magnificent example of that spirit of Southern patriotism that animated
> the hearts.
>
> —DUNBAR ROWLAND[1]

Of all the former Confederate states that adopted new constitutions during
Reconstruction, Mississippi was the only one in which the ratification vote
failed at the ballot box.[2] As some had predicted, it was the proposal to disqualify tens of thousands of white Mississippians from registering to vote and
from serving in public office that formed the centerpiece of the successful
campaign by white Democrats to defeat the proposed constitution.[3]

The events in the spring and summer of 1868 in the state were among the
most dramatic in all of Reconstruction and moved very fast. The day after the
convention adjourned, the military commander, Alvan Gillem, called for an
election in less than five weeks, on June 22. Seven days later, the United States
Senate acquitted President Johnson of the impeachment charges against
him. That same week, buoyed by Johnson's victory in the Senate, Mississippi
Democrats began their campaign to defeat the constitution, urged on by
editors like Ethelbert Barksdale of the Jackson *Daily Clarion*: "the twenty-
second of June as the day of commencing the election on the question of
ratifying the proposed bastard and mongrel constitution. The week commencing with that day will be fraught with momentous consequences to the
people of Mississippi."[4]

Two factors would work in favor of white Democrats during the ensuing
month-long campaign.

First, also appearing on the ballot would be candidates for all of the state-wide and legislative offices authorized by the proposed constitution. It was with the choice of their candidates that Republicans made a critical campaign error: they failed to nominate even one Black candidate for any statewide position. As a result, they deprived their party of a key ingredient any successful campaign needs—a well-known and recognizable figure to motivate turnout. The Democrats held their convention in May and nominated the incumbent governor Benjamin Humphreys as their candidate for the top position on the ballot, along with other popular white moderates for the other positions.[5]

Second, and more importantly, the general in charge of managing the election, Alvan Gillem, was a close friend of President Johnson, having been appointed to that post by the president earlier in the year. Conservative by nature, an ally of Johnson's from their service together in Tennessee, and sympathetic to whites in general, Gillem used his authority to establish election procedures to aid the campaign of the Democrats, including the appointment of supportive county election officials.[6]

For Democrats, the danger inherent in the disqualification of large numbers of white voters transcended any divisions among the various constituencies that constituted their coalition. They would work and they would work together. As one historian described the campaign: "speaking opportunities abounded for everyone; numerous mass meetings were held in every county. When the Democratic campaign crested in June, the white masses, now thoroughly behind their leadership, were attending political rallies in larger numbers than at any time since 1860. The candidates for state office toured Mississippi, speaking in open fields before huge, enthusiastic audiences."[7]

Moreover, like-minded newspapers provided a constant stream of rallying cries for the Democratic slate. A Jackson newspaper editor exclaimed, "The cunning agents of despotism and social evils, well knew they would fail in their undertaking, unless they deprived a large class of the white population of their right to have a voice in the legislation of their state," while the Vicksburg newspaper made its appeal directly: "White Men! If you would escape political degradation, negro equality, carpet-bag domination, unlimited taxation, and the worst bondage to which a white man could possibly be subjected, work to defeat the mongrel constitution."[8]

The editor of the Natchez newspaper offered a startlingly unique rationale for a vote against the constitution when he argued that if Republicans ever got into power, the only way to get them out would be through a revolution that would surely involve "shooting and hanging." Whites could avoid having to carry out that violent option by simply defeating the constitution.[9]

Against unified and energized white voters, the Republicans were the underdogs: Republicans in Mississippi were a new thing, as was Black voting. The Union Leagues were organized in some counties, but not in all. Not only were Republican leaders overconfident—because of the edge in registered voters and because of the November convention election—they had failed to build a ticket of candidates that would appeal to all voters. Moreover, Gillem, underestimated by Republicans, failed to rein in his soldiers who often sided with local planters and county officials. The absence of Army protection was one of many reasons, for example, Union League members met in secret.[10]

THE 1868 ELECTION

Notwithstanding all that Democrats had going for them, they were confronting a registration disadvantage—86,972 Blacks compared to 68,547 whites according to the military's tally leading up to election day. There were only two ways to overcome those numbers: either intimidate the newly enfranchised Black voters and work to prevent them from showing up at the polls or, if they did show up, steal their votes.[11]

The most exhaustive analysis of primary sources from the 1868 election has come from William Harris, who reviewed newspapers, government reports, letters, and correspondence and identified a number of tactics used by white Democrats: having whites at the polls recording the names of the Blacks coming to vote, intimidating Black voters at the polls, and meeting Blacks in route to vote and urging them to turn around or lose their jobs, or, in other cases, actually preventing them from getting to the polling locations. Moreover, Harris found that in many cases this kind of intimidation was allowed to take place because many of the "troops openly sympathized with the conservatives . . . and aided the Democratic cause by simply refusing to act on Republican complaints of intimidation and irregularities" and because "many election officials, originally appointed by Gillem as registrars, were selected after their conservatism had been ascertained, and when the chips were down they permitted their conservative leanings to influence their official behavior."[12]

Then, on the eve of the election, Democrats were handed a campaign gift. Less than two weeks before the election, Gillem was temporarily replaced by General Irvin McDowell. The day after his appointment, McDowell received a telegram from Grant, by then General of the Army, suggesting he remove Governor Humphreys from his position as provisional governor and

replace him with "an officer of the Army." Grant was apparently worried that
Humphreys should be removed because "he was a candidate in the upcoming
election" and should not "control the state pending the approaching election."
In a very astute response, McDowell telegrammed back to Grant, making the
case against removal, because Humphreys "has only bare prestige of his nomi-
nal office, and the loss of this would, I think, be more than made up by the
prestige he would acquire of political martyrdom." Five days later, McDowell
sent a message to Grant that if he persisted in his request for a removal, he
would suggest General Adelbert Ames as Humphreys's replacement. Grant
replied two days later: "No one would be more suitable for Governor than
Gen. Ames. I leave it to your judgment however whether a change should
be made." On June 15, McDowell, apparently against his better judgment,
sent a telegram to Grant saying he had removed Humphreys. He defended
his action by claiming that a provision of the Reconstruction Acts required
him to make the change: "It shall be the duty of the [district commander] to
remove from office all persons . . . who use their official influence in any manner to . . . obstruct the due and proper administration of this act." Maybe so,
but the timing could not have been better for the Democrats.[13]

By making this move so close to the election—"the bloody guillotine of
despotism," as the Natchez newspaper called it—Grant and McDowell gave
whites yet one more reason to fully engage in the election. Even if McDowell
was retaliating for the Democrats nominating Humphreys as their candidate for governor or for Humphreys campaigning against the constitution or
if he felt the law required the expulsion, making this move, in the heat of a
campaign, would be nothing less than throwing gas on a fire. As the *Grenada
Sentinel* predicted, "Whether General Grant or General McDowell is the despot who has placed his foot on civil liberty, it will increase the Democratic
majority by at least ten thousand votes in the state at the coming election."[14]

A week later, the new constitution was defeated by a margin of 63,860 to
56,234. Humphreys was elected governor and Democrats assumed a majority of the Legislature, none of whom were ever inaugurated since the defeat
of the constitution meant Mississippi would remain under military control.[15]

As for the authors of the proposed constitution, the editor of the *Natchez
Democrat* hoped, "Their filthy tongues should blister when they speak," while
the Meridian newspaper spoke for the vast majority of whites when its editor
wrote, "With a sigh of relief, thank God, we can announce it is over; the election, the most disgusting, disgraceful, and degrading thing ever devised by the
malice of man. Thank God, it is over! And pray his Holy name to remove the
sin-created and sin-creating thing, negro suffrage."[16]

Notwithstanding the possibility of divine intervention, something out of the ordinary had happened in the intervening eight months since the 1867 election. The registration numbers conform to what would be expected to happen over that period. Black registration grew from 79,179 to 86,972. White registration had increased from 58,385 to 68,547.

But it was the actual election returns that were suspicious. Not only was the AGAINST count (63,860) unrealistically close to the total number of white registered voters (68,547), but the FOR vote (56,234) was significantly less than the number of Black registered voters (86,972). The FOR vote of 56,234 represented a drop-off of 13,500 from the November 1867 turnout and 30,000 less than the number of registered voters.

What explains these turnout figures and the reversal from 1867? To answer that question, political scientist Lawrence N. Powell made use of a quantitative and statistical analysis process, using individual county returns and census data, to determine if the fraud and intimidation that took place during the election "ensured the constitution's defeat." He concluded, "Using ballot-box stuffing and other coercive methods, thousands of black ballots were recorded for the Democrats." In other words, "the contest did not turn on the suppression of the black vote," Powell wrote, but in the 1868 election, "the swing vote was a stolen vote, and it was the decisive vote. The constitution lost in the actual election by roughly the same margin by which it probably would have won with a fair and free canvass."

Apart from using intimidation to keep Black voters away from the polls, and as Harris and others have demonstrated, there was plenty of that, what Powell discovered in his analysis of the 1868 election was that despite the threats, Black voters cast their ballots. While there were surely some voters who opted to stay home because of the pressure, the damage was done at the polling places, where either Blacks were intimidated and forced to vote for the Democratic ticket or the ballots were changed after they had been cast.

While in most counties the vote mirrored the racial registration numbers, in a significant number of counties the vote for the constitution was much less than would be expected while the vote against it was much higher—in some cases higher than the total number of white registered voters. What appears to have happened, more often than not, is that Black votes for the constitution were fraudulently switched to be votes against it.

For example, in Smith County, with 332 Black registered voters and 650 white registered voters, only three votes were recorded for the new constitution while 827 votes were cast against the constitution (substantially more than the number of white registered voters). In Newton County, which had

588 Blacks registered and 1,201 whites, the outcome was similar: only 115 for the constitution and 1,182 against the constitution. Consider Amite County, which had 1,059 Black registered voters and just 813 whites registered: the final tally showed 228 for the constitution and 1,093 against it. Perhaps the most blatant, though, was in Carroll County, with its 2,295 Black voters and 1,742 whites: just 276 voted for the constitution while 2,727 opposed it. These numbers stand out because, in most counties, the election outcome mirrors the percentage of Black and white registered voters. It is in only about fifteen to twenty of the counties where fraud, like this, occurred. When the Reconstruction history of Newton County was written for the Mississippi Historical Society in 1910, the author interviewed a local citizen who admitted that "the usual way of carrying elections [in the county] was by stuffing the ballot boxes."[17]

The 300-page report issued in January 1869 by the Congressional Committee on Reconstruction that investigated the 1868 Mississippi election had no similar analysis or comparison of election outcomes with registered voters. Instead, it focused almost exclusively on threats, intimidation, and harassment of Black voters and white Republicans, and its findings confirmed Harris's findings that many of the soldiers either looked away or actively participated with the Democrats, especially at the polling places. A common complaint was that Democrats would hover around the polls and watch to see how people were voting, as a registrar in Yazoo County testified: "Parties opposed to Reconstruction insist upon remaining about the polls as challengers, and take the names of all parties voting, and inquire very particular how every man votes. The voters are watched so closely that many of them say they cannot vote as they wish to. They are informed by people away from the polls that these men are taking their names, and are finding out how they vote, telling them that if they do not vote as they wish them to, that they (the freedmen) will regret it." In heaping praise on the election outcome and, in particular, explaining away the ability of Black voters to use their majority to carry the day, the Jackson *Clarion* let down its guard a little when it declared, "The election on our part was fairly conducted. Freedmen were reasoned with, it is true."[18]

At this point, the reader might be asking: How could the election officials do this? Voting during Reconstruction was unlike anything experienced today. An official ballot was not printed by either the local or state government. Each voter brought his own ballot. While voters were allowed to bring their handwritten ballots, by the late 1860s and into the 1870s, voters typically brought a preprinted and prechecked ballot that had been produced by either the Democratic Party or the Republican Party. Voters either cut the ballot out of the local newspaper, where it had been placed as an advertisement, or made use of sample ballots printed by local parties and handed out at the polls or meetings before election day. As a result, there was little secrecy afforded voters when they went to deposit ballots into the box or container, especially since there was no private place for the voter to use to deposit his ballot. The widespread use of preprinted ballots made it easy to exchange Democratic ballots for Republican ballots as they were being counted.[19] The kind of voting procedures used today didn't take root in Mississippi until the late nineteenth century as part of a nationwide trend against the very loose, very public balloting that had characterized voting in the country since its inception.[20]

Republicans complained vigorously to General Gillem, now once again back in charge of the military in Mississippi. Through his appointments of precinct officials, his failure to deploy sufficient security, and now his refusal to investigate the election, Gillem "had done his best," as historian Brooks Simpson observed, "to help Mississippi conservatives to beat back the proposed constitution."[21]

As a result, a small group of convention delegates petitioned the Congressional Committee on Reconstruction to conduct an independent investigation. In the meantime, the local Republican organization commenced its own inquiry. Later that fall, the group declared the returns from seven counties were void because of fraud and intimidation, which would have allowed the constitution to pass by 3,380 votes. The Republican State Convention, following rallies of Republican activists around the state, met on November 25, adopted the report, and urged Congress again to investigate and unilaterally declare the constitution legal and adopted in the state. A committee was sent to Washington to personally deliver the report.[22]

For officials in Washington, however, the Mississippi election took a back seat to the national election.[23] The outcome of that election would determine Mississippi's future.

THE 1868 PRESIDENTIAL CAMPAIGN AND THE FIFTEENTH AMENDMENT

The 1868 presidential campaign began in the fall of 1867, when Ohio held its state elections. On the ballot was an amendment to the state constitution guaranteeing Blacks the right to vote. As one historian pointed out, "It became standard political fare for each party to pander to a particular phobia—Republicans to the distrust of the South and the danger of reaction, and Democrats to the hatred of the Black race and the danger of radicalism. For every wave of the 'bloody shirt of rebellion' by Republicans, Democrats answered with a shriek of 'white man's country.'" On election day, Republicans lost the amendment, lost both houses of the Legislature, and barely held onto the Governor's Mansion. Political commentators from both parties blamed the losses on the opposition of white voters to Black suffrage.[24]

Consequently, the presidential election of 1868 represented the great hope of deliverance from Reconstruction for Mississippi Democrats. By November of 1868, virtually all of the former Confederate states had been readmitted, with only Mississippi, Virginia, and Texas not participating in the presidential election.

Whites in Mississippi hoped Democrats would regain the White House, loosen the Radical hold on Congress, and bring Reconstruction and the military occupation to an end. After President Johnson survived impeachment and after several Northern and Midwestern states followed Ohio's lead and failed to approve referenda on Black voting, the "Radical Republicans" were beginning to lose their influence and hold on power in Congress and within the party. Consequently, they would not have one of their own as the presidential nominee. That title went to Ulysses S. Grant, who had "emerged from the [War] as the preeminent Union military hero" and one of the most popular men in the North. While the party maintained a platform that endorsed the Reconstruction policies in the South, it did not push for universal Black suffrage. While Grant's Democratic opponent was former New York governor Horatio Seymour, it was Seymour's running mate, Frank Blair, who provided much of the fireworks for the Democratic ticket, most of which significantly weakened their chances of victory on election day. Blair campaigned against Reconstruction, urged the restoration of "white people" to power in the South, and criticized Republicans for placing the South under the rule of "a semi-barbarous race of blacks." Blair even urged a vote for Seymour so the newly elected president could, on his own and without consent of Congress, "declare the Reconstruction Acts null and void . . . and allow the white people to reorganize their own governments." It was the last presidential campaign that featured white supremacy as a core value.[25]

Given all the country had been through since the end of the War, Grant's theme of "Let us have peace" resonated with enough voters to give him a strong Electoral College victory and returned majorities of Republicans to both houses of Congress. It also put to rest that Reconstruction would be upended in Mississippi, or as one legal scholar wrote, "Reconstruction had reached a point of no return. With the Republicans in firm command of the national institutions, the remaining states of the South had little choice but to ratify the Reconstruction amendments as the price for readmission to Congress."[26]

A political cartoon published during Ulysses S. Grant's 1868 presidential campaign. Library of Congress, Prints and Photographs Division, LC-DIG-ppmsca-65157.

Following Grant's victory, the *New York Times* headlined its main editorial with "Grant's Great Triumph": "Not during this generation, nor during the next, will the people of this country lose sight of the great war, or forget the part played in it by those who have been leaders, or who may aspire to be leaders. To have been false to the Republic in that tremendous crisis, or to have been lukewarm in its service, will be a brand of political ruin for many a year to come."[27] Nevertheless, the popular vote was much closer, with Grant polling 3,013,650 votes to 2,708,744 for Seymour. "Grant's substantial Electoral College majority," observed one historian, "was belied by his thin margin of 300,000 popular votes. Since more than half a million African Americans voted under the terms of the Reconstruction Acts, this meant that most whites voted for Democrats Horatio Seymour and Frank Blair."[28]

Startled by that outcome, and knowing the remaining three Confederate states would soon rejoin the Union and that formerly disqualified whites in the other states would soon regain the right to vote, Republicans in Congress became convinced that universal Black suffrage was the only way to avoid becoming a minority party. "Although egalitarians had begun the advocacy of Negro enfranchisement," wrote one scholar, "political strategists had made its achievement possible." That led to Congress approving the Fifteenth Amendment on February 26, 1869. And much like the Fourteenth, what went to the states ended up as a compromise between Radical and moderate congressional Republicans. While the amendment prohibited Congress or any state from denying the right to vote based on "race, color or previous condition of servitude," it did nothing to ensure Blacks could hold office, nor did it contain provisions to prevent states from using poll taxes or literacy tests or property qualifications to restrict suffrage. Republicans rejected a broader amendment that would have barred discrimination in voting and office holding based on "race, color, nativity, property, education, or religious beliefs" because it would have jeopardized the amendment's ratification in many Northern states. And the blanket ban on all suffrage restrictions was shelved because Northern states wanted to retain their own qualifications while in the West, for example, Chinese immigrants were not allowed to vote. Pennsylvania required the payment of all state taxes to vote, while Massachusetts and Connecticut had literacy tests. As historian Eric Foner once wrote, "Thus, it was not a limited commitment to blacks' rights, but the desire to retain other inequalities, affecting whites, that produced a Fifteenth Amendment that opened the door to poll taxes, literacy tests and property qualifications in the South." It took less than a year for the necessary twenty-eight states to ratify the amendment, starting with Nevada on March 1 and ending with Iowa on February 3, 1870.[29]

In one of his last acts as president, Andrew Johnson gave the South a Christmas gift when on December 25, 1868, he issued an unconditional pardon and amnesty "to all and to every person who directly or indirectly participated in the late insurrection or rebellion . . . with restoration of rights, privileges, and immunities under the Constitution."[30]

THE 1869 RATIFICATION ELECTION

With Grant scheduled to take the oath of office as the country's eighteenth president in March, and with Congress in a lame-duck session, the Congressional Committee on Reconstruction held hearings in December and January on the 1868 Mississippi election. General Gillem testified, as did a host of others, both Republican and Democrat. Without providing any justification or explanation for the low Black turnout, the consensus among the white Democratic witnesses was that the disqualifying clauses had been the

Ulysses S. Grant, circa 1870–1880. Photo No. 87, Bultema-Williams Photograph and Print Collection, Ulysses S. Grant Presidential Library, Mississippi State University Libraries.

reason for the defeat: whites had turned out in massive numbers to offset the Republican vote. Congress, on the other hand, divided about how to proceed, opted to postpone any decision until after Grant's inauguration and the convening of a new Congress.[31]

The day after he was sworn in, Grant issued orders removing Gillem and replaced him with Adelbert Ames, making Ames not only the state's provisional governor but also the military commander. Ames took charge on March 17 and promptly moved the military headquarters to Jackson to link his gubernatorial office to his new military responsibilities. "In the two capacities of the civil governor and military commander," observed a historian, "there were few limitations upon his power. . . . His power as military governor gave him supremacy in Mississippi, and he allowed no law to stand in his way."[32]

A native of Maine, West Point graduate, and Union soldier, Ames would figure prominently in the remainder of Mississippi's Reconstruction story. He was all of thirty-four when he received Grant's appointment.[33]

Back in Washington, a stalemate soon developed in Congress between the "Radical" Republican members, who wanted to acknowledge election irregularities among Mississippi Democrats and unilaterally enact the full 1868 Constitution, and moderates, who favored either a call for a new convention or separate referenda on the provisions that would disqualify white voters. Notwithstanding his decision to remove Gillen, Grant ended up siding with the moderates. He became convinced that supporting the "Radical" members of his party posed too great a political risk and that the nation needed to move beyond Reconstruction and concentrate on economic issues. Moreover, Grant believed, removing the disqualifying provisions from the constitution might facilitate the development of a broader-based Republican Party. For all those reasons, he wrote to Congress on April 7 and urged a compromise: "The authority of the United States, which has been vindicated, but whenever the people of a rebellious State are ready to enter in good faith upon the accomplishment of this object, it is certainly desirable that all causes of irritation should be removed as promptly as possible, that a more perfect union may be established and the country be restored to peace and prosperity."[34]

Eager to move beyond Reconstruction, Congress sent Grant legislation that not only resolved the Mississippi stalemate, but authorized new elections in Texas and Virginia as well. On the floor of the Senate, an amendment was adopted requiring the Legislatures of the three states to approve the Fifteenth Amendment (at this point, the amendment was sixteen states shy of what was needed for ratification). After the amendment passed 30-20, the final bill was approved 49-9, the House concurred with the Senate amendments, and President Grant made it official with his signature. The legislation—endorsed by the *New York Herald* as the work of "a practical statesman, who seeks to temper justice with kindness and conciliation"—allowed Grant to choose which provisions would be subject to a special vote, when to set the election, and whether to allow a vote on all statewide and legislative officials authorized by the new constitution.[35]

On July 13, President Grant set the special Mississippi election for November 30, 1869, calling for a vote on the constitution except for those provisions that sought to disqualify the former Confederates. Those would be subject to separate votes along with the statewide and legislative offices created by the new constitution. Grant had been under some pressure to hold the election in the summer, but ultimately took the advice of Republicans in the state to push it back to the end of the year, once the crops had been harvested, so that Black voters under contract with planters would be less vulnerable to threats.[36]

For the remainder of 1869, politics in the state could be described as a big letdown, from the "high" white Democrats experienced in the summer of 1868. Notwithstanding Grant's willingness to compromise, Democrats in the state realized there would be no wholesale repeal of Reconstruction, no chance the 1868 Constitution would fail to take effect, and no possibility Blacks would lose the right to vote. The time had come to pull back, wait, and regroup.[37]

With Grant in the White House, Republicans in control of Congress, and Ames exercising the full powers of both his offices in Mississippi, many white Democrats in the state opted to join forces with some moderate Republicans and create a one-time party coalition, called the National Union Republican Party, to support a slate of candidates for the statewide and legislative offices that would also be on the November ballot. The party hosted its first convention on June 23, endorsed the new constitution, opposed the separate disqualifying provisions, and nominated Republicans for most of the major state offices, including Louis Dent for governor (a Coahoma County farmer and President Grant's brother-in-law) and Thomas Sinclair for secretary of state (a Black man from Copiah County). It was a recognition that the 1869 campaign would be less about ratifying the new constitution and more about who would fill the statewide and legislative positions created by the constitution, as well as the seats available to Mississippi in the US House of Representatives.[38]

White and Black Republicans met the following month and this time did a better job choosing candidates, nominating James Alcorn to head the ticket as their gubernatorial candidate; Ridgley Powers, a Northern white planter from Noxubee County, for lieutenant governor; and a Black minister and organizer, James Lynch, as their candidate for secretary of state. Joining Grant in seeking to build a broader base of voters, the Republicans also urged NO votes on the separate disqualifying provisions of the constitution, explaining in its party platform that "in the same measure as the spirit of disloyalty may die out and as may be consistent with the safety of the loyal people, and we shall hail with unfeigned delight, the day with the spirit of toleration now dawning upon our state."[39]

With the power of both the provisional governor and military commander, Ames replaced local and state officials with "men who were in sympathy with the Congressional program," including naming Blacks to key official positions. For the Democrats, they more or less threw in the towel, and as historian Vernon Lane Wharton wrote, with Ames in charge, "No longer was military government preferable to Negro suffrage. The policy of the opposition now came to be that of accepting Reconstruction on the best terms that could be obtained, and of continuing the fight from a better position after the restoration of the state to the Union."[40]

Ames even appeared at the Republican convention in July and expressed his support for the platform and their campaign, after which he removed anyone from local office who had any connection with the rival National Union Republicans. Risking backlash from Washington, Ames explained his decision to get involved: the National Union Republicans were a "stalking horse" for the Democrats, "they are the tools by [which Democrats] propose to deceive the world. They are important only so far as they aid in that scheme. . . . They actually have no power in the state—it is with those who use them."[41]

Grant agreed and in choosing to endorse Alcorn, Grant wrote his brother-in-law with the bad news:

> I am so thoroughly satisfied in my own mind that the success of the so-called Conservative Republican party in Mississippi would result in the defeat of what I believe to be in the best interest of the State and the country, that I have determined to say so to you in writing. . . . I would regret to see you run for an office, and be defeated by my act, but as matters now look, I must throw the weight of my influence in favor of the party opposed to you. Personally, I wish you well, and would do all in power proper to be done to secure your success; but in public matters, personal feelings will not influence me.[42]

With the election day set for November 30, the fall campaign lacked the same level of energy and excitement of 1868. Ames, fully engaged and in full control of the election machinery, used his power to ensure a fair election by appointing neutral officials to handle the balloting, adopting strong measures to prevent intimidation of Black voters, and deploying more soldiers to key precincts to keep order.[43]

While the constitution was approved 113,735 to 955, the disqualifying provisions all were defeated. The more significant outcome involved the candidates for the seven statewide offices and five seats in Congress, all of which Republicans won, and the state Legislature, in which Republicans won a majority of both houses. In winning the campaign for secretary of state, James Lynch became known to history as the first Black person elected to a statewide post.

The turnout of Black and white Republicans hit a historic level when Alcorn received 76,143 votes to 38,133 for Dent. The previous high was in the 1867 convention election, which garnered 69,739 and was not far off the

REPUBLICAN TICKET.

Coahoma County.

FOR THE CONSTITUTION.

For Governor,
JAMES L. ALCORN.

For Lieutenant-Governor,
RIDGLEY C. POWERS.

For Secretary of State,
JAMES LYNCH.

For Auditor of Public Accounts,
HENRY MUSGROVE.

For State Treasurer,
WILLIAM H. VASSER.

For Attorney-General,
JOSHUA S. MORRIS.

For Superintendent of Public Education,
HENRY R. PEASE.

FOR CONGRESS—1st District,
GEORGE E. HARRIS.

For Senator—23d District.
ANDREW S. DOWD.

For Representative,
BART HARRINGTON.

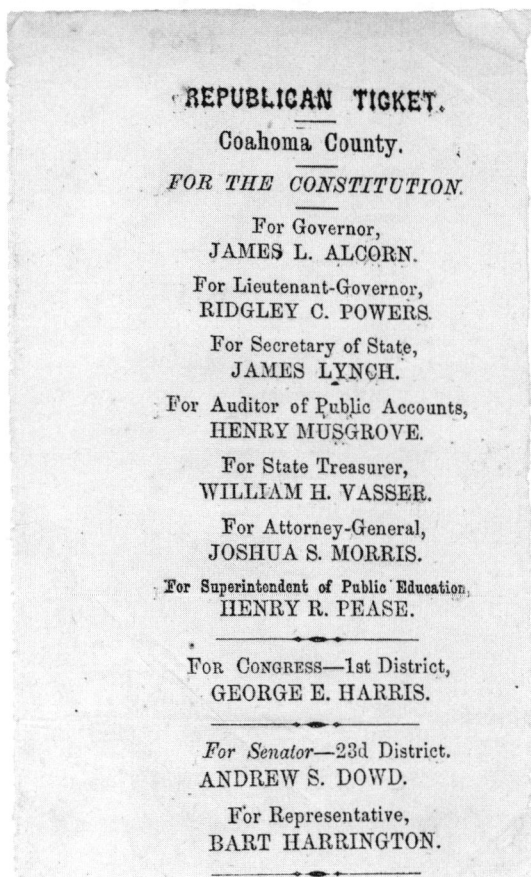

A Mississippi Republican Party Ballot, November 1869.
Courtesy of the Archives and Records Services Division,
Mississippi Department of Archives and History.

record 82,406 votes Grant would receive in Mississippi in his 1872 reelection bid for the presidency. Alcorn carried all but two of the majority-Black counties and all but nineteen of the state's sixty-one counties.[44]

In the meantime, the Grant and Alcorn strategy of appealing to moderates would depend almost entirely on the willingness of Southern whites to cooperate. Moderate white Republicans and some Democrats had promised the development of a strong Grant party among whites if the new administration abandoned the proscription of former Confederates. Grant and his party in Washington had taken that step. Would the whites respond positively? The challenge for the newly elected Republicans would be to grow and strengthen their coalition, avoid internal disputes, and wait for an answer from the Democrats.[45]

Hints of the answer came in December from editors of the Forest newspaper—"We must look to the interests of our own race. The issues will henceforth be mainly based upon color."—and the Meridian paper: "Henceforth, the lines will be drawn sharply between the races in this State. The white men are not likely again to fraternize with the negro but accept sternly the issue of the irrepressible conflict of [the] races."[46]

With 1869 drawing to a close, Congress would soon end its oversight of the South. Mississippi would join Virginia and Texas in having their constitutions approved and delegations seated by Congress, all within the next three months. The Freedmen's Bureau had already shuttered its operation, while the Army would soon disband its command in Mississippi. Other national and international demands, especially those involving the economy, would begin to consume the federal government.[47]

Mississippi would be on its own, as would the new Black citizens and voters. That attitude was perfectly conveyed at the end of the year by Ohio Congressman James A. Garfield: "The Fifteenth Amendment confers upon the African race the care of its own destiny. It places their fortunes in their own hands." Or, more succinctly an Illinois newspaper editor wrote, "The negro is now a voter and a citizen. Let him hereafter take his chances in the battle of life."[48]

Were it that simple. For the Black men, women, and children who emerged from slavery with no land, housing, farm equipment, money, and little to no clothing or other personal belongings, they confronted a white society opposed to sharing economic assets or political power with them. By failing to support a constitution that would prevent a substantial number of former Confederates from participating in the political life of the state, Grant, Alcorn, and other moderate Republicans allowed white Democrats to regroup for another day. The 1868 election provided the means and the 1869 election set the stage for 1875.

FISK AUTOGRAPH BOOK

In his master's thesis on the 1868 Constitution, Walter Howell described how the official printer for the convention, James Dugan, spent the final hours before adjournment passing around an autograph book among the delegates for each of them to sign. That book is known as the Fisk Autograph Book, because Dugan gave it to A. C. Fisk, one of the delegates, as a memento. The book can now be found in the collections of the Mississippi Department of Archives and History. When white delegate N. B. Bridges of Choctaw County

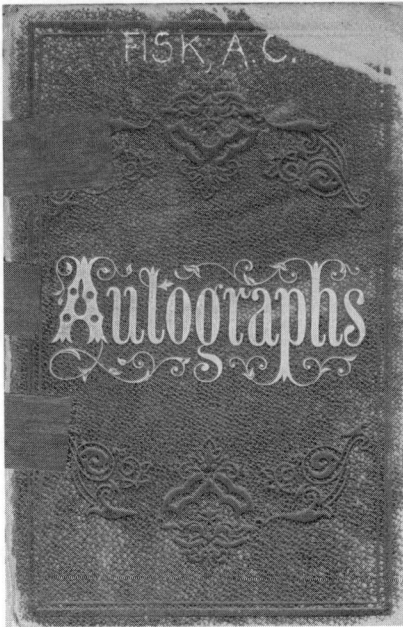

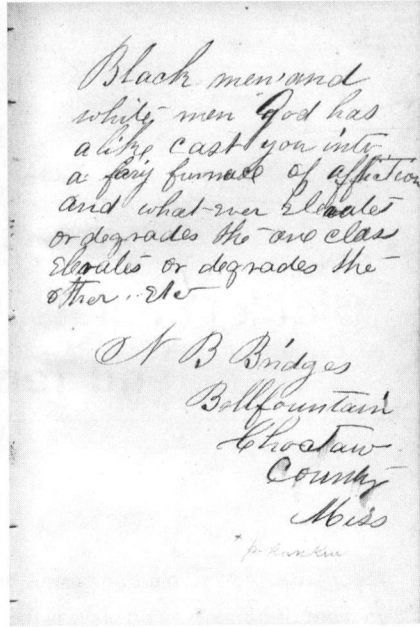

Cover of the Fisk autograph book, dated May 18, 1868. Courtesy of the Archives and Records Services Division, Mississippi Department of Archives and History.

signed his name in the book, he wrote, "Black men and white men God has alike cast you into a fiery furnace of affliction and whatever elevates or degrades the one class elevates or degrades the other."[49]

That observation was reduced to writing 137 years before I found myself reading an oral history Gil Carmichael had recorded at Mississippi State University. Carmichael had been a leader in the Mississippi Republican Party for three decades, starting in the mid-1960s. He told the interviewer that in thinking about the years since the Civil War in Mississippi, he had never forgotten what a young Black girl had once said to him: "If you keep your foot on my neck and keep me in the ditch, you ain't going anywhere either."

CHAPTER 8

1870–1872
Black Officials, Public Schools, and Terrorism

Anyone devoted to his books was on the road to freedom, and anyone ignorant of books was on his way back to slavery.
—JOHN EATON[1]

Public education for all at public expense, was, in the South, a Negro idea.
—W. E. B. DuBois[2]

The military occupation of Mississippi ended on February 26, 1870, three days after President Grant signed the congressionally approved bill entitled "An Act to Admit the State of Mississippi to Representation in the Congress of the United States."[3]

For nine years, Mississippi had been without representation in Congress. The popular phrases used to describe that gap include "separation from the Union" or "secession from the Union" or "what is needed to rejoin the Union." They all imply that Mississippi, the state, was for that period no longer a constituent member state of the United States of America.

This is certainly what Governor John Pettus, Congressman L. Q. C. Lamar, and all the other white men who attended and supported the 1861 secession convention believed at the time. They argued Mississippi had a fundamental right to withdraw from the United States of America and either go it alone or join with other states to form a new country. The language of the secession ordinance that Lamar wrote and that the delegates approved on January 7 of that year was as clear and definitive as they could make it: "That all the laws and ordinances by which the said State of Mississippi became a member of the

Federal Union of the United States of America be, and the same are repealed . . . and [Mississippi] shall henceforth be a free, sovereign, and independent state."[4]

On April 12, 1869, the United States Supreme Court disagreed. In a case involving a dispute over bonds issued by Texas after it had seceded, the court declared all of the secession ordinances unconstitutional, or to quote Chief Justice Salmon Chase, who wrote the majority opinion: "The union between Texas and the other States was as complete, as perpetual, and as indissoluble as the union between the original States. There was no place for reconsideration, or revocation, except through revolution or consent of the States."[5]

Consequently, Mississippi never left the Union. It was the state's congressional delegation who left. Mississippi's troubles began in January 1861 when its two senators (including Jefferson Davis) and five representatives (including L. Q. C. Lamar) resigned from Congress in the wake of secession. Since Congress has near unilateral authority under the Constitution to determine the eligibility of its members, it withheld the privilege of representation from Mississippi until the state (and all other Southern states) had vested with Black men the right to vote, adopted a new constitution that prohibited slavery, and ratified the Fourteenth and Fifteenth Amendments to the Constitution. By January 1870, all of those requirements for Mississippi had been met except for the ratification votes.[6] It was for that purpose that the new Legislature convened in Jackson on January 11, 1870. The meeting was extraordinary for two reasons.

First, it was the only time in the history of the state, before or after, that the Legislature's call to meet was authorized and sanctioned by orders of a military commander. The opening page of the Senate legislative journal for Tuesday, January 11, begins with *General Orders No. 60*, issued on December 20, 1869, by General Ames, in response to the relevant congressional and presidential proclamations, authorizing the Legislature to convene. Addressing the Senate, Lieutenant Governor Ridgley Powers recognized that fact: "We are here, gentlemen of the Senate, by order of the Commander of the 4th Military District, and in accordance with the Reconstruction Acts of Congress of the United States to perform the remaining conditions whereby the state of Mississippi is to be restored to her place in the Federal Union."[7]

Second, for the first time in the history of the state, Black Mississippians had participated in the election of the members and had elected some of their own color and race to serve in the Legislature. Of the 107 representatives, 32 were Black, and of the 33 senators, 5 were Black. More importantly, from the perspective of controlling the Legislature and passing bills, those 37 Blacks were part of the 110 Republicans who held membership in the 140-seat Legislature.[8]

Soon after assembling, the Legislature approved the Fourteenth Amendment that Saturday afternoon by a 24-2 margin in the Senate and 87-6 in the House. A few minutes later, the Fifteenth was ratified unanimously in the Senate and by 93-1 in the House.[9]

The business of the Legislature then turned to the election of United States senators. Until 1913, when the Seventeenth Amendment to the United States Constitution was ratified by the states to provide for the direct election of US senators, the selection of those senators was the responsibility of state Legislatures. As a result of the nine-year gap since secession, the 1870 Legislature had three Senate appointments to make.

The first was the unexpired term of Jefferson Davis, who, when he resigned his Senate seat, would have had five years remaining on his term, or ending on March 3, 1875.

The second was the unexpired term of Albert Gallatin Brown, who, when he resigned his Senate seat, would have had about a year left on his term, or ending on March 3, 1871.

And, finally, the third appointment would serve the full term of the Brown seat once the interim term expired. That term would begin on March 4, 1871, and end on March 3, 1877.

On Wednesday, January 19, the Senate and House members met in a joint session to finalize the choices. The two most prominent white Republicans would be rewarded with the two longest Senate terms: Alcorn received 120 votes for the full Brown term ending in 1877 while Ames, who no longer held any appointed state or federal office, was selected for the open Davis seat by a vote of 94 to 24.[10]

For the one-year Brown term, ending March 3, 1871, Black legislators insisted on one of their own receiving this appointment. After working their way through five separate ballots, with no one gaining a majority of the votes, Hiram Revels, a Black state senator from Adams County, emerged as a compromise candidate and was approved by a vote of 81 to 38.[11]

John Roy Lynch was a fellow legislator from Adams County, one of three representatives from that southwest Mississippi county. Unlike Revels, who was born free, Lynch was born into slavery in 1847 and was freed by Lincoln's 1863 Emancipation Proclamation. He had a talent for business, did well in Natchez as the War was winding down, and became involved with the Republican Party. In 1873 he would be chosen by his colleagues as the first Black Speaker of the House of Representatives and go on to wage a successful campaign to become the state's first Black congressman. But in 1869 he had persuaded Revels to run for the state senate and in 1870 worked to give him a promotion to the United States Senate. Lynch once wrote how Revels became the favored candidate: "Rev. Dr. Revels opened the Senate with prayer on the opening day. That prayer, one of the most impressive and eloquent prayers that had ever been delivered in the Senate chamber, made Revels a United States senator. He made a profound impression upon all who heard him."[12]

Born in 1827 in North Carolina, Revels enrolled in a Quaker seminary in Indiana and later was ordained a minister in the African Methodist Episcopal Church in Baltimore. In late 1864, he left a church in St. Louis and moved to Vicksburg to begin work with the Freedmen's Bureau, while serving as a minister at the local AME church. He then moved to Natchez when General Ames, in his capacity as the military governor, appointed him to the Board of Aldermen in that city. It was there he met John Roy Lynch.[13]

Revels would resign his state Senate seat and travel to Washington to soon take the oath of office in a historic occasion on the floor of the United States Senate. As for the Legislature, they recessed subject to the call of the chair, after Rev. Johnson offered a benediction, to await action by Congress.

CONGRESS WELCOMES MISSISSIPPI

A few days after the Legislature had adjourned and the official documents recording its actions had been delivered to Washington, Massachusetts Congressman Benjamin Butler introduced HR 1096, legislation to restore the state's representation in Congress. It was approved on February 3, 1870, by a vote of 134-56 in the House and 50-11 in the Senate on February 17. President Grant signed it into law on February 23, 1870.[14]

For all the other Confederate states that had been readmitted the next step was to have their delegation members take oaths of office and assume their seats in the House and Senate. For Mississippi, that step was anything but anticlimactic because Hiram Revels was waiting to be sworn in as the first Black man to ever serve in the United States Senate.

No sooner than Massachusetts Senator Henry Wilson had moved to seat Revels, Democratic senators objected and began a three-day campaign to undermine his qualifications for the position. They maintained Revels's election had not been properly certified, nor had he been a legal resident of the state. One senator used the infamous *Dred Scott* decision to argue Revels had not been a citizen for nine years, as required by the Constitution. Finally, on

Hiram Revels, 1870. Library of Congress, Prints and Photographs Division, LC-BH83- 1823.

the third day of debate, Senator Charles Sumner had had enough and rose to address each of the points against Revels:

> Mr. President, the time has passed for argument. Nothing more need be said. I doubt if anything more can be said in the way of argument. . . . All must be equal before the law, without any distinction of color. . . . It is use-less to interpose ancient pretensions. They are dead beyond resurrec-tion. It is useless to interpose the Dred Scott decision. Born of a putrid corpse, this decision became at once a stench in the nostrils and a scan-dal to the court itself, which made haste to turn away from its offensive offspring. . . . The vote on this question will be a historic event, marking the triumph of a great cause. . . . All men are created equal says the great Declaration, and now a great act attests to this verity. Today we make the Declaration a reality. For a long time a word only, it now becomes a deed. . . . What we do today is not alone for ourselves, not alone for that African race now lifted up, it is for all everywhere who suffer from tyr-anny and wrong, for all who bend beneath the yoke. . . . It is for all mankind;

it is for God himself, whose sublime fatherhood we most truly confess when we recognize the Brotherhood of Man.

A few minutes later, the motion to seat Revels was approved 48-8. Schuyler Colfax, vice president and presiding officer of the Senate, announced that the "Senator-elect will present himself at the chair of the Vice President to take the oaths of office." As recorded in the dry transcript of the Senate proceedings, "Mr. Revels was escorted to the desk by Mr. Wilson, and the oaths prescribed by law having been administered to him, Mr. REVELS took his seat in the Senate."

The *New York Times* put some life into the occasion:

> In a dramatic moment before a packed and silent gallery, the first black to be selected to the US Senate was escorted down the aisle of the chamber to take his seat—the seat that some delighted in saying Jefferson Davis had vacated in 1861. Mr. Revels, the colored Senator from Mississippi, was sworn in and admitted to his seat this afternoon at 4:40 o'clock. There was not an inch of standing or sitting room in the galleries, so densely were they packed; and to say that the interest was intense gives but a faint idea of the feeling which prevailed throughout the entire proceeding. When the Vice-President uttered the words, "The Senator-elect will now advance and take the oath," a pin might have been heard drop. But, as Senator Wilson rose in his seat and stepped to the lounge immediately behind the desk, where Mr. Revels was sitting, to escort that gentleman to the Speaker's desk, the galleries rose to their feet, that they might miss no word or lose no glimpse of what was being enacted below."

A Black constituent of Sumner's wrote to him after the swearing-in, "The Great Battle is over—victory has been proclaimed. . . . See how the chains are broken."[15]

The five Republican members of the House were sworn in on the other side of the Capitol, while Adelbert Ames was the last to officially take his seat on April 1, 1870, after resolving disagreements about his residency.[16]

Mississippi was now official. The Legislature could reconvene and begin its work. Meanwhile, William Whitehurst received an irascible letter at his home in Washington, Mississippi, from an out-of-town friend who had been reading the coverage about Revels: "Well I see Mississippi has filled the Senatorial seat of President Davis with a distinguished 'man and brother' from Africa. I suppose he is preferable to a Yankee, and as you were compelled to have one or the other, you ought to rejoice at the success of the nigger."[17]

THE LEGISLATURE RETURNS

Lieutenant Governor Ridgley Powers greeted the members of the Senate on Tuesday, March 8, when the Legislature reassembled to conduct business and attend the inauguration of Mississippi's first Republican governor, James L. Alcorn. Powers shared some optimism with his colleagues: "Our political status, which has been so long a source of anxiety and doubt, is at last fixed, by the readmission of the State into the fold of the Union and the restoration of civil law. Although the last few years have wrought material alterations in the structure of society, the change has been in keeping with the spirit of freedom and progress that characterizes the age in which we live."[18]

For nearly a decade, Mississippi's state government had been largely nonfunctional. Given four years of civil war and five years of military occupation, the ability of state government to collect revenue, manage a judicial and criminal justice system, build roads, care for the State Capitol, the Governor's Mansion, and other state buildings, and support the needs of farmers had largely eroded. For the next five months, the Legislature began the painstaking task of writing laws, developing budgets, and approving programs to address each of those needs, including the elimination of any statutes that sanctioned discrimination and segregation.

As for the one new program the Legislature would enact, the newly adopted Constitution resolved whether or not Mississippi would have a statewide system of public education for all white and Black students. The question was what would it look like.

Even by today's standards, the task was daunting: create nearly from scratch a comprehensive and statewide system of public education. In the winter of 1870, though, the state was still recovering from the War's destruction. The few school buildings that survived were a far cry from what was needed to educate all of the eligible children. Teachers had to be recruited and trained. Grading, curriculum, salary schedules, and reporting systems had to be prescribed. A funding mechanism had to be developed and implemented. Land had to be obtained and buildings erected, and governance issues had to be resolved. In addition, the state government would be educating Black students, a first in the history of the state.

Ridgley Powers, circa 1871–1874. Courtesy of the Archives and Records Services Division, Mississippi Department of Archives and History.

The framework for the new system was developed by Henry R. Pease, the State Superintendent of Public Education. Originally from Connecticut, and as a former teacher and administrator, Pease had come to Mississippi to work in the Freedmen Schools. He submitted his report and recommendations on March 26, 1870, which were incorporated into legislation designated as House Bill 352 and referred to the Education Committee.

In his recommendations, Pease outlined a system that is fundamentally the same one Mississippi uses today: a state superintendent, based in Jackson, would coordinate the work at every local district; each county would form a district, though a municipality could establish a separate district; a local board would govern the county or municipal district, including the hiring of teachers, acquiring and furnishing the facilities, and setting the curricula and standards; each district would be headed by a superintendent; and county supervisors would be required to levy a local property tax to pay for the district's operations, with supplemental funding from the state. Pease proposed a State Board of Education, composed of the secretary of state, attorney general, and state superintendent, and that's the way the board was enacted in 1870 and remained until the voters changed it in 1982.

The legislation that was ultimately adopted in 1870 stipulated each county superintendent would be appointed by the state board, though the Legislature had the option to make the position elective. Each county district or municipal separate district would have a board of six school directors chosen by the board of supervisors or the city board of aldermen. County supervisors would levy a local property tax to fund the schools, at the request of the school board. The free public schools in each district had to serve students for a period of at least four months of the year.[19]

Of the hundreds of details that had to be worked out, ultimately two would consume the most debate: go fast or go slow and segregate or integrate.

In early May, Governor Alcorn weighed in on both issues, with a special message to the Legislature, making the case against implementing a comprehensive system all in the first year, while making the case for an explicit provision to require the separation of the races. A slaveholder and prosperous Coahoma County farmer before the War, Alcorn had believed preserving the Union was the safest way to protect his economic standing and those of his peers. Nevertheless, as a delegate to the secession convention he had voted to leave. He served in the Confederate Army but upon returning to Mississippi gradually began to align himself with the national Republican Party and through shrewd campaigning maneuvered himself to the top of the ticket in 1869 and won the campaign for governor.[20]

Alcorn knew ramping up a full-scale system of public schools would be expensive and he doubted it was something the state could afford, especially given the other demands on the treasury. As for his argument that Black children and white children should attend separate schools, he may have had an "R" after his name on the ballot, but he had lived and worked in Mississippi for nearly thirty-two years and had been involved in politics for half of those. He knew what the average white Mississippian would tolerate, and sending his or her children to an integrated classroom was not one of them. Consequently, he was unwilling to jeopardize the entire education program on that one point. A conservative at heart, his instincts were to go slow, taking changes to public policy one step at a time, though that was certainly not the prevailing spirit among Republicans at the Legislature.[21]

Alcorn's message represented the essence of conservatism:

Great systems should be set in operation by steps cautious and slow. I recommend, given this consideration, and in view, further, of the pressure of the common schools upon our available resources, that, for the present, we stop short in legislating on the question of education at the limit to which we are commanded absolutely to go by the letter of the Constitution. . . . Beyond that, it appears to me that, the whole work being thus set in motion on the smallest possible scale, we ought to await observation of its working before legislation shall attempt a further approach to the completeness.[22]

Nothing threatened the status of white Mississippians more than the education of Black Mississippians. Both white and Black knew education was essential in casting an informed vote, negotiating labor contracts, becoming landowners, accessing the legal system, and managing the everyday affairs of one's family. As one historian wrote, education "put black children in schoolhouses rather than cotton fields and inspired them to be more than a cotton picker for someone else's profit."

For white Democrats, resigned to the establishment of a statewide public school system, the key to creating a legal inequality between the races was to separate the races. That formed the heart of white supremacy in the years following the War, a way of life that became known as Jim Crow. The first, and easily the most important, battle in that long war in Mississippi was whether the new school legislation would allow Black and white children to attend the same classrooms.[23]

The struggle began on Tuesday, June 7, when HB 352 was approved by the Education Committee and set for special order of the day on the floor of the House of Representatives. By Friday afternoon, legislators had worked their way through forty-eight sections of the bill, only to come to Section 49, the one that prohibited segregated schools. A Democrat offered an amendment to require each school board to "lay down such rules and regulations for the distribution of scholars of the district as shall avoid any mixing of white and colored children." A Republican countered with a substitute that merely allowed the boards "of each district shall be authorized to establish schools to meet the wants or the different conditions of the children." After both amendments lost, the House adjourned for the weekend.[24]

When the House resumed business on Tuesday, June 14, Section 49 was still before the members. Another Democrat tried a different approach, letting each school board set its own policy. That amendment was defeated.[25] Finally, the Democrats convinced enough white Republicans to join them in approving an amendment to just delete the entire section. Hence, the legislation would be silent on the thorny subject. Worn out and on edge, the House approved the final bill by a vote of 48-22 and adjourned at 6:15 that evening.[26]

A week later, on Tuesday, June 21, the full Senate began consideration of the historic legislation. Seven days later, the senators remained at an impasse on the two issues Alcorn had raised several months earlier. And that's when Lieutenant Governor Ridgley Powers used his position as presiding officer of the Senate to address his colleagues. Unlike the governor, Powers, a native of Ohio, had arrived in Mississippi only after the War, in which he served in the Union Army. He acquired a plantation in east Mississippi and joined the Republican Party to campaign for the adoption of the new Constitution, which earned him a position on the 1869 Republican ticket as lieutenant governor. On both points, Powers offered a stark alternative to the Alcorn's viewpoint:

> I think a correct view of this subject is that property is held by the individual for the good of society. No man has more than a life lease upon anything in this world; he uses his means to best advantage who contributes most freely to the happiness and advancement of those about him. It is true, it will require a large amount of money to establish and maintain a system of public schools throughout the state, but it will cost more not to do so. Schoolhouses and colleges are not so expensive buildings as jails and prisons. But there is another obstacle that stands in the way of carrying the provisions of the bill before us into effect: The Social Question enters into this discussion, as it has into many others that have come before this legislature. I can see some reason for refusing to ride in the same steamboat, or for declining to sit in the same assembly with drunkards, gamblers, robbers, and murderers; but to refuse to come into such proximity with men because they happened to bear a different complexion from my own would be to acknowledge a mean prejudice, unworthy of an age of intelligence. The time has passed for estimating a man by the color of his skin rather than by the qualities of his heart, or the strength of his intellect.

After hearing the Powers speech, the Senate approved the legislation, implementing a statewide system of schools all in the first year. As for the troublesome Section 49, the senators found a way to make almost everyone happy. They opened the section with a ringing endorsement of a color-blind classroom: "All of the children of this State, between the ages of five and twenty-one years of age, shall have, in all respects, equal advantages in the Public Schools."

Then, later in the paragraph, they provided a way around the color-blind class-room by authorizing a local school board to establish a separate school in the district if the parents of at least twenty-five children of legal school age petition the board with that request. That state-of-the-art political compromise generated only five "no" votes on the final passage of the bill. The House quickly concurred with the Senate amendments and sent the bill to the governor.[27]

Whether by luck or simple coincidence or divine inspiration, Governor Alcorn signed the education legislation into law on July 4, 1870.

Alcorn himself engineered a higher education compromise when alumni, staff, and supporters of the University of Mississippi became alarmed, as a result of the debate on the public school legislation, that the university might be forced to admit Black students. The answer, of course, was to establish an entirely new postsecondary school for Black college students, or as historian William Harris wrote, "Alcorn University arose out of the need of white Republicans, principally Governor Alcorn and his moderate associates at the capital, to relieve black pressure for the racial integration of the University of Mississippi."

The Legislature created the all-Black Alcorn University—named after the architect of the compromise—in May of 1871 on the site of what had been Oakland College in Claiborne County. And for the college's first president, Alcorn chose Hiram Revels, whose term as a United States senator had expired the month before. In justifying the compromise, the editor of the Republican-leaning Jackson *Pilot* wrote approvingly, "We have to take mankind as we find it; and what we would like to have, and what we can obtain, maybe two [different] things, owing entirely to circumstances beyond our control."[28]

TERRORISM IN MISSISSIPPI[29]

For as long as Mississippi had been a state, white-on-Black violence was the norm, was culturally acceptable, and was even viewed as necessary. Using violence and threats of violence to control the actions of Black Mississippians was the norm because slavery was the norm. Violence was legally sanctioned to keep the enslaved Black men, women, and children "in their place." Generations of white Mississippians knew nothing else. Moreover, these white Mississippians lived in a society that devalued Black lives to the point that they were considered expendable as inferior human beings.

By the time a new Legislature convened at the State Capitol in early 1870, Black Mississippians, once deemed second-class citizens unworthy of citizenship in the United States and of the rights conferred on citizens by the Constitution, were now voting on new laws, enacting new taxes, and creating a new society where Blacks were the equal of whites.

While the rage by whites at this extraordinary turn of events had been kept largely in check by the Freedmen's Bureau and the soldiers of the military occupation for the previous five years, those federal officials were mostly all gone by the time Governor Alcorn delivered his inaugural address. The white and Black Republicans in Mississippi were on their own at the beginning of the new decade.

About the time the federal government was leaving Mississippi, the Ku Klux Klan was five years old; had seeded local organizations throughout the South, beyond its founding town of Pulaski, Tennessee; and had developed a widely recognized reputation for terror. For white men in Mississippi who needed a reason to join the Klan or to engage in local violent activity independent of the Klan, beyond simple disgust of the new role of Blacks, three events gave them that reason: the statewide effort to build a public school system, the 1871 elections for the Legislature and local offices, and the 1872 presidential election.

The goals were simple: disrupt Black education by threatening teachers and other school officials, win elections by intimidating and frightening Black voters, and restore white supremacy by driving Black men from their land and businesses and sexually molesting Black women.

The rewards for white men included the care and feeding of their resentment of "outsiders" and "Negroes who didn't know their place" and reaffirmation of their Southern identity. As one historian wrote, "The Klan emerged after the Civil War as a solution to the problem of Southern white defeat. We know now that white political, economic, and social dominance of black Southerners would long outlast slavery, but white Southerners, lacking the benefit of hindsight, were not at all certain. . . . White Southerners shared a widespread fear that their former slaves would rapidly overtake them. They worried that all of the remaining pillars of their power could be chipped away if freed people took full advantage of their new freedoms." A lawyer in Meridian, when asked to describe the KKK, had a simpler explanation: "They are Confederate soldiers killed in the war who cannot rest in their graves."[30]

Vigilante violence was the preferred method whites in Mississippi chose to try and curtail the newly won freedoms of Blacks. While schools were burned, and Black businesses and farms were destroyed, the harassment most feared and publicized were the raids by groups of local men, wearing hoods, robes, costumes, and other disguises, typically done at night, at homes, and focused

MISSISSIPPI KU-KLUX IN THE DISGUISES IN WHICH THEY WERE CAPTURED.
(FROM A PHOTOGRAPH.)

A drawing that depicted Klansmen in Mississippi, circa
1872. Library of Congress, Prints and Photographs Division,
LC-USZ62-49988.

mostly on Black leaders, farmers, store owners, or teachers in the community,
though some white Republicans, especially teachers in Black schools, were
also targeted. Whippings and beatings were more commonplace in these raids,
though murder, disfigurement, and lynching were certainly not exceptions.

White men from all walks of life joined the Klan or otherwise participated
in local acts of intimidation or violence, and they were allowed to engage in
these violent activities because other white men and women in the towns and
rural areas let them. There was rarely any pushback from white Democrats
who held elective office or ran local businesses or edited newspapers. An
investigator with the state once infiltrated the Klan organization in Lafayette
County and reported, "Almost every young man in the county is a member of
the organization or in sympathy with those who are in it."[31]

Newspapers known to support the Democratic Party either complained
about the coverage Republicans gave to the violence or tried to explain it
away, offer excuses, or even justify the behavior. The attitude was best captured by A. J. Brown when he chronicled the history of Newton County in
1894: "In the year 1870, there was a secret political organization in the State,
well known to most of the prominent citizens. This organization had for its

purpose nothing more than the good of the country and the advancement of the Democratic Party. There was nothing disloyal in it to the United States Government. . . . This secret society of Democrats were white men, had for one of its main features the ruling of the country by the Anglo-Saxon race."[32]

What happened to Cornelius McBride, a white teacher from Ohio leading a Black school in Chickasaw County, typified the Klan approach. McBride lived to tell about it:

Between 12 and 1 o'clock on Thursday night, in the last week of March, a body of men came to the house, burst in the doors and windows, and presented their rifles at me. I asked them, "What are you all coming here this time of night for?" The leader of the party said, "You God damned Yankee, come out here. . . ." They took me scarcely a quarter of a mile from the house, to a field near the road. Two of them held me down and one of them took a bundle of black-gum switches . . . a peculiar kind of stick, which stings and raises the flesh when it hits. One of them took the bundle of switches and commenced to hit me. One man gave me a hundred and then handed the bundle of switches to another, who gave me about seventy-five. I asked them while they were whipping me what I had done to merit that treatment. They said I wanted to make these niggers equal with the white men; that this was a white man's country. They said, "God damn you! Don't you know this is a white man's country!" When he told them he also taught Sunday school at a white church, they replied, "Yes, God damn you, that is the worst feature in it, having a nigger teacher to teach the white school on Sunday!"[33]

McBride was able to escape when neighbors heard the racket and came to his rescue. Jack Dupree, the Black president of the local Republican club in Monroe County, was not so lucky. His story of a Klan raid was disclosed by a witness to the execution:

Some sixty disguised men took him from his house, and from his wife, who had been confined not two weeks before with twins, and who had a child about a year old beside; they took him from his bed, took him out into the yard, stripped him of his shirt and drawers, all the clothing he had on, and beat him there in the yard. Then they took him some five miles . . . took him into the woods and beat him until he was nearly dead. . . . They then cut him open from the throat to the straddle, took out all his insides, and then threw his body into McKinley's Creek, that runs near Ross's mill.[34]

Forty years later, when E. F. Puckett, a teacher in Oxford sympathetic to white Democrats, wrote a history of Reconstruction in Monroe County for the Mississippi Historical Society, he didn't shy away from the role of the Klan. He described Dupree as "exerting some authority and influence over the colored brethren in a way not pleasing to the white Democrats." Puckett provided a dispassionate account of the murder that corroborated the account above, and then had this to say about the Klan in that county: "The purpose of the organization was primarily to quell the negroes and to keep them in their proper places. It served as a kind of police force which prevented the Radicals from having undisputed control over the negroes. . . . Every old citizen of the county I have consulted on the subject says that the Ku Klux organization was indispensable to the public welfare."[35]

In Yalobusha County, after Klansmen lynched three Black men accused of various crimes and murdered a white informer, a local law enforcement officer told the killers "that they had done right, but that . . . burning [the body] was wrong." In neighboring Grenada County, a Black man was assassinated for no reason other than he had campaigned for the Legislature. A local Carroll County historian wrote that bands of young white men were active all over the county "in regulating negroes." In Scott County, "a freedman named Berry Smith became a little too impudent, and several white men caught him at the depot in Forest and proceeded to give him a good thrashing behind closed doors." After a Black farmer from north Mississippi "fell out with a white neighbor over the division of the season's crop, masked men took away his two sons, shot them in the face, and dumped their bodies in the Tombigbee River."[36]

A farmer in Noxubee County reported that no Klan member in his county had been arrested or prosecuted for the fifteen to twenty murders he knew about, including a Black minister: "There was a Negro killed over on the far edge of the county. . . . He was a Negro preacher. They wanted to prevent him from preaching. They went to his house, took him out, and whipped him. He hallooed very loudly and alarmed the neighborhood; and they thought the better way would be to kill him, which they did." When asked why these murders were taking place, the farmer replied, "Merely as they called it there, to 'straighten' the neighborhood—to make the negroes subservient, and make them fear them."[37]

In her 1913 history of Lafayette County, a local teacher described Klan activities in the area in the early 1870s:

For a long time, it was dangerous to go fishing in Yockana [Lake], provided one had a horror of coming in contact with a human skeleton when alone;

for it was no uncommon thing to get a fishhook fastened on the bones of a dead negro. The body of a negro who lived on Mr. Ragland's place was once found in the river. One day, so they say, the cook went to the spring about dinner time for water and was never seen again. In this way, the Ku Klux Klan made way with a number of negroes. We are told that from seventeen to thirty negroes were drowned.[38]

A teacher in Holly Springs, Elise Timberlake, writing an article for the Mississippi Historical Society in 1912, unwittingly revealed the motives behind some of the violence:

Why were the schoolhouses burned in some localities and the teachers of negro schools whipped or driven away? This state of affairs seems to have risen not from opposition to the negro schools but to the demoralizing effect on labor. In many counties, old, gray-headed negro men and women, fired with a zeal for learning, refused to work in the field and, procuring blue-backed speller, insisted upon spending their time in school. The farmers, still dependent as they were upon negro labor, became desperate and resorted to the only means they knew to put the negroes back in the field.[39]

By the time the House of Representatives had approved the public education bill, violence around the state had become so publicized and widespread that Governor Alcorn urged the Legislature to take action. Legislators responded by approving a law making it illegal for any person to appear in public or travel in a mask or disguise, enter into any home in disguise, or assault a person in disguise. The bill allowed the governor to offer monetary awards for the apprehension of violators. A separate act gave the governor unprecedented power to investigate charges of violent behavior, arrest the suspects, and refer cases to the local prosecutors, along with a specific appropriation to fund that work. Alcorn was given enough money to hire a director and some half a dozen investigators. While the small staff was able to solve some cases, the violence ultimately became so pervasive that more resources were needed. And those came from the federal government.[40]

With violence continuing to escalate through the winter and spring of 1870, with Grant in the White House and a Congress controlled by Republicans, and with the national press giving full coverage of the terrorism throughout the South, Congress was moved to act. For twelve months, from May of 1870 to May of 1871, Congress enacted three major new laws, known as the Force

Acts, that authorized federal oversight of state and local elections; created a series of federal crimes to deter the use of obstruction, intimidation, or bribery in preventing Blacks from voting or registering to vote; allowed the president to appoint election supervisors; defined and described the intimidation tactics then employed by the KKK and similar groups; and gave new legal powers to federal prosecutors to investigate and indict people who engaged in those activities.

If states failed to act to protect the voting and civil rights of their new Black citizens, for the first time in the history of the country, the federal government could intervene. Just as important, on June 22, 1870, President Grant approved legislation establishing the United States Department of Justice. It authorized the attorney general to supervise federal prosecutors assigned to each of the states and to employ staff to prosecute the crimes enacted by the Force bills. The new law also created the position of solicitor general to represent the federal government before the Supreme Court. As one writer described the congressional action, "These are momentous changes. . . . They not only increase the power of the central government, but they arm it with jurisdiction over a class of cases of which it has never hitherto had." Democrats, on the other hand, denied the extent of the violent activities and complained bitterly that the legislation infringed on their sacred "state's rights" with one Democratic congressman from Illinois calling Grant, who lobbied hard for their passage, "a despot, a dictator" who would "override the liberties of this great people."[41]

But it was a slaughter in Meridian during the first week of March 1871 that provoked Congress to enact the Third Force Act, by far the most aggressive federal legislation approved by Congress to combat the Klan violence in the South. It came to be known as the Civil Rights Act of 1871 because of its powerful preamble: "An act to protect all persons in the United States in their civil rights, and to furnish the means of their vindication."[42]

The "Meridian Riot" occurred over the first days of March 1871. For several months into the new year, Black leaders had complained about rampant Klan activity, including the assassination of two Black county supervisors. When local white leaders refused to denounce the violence, a rally was scheduled for March 4 in downtown Meridian. In the wake of a fire at the site of the rally, marches by Blacks from throughout the community, and a deadly shooting at the courthouse two days later, a mob of more than 300 whites took matters into their own hands. By the time a small contingent of federal troops arrived to quell the violence, at least thirty Blacks had been killed. White gunmen found one of the Black leaders, who had escaped the melee in the courtroom, hiding in another room. According to one account, "They carried him upstairs and tossed him from the second-story balcony, then cut his throat when the drop failed to kill him."

By this time, Klan activity was getting enormous coverage in state and national newspapers. For her history of the Ku Klux Klan, historian Elaine Parsons examined four newspapers—one each in Chicago and Milwaukee and two in New City—and found that those four papers alone had published more than 3,000 articles mentioning the KKK before 1873. The murders in Meridian generated headlines all over the country, and as one observer wrote to Governor Alcorn, "The negroes have acted badly, [but] the whites have committed & applauded outrages committed which History must hand down as only equaled by the most uncivilized of the Human Race." Two weeks later, Grant sent a message to Congress asking for more executive authority to counter Southern violence.[43]

In Mississippi, enforcement of the Force Acts fell to the United States attorney in the state, Wiley Wells, who over the ensuing months secured almost 600 convictions, and his marshals, who were charged with investigating the crimes, making the arrests, and working with the witnesses. Wells and his staff were aided by Grant's attorney general, Amos T. Akerman, who had become convinced that eradication of the KKK required "extraordinary means."[44]

By the end of 1872, the passage of the federal Force Acts, the creation of a Department of Justice led by an aggressive attorney general, and the vigorous prosecution of violence in Mississippi had largely eroded the power and reach of the Klan. Historian Eric Foner concluded that "in terms of its larger purposes—restoring order, reinvigorating the morale of Southern Republicans, and enabling blacks to exercise their rights as citizens—the policy proved a success."[45]

While Foner recognized the short-term success of the program, he identified a longer-term vulnerability in the South for Republicans when he observed, "The Ku Klux Klan Act pushed Republicans to the outer limits of constitutional change. . . . The need for outside intervention was a confession of weakness for the Republican regimes" in the South. Albert Morgan, a Yazoo County Republican activist during Reconstruction, came to the same conclusion about the need for "outside intervention" when he wrote, "The Enforcement Act has a potency derived alone from its source; no such law could be enforced by state authority, the local power being too weak . . . [only] steady, unswerving power from without."[46]

Nevertheless, six months after Grant signed the law and hundreds of prosecutions were underway, Ames wrote to his wife: "Had it not been for the Ku Klux law . . . we would not have had any showing in the election. At one time, just previous to the passage of that law, the K. K. organizations were being perfected in every county in the state. As it is, the K.K.'s cowards as they are, have for a time suspended their operations in all but the eastern parts of the state."[47]

THE AFTERMATH

While the documented cases of harassment, intimidation, and violence against Black Mississippians in the years 1870–1872 were numerous, vicious, and heartbreaking, in the end, the campaign of terror waged by the Klan and their cousin organizations failed to undermine the education of Black children and failed to prevent Black men from exercising their newly established right to vote.

By the end of 1871, a year after the enactment of the public school legislation, Mississippi could boast of having 3,450 schools in 75 districts, employing close to 3,600 teachers, and enrolling 117,000 students in all grades. Two years later, the number of children attending schools in just grades 1–3 had alone grown to 80,000. The State Superintendent of Public Education declared in his 1874 Annual Report: "As the people become familiar with the workings and results of our system of schools, they are convinced not only of its practical utility as a means of educating their children but that universal education, secured by a system of public instruction, is necessary to the very existence of a government like ours."[48]

For the 1871 elections, in which members of the Legislature and hundreds of local offices were on the ballot, a record number of votes (83,588) were cast for Republican legislators. Turnout was up 10 percent over the number of Republicans who went to the polls in 1869 to support Alcorn for governor, and the number of Black representatives in the House increased from thirty-two to thirty-eight.[49]

During the presidential campaign the following year, when Grant was up for reelection, the Republican incumbent received 82,406 votes compared to 47,287 for his opponent in Mississippi. It would be the only time in the state's record of participating in federal elections, from its founding in 1817 until the Barry Goldwater campaign for president in 1964, that Mississippi's electoral votes would go to the Republican nominee for president.

In the face of unremitting violence, Black men and women were undaunted. Their children attended schools and they married whom they wanted to marry, opened their own businesses, attended the churches of their choice, and ran for office and voted. It would take more than raw violence for white Democrats to regain power.

JAMES LYNCH

One of the half dozen most consequential meetings during the Civil War that affected the future of Black Southerners occurred on January 12, 1865, in Savannah, Georgia, when General William Sherman and Secretary of War Edwin Stanton met with twenty Black ministers and missionaries, many of them formerly enslaved, "to learn their views as to what they desired should be done in their behalf by the government." James Lynch was there as one of the twenty.

Stanton later remarked that the extraordinary meeting was the "first time in the history of the nation" that the federal government had solicited the views of ex-slaves. When asked by Sherman to "state in what manner you think you can take care of yourselves" the spokesperson for the religious leaders responded by saying, "The way we can best take care of ourselves is to have land, and turn it and till it by our own labor."

Four days later, Sherman issued Special Field Orders No. 15, which reserved several hundred thousand acres of land comprising a strip of coastline stretching from Charleston to northern Florida for the "exclusive use of ex-slaves" and provided for the allotment of forty-acre "homesteads." By June, some 40,000 Black families had settled on 400,000 acres of "Sherman" land.[50]

James Lynch[51] was born in Baltimore in 1839 as a free man, was ordained as an African Methodist Episcopal minister at the age of twenty, and ended up following Sherman through Georgia as a pastor to the newly freed slaves. He joined with a friend and fellow minister Hiram Revels in 1867 and moved to Mississippi to organize Black churches. Lynch settled in Jackson, became active in local politics, engaged in a statewide speaking tour on behalf of the new constitution, and joined the local Republican party organization. His skills as a public speaker became so well known and admired that he was the only Black candidate given a slot on the 1869 Republican ticket for a statewide office. Years later, when William Harris Hardy, a notorious white Democrat, wrote his autobiography, he remarked that Lynch was "the greatest orator he had heard during his long public life." When Lynch was elected secretary of state in 1869, getting more votes than James Alcorn received in his winning campaign for governor, Lynch became Mississippi's first Black statewide officeholder. After campaigning for Republican candidates in Indiana in late

James Lynch Memorial in the Greenwood Cemetery, Jackson, Mississippi. Photo by
Linda Thompson Robertson for the Greenwood Cemetery Association, used with the
Association's permission.

1872, Lynch was unexpectedly struck by a debilitating kidney disease and died
several days later, on December 18, at the age of thirty-four.

As early as 1870, Lynch began to speak out against the sharecropping system and its reliance on credit from merchants and landowners. Ahead of his
time, he saw the future when he declared in one speech that sharecropping
"leaves the laborer at the mercy of the planter, the merchant. . . . The result is
that every year will find them in debt, and with no faith in the future."

Lynch was given a state funeral and buried in the city's predominantly
white Greenwood Cemetery, a few blocks from the State Capitol, the last resting place of many of the state's elite, and numerous Confederate soldiers. Two
years later, the Republican-controlled Legislature appropriated funds to erect
a monument at his gravesite, which displays his profile and the simple inscrip-
tion, "True to the Public Trust."[52]

All was well until 1900, when the Ladies Auxiliary Greenwood Cemetery
Association petitioned the state Legislature, now thoroughly controlled by

white Democrats, to appropriate $1,000 to have Lynch's remains relocated to the newly established Black cemetery in Jackson. While the original bill in the House would have authorized the expenditure of that money, the final bill that was signed into law authorized the association to "remove the monument and remains of the late Secretary of State Lynch from the white cemetery to the negro cemetery in the city of Jackson; provided, that it be done without expense to the state of Mississippi."[53] There is no evidence Lynch's remains were ever moved, and the monument and his gravesite are still there and are now a prominent feature of the self-guided walking tour of the cemetery.

THE END OF THE THREE-FIFTHS CLAUSE

After the Census of 1870 was completed and the population totals for each state were sent to Congress to determine the number of representatives that would be apportioned or allocated to each of the states, Mississippi gained a Member of Congress, going from five to six representatives. Along with all of the other Southern states, Mississippi's membership in Congress increased because, for the first time since the United States Constitution was ratified in 1789, a provision in Section 2 of Article I requiring an enslaved person to be counted as three-fifths of a free person was no longer applicable. The Fourteenth Amendment eliminated that stain from the Constitution and automatically increased the number of people in Mississippi who would be used to determine their representation in Congress.[54]

CHAPTER 9

1873
Cotton, Economics, and Politics

Neither cotton nor slavery will [emerge] from this war as they went into it.

—A COLUMBIA UNIVERSITY POLITICAL SCIENTIST WRITING AFTER FORT SUMTER[1]

Three years into the new decade, with the state governed by a coalition of white and Black Republicans, Black Mississippians had achieved full citizenship in the United States, modest political freedom, and some essential civil and social freedoms.

Economic freedom, though, was proving more elusive.

Once President Andrew Johnson shut off any opportunity, in September 1865, for Black men and women to claim ownership of property once held by Confederate soldiers, they had only their labor to use as a means to achieve economic prosperity. And in Mississippi that meant, for the most part, using one's labor to grow and harvest cotton. Consequently, the worth of that labor was tied directly to the price of a bale of cotton. The higher the price of cotton, the more valuable labor became; the higher the price of cotton, the more real the possibility of saving money to acquire a tract of land, or other assets, became. Just as important, the higher the price of cotton, the easier it would be for the nascent Republican Party to hold onto political power and finance the public school system and the rebuilding of state government.

For formerly enslaved Mississippians to achieve economic independence, they needed cotton grown in the state to draw a high price on the world market. Without the ability to successfully gain ownership of land in the early years of Reconstruction, they needed a high price of cotton to bargain effectively with their labor. They never got it.

The economy of the United States in the years following the Civil War undermined the Reconstruction experiment. The world price of cotton fell to levels that never gave Black farmers a chance to translate their labor into anything more than subsistence living. Moreover, in September of 1873, a bankruptcy in New York City triggered a national economic crisis that weakened the Grant Presidency, cost the Republicans control of the US House of Representatives in 1874, and contributed to the disillusionment on the part of Northern voters and politicians about the future of the Republican Party in the South, which ultimately gave Grant the excuse he needed for the federal government to stay out of Mississippi during the critical 1875 legislative elections.

BACK TO THE WAR

Ironically, it was a series of strategic blunders on the part of Jefferson Davis and other Confederate leaders in 1861 that helped to create the dynamic for a low price of cotton in the years following the War. In his sweeping history of the prominent role of cotton in the world's economy, Sven Beckert described why the mistakes would prove so costly: "By the time the shots were fired on Fort Sumter in April 1861, cotton was the core ingredient of the world's most important manufacturing industry. By multiple measures—the sheer numbers employed, the value of output, profitability—the cotton empire had no parallel. Whole regions of Europe and the United States had come to depend on a predictable supply of cheap cotton. On the eve of the Civil War, raw cotton constituted 61 percent of the value of all U.S. products shipped abroad."[2]

Not only did most of that cotton come from the American South, but Mississippi was its leading producer. For the 1860 crop year, the country harvested nearly 4.9 million bales of cotton, of which 1.2 million or 20 percent came from Mississippi. It was a record the state would not surpass for thirty years.[3]

At the time, upwards of a million people were employed in England in a textile manufacturing industry that relied on nearly 80 percent of its cotton coming from the American South. Cotton was the largest single sector of the global economy, and the textile industry dominated the British, and the larger European, economy. Confederate leaders had every reason to believe cotton would bring England and France into the Civil War on their side and give them the advantage in any conflict with the North. As one cotton planter remarked, "We hold a power over the North more powerful than [any] army in the field."[4]

The clearest expression of this Southern cockiness came from South Carolina Senator and plantation owner James Henry Hammond, in a speech on the floor of the United States Senate:

Without firing a gun, without drawing a sword, when they make war on us
we can bring the whole world to our feet. The South is perfectly competent to go on, one, two, or three years without planting a seed of cotton. . . . What would happen if no cotton was furnished for three years? I
will not stop to depict what everyone can imagine, but this is certain: old
England would topple headlong and carry the whole civilized world with
her. No sir, you dare not make war on cotton. No power on earth dares
to make war upon it. Cotton is king.[5]

At the outset of the War, Southerners came to believe that withholding cotton
would be the key—halt cotton shipments, impose economic pain on England
and France, and wait for them to capitulate in favor of the Confederacy. In
July 1861, Confederate States of America Vice President Alexander Stephens
confirmed this approach: "Our cotton is . . . the tremendous lever by which we
can work our destiny."

While the move was never officially adopted by the Confederate Congress,
farmers all across the South regarded the withholding of cotton that summer and fall from the export wholesalers as an act of Southern patriotism.
The unofficial stoppage resulted in cotton exports plummeting from 3.7 million bales in 1860 to 640,000 bales in 1862. Davis and other leaders tacitly
endorsed the ban.[6]

Southerners, however, miscalculated on three fronts.

First, in encouraging the ban on cotton sales, Confederate leaders failed
to realize that England boasted a surplus of cotton after the historic 1860
crop. As one historian remarked, not only did "many Englishmen resent
the Confederacy's attempt at economic blackmail, the South's embargo
turned out to be a blessing in disguise for textile manufacturers in 1861." The
Confederacy's cotton diplomacy was based on the miscalculation that a shortage of cotton would determine British and French diplomacy in the months
after secession, when, in fact, there was no shortage. Only in the summer of
1862 did the pain hit as the number of bales in Britain fell to one-sixth that of
1861. By then, though, the blockade was in place.[7]

Second, the Confederate leadership failed to anticipate a Northern blockade on shipments from Southern ports. Nevertheless, on April 19, six days
after Fort Sumter, President Lincoln issued just such a proclamation, ordering a blockade of the 3,600 miles of shoreline from South Carolina to Texas.
On April 27, the blockade was extended to Virginia and North Carolina. The
purpose: isolate the South from European trade to weaken the South's economy. And while there were close to 190 harbor and river openings along that

shoreline, there were only ten seaports that had rail or water connections to the Southern interior. These locations became the focus of the federal effort. Gradually, over the course of three years, the Union Navy sealed the ports, effectively denying the South the means to export its cotton and import the armaments, ammunition, and other supplies it so desperately required. The blockade reduced the South's seaborne trade by two-thirds. The 500,000 bales that slipped through the blockade during the last three years of the War paled in comparison to the ten million exported in the last three antebellum years. Once New Orleans fell to the North on May 1, 1862, Mississippi was largely without an outlet for any of its wartime cotton. The economic damage to the region was unprecedented. In 1860, the New Orleans port supported more than 3,500 steamboat arrivals, shipped out 2 million bales of cotton, 85 percent of which went to British manufacturers, and processed accounts exceeding $185 million. That economic engine collapsed on May 1.[8]

Surveying the damage done to the Natchez area, historian Aaron Anderson wrote that "the war and ensuing blockade quickly destroyed the supply chains and credit sources emanating from New Orleans and elsewhere. While a handful of local merchants eked out a living as smugglers or purveyors of scarce goods, the first two years of war largely destroyed the large local cotton commission houses and plantation supply firms."[9]

Third, and what turned out to be the South's greatest long-term threat to profitable cotton farming, England and France, in response to the self-imposed Southern embargo and the Northern-imposed blockade, developed other sources for their cotton manufacturers, including India, Egypt, Brazil, Argentina, and Turkey. As one magazine reported, "The American slaveholders have done more to promote the development of resources of India by British capital than British capitalists would ever have done without their interference." Without ever stopping to analyze the economic implications of secession, the South effectively ended its cotton trading monopoly with Europe.[10]

As Beckert observed, "The Civil War in the United States was an acid test for the entire industrial order: could it adapt to the even temporary loss of its providential partner—the expansive, slave-powered antebellum United States—before social chaos and economic collapse brought the empire to ruins?"[11] The answer, unfortunately for the South and for the newly freed Black workers looking to translate their labor into economic independence, was yes.

COTTON

In the years following the end of the War, Black and white Mississippians had little choice but to turn to the growing and harvesting of cotton as a way to overcome the devastation of the land and survive economically and financially. It was the only way of life the vast majority of them knew.

During the Reconstruction era, Mississippi had more of its population engaged in farming—81 percent—than any other state in the country. And no state had fewer workers engaged in either manufacturing or trade occupations. Consequently, only 8 percent of Mississippians lived in any of the state's towns or villages. The state had no urban center, unlike Louisiana with New Orleans or Tennessee with Memphis. Vicksburg was the largest city at 12,443 compared to the New Orleans population of 191,418. Only fifteen of the state's sixty-nine towns had more than 1,000 people living in them. Major cities we know today, like Biloxi, Tupelo, Starkville, and Brandon, all had fewer than 1,000 people in 1870. Others, such as Cleveland, Clarksdale, Indianola, Yazoo City, and Belzoni had yet to be settled. In fact, of the sixty-seven counties in Mississippi at the time of the 1870 Census, incorporated towns were absent in fourteen.[12]

Living and working on farms is what Mississippians did. In 1860, they set records for producing 1.2 million bales of cotton for export, 29.1 million bushels of corn, and 4.5 million bushels of sweet potatoes. The corn and potatoes were for domestic consumption, with much of the grain used to feed livestock, horses, and mules. Cotton was the money crop. Thanks to the soil, the climate, the cotton gin, and the enslaved laborers, white farmers and plantation owners had converted Mississippi into the country's leading producer of raw cotton. A decade later, cotton, corn, and potatoes were still the three main crops, and even though the yield amounts were cut in half, Mississippi remained the leading cotton producer. The problem, of course, was that cotton was the only money-maker for the state.[13]

For Mississippians, cotton was akin to currency. There was always a market for the staple crop. It could always translate into cash, even if the returns were small. Merchants and other sellers would honor it as collateral for loans or credit purchases. As economist Gavin Wright pointed out, "There were many pressures and incentives toward specialization in cotton, but behind them all lies the fact that cotton was far more valuable per acre than were alternative uses of land." Unlike corn, cotton could not be eaten for food by those raising the crop, and stealing a lot of it was difficult. Fundamentally, though, cotton was the crop Black and white farmers knew best, at a time when the state was in shambles.[14]

Cotton gin in Dahomey, Mississippi, circa 1890. Library of Congress, Prints and
Photographs Division, LC-USZ62-9366.

As fate would have it, for whites returning to their farms following the
Confederate surrender and for Blacks entering the labor force as free men
and women, the lure of cotton was the price. In 1865, the average price for
a bale of cotton on the worldwide market was $83. That was eight times the
price five years earlier. So long as growers could keep the worms, insects, and
rain at bay, they could make money at that price. Unfortunately, the price that
year was an anomaly. As Southern cotton returned to the worldwide market,
the price fell by half in 1866, and by half again two years later. By 1871, the
average price of a bale of cotton was down to $17. By the end of the decade, it
had dropped even further, to $12.[15]

To put that price in perspective, a bale of cotton before the outbreak of the
War averaged $10 to $11. Farmers and plantation owners could make money
at the price because of the free labor provided by Black men, women, and
children. Those days were, of course, history.

The price decline moved in lockstep with the Southern production of cotton. The last year of the War saw Europe import a little more than 3 million bales of cotton, all from markets outside the South. In 1866, the South

managed to export 1.5 million bales, which Europe purchased, but at half the 1865 price. By 1871, the South had increased its exports by a staggering 100 percent, but the price had dropped from its high at the end of the War by 80 percent. And that was the average price. Poorer quality cotton went for less. Even though there were always buyers for American cotton, it was now competing with cotton worldwide—half of Europe's cotton imports in 1871 came from outside the United States—which translated into much lower prices.[16]

While it may defy common sense, as prices continued to drop, farmers in the South continued to plant cotton, even at the expense of grain and other food crops. In Mississippi, the first full year after the War, farmers produced 300,000 bales of cotton. Ten years later, farmers produced twice that number, even though the price had dropped to $15 a bale. By the start of the new decade in 1880, Mississippi cotton growers were exporting close to one million bales, but at an average price of $11 a bale, down 86 percent from fifteen years earlier.[17]

Why farmers stuck with cotton—or as some would argue, why farmers couldn't get out of cotton—in the face of market gluts and falling prices, is something economists, historians, and agricultural experts have debated in books, research papers, and conferences ever since Reconstruction. The causes they have identified have been many, complex, and interconnected: financial and legal constraints, cycles of poverty and dependency, accumulation of debt, dearth of capital to invest in new equipment, an inadequate banking system, sharecropping arrangements, and lack of innovation in land use, conservation, and farming techniques.

Even though government agencies, private organizations, and university researchers during this time argued for a diversified approach to crop choices and more reliance on growing crops for food rather than export, that advice was generally ignored. Even with the introduction of fertilizers, farmers used the chemicals in a way to increase short-term crop gains rather than to improve the soil over the long term. As one author observed, "The spirit of improvement the agency hoped for had been overshadowed by the need to simply make a living." Or, as a pamphlet touting the benefits of moving to Mississippi, proclaimed: "Her cotton, the staple product of the State—the culture of which offers to the man of small means a sure and profitable return." In short, there is no consensus about why it happened, just that it happened.[18] Economist Harold D. Woodman captured the dilemma when he wrote that funds moving into the South to buy cotton or pay for the shipment of cotton to the North and Europe allowed merchants, storekeepers, and planters to begin the reconstruction of their economic lives. That being said, what came was just a fraction of what was needed."[19]

In fact, what came to Mississippi farmers when they sold a bale of cotton during the Reconstruction era, and in the decades that followed, was never enough of what was needed. The consequences were devasting for the white and Black Republicans trying to hold onto political power. Farmers simply had less money. Higher property taxes enacted to fund the public school system and the rebuilding of state and local governments competed with daily living expenses. Decisions about investing in new equipment or fertilizers were postponed, while small farmers incurred more debt, hoping against all hope the price for a bale of cotton would increase. It never did.

LABOR AND SHARECROPPERS[20]

Even today, some 150 years since the Reconstruction era, a few descriptive words and phrases from that time remain part of our popular culture, such as "forty acres and a mule" and "carpetbagger" and "sharecropper."[21] Ask a dozen random people what it meant to be a sharecropper, and you're likely to get a dozen different answers, though the term has come to embrace the entire economic experience for the small farmer in the decades following the end of the War. The reality, of course, was more complicated.

Between 1866 and 1869, sharecropping emerged as an arrangement for many of the newly freed slaves to provide white landowners with their labor to grow cotton. It developed as a compromise, though generally required of white landowners by Blacks who demanded a work environment that was fundamentally different from what they experienced in bondage.[22] The tragedy is that the scheme would have led to a chance at financial freedom but for the unrelenting low price of cotton and, later, the imposition of Jim Crow.

The focus of the Freedmen's Bureau in the early years after the War's end, as described in Chapter 4, was developing and enforcing contracts for the payment of wages by farmers. It was called a fixed-wage system but proved unacceptable to many of the Freedpersons. White landowners would cheat on the amounts or withhold payments as punishment for some petty or unrelated reason simply as a way to impose control over the lives of their former slaves, or, as one writer observed, "the wages became the whips."[23]

Freedpeople rebelled at anything that resembled slavery: close supervision, work gangs, the whip, and rigid control of their time. They sought their independence and the freedom to be on their own. If they wanted to take a break during the day to go hunting for their evening meal or to play with their children, they wanted to do that. Many of the men wanted their wives out of the fields and their children in schools. Since they were denied ownership of land, they at least wanted to plan their own labor on a plot of land they could call their own, even if it was rented. They used contract negotiations and share-cropper arrangements to bargain for their autonomy and that of their family, a privilege they were denied during slavery.

What gradually developed were variants of an arrangement that was popularly called sharecropping. The variations could take many forms, including arrangements where the worker (and his family) rented a portion of land (twenty to forty acres) in turn for a fixed dollar amount or a fixed amount of cotton (so many pounds or bales) or a fixed share amount in cotton (such as one-third of the crop). Other variations reversed the process, where the worker received a share of the crop as payment for his labor. The cash rent or share amount was paid when the crop was delivered at the end of the year. In some cases, workers provided their tools and work animals, but more often than not the landowner provided the equipment along with seed, supplies, and, of course, a cabin.

In reviewing labor contracts over a three year period, historian Ted Ownby showed how Freedpeople used the purchase of clothing to demonstrate their freedom. Rather than let landowners provide work clothes, which were almost always similar to what they were required to wear during slavery, Black men and women stipulated in the contracts that they would choose what to wear. "This change," Ownby determined, "became part liberating but also a very threatening part [to the landowners] of the meaning of freedom." A Freedwoman once recalled that her "greatest pleasure was independence—making my money, go and spend it as I see fit."[24]

All of these details and the worth of each as part of the rent or shares were subject to negotiation. For Black men and women, who had few assets to bring to the table, the arrangement gave them and their families their own plot of land to manage as they saw fit, along with autonomy for their family. And even though they didn't own the land, they had responsibility for the quality of the crop on their parcel: their labor was therefore related to the profit they may receive at the end of the year. By using rent or shares as the point of negotiation, and by farming their own plot of land, Freedpeople were claiming ownership of their time. As Richard Sutch and Roger Ransom put it, "Freedom allowed blacks to determine how they wished to spend their time. Not surprisingly, once free they elected to work less than they had as slaves. . . . They did not choose to double their material income; they chose to forego some of their potential income to 'purchase' the free time that had been denied them as slaves."[25]

It was the "free time" Black men and women sought that unnerved whites. They were so accustomed to exploiting slave labor that a free Black man, choosing to play with his children or tend to his garden rather than work in the fields, shocked whites to their core. This disbelief and disdain shows up time and time again in the letters, memoirs, and newspaper columns of the day and formed the myth of the "lazy Negro" that so permeated the writing of white Southern historians and politicians in the decades following Reconstruction.

The frequent letters Julia Dixon, wife of a Washington County planter, wrote to her son are preserved at the Mississippi Department of Archives and History and offer but one sample of the white reaction. A letter written on November 5, 1869, complained that "the negroes are so independent & behaving so badly." Another one sent a few months later was more contemptuous: "the negroes are becoming more worthless every year."[26]

While the 1870 Census revealed how quickly sharecropping was altering the organization of Mississippi's agricultural economy, the process was just beginning. Ten years earlier, at the height of slavery, there were only 3,079 farms in Mississippi under twenty acres. In 1870, that figure had exploded to almost 20,000, with the vast majority of them plots of land being rented to sharecroppers. At the other end of the spectrum, the number of farms with acreage over 500—farmed in the traditional way by wage earners—had fallen by 54 percent to less than 1,100. By the time the Census data was gathered in the summer of 1870, the number of small farms had increased by 58 percent from 1860 while the total acreage devoted to farming had declined by nearly 800,000 acres or more than 21 percent.[27]

That being said, the 1870 Census for Mississippi reported, in addition to 77,000 farmers, another 181,000 men and women were classified as agricultural laborers. These workers were almost all Black, all dependent on farmers needing seasonal employment during planting and harvesting times, and all hoping for a high price of cotton to provide them with high wages.[28]

Notwithstanding all the benefits that a sharecropping arrangement initially brought to the new Black farmers, potential problems soon developed. Since payment was made at the end of the year, after the delivery of the crop, the farmer, especially the ex-slave who was beginning a new life with no income and no assets, needed money to live on in the interim. They borrowed money for living expenses from either the landowner, who had his store, or from a merchant who owned a nearby store. Typically, the sharecropper was given credit at the store as he made purchases throughout the year.

So, at the end of the year, when the farmer had to use his crop to pay rent for the land, the equipment and supplies, and store purchases or advances for living expenses, if the price of cotton was not high enough to cover that total, or if worms or insects or rain had diminished the amount of cotton produced per acre, then the worker would be forced into owing money for the next year, on top of what he would have to borrow for the ensuing year. Since most share-croppers had no collateral, other than their labor, the landowner or merchant would use the future cotton crop as collateral. Thus began a never-ending cycle of debt because the price of cotton never recovered from its postwar highs.[29]

Sven Beckert summed up the dilemma that confronted Mississippi farm-ers: "High debts to merchants and landlords, in turn, forced sharecroppers to grow ever more cotton, the only crop that could always be turned into money, even though its proceeds per bale diminished. Operating in an environment of expensive credit, a marginal position in the nation's political economy, and falling prices, rural cultivators watched their incomes deteriorate."[30]

For the economy in Mississippi, the years of Reconstruction witnessed an unprecedented transformation from slave labor to free labor; the devel-opment of compensation arrangements between landowners, farmers, and workers that would persist well into the twentieth century; and the worldwide production of cotton from many competitive markets that drove the price per bale down to record lows.

While sharecroppers and wage earners were mostly Black, there were plenty of whites in both categories. And while landowners were predomi-nantly white, some Blacks were able to gain ownership of land. The for-mative years of Mississippi's postbellum economy took shape during the Reconstruction era, but its health was dependent on cotton. Even though global demand for cotton doubled from 1860 to 1890 and doubled again thirty years later, the average price never surpassed $12.00 a bale and more often, in the years between 1880 and 1920, hovered around $10.00 and dipped as low as $6.50. These were the years when Mississippi's per capita income sank to the bottom of the national ratings—and never recovered.

DAVIS BEND[31]

Before the spring of 1867, the Mississippi River took a long, circular path, or bend, west around a peninsula attached to Warren County, some eighteen miles south of Vicksburg. The 11,000-acre peninsula was known as Davis Bend, named after Joseph Davis, who began to acquire the land in 1818 from the federal government. Some years later, Joseph Davis convinced his younger brother Jefferson to join him there in growing cotton. While Davis sold sections of the peninsula to friends in the ensuing years, he retained about 5,000 acres for his own operation.

By 1827, when he moved his family to Davis Bend to build a cotton plantation, together with a group of enslaved men and women he had inherited from his father, Davis was a successful Natchez lawyer, founder of the Mississippi Bar Foundation, delegate to the 1817 Constitutional Convention, and former legislator. Nevertheless, at the age of forty-two, he decided he wanted to grow cotton.

Thirty years later, the Davis brothers, together with close to 460 enslaved Black men, women, and children, had created a hugely successful cotton growing operation. What was unusual about Davis Bend, however, was the approach Joseph Davis brought to the management of his enslaved population. Davis disagreed with the prevalent school of thought that the way to manage his enslaved workers was to keep them in "unconditional submission." Davis, instead, believed he would gain their cooperation, and thus increase their productivity, by allowing some to exercise limited self-government. Unlike virtually every other slaveholder in the state, for example, Davis established a private court to adjudicate infractions of slaves, heard by a jury of their peers, and presided over by a Black judge. Davis allowed slaves to run the plantation commissary store, and empowered a Black man, rather than a white man, to oversee the planting, cultivation, and harvesting in the fields. That man was Benjamin Montgomery.

Born into slavery in Virginia in 1819, Benjamin Montgomery was "sold" to a trader in 1836 who then took him to Natchez, a major slave trading area at the time. It was there that Joseph Davis "purchased" him, among many others, when he was building up his labor force on Davis Bend. Davis gave Montgomery access to his library and there he learned to read and write. As Montgomery displayed an interest and talent in business and mechanics, Davis gave him more and more responsibility, with Montgomery ultimately becoming his unofficial business manager, all the while remaining enslaved. Davis permitted Montgomery to open his own dry goods store on the plantation, buying from vendors, based on Davis's reputation and credit, up and down the river, from New Orleans to St. Louis. It was an extraordinary and unprecedented way to manage an antebellum plantation for the time, was hugely successful, and bestowed on Joseph and Jefferson Davis and their families wealth and prestige.

The War brought it all to a crashing end. Jefferson left first for Montgomery, Alabama, and then to Richmond, Virginia, in 1861 to assume the presidency of the Confederate States of America. After Union forces took New Orleans

Benjamin Montgomery, from a family album, date unknown. Courtesy of the Archives and Records Services Division, Mississippi Department of Archives and History.

and began raids upriver, Joseph, then seventy-eight, fled to Alabama for his safety. General Grant learned about Davis Bend during the Vicksburg campaign and, appreciating the irony of the situation, told John Eaton, his officer in charge of the refugee camps, to convert the land into a "Negro paradise," a haven for refugees who were escaping from the Confederacy championed by Jefferson Davis.

The Union Army appropriated the Davis plantations and by 1864 more than 1,000 formerly enslaved men, women, and children had made Davis Bend their home, while more than thirty teachers and other missionaries, representing fourteen different churches and other organizations, were on the peninsula teaching more than 250 children. By the end of the War, the population of Davis Bend had grown to more than 4,000. In a practice utterly unique for its day and time, Black families, headed by Benjamin Montgomery, were managing the farming operation. While under the supervision of the military, Montgomery and other Davis Bend residents were generally left to make their own decisions. A reporter for the *New York Times* wrote from Vicksburg in November 1864, "The nest in which the rebellion was hatched is to be the Mecca of The Freedmen. The home of Jeff. Davis, who represents the rebellion for slavery is consecrated . . . as the home of the emancipated."[32] For the 1865 season, the Davis Bend operation showed a net profit of about $200,000, with many of the families receiving payment for their work for the first time in their lives.

A federal official touring Davis Bend in the summer of 1866 reported, "Their crops are better than those generally surrounding them, their houses are more comfortable than the quarters occupied by Freedmen usually, and finally they appear contented and happy, industrious and energetic."[33] The official found that schools had been established throughout the peninsula, all self-supporting.

That fall, the "Mecca of the Freedmen" came to an end when President Johnson officially returned the land to Joseph Davis. But Benjamin Montgomery knew things few others did: Joseph Davis was past the age of eighty and in no shape to resume management of the business; notwithstanding the decision of Johnson, Davis was worried Radical Republicans in Congress might appropriate the land anyway, because of who he was and who his brother was, especially since Jefferson had been arrested and was facing prosecution and possible imprisonment; moreover, Davis needed money. So, in early November Davis sold his Davis Bend acreage to Benjamin Montgomery. A few days after the purchase agreement was signed, the following advertisement appeared in the Vicksburg newspaper:

ADVERTISEMENT
TO THE COLORED PEOPLE

The undersigned having secured for a term of years the [Davis Bend] plantations in Warren County, in this State, from Joseph E. Davis,

Esq., the proprietor thereof, proposed on the 1st day of January 1867, to organize a community composed exclusively of colored people, to occupy and cultivate said plantations and invites the cooperation of such as are recommended by honesty, industry, sobriety, and intelligence, in the enterprise. He hopes by the pursuit of agriculture, horticulture, and manufacturing and mechanical arts, as well as the raising of stock, to attain as much prosperity and happiness as are consistent with human nature . . . the government of the association will be confined to a council, selected by the community, whose duty it shall be to adopt such rules and regulations as experience shall show to be necessary for its welfare . . .

B. T. MONTGOMERY, COLORED, FORMERLY A SLAVE AND
ONE OF THE BUSINESS MANAGERS OF JOSEPH E. DAVIS, ESQ,
ON THE PART OF THE ASSOCIATION.[34]

The appeal by Montgomery heralded an extraordinary opportunity for Mississippi freedmen and freedwomen. Unfortunately, nature put the entire enterprise at risk. In the spring of 1867, just a few months after Montgomery had acquired the land, the seasonal flooding exceeded anything in recent times. The river not only broke through the levees but opted for a shorter route south by cutting the half-mile neck off the peninsula, converting Davis Bend from a peninsula to an island on the Louisiana side of the river. The problems for Montgomery were immediate and potentially disastrous. Not only did he have to repair levees and drain the land for planting, but the land for his crops were on the west side of the island and were no longer accessible to the river and the large vessels required to transport the heavy bales of cotton to New Orleans. Montgomery's docks were now on a shallow river, rendered worthless by the river's change of direction. There would be added cost of having to move his cotton over land and pay others on the island whose docks now fronted the river. It was a heartbreaking development.

Montgomery's first year as a landowner could not have been more challenging: levees needed repair, delayed planting, declining cotton prices, and livestock lost to flooding. Moreover, his new association members were unsettled. They saw the same devastation Montgomery saw. But in a demonstration of "astonishing management skills and unbridled optimism," Montgomery rallied his farmers and harvested close to 600 bales of cotton by the end of the year. While it was barely enough to satisfy the families who had stayed for the harvest and to pay Davis the annual interest charge on the loan, it was a heroic standoff with nature and the river. The year was also notable in

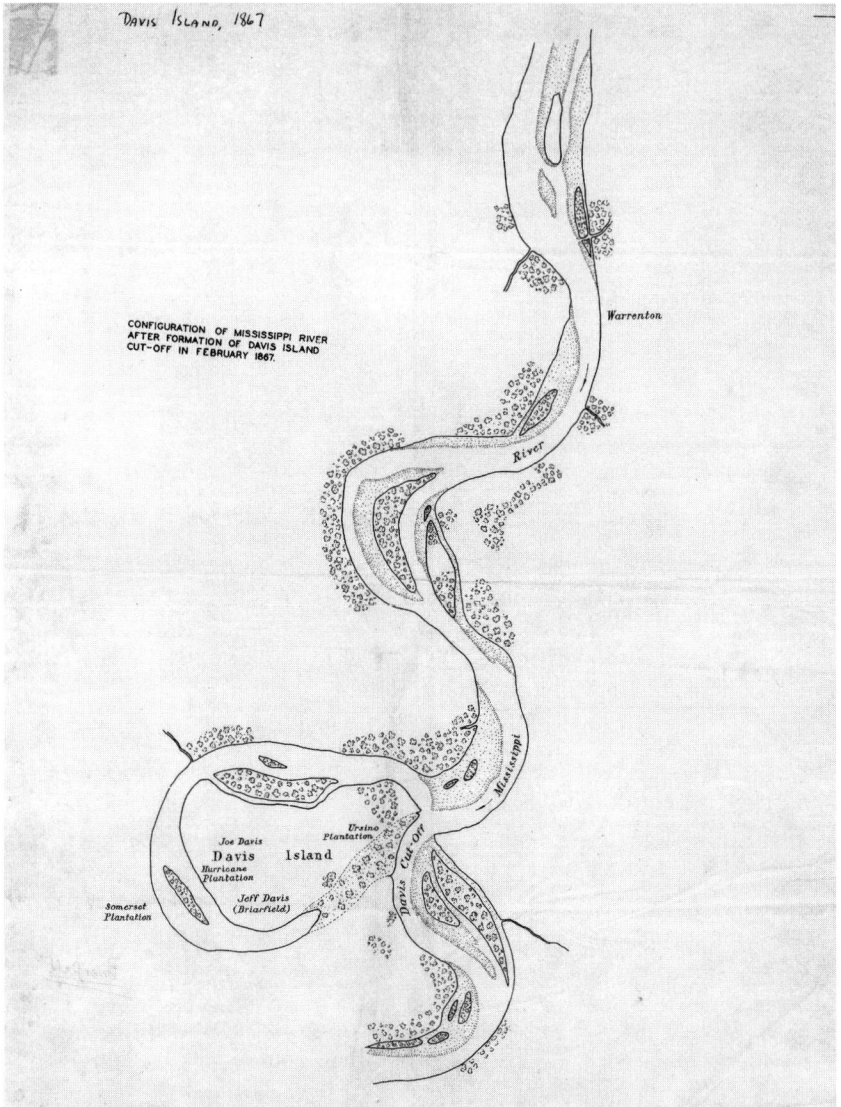

An engineer's drawing of the Mississippi River after it had altered course and turned the Davis Bend plantations into an island, circa 1867. Courtesy of the Archives and Records Services Division, Mississippi Department of Archives and History.

that Benjamin Montgomery was named by the military commander for the state as justice of the peace for Davis Bend, while one of Montgomery's sons, Thornton, was named constable. They became the first two Black men to ever hold public office in Mississippi.

The 1870 Census found 1,628 people on the Bend, of whom thirty were white. Later that year, on September 18, Joseph Davis died, at the age of eighty-five. He was buried on the site of his original plantation. During the early 1870s, the Montgomery Association was harvesting close to 2,500 bales of cotton, though the declining price of cotton never gave Montgomery the profit he needed to cover his expenses, pay the association members, and cover the interest and principal he owed to the heirs of Joseph Davis. Continued flooding and the relentless pressure of interest and principal payments took their toll on Benjamin Montgomery, who died on May 12, 1877. Leadership for the association fell to his son Isaiah Montgomery. The next year, the Mississippi Supreme Court, now in the hands of white Democrats, forced the Montgomery Association to return the old land Joseph Davis had given to his brother Jefferson. Davis promptly filed foreclosure on the grounds that the association had failed to honor the original purchase agreement because of delinquent interest and principal payments.

Isaiah and Thornton Montgomery lost the plantations in 1881 when they were auctioned to the Jefferson Davis family and the grandchildren of Joseph Davis. The challenges of trying to grow cotton on an island in the middle of the Mississippi River, together with the constant flooding, low worldwide price of cotton, and unrelenting loan payments were too much to overcome.

The Davis plantations are now deserted, with the entire island now functioning as a game preserve privately owned by Louisiana hunters and lawyers. Even though it remains part of Warren County, Mississippi, the land now resides on the Louisiana side of the river. As historian James Currie wrote, "Except for a few crumbling chimneys and the ill-kept Davis family cemetery, the lands which now form Davis Island look much as they did in 1818 when Joseph Davis first took possession."[35]

Not until 1947 was a book published that began to accurately record and portray the history of Black Mississippians in the Reconstruction era. It was called *The Negro in Mississippi: 1865–1890* and was written by Vernon Lane Wharton, a native Mississippian, based on his doctoral dissertation in history at the University of North Carolina. Wharton summed up his section on Montgomery and Davis Bend in the book in this way: "A wiser and more benevolent government might well have seen in Davis Bend the suggestion of a long-time program for making the Negro a self-reliant, prosperous, and

Isaiah Montgomery, from a family album, date unknown. Courtesy of the Archives and Records Services Division, Mississippi Department of Archives and History.

enterprising element of the population. It would have cost a great deal of money for the purchase of lands or would have involved an attack on the sacredness of property rights in their confiscation, but it would have certainly altered the future of the South, and it might have made of her a much happier and more prosperous section."[36]

In the intervening years, Isaiah Montgomery came to realize the one fundamental mistake his father had made in organizing the association: he ignored the overwhelming desire of Black families to own a plot of land, and, instead, required his association members to rent the land. In 1886, Isaiah learned of an offer that a new railroad—the Louisville, New Orleans, and Texas Railroad from Vicksburg to Memphis—was making for land it had acquired inside their right-of-way. To spur economic development along its railroad, the investors were selling the land at bargain prices. Isaiah made several trips through the area, and in 1887, he purchased an 840-acre site four miles west of the Sunflower River in the upper part of the Mississippi Delta. He called it Mound Bayou for the large Indian mound that dominated the property. In his advertisement to prospective settlers, he offered plots of forty acres for sale.

THE 1873 ELECTION[37]

When two politicians of the same party grow to loathe each other, the rational or policy reasons for the breakup come to have, over time, less consequence than the irrational: petty insults, family connections, one's perceived honor or public standing, or even where one was born. Writing this account a century and a half after the election of 1873, the full story of what led the two most important white leaders of the Mississippi Republican Party in the years following the Civil War to engage in a brutal campaign against each other will likely remain a mystery. The fallout was predictable, and permanent: a political party that sought to combine Black and white voters in the years following the Civil War into a governing majority lost its unity. Rifts developed that created opportunities for white Democrats to successfully exploit in 1875.

Given that Mississippi's new constitution prescribed a four-year term for governor and allowed an incumbent governor to succeed himself, the general election of 1873 would serve as the first election to fill statewide offices since Mississippi emerged from military occupation. The modern reader is familiar with political parties using primary elections to choose their nominees, but there were no primary elections in the state until 1903. Prior to that time, party nominees were chosen by delegates elected from the various counties to a state convention. The Republican and Democrat conventions were scheduled for August and September of 1873.

As for James Alcorn and Adelbert Ames, their personal backgrounds left them on opposite sides of the Republican Party in Mississippi. Alcorn owned a huge plantation operation in Coahoma County before the War, and while he supported the secession movement, he left the service of the Confederate Army midway through the War to return to his home and clandestinely farm cotton. Even though he joined the Republican Party after realizing white Democrats had learned nothing from the War, Alcorn came to believe the future of the state could only be guaranteed by a coalition of Freedpeople and moderate whites. Ames, on the other hand, grew up in Maine; graduated fifth in his class from West Point in 1861; saw action throughout the War;

was promoted to Major General in the Union Army at the age of twenty-nine; married Blanche Butler, the daughter of prominent Massachusetts Congressman and Radical Republican Benjamin Butler; and in 1868 was appointed military governor of Mississippi. He befriended Freedpeople and quickly developed a reputation for refusing to compromise away their rights. A Black sharecropper once spoke for many when he said, "Gov. Ames Dar Father of the State."[38]

While there were early—and petty—disagreements among the two, Lillian Pereyra, Alcorn's biographer, makes a compelling case that it was the Ku Klux Klan violence that ultimately tore them apart. The Klan violence reached its height in 1871 when Alcorn was governor and Ames was in the Senate. As the violence in the South, including Mississippi, reached a national audience, Alcorn the governor became defensive about the Mississippi crisis, tried to contain it using Mississippi resources, and took it personally when Northern newspapers and politicians complained about the inability of state government—and thus Alcorn—to curtail the KKK. Rather than seek federal help, Alcorn sought to minimize the violence and went so far as to publish statistics allegedly demonstrating that crimes were down. When a private letter Ames had sent to a friendly legislator was made public—claiming Alcorn was allowing Blacks to be murdered by the "tens and hundreds" to gain favor with the Democrats—Alcorn countered that Ames was inflaming the passions "of a poor people struggled up amongst us to the moral and intellectual level of free Government."

As Alcorn's biographer wrote: "In all his public utterances Alcorn denied the presence of organized Klan activity, in contradiction to his own Secret Service reports, and he insisted that the state government could handle the situation. No doubt he was anxious to forestall outside interference, not only from the Federal government but also from Adelbert Ames."[39]

The March 1871 Meridian Riot, the national outcry that followed, and Alcorn's tepid response gave Ames the opening he needed, especially after Alcorn wired the members of the congressional delegation on March 17: "A riot occurred recently in Meridian, but was promptly suppressed. . . . Some minor outrages have been committed on other points of the Alabama border in the night by parties in disguise. . . . Save in those cases, Mississippi presents unbroken evidence of civil obedience and order."

Ames took to the Senate Floor four days later: "We have upon us there the natural consequences of slavery and rebellion. Slavery denied the right of human liberty; rebellion had as its corner-stone, slavery; and now in their ruins are found hostility to the Government and a disregard and denial of all rights, even that of life itself. . . . Outrage upon outrage is being committed, and the Republican members of the Legislature have petitioned Congress for protection. . . . As a different opinion as to the condition of Mississippi has recently been expressed." After reading into the record Alcorn's message about Meridian, Ames quoted from a dramatically different telegram wired to him from Republican members of the Legislature, signed by H. W. Warren, president of the Republican caucus: "The caucus 'earnestly urges on Congress the necessity of prompt and thorough measures to suppress outrage and violence in all parts of the state.'"[40] Ames went on to explain how he had heard from desperate people all over the state, pleading for help from the federal government. Soon thereafter, Congress enacted a sweeping Civil Rights bill that empowered federal prosecutors to crack down on the KKK violence.

The rift continued to simmer until Alcorn, per the January 1870 legislative agreement, resigned his position as governor in December 1871 and assumed the Senate seat vacated by Hiram Revels. During congressional debate in the spring of 1872, over the extension of legislation designed to curtail KKK activities, the fracture between the two spilled over onto the floor of the Senate. In late May 1872, the entire country witnessed the two senators from Mississippi, the two most influential white Republican politicians in the state, attack each other, argue with each other, and berate each other, in person, all on the floor of the United States Senate. The episode took up seven full pages, over two days, in very small print, in the verbatim record of the proceedings on the Senate floor.

In response to an earlier speech by Alcorn, Ames declared Alcorn was a liar: "When my colleague was not pronouncing the personal pronoun 'I,' when he was not telling of his plantation in Coahoma County, when he was not misrepresenting the State of Mississippi—and I now declare that he has misrepresented it in nearly everything he has uttered here tonight."

And then Ames made it personal: "I imagine that my colleague's Ku Klux friends could prove almost anything they pleased in reference to this man; they usually do."

The next day, Alcorn could barely contain himself: "But [Ames] stands here, I regret to say, a representative of the class of men who occupy positions under the abnormal condition of things incident to revolution. No one present supposes that he could by any possibility become clothed with the honor of representing Mississippi in this Chamber in a period of repose and concord. . . . In the duty which demands these statements I regret to be constrained to say that the gentleman must be therefore open to some distrust. . . . My colleague is not connected with my State by any of the ties that make up the genuineness, the reality of the representation."[41]

Over the next twelve months, the two politicians continued to argue and embarrass each other. The fight was covered by newspapers and talked about among friends and party activists. Receiving approval from Black voters became one of many reasons Ames began to gravitate to the governor's election. As his daughter wrote in her memoir, her father's "desire was deepening for endorsement by the votes of the people to uphold the action taken by the Mississippi Legislature which had sent him to the Senate."[42]

In the midst of this titanic struggle, the incumbent governor and successor to Alcorn, Ridgely Powers, took a back seat. Even though he actively campaigned for reelection, Ames's stature among the Black convention delegates, who formed a majority, had become unassailable. At the August 27, 1873, Republican Convention, Ames was nominated by a vote of 187 to 40. As John Lynch observed in his memoir, Ames "proved to be too popular among the party faithful."[43]

Afterward, Ames wrote to his wife: "Alcorn intends to run against me. At least, that is what he says. I only wish he would. It would be the last of him."[44]

Alcorn obliged and "blind with rage," as one writer put it, announced on September 18 on an independent ticket. The white Democrats smartly decided, at their convention that month, to decline to officially nominate a candidate. Though many announced their support of Alcorn, the party leaders reasoned the timing was not ripe for a full-scale effort.

As the campaign developed over the fall, the more Ames consolidated his support among Black voters, the more Alcorn was left to make up the electoral ground by appealing to white Democrats. His lines of attack became predictable and counterproductive: Ames was an "irresponsible non-resident" who had accomplished nothing in the Senate and had none other than the Radical Republican and despised Benjamin F. Butler as a father-in-law. The more Alcorn tried to separate Ames from the state's traditional white voters, the more he solidified Ames's support among the newly enfranchised Black voters.

By this time, Alcorn's fight with Ames had become personal and he missed something about himself that was so poignantly captured by his biographer: "Having lived for years in the Delta where the Negro was accepted as necessary and often a welcome part of the economic scene, and, having achieved a secure position in the aristocratic planter class, Alcorn did not appreciate the antagonism of the lower class whites for whom slavery had offered the consoling reminder that they were not at the bottom of the social ladder."[45]

In the end, Ames was elected governor by a margin of 58 percent, or 69,870 votes to 50,490 for Alcorn. Of the state's seventy-two counties, Ames won all of the thirty-five majority-Black counties, except three. Alcorn, on the other hand, won all of the thirty-seven majority-white counties, except four. The overall outcome mirrored Mississippi's racial population as well as the 1871 and 1872 election returns. Alcorn could only muster 18 percent of the vote in his majority Black home county of Coahoma.[46]

The other six statewide offices were also won by Republicans, and, as for the Legislature, Black candidates made spectacular gains, increasing their number to record levels: 9 in the Senate and 55 in the House. Going into the 1874 Session, Republicans controlled 25 of the 37 Senate seats and 77 of the 115 House Seats.[47] The Senate would be led by a Black Republican lieutenant governor while the House would elect a Black Republican, I. D. Shadd, to serve as its Speaker. It was a stunning show of party strength, though it would last only two short years.[48]

In the broadest sense, setting aside the personal recriminations in which Alcorn and Ames engaged, Alcorn in his most lucid moments was making the case for a Republican Party that should be a home for Blacks and whites and that the party should work at expanding its tent. To do that meant compromising from time to time on policy and legislation. Ames, on the other hand, wanted none of those compromises and argued that Blacks were a majority in the state and an overwhelming majority of the Mississippi Republican Party. Consequently, it should stay pure, he argued. These kinds of strategic political considerations have confronted party leaders and activists since the dawn of time. Even today, the fundamental argument among party leaders is this: "Do you stick with the base or compromise on policies to grow the party beyond the base?"

We can only speculate what the right course should have been in the summer and fall of 1873. Given that the pool of available voters in Mississippi left little room for error—about 90,100 Black men age twenty-one years and over and 84,700 white men twenty-one and over—Alcorn's approach would have been the smart approach.[49] That being said, it is hard to make the case that in that particular time in our state's history, white voters in any significant number would have ever agreed to join with Black voters to form a working majority at the state Legislature. These were the same white voters who started a war to preserve slavery and the same white voters who would impose the harshest Jim Crow regime imaginable in the decades following Reconstruction.

Regardless, the Alcorn/Ames rupture within the Republican Party ended any possibility of that kind of strategic campaign planning. To succeed, Ames and his allies would need a healthy and growing economy and the continued protection of the federal government. The ever-declining price of cotton undermined the economy, and the Panic of 1873 not only created economic

turmoil in Mississippi, but its effect was so deep and widespread throughout the country that Grant and the Republicans lost control of the House
of Representatives in the 1874 congressional elections. Consequently, Ames
never got a robust economy and he would ultimately lose the federal intervention he would desperately require to prevail in the 1875 legislative elections.[50]

CHAPTER 10

1874
The Beginning of the End

It was the State and Congressional elections of 1874 that proved to be the death of the Republican party in the South.
—JOHN R. LYNCH[1]

For three election cycles in a row—1871, 1872, and 1873—neither the political dynamic in the country nor the state had fashioned issues and emotions that white Democrats in Mississippi could effectively use in their favor. Not since the 1868 election to ratify the constitution—which threatened to disqualify most white voters in the state—had white Democratic leaders been able to organize and motivate their base of voters. Their next opportunity was the 1875 general election, when members of the Legislature would be on the ballot. Winning a majority of those races would give the Democrats control of state government. Five states had already returned to the Democratic fold—Tennessee, Virginia, Georgia, North Carolina, and Texas—and two more—Alabama and Arkansas—would go in 1874.

Those states were relatively easy as white voters were in the majority. The challenge for white Democrats in Mississippi: Black voters outnumbered white voters 53 to 47 percent.[2] For 1875, Democratic leaders would need a campaign issue to rally their voters, and, even more importantly, they would need President Grant to remain neutral and refrain from sending federal soldiers to the state during the campaign. Soldiers at the precincts enforcing a fair election were to be avoided at all costs. The Panic of 1873 took care of both.

The turmoil began on September 18, 1873, when the investment firm Jay Cooke & Company collapsed after failing to sell bonds to cover its holdings in the Northern Pacific Railroad, the new transcontinental undertaking in which it had invested heavily. The economic crisis that followed—and which came to be known as "The Panic of 1873"—set off what would turn out to be the most extensive economic depression in the country until the Great Depression of 1929. By most accounts, the nation's economy would not fully recover until well into 1879. Wall Street panicked not only because the Cooke & Company default took it by surprise but also because traders began to question other speculative railroad investments. After a brutal run on the market, the exchange shut down for ten days, for the first time in its history. Even though President Grant took the unusual step of traveling to New York City to offer assurances to the country, it would take several months for the market to return to normal. Nevertheless, the damage would stretch beyond New York, and instigate a deep economic downturn.[3]

By the time the thirty-eight-year-old Adelbert Ames delivered his inauguration speech in Jackson on January 22, 1874, railroad operating companies across the country and throughout the South were threatening bankruptcy. More than half shut down by the end of 1876. Iron and steel industries that supplied the railroads, plus many other businesses that were caught in the economic trap, laid off thousands of workers, banks called in loans, wages tumbled, and business confidence collapsed.[4]

In Mississippi, the price of cotton had been on a downward trajectory for years, and the Panic only hastened its decline. Meanwhile, for those farmers needing access to bank credit, the crisis largely took away that option. As for state government, in his January 1, 1874, annual financial statement to the Legislature, the auditor of public accounts reported revenues were down substantially, partly due to the "severe monetary panic that recently swept the length and breadth of the land and sends distress to nearly every home."[5] The fallout from the crisis helped the Democrats consolidate and simplify their message: state government was spending too much money and taxes were too high. In the face of the depression, both needed to be cut.

This message had the added benefit of having real meaning for virtually all of the white men in Mississippi who would be voting in November of 1875. Land ownership had been in white hands, but by the end of 1874, state government and levee boards held title to at least 6,000,000 acres of land forfeited for nonpayment of taxes, or about one-fifth of the entire area of the state.[6] While these voters could do nothing about the price of cotton or the stock market in New York City or the big banks, they could do something about the high taxes they had been paying under "Radical Republican" rule.

In Mississippi during Reconstruction, cutting taxes meant cutting property taxes, as there were no sales or income taxes. Property taxes were levied by the Legislature to cover appropriations for the new public school system, as well

Adelbert Ames, circa 1900–1920. Courtesy of the Archives and Records Services Division, Mississippi Department of Archives and History.

as to pay for the operations of state government, the two universities, all of the local courts, the state prison, and the state hospital system. The state was not in the highway construction business; that responsibility fell to county governments, who levied their own set of property taxes to cover the rebuilding of local roads, school buildings, and local courthouse operations. There is no question that a landowner's property tax bill during this time, depending on the county, would have been much larger than anything else he had ever had to pay. Not only was it larger because of the increased millage levied to cover additional spending, but it was larger to cover the absence of a significant source of antebellum tax revenue, and that was the per capita tax on slaves. In the years leading up to the War, that tax accounted a third of total state tax revenues. Since that tax had been largely borne by wealthy slaveholders, the Reconstruction tax burden fell even harder on the average white landowner.[7]

In his annual report to the Legislature, issued on January 1, 1874, the auditor of public accounts recommended broad cuts in state government spending, tax relief, a change to biennial legislative sessions, and other financial management reforms.[8]

Ames addressed all of these concerns in his inauguration speech three weeks later.

> Our party has pledged itself to retrenchment in expenditures and to a rigid economy and so far as it may be in my power its wish as well as that of the entire people, shall be executed to the very letter. Rigid economy and a strict accountability in all expenditures of public moneys are due the people who are taxed to support the Government. . . . Political organizations can no better afford than individuals to screen or shield corruption or malfeasance in office. I invite all good citizens to join me in my efforts at an economical, impartial, and liberal administration of the laws.[9]

On February 7, Ames was concerned enough that he delivered to the Legislature a special message on state finances. He repeated many of the auditor's recommendations and urged the Legislature to consider them.[10]

The money spent by the state government and by county governments during the five years between 1870 and 1875 when Black and white Republicans were in charge, and the taxes levied to pay for those expenses, constituted the major public policy complaint white Democrats used in the ensuing years and decades to undermine the memory and history of Reconstruction. Even though spending by the Legislature was down 23 percent from a high in 1871, millage rates applied to the real and personal property were higher than white farmers had ever experienced. The relentless decline in the price of cotton and, for 1874, the effects of the economic crisis added to the misery. Taxes and spending became the putative rallying cry.[11]

Whether it was a legitimate rallying cry depends on your perspective.

A sample of the white Democratic perspective came from Dr. Charles Brough, who wrote a "History of Taxation in Mississippi" for the state historical society in 1899 and claimed that "with the election and inauguration of Adelbert Ames as governor in 1874, the spirit of plunder and revenge which animated the aliens and negroes burst forth with a fresh fury. The tax on land was increased to 14 mills, a rate which virtually amounted to confiscation." This was after Dr. Brough had characterized Republican Reconstruction in the state as the "reign of mongrelism, ignorance, and depravity."[12]

Historian William Whitley offered a description of the Republican perspective: Because very few African Americans owned land, Black voters rarely felt the sting of the taxes that the governments they elected imposed on landholders. On the contrary, taxes in the eyes of most Black voters were insufficient to pay for the services, mainly schools, that the state's newest citizens required.

That some white landowners were forfeiting land to the state because of taxes would no doubt have struck Black Mississippians as poetic justice.[13]

Consistent with Whitley's interpretation, the Legislature adjourned in April without addressing any of the fundamental recommendations made by either the auditor or the governor. Would they have taken a different course of action if they had known the outcome of the midterm federal elections later that year and that President Grant would abandon them in the election the following year? Would it have made a difference? While the answers to those questions are unknowable, once the Legislature left Jackson without enacting any tax and budget reforms, white Democrats throughout the state started organizing. To the extent the average white voter had been apathetic through the earlier election cycles, they now were energetic and eager to hear from their leaders.[14]

GRANT, THE PANIC, AND THE 1874 ELECTIONS[15]

Back in Washington, the panic on Wall Street had left the nation's economy in a tailspin. At this time and place in the country's history, there was no clear precedent for the federal government to assume responsibility for manipulating the economy to soften the impact of the expanding recession. As Ron Chernow, Grant's recent biographer, observed: "In this heyday of laissez-faire economics, citizens didn't automatically expect the president to manage the economy or cushion downturns. Economic fluctuations were regarded almost like vagaries of weather."[16]

That being said, the politicians in Congress, facing reelection campaigns in less than ten months, were under intense pressure to respond. Moreover, Northern voters, increasingly weary of the administration's focus on the South, were watching their jobs disappear. In many cities, the newly unemployed organized protests and marches. The debates among Members of Congress, businessmen, workers, and editors were no different 150 years ago than they are today: does the government engage in a tight money program to "cleanse the system of speculation" or combat unemployment through a public works and expansive money supply program? Tight money would straitjacket the economy; loose money would lead to inflation—those were the arguments. The representatives up for reelection, along with workers, speculators, and entrepreneurs building railroads out west sought a stimulus. Bankers and industrialists in the Northeast, wary of inflation, demanded tight money.

On April 14, 1874, Congress adopted a compromise measure that authorized Grant's Treasury Department to inject a modest amount of new paper

currency, or Greenbacks, as they were called, into the country's money supply. When Grant took office, there were about $356 million of Greenbacks in
circulation. The congressional rescue plan would have boosted the Greenback
currency to $400 million. The fight over President Grant's pen was on:
Democrats, factory workers, farmers, and Westerners pressed for a signature;
most businessmen and banks, and some key Republicans, were hoping for a
veto. Republican party leaders, however, urged their president to sign the legislation to protect their majority status in Congress.

While virtually everyone expected Grant to sign it, on April 21, he surprised even his cabinet at the last minute and issued one of the few vetoes
of his administration. Three of Grant's biographers addressed the veto and
agreed that Grant, a fiscal conservative by instinct, came down on the side
of fiscal restraint and believed any short-term hardship would be offset by
a stronger economy over the long term. While the biographers made clear
that party politics was mentioned by some in encouraging Grant to sign the
bill, and that Grant took those considerations into account, in the end, he
"resolved to do what I believed to be right."[17]

Nevertheless, seven months later, with the recession spiraling into a depression, voters took their frustrations out on the party in power: the Republicans
lost ninety-two seats in the House of Representatives. That gave Democrats
control of the lower chamber for the first time since 1860. No senators were
on the ballot in 1874, as state Legislatures continued to appoint US senators,
but losses in legislatures in seven states meant that seven incumbent GOP
senators would not be returning when their term was up. Only five Southern
states remained with Republicans in power.

Historian Richard White summed up the consequences: "The veto was a
political disaster. Rarely has an American political party suffered a defeat on
the scale that the Republican Party did in the congressional elections of 1874.
In the House, they went from a 70 percent majority to a 37 percent minority
in a single election."[18]

For white Democrats in Mississippi, the election was all they could have
hoped for. Northern editors, politicians, and party leaders called on Grant
to turn his energy and attention to the North, where the economic crisis was
having real consequences. "Busted. The Radical Machine Gone to Smash" was
the headline in a Louisville, Kentucky, newspaper. The *New York Herald* interpreted the election to mean that white Southerners would be welcomed back
as "our brothers and our fellow citizens." Public officials were openly admitting their constituents were "sick and tired of carpet-bag governments."[19]

Reviewing the economic crisis, the Grant veto, the 1874 midterm elections, and continued Southern violence, historian James McPherson explained the relatively sudden loss of interest on the part of Northern voters: "The Republican commitment to black rights had never been very deep. . . . The revolutionary achievements of the war and reconstruction—emancipation, civil equality, Negro suffrage, black participation in Southern governments—owed more to anti-Southern than to pro-black motivation. They sprang primarily from the military exigencies of war and the political exigencies of peace, rather than from a considered social purpose." Henry Louis Gates Jr. once offered a similar explanation: "Being an advocate of the abolition of slavery was not the same thing as being a proponent of the fundamental equality of black and white people."[20]

As for the "Radical wing" in Congress, the stark reality for Blacks in Mississippi was that almost all of them were gone: not only Charles Sumner and Thaddeus Stevens, but Senators Benjamin Wade of Ohio, Henry Wilson of Massachusetts, and Zachariah Chandler of Michigan and Representatives James Ashley of Ohio, William Kelley and John Broomall of Pennsylvania, and George Julian of Indiana. Moreover, when Congress convened in March of 1875, with Democrats in control of the house, newly elected Southern Democrats would receive half the committee assignments.

If the results of the November elections were not enough of a signal to President Grant to divert his attention away from the South, Congress delivered him another one in January. In response to continuing violence in Louisiana, Grant sent a sternly worded message to Congress, urging them to renew the Ku Klux Klan enforcement and prosecution legislation that had expired at the end of 1872 and declaring, "to the extent that Congress has conferred power upon me to prevent it, neither Ku-Klux-Klans, White Leagues, nor any other association using arms and violence to execute their unlawful purposes, can be permitted in that way to govern any part of this country." Congress ignored Grant's plea and never acted on his proposal.[21]

One of Grant's biographers, Geoffrey Perret, captured the political shifts in the country when he wrote that "The Panic of 1873 revealed as nothing else could that Reconstruction had lost its primacy as the touchstone of party politics. American political life had been realigned. The political divide was no longer North versus South, but East versus West, cities versus rural areas, and hard money—gold—versus soft money—greenbacks."[22]

For white Democrats in Mississippi, looking ahead to the November elections, that was a realignment they welcomed.

VICKSBURG[23]

Heading into the 1875 legislative elections, white Democrats in Mississippi had accumulated a number of advantages: the Alcorn/Ames 1873 gubernatorial election had divided the Republican Party and given an excuse to many whites to look for another political home; the economic slump, continuing decline of the price of cotton, and taxes and spending by the Republican-controlled Legislature had combined to provide the central issue; and the federal midterm elections had given Democrats control of the House while helping to solidify Northern opposition to continued Southern intervention.

What more could the white Democrats possibly need? A dry run, of course. And Vicksburg gave it to them.

After the 1874 Legislature adjourned in April without acting on much of the reform program proposed by Ames in his inaugural address and in his special message on state finances, whites in the state, mostly Democrats but including some disaffected Alcorn Republicans, began to organize local "taxpayers' leagues" in towns and counties to campaign for relief from high taxes. As a Natchez newspaper put it: "The great cardinal principle of the movement is that the State and county taxation to which our people have been and are now subjected is enormously excessive, unequal, unjust, oppressive, and incompatible with good government and the natural rights of men."

As it happened, Vicksburg, the state's largest town, would be having municipal elections in early August. White Democrats, moved by the Legislature's failure, the excitement generated by the taxpayers' leagues, and encouragement from local newspapers, organized a group of candidates to oppose the Black-and-white Republican ticket for city offices. At a July 4 anniversary celebration of Grant's Vicksburg victory, several Blacks were murdered when white militants opened fire during the march. Tension ran so high as armed men, both Black and white, began patrolling the city that Lt. Governor A. K. Davis and Governor Ames both wired President Grant begging for federal troops to bring calm to the city and to ensure a fair and safe election.

Grant, less than three months from election day, worried about the political ramifications of sending federal troops, once again, to the South. The president listened to his party leaders this time and denied the request. Ironically, given the absence of federal troops, both sides backed down from armed warfare, and election day passed without any violent confrontations.

As it turned out, Democrats were far more motivated to vote than Republicans—a good number of whom stayed home to avoid physical intimidation—and the Democratic ticket prevailed by a small 350-vote margin.

A few days later, Grant received a telegram from a local official reassuring him that "the election just closed was the most peaceable and orderly ever held here." Grant biographer Ron Chernow noted that "White Democrats had demonstrated that without the protection of federal troops, they could resurrect the prewar power structure. The Vicksburg vote showed the fundamental weakness of a political revolution that had relied heavily on force applied by outsiders in Washington." Consequently, Chernow called the vote "a turning point in Reconstruction." In the meantime, Ames wrote to his wife and predicted that if Grant continued to refuse to send federal troops, "Republicanism must go down in the South."[24]

Buoyed by their success in the municipal election, and urged on by their local editors—one of whom wrote in October that the only way to win was to "put pressure on the darkeys"—white Democratic leaders in Vicksburg decided to make a play for the more powerful county offices that were in the hands of the Republicans: the sheriff and the five members of the board of supervisors. The incumbent sheriff and four of the five supervisors were Black.

Rather than wait for the fall elections, however, on December 2, a white mob numbering more than 500 marched on the courthouse and demanded the resignation of the Black sheriff, Peter Crosby. After fleeing to Jackson and consulting with Governor Ames and his cabinet, Crosby returned to Vicksburg to organize his own posse of armed Black men. Monday morning, December 7, Crosby's volunteer militia was seen by whites in Vicksburg marching toward the city, so the new white mayor declared martial law and appointed a former Confederate officer to take charge. As the Black marchers began to retreat, a deadly firefight ensued with a white mob eventually overrunning Crosby's marchers. For the next several days, armed white militants roamed the county indiscriminately killing Black farmers and their families. Days later, at least 300 Blacks lay dead and the white mob had assumed control of the county.

A desperate Ames called the Legislature into a special session on December 17, which immediately appealed to President Grant to send federal troops to restore order in the county. On January 5, 1875, Grant did just that and within several weeks the Republican officeholders were returned to power and the armed bands of white militants had been broken up. Grant's biographer described the distinction between the summer incidents in Vicksburg—and what would take place in connection with the fall elections in the next year—and the December takeover by militant whites: "There was no way Grant could back down before a military putsch on American soil."[25]

The violence was so rampant and so thoroughly reported by newspapers across the country, especially after Grant dispatched troops, that a special five-person committee of the United States House of Representatives was ordered to Vicksburg to conduct an investigation and report back to the full body. The report was submitted on February 27, 1875, with the committee finding the violence was instigated by an offshoot of the Taxpayers' League, which went by the name of White League and whose avowed purpose was "to set aside, by whatever means necessary, the election of colored men to office" and to "allow none but white men to be elected to office or to hold office." The committee determined the white mob had fired on Black marchers without provocation: "The killing of these men, thus retiring in good faith, was murder, willful, cowardly, and in violation of all laws of peace and war." One witness told the committee members that after the carnage the easiest way to locate those who had been shot was to "watch where the buzzards hover." The report's conclusion: "It was no battle; it was a simple massacre."

Nevertheless, while newspapers around the state condemned Ames for calling in troops, Senator Alcorn observed dryly, Ames "has dedicated his life to the cause of impoverishment and ruin of Mississippi, and it does seem that he and his henchmen are doing their work well."

Historian William Gillette described the results of the dry run: "The Democrats learned a valuable lesson from the Vicksburg eruptions: they had succeeded in capturing city hall by the covert means of election trickery but had failed to secure the county courthouse by overt mob action. Control of all of Mississippi was their goal; all they needed was to evolve an appropriate strategy.[26]

Democratic leaders would not make the same mistake in November of next year.

L. Q. C. LAMAR, CHARLES SUMNER, AND HISTORICAL MEMORY

In the middle of the 1874 Mississippi legislative session, Massachusetts Senator Charles Sumner took his last breath on March 11 and passed away. He was sixty-three and had served in the United States Senate since 1851. Together with Pennsylvania Representative Thaddeus Stevens, who died in 1868, they came to embody everything white Democrats in Mississippi hated about losing slavery, the War, and their way of life. These two leaders of the Radical

Copyright by Geo. Prince, Photo.   Pa. Ave. and 11th St. Washington, D. C.
W. F. VILAS.   W. C. WHITNEY.   W. C. ENDICOTT.   A. H. GARLAND.
F. T. BAYARD.   PRESIDENT CLEVELAND.   DANIEL MANNING.   L. Q. C. LAMAR.
THE PRESIDENT AND CABINET.

L. Q. C. Lamar, seated far right, as a member of President Grover Cleveland's cabinet, circa 1886–1887.

Republicans became the public face of Reconstruction, and they were loathed by white Democrats.

On the other hand, two days later at the State Capitol, on a Friday afternoon, both the House and Senate, controlled by Black and white Republicans, devoted several hours to honoring Sumner, one of the men they believed helped to end slavery and ensure suffrage for the formerly enslaved. Thirteen pages in the *House Journal* and a similar number in the *Senate Journal* were filled with speeches thanking Sumner for his service. Both houses adopted resolutions praising his accomplishments and then adjourned in his memory. The House resolution declared the "world has lost one of the brightest and best intellects, our country one of her greatest statesmen, liberty one of her ablest champions, and human rights the most faithful, untiring and efficient advocate."[27]

Three weeks later, the Legislature carved out portions of Chickasaw, Montgomery, Choctaw, and Oktibbeha Counties in the northeast part of the state to create a new Sumner County. Not until 1882, when the Legislature was controlled by white Democrats, would the county name be changed to Webster.[28]

But the highest drama associated with Sumner's death was a speech that Mississippi Congressman L. Q. C. Lamar delivered on the floor of the United States House of Representatives on April 28, 1874. It came to be known as "Lamar's Eulogy of Sumner" and caused a sensation throughout the country.

Other than Jefferson Davis, Lamar may have been the best-known Mississippi Democratic politician at the time. We know much about Lamar because of three biographies and the many letters he wrote and hundreds of speeches he gave that have been preserved and documented.[29]

An educator, lawyer, planter, and slaveholder in Lafayette County before the War, Lamar ran for and was elected to the United States House of Representatives in 1856. Along with the entire Mississippi delegation, he resigned from Congress in January 1861 and returned to Jackson to draft the Ordinance of Secession that the convention adopted later that month. One scholar referred to Lamar as "the soul of secession at the convention." After Lamar rose to the rank of colonel, Jefferson Davis appointed him as an envoy to Europe as a representative of the CSA. After the War, he returned to Oxford and resumed the practice of law. During the congressional elections of 1872, he was encouraged by many friends and supporters to seek reelection to the House. That year was the first year Mississippi had six seats in the House, and the first district, which included Oxford, had fewer Black voters than any other district, which allowed Lamar to become the first Democrat from Mississippi to represent the state in Congress since 1860. Lamar would later move to the Senate when Alcorn's term expired and then accept two appointments from President Grover Cleveland: first, as secretary of the interior in 1885 and then as an associate justice on the United States Supreme Court in 1887.[30]

In the spring of 1874, though, Lamar was looking for an opportunity to publicly advance an approach to ending Republican control of the South he had been working on for several years. His desire was for Southern white men like himself to govern Mississippi. Any thought that Northern Republican businessmen and speculators—the dreaded Carpetbaggers—or the new Black citizens of the state could enjoy equal footing in the work to help Mississippi recover and perhaps even prosper was foreign to him.

Only if the federal government left his home state alone could Lamar realize his dream. He achieved that by successfully articulating a case for postbellum relations between the North and South that would help guide Southern Democrats until the advent of World War II.

Lamar's rather brilliant approach consisted of the following: never admit slavery or secession was wrong, but do admit the North had won the War and thus the South should submit to a new political reality, which was defined by the Thirteenth, Fourteenth, and Fifteenth Amendments. That reconciliation process meant admitting defeat and assuring the North that what their husbands, brothers, and sons died for—to preserve the Union and end slavery—would never be at risk again. His appeal was disarming: were it not for the

Radical Republicans in the North and the newly enfranchised "Radical" Black leaders in the South, the great bulk of Northern and Southern white people had much in common and should reconcile with each other. The deception and cynicism of this approach was that it divorced the cause of the ex-slaves from the reconciliation process. Going forward Blacks would be forgotten.

Two years before the Sumner speech, Lamar wrote to a friend, wondering aloud if he could appeal to Northern voters by going around their Republican party leaders: "Our people are under the supreme necessity of getting into harmonious relations with the Federal government. . . . Is it possible for a secessionist from the South to convince a Northern audience that there is still a common ground on which the state sections can stand and live in harmony. . . . In my opinion, the two sections are estranged simply because each is ignorant of the inner mind of the other, and it is the policy of the party in power to keep up and exaggerate the mutual misunderstanding."[31] Notwithstanding his interest in reaching an accommodation with Northern voters and the federal government, later in the letter he couldn't contain his loathing for the Northern Republicans, or Carpetbaggers, who had migrated to his home state: "Such being the condition, the thought which presses upon every aching heart and head is not how to restore the constitutional faith of our fathers, but how to get rid of these creatures, defiled by blood, gorged with spoil, cruel, cowardly, faithless, who are now ruling the South for no purposes except those of oppression and plunder."[32]

In a different letter a few months later, his aim was becoming clearer: "If I say or do anything, it will be to give to the North the assurance it wants that the South comprehends its own great necessities, and wishes to be no longer the agitating and agitated pendulum of American politics. . . . The object has been to have an election that would secure for our people harmonious and restored relations with the Federal administration. . . . The real object of both sides was to secure the goodwill of the power at Washington."[33] Fast forward to April 28, 1874, when time had been reserved on the floor of the House for members to offer their praise of Sumner and their condolences to his family.[34]

There was Lamar's opportunity. The floor and the galleries were packed when Lamar rose to speak. After spending ten minutes praising Sumner's intellect, commitment, energy, and scholarship, Lamar then honored Sumner's love of freedom while, very discretely, undercutting the very people for whom Sumner had sought freedom:

To a man thoroughly permeated and imbued with such a creed, and animated and constantly actuated by such a spirit of devotion, to behold a

human being or a race of human beings restrained by their natural right to liberty, for no crime by him or them committed, was to feel all the belligerent instincts of his nature roused to combat. That fact was to him a wrong which no logic could justify. It mattered not how humble in the scale of rational existence the subject of this restraint might be, how dark his skin, or how dense his ignorance. . . . It mattered not that the slave might be contented with his lot; that his actual condition might be immeasurably more desirable than that from which it had transplanted him.

Lamar was speaking directly to the average white Northern voter, seeking grounds for understanding and reconciliation. Then Lamar sought to put the War behind his listeners while never admitting the South was wrong: "But here let me do this great man the justice which, amid the excitement of the struggle between the [North and South]—now past—I may have been disposed to deny him. In this fiery zeal, and this earnest warfare against the wrong, as he viewed it, there entered no enduring personal animosity toward the men whose lot it was to be born to the system he denounced."

Toward the end of the eulogy is the inspired heart of Lamar's approach. The Civil War was a "war of ideas" and principles, neither of which was wrong, immoral, or illegal:

Both [the North and South] should gather up the glories won by each section: not envious, but proud of each other, and regard them as a common heritage of American valor. Let us hope that future generations, when they remember the deeds of heroism and devotion done on both sides, will speak not of Northern prowess and Southern courage, but of the heroism, fortitude, and courage of Americans in a war of ideas; a war in which each section signalized its consecration to the principles, as each understood them, of American liberty and of the constitution received from their fathers.

The response to the speech, both in the packed chamber and throughout the editorial pages of the nation's newspapers was overwhelming. Lamar received a sustained standing ovation while in the weeks that followed the speech was reprinted in newspapers around the country. Lamar's contrition and appeal to reconciliation were celebrated, while his rationalization and defense of the cause Sumner so vigorously condemned was overlooked. By arguing, in effect, that "both sides were good people," he sought to remove any obstacle to a return of white control in the South.

That evening, after the speech, Lamar wrote to his wife: "I never in all my life opened my lips with a purpose more single to the interests of our Southern people than when I made this speech."[35] A week later, in another letter to his wife, Lamar basked in his new position on the national stage: "My eulogy has given me a reputation that I have never had before. The whole world is my audience."[36]

In a subsequent speech to the House of Representatives, Lamar continued with his sly denial that the South was wrong about slavery: "The Southern people . . . fully recognize the fact that every claim to the right of secession from this Union is extinguished and eliminated from the American system. . . . They believe that the institution of slavery, with all of its incidents and affinities, is dead. . . . They cherish no aspirations nor schemes for its resuscitation. With their opinions on the rightfulness of slavery unchanged by the events of the war, yet as an enlightened people accepting what is inevitable."[37]

When a constituent complained that Lamar had been too soft on the Republicans in Congress, Lamar explained his purpose: "Never was there a more critical period in our history than the present. The only course I, in common with other Southern representatives, have to follow, is to do what we can to allay excitement between the [North and South], and to bring about peace and reconciliation. That will be the foundation upon which we may establish a constitutional government for the whole country, and local self-government for the South."[38] And he assured a friend in a different letter that his eulogy "was dictated by no pseudo 'magnanimity,' but by a concern for the Southern people, a love for them with their helpless families."[39] There it was: praise the North to deliver the South from federal troops.

Maine Congressman James G. Blaine was Speaker of the House when Lamar gave his Sumner eulogy. Twelve years later, Blaine wrote his memoirs and included this analysis of Lamar's speech, which was spot-on: "It was a mark of positive genius in a Southern representative to pronounce a fervid and discriminating eulogy upon Mr. Sumner, and skillfully to interweave with it a defense of that which Mr. Sumner . . . believed to be the sum of all villainies. . . . He pleased the Radical antislavery sentiment of New England. He did not displease the Radical proslavery sentiment of the South."[40]

In the ensuing decades, erecting monuments of soldiers on courthouse lawns and engaging in battle reenactments between "Blue" and "Gray" soldiers were just two of the many ways the memory of the Civil War came to be defined by the War and not the cause of the War. The new Black citizens of the South were ignored and forgotten.

In 1961, Mississippi joined with other states to commemorate the Civil War Centennial. The Mississippi Centennial Commission published a booklet, called "Mississippi's Greatest Hour," to outline the purposes of the commemoration and to provide guidance for local communities that wanted to host events in connection with the state celebration. Lamar would have been pleased with the fourth paragraph under the heading, "The Meaning of the Centennial": "If any one goal is paramount in this commemorative undertaking, it is to inform all people that there was a dedication to ideals and honest beliefs on both sides, North and South."[41] Absent from the forty-eight-page booklet are words such as "negro" or "freedman," terms that might indicate some role Black Mississippians may have had in events of a hundred years earlier.

Less than two months after the March 28, 1961, formal opening of the Mississippi Civil War Centennial commemoration, on May 24, the first wave of Freedom Riders arrived at the Greyhound Bus Station in downtown Jackson. It was the beginning of the end for everything being celebrated by the Centennial.[42]

BLANCHE K. BRUCE

With Adelbert Ames's election as governor, the 1874 Mississippi Legislature had his seat to fill in the United States Senate. To complete the remainder of his term—from February 3, 1874, to March 3, 1875—the Legislature gave the honor to Henry R. Pease, the white man who devised and implemented Mississippi's first comprehensive system of public schools. A year later, as his term expired, Pease settled in Vicksburg where President Grant appointed him postmaster and where he established and edited the *Mississippi Educational Journal*.

For the full six-year term, beginning on March 3, 1875, the Legislature elected Blanche Kelso Bruce to the post.[43]

Born in 1841 as an enslaved man in Virginia, Bruce and his family were moved from Virginia to Missouri, back to Virginia, then to Mississippi, and finally back to Missouri over the ensuing twenty-one years. Bruce managed to escape in 1862 and became a free man in 1863 when President Lincoln issued the Emancipation Proclamation. After attending Oberlin College in Ohio for several years, Bruce heard about Benjamin Montgomery and Davis Bend and began to make his way to Mississippi to take advantage of new opportunities made available to Blacks by the Reconstruction initiatives. Once he made a home in the Delta, Bruce befriended both Alcorn and Ames and received the appointment as tax assessor for Bolivar County. In 1871, he was elected sheriff of the county and, at the same time, became superintendent of education for the county. Over the next four years, he built a formidable base of political

Senator Blanche Bruce, circa 1875–1880. Courtesy of the Archives and Records Services Division, Mississippi Department of Archives and History.

power in Bolivar and the surrounding counties and earned enough money to start buying farmland. Later in 1874, after his election to the Senate, he secured a bank loan to acquire a 600-acre plantation in Bolivar County.[44]

The swearing-in of Bruce on the floor of the United States Senate on March 4, 1875, gave us one of the most poignant and moving anecdotes of this entire history of Reconstruction. It is told by Lawrence Otis Graham, Bruce's biographer:

Vice President Henry Wilson, himself a former senator from Massachusetts, had already asked more than a dozen newly elected senators to proceed to the front of the grand room, each escorted by the senior senator from the same state. For this group of senators-elect, the tradition of using escorts was, indeed, necessary since nineteen of the twenty-three senators to be sworn in that day were completely new to the governmental body.

Then it was Bruce's turn.

Senator-elect Blanche Kelso Bruce of Mississippi, called Vice President Wilson's voice into the large ornate chamber.

Bruce unclasped his hands and stood slowly as he looked at the men around him.

"Senator-elect Blanche Kelso Bruce" the loud voice at the front repeated, "of Mississippi."

Three long rows of men, many of them white-haired, turned to Bruce and waited with curious expressions. They watched and waited for Bruce's escort to come to the black man's side.

But no escort came. The senior senator from Mississippi, James Lusk Alcorn, did not move. He remained in seat number fourteen, his face hidden behind a newspaper.

The lone black man in the room, Bruce finally moved to the end of his row and then glanced back at Alcorn, who remained in his seat. Seeing that Alcorn was not going to follow proper protocol and lead the senator-elect to the front, Bruce looked to the front, adjusted his coat, and strolled slowly down the purple carpeted aisle by himself.

As Bruce advanced a few steps, he was suddenly joined by a thin, full-bearded man with a receding hairline.

"If I may, Mr. Bruce," the courtly white gentleman said with a slight nod as he took Bruce's arm, "Permit me. I am the senator from New York, Roscoe Conkling."

The room of white men watched in stunned silence as the two reached the front.

He and Conkling would eventually enjoy a long friendship in the Senate. Bruce would ultimately name his own son after the white Republican senator from New York, and Bruce would never again feel so vulnerable in the Senate Chamber as he felt that day. For even though he was reaching the greatest heights of power and dignity possible for a black man in America, he simultaneously could see how easily all of it could be taken away—both in that chamber and back home in Mississippi.

Bruce later shared his experience with a newspaper reporter: "I took the oath and then he escorted me back to my seat. Later in the day when they were fixing up the committees, Conkling asked me if anyone was looking out after my interests, and upon my informing him that there was not and that I was myself more ignorant of my rights in the matter, he volunteered to attend to it, and as a result, I was placed on some very good committees."[45]

In 1881, as Bruce was leaving the Senate at the end of his term, President James Garfield appointed him register of the US Treasury and in that capacity, Bruce became the first Black person to have his signature on the currency of the United States. In 1884, when Frederick Douglass and Helen Pitts were married in a private ceremony in Washington, by the abolitionist preacher Francis J. Grimke, the only witnesses to the marriage were Blanche Bruce, his wife Josephine, and Grimke's wife Charlotte. Bruce later joined the board of Howard University and opened an insurance and investment business in Washington. Bruce died on March 17, 1898, at the age of fifty-seven, one year after accepting another appointment to the Treasury post, this time from President William McKinley. His son Roscoe Conklin Bruce would graduate from Harvard University, Phi Beta Kappa, where he was president of the debate team and was chosen as class orator.

After Blanche Bruce left the Senate in 1881, no other Black person would serve in the Senate until Edward Brooke was elected as a Republican by the voters of Massachusetts in 1966. Almost ninety-three years to the month of Charles Sumner's death, Brooke would take the oath of office. No doubt Sumner would be pleased that the first African American elected to the Senate since the two Black members from Mississippi had served came from his party and from his home state.

When Alcorn's term in the Senate expired, the Mississippi Legislature appointed L. Q. C. Lamar to take his place. When Bruce's term expired, J. Z. George was elected as his replacement. It would be those two men who would lead the Democrats in 1875 in the most important and consequential election in the history of the state.

CHAPTER 11

1875
The End
White Democrats Reassert Their Power

In the domestic history of Mississippi, the year 1875 is the supplement of 1861.
—EDWARD MAYES[1]

The state was "sickened at an orgy of negro and 'carpet-bag' control that reads like the record of some unhappy planet. Then the scene shifted and retribution came.
—DUNBAR ROWLAND[2]

Of all of the state and federal elections that have taken place in Mississippi since 1817—perhaps as many as 200—only four fundamentally altered the direction of the state: the 1861 election for secession; the legislative campaigns of 1875 that ended Reconstruction; the 1911 election that elevated James K. Vardaman to the US Senate and Theodore Bilbo to the office of lieutenant governor and gave those two men vast public platforms to define race relations in the state for nearly forty years; and the 1959 election of Ross Barnett as governor, leading to the debacle at the University of Mississippi that he engineered in 1962 and that left a stain on the state for decades. Of those four, the election of 1875 had the longest reach and would ultimately prove the most consequential.

There were legislative elections in 1875 because of the odd date on which Mississippi's Constitution—and the first slate of statewide and legislative office-holders—was approved by the voters. That was in 1869. In addition, the new constitution prescribed two-year terms for state representatives and four-year terms for state senators, but with the requirement that half of the senate seats would be up for reelection every two years. Given that framework, and the four-year terms for the governor and the other six statewide offices, only the full House and half the Senate would be on the ballot in 1875, though even that would change in the coming months. Election day in 1875 would fall on Tuesday, November 2.[3]

Timing is everything in politics and as the political calendar moved from 1874 to 1875, white Democrats enjoyed an election dynamic that was finally in their favor: the breakup of the state Republican Party, leading to disaffected white Alcorn supporters joining with Democrats to oppose Ames; tough economic times, leading to the kind of supercharged issue that can motivate people to vote; and a largely disinterested federal government and broader national audience, leading to the greatly diminished possibility of federal military intervention on election day.

Given the racial composition of the eligible voters—eligible Black voters outnumbered white voters 53 to 47 percent—how the Democrats converted their advantages into a winning campaign is the subject of this chapter.[4]

By and large, though, the Democrats would repeat the successful approach they used in the 1868 campaign to defeat the adoption of the new constitution. There, they had an issue that motivated their base—the elimination of voting rights—and a federal oversight official sympathetic to white Democrats. Their 1875 campaign, though, would be more centralized, more organized, more energetic, and more violent.

For 1875, three men would primarily determine the outcome of the election: President Ulysses S. Grant, Governor Adelbert Ames, and James Z. George, the Jackson lawyer chosen by the Democrats to manage their campaign operation. Given the modest Black voter advantage, the ultimate goal of both Ames and George was to manage Grant. Ames would need the president to provide federal troops to ensure a fair election; George would need the president to withhold federal troops from Mississippi to ensure an unfair election. George proved the more capable.

James Zachariah George, born in 1826 in Georgia, moved to Mississippi with his family as a child and, after serving with Jefferson Davis in the Mexican-American War, settled in the Delta town of Carrollton where he opened a law practice. By 1861, George's work in the area had impressed the voters so much that they elected him as a delegate to the secession convention. After serving in the Civil War for several years, he ended up in Jackson to resume his law practice. His biographer, Timothy Smith, captured the essence of the future campaign manager, by describing him as someone who "generally shunned the spotlight, . . . much preferred to work behind the scenes, . . . and [was] extremely careful in what he said and did, and to whom he spoke."

A drawing of James Z. George, circa 1880–1885. Courtesy of the Archives and Records Services Division, Mississippi Department of Archives and History.

This characteristic, so critical to an effective manager, came through once in a letter to Congressman Lamar, to whom he wrote complaining about the "inexorable demands of the legislature" and labeling the Ames government the "most corrupt government which ever existed in a capital city," but, at the same time, telling Lamar that while he "would like to write you a long letter about public affairs," he thought better of it: "I do not think it opportune to talk about [it] now publicly." Critical to a successful campaign is planning, apparently another habit of George. After assuming control of the Democratic campaign, one of his lieutenants remembered: "how carefully every possible phase of the situation was discussed . . . how fully every possible outcome of that course was considered." George was at the early meetings of Democrats, and by the August convention had demonstrated enough interest and ability that he was chosen the leader.[5]

PREFACE TO THE ELECTION

The 1875 election in Mississippi has been covered in virtually everything written about Reconstruction in America, including popular and scholarly historical accounts, biographies, graduate dissertations, autobiographies, and memoirs. Moreover, by the end of the election, the campaign had been extensively documented by national newspapers, magazines, and journals, not to mention the wall-to-wall coverage by local newspapers in the state.[6]

It was then the subject of a massive congressional investigation during the first nine months of 1876, resulting in a report exceeding 2,000 pages of documents and testimony from 162 witnesses.[7]

In addition to the dynamics of the election season that George inherited and of which he took full advantage, he employed two campaign tactics very successfully:

- The term "color line" was ubiquitous in all of the contemporary coverage of the election. It denoted the overt use of race by white Democrats to motivate their base of voters by blaming the newly enfranchised Blacks for problems in Mississippi. J. Z. George, L. Q. C. Lamar, and other leaders knew instinctively that whatever support they were slowly building among Northern whites—as a firewall to keep the federal government from sending troops—would disappear if a "race war" were to engulf the state. Throughout their speeches and written communications, these leaders implored their voters to reject the "color-line" and instead make the election about Ames and taxes. Ironically, Grant was less likely to come to the rescue of a fellow Republican than innocent Blacks: white Union soldiers may have given their lives to free enslaved Mississippians, but they most assuredly did not make the ultimate sacrifice to protect allegedly incompetent Republican governors.
- When George was confronted with violent outbursts from whites, his only hope of containing Grant was to confuse the situation. And in this task, George was brilliant. He took advantage of prominent Republicans who abandoned Ames after the Alcorn election, including former superintendent of education and former US Senator Henry Pease, state attorney general George Harris, Congressman George C. McKee, former state auditor Henry Musgrove, former US attorney G. Wiley Wells, and even former US Senator Hiram Revels. At various times during the fall campaign, these individuals, as well

as others, on their own or in concert with George, assured Grant and other officials in Washington that any violence was confined and the election would remain fair.[8] At the same time, George, Lamar, and other well-known Democrats would send their own telegrams and letters to the White House offering accounts that were contradictory to other published reports, offering excuses that involved Ames, and giving assurances for a fair election. Given the rudimentary ways in which people communicated—through telegrams, letters, and delayed newspaper reports—it was relatively easy to present a given situation as confusing, contradictory, and inconsistent. Without clarity, it was difficult for Grant to act.

Whether George overtly coordinated with friendly editors, disaffected Republicans, county Democratic leaders, and state officials like Lamar to create the successful campaign operation, or whether the events unfolded because people acted on their own or took cues from others, George took advantage of all the breaks that fell his way.

A very, very small sampling of the available evidence is presented in the pages that follow, with snippets of speeches, editorials, letters, news articles, telegrams, and memoir passages presented in chronological fashion to give the reader a sense of how the campaign evolved, how seemingly independent initiatives contributed to the larger purpose, and how each side compensated for its mistakes.

THE 1875 ELECTION

Both sides opened the new year by defining the core issues of the upcoming election.

On January 4, a large group of Democrats, along with some disaffected white Republicans, hosted a State Taxpayers Convention in Jackson. After agreeing that "every day the people have grown poorer, lands have diminished in value, wages have grown less, and all industries have become more and more paralyzed," the delegates issued a petition demanding a reduction in taxation from the upcoming session of the Legislature.[9]

The next day, the Republican-controlled Legislature convened for its regular session. Later that afternoon Governor Ames delivered a message that noted the continuing economic crisis, called on legislators to exercise "the most stringent economy in appropriations ... in the direction of retrenchment

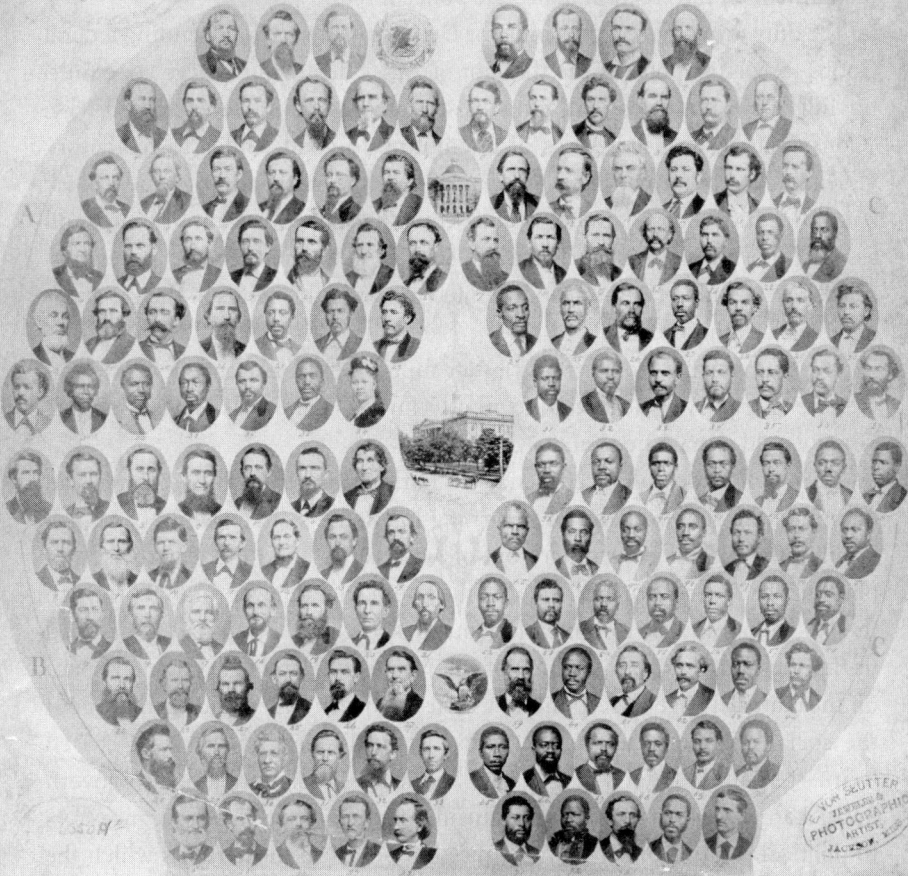

The membership of the Mississippi Legislature, 1874–1875. Library of Congress, Prints and Photographs Division, LC-USZ62-33248.

and reform" and to reduce expenses by adopting biennial legislative sessions, limiting the number of local judges, cutting property taxes and payments to the two state universities, and pushing some state costs to the counties. Toward the end of his message, though, he referenced the Vicksburg riots and recommended the creation of "a state police force."[10]

The only thing more worrisome for Democrats than Grant sending federal troops to Mississippi was the thought of Ames deploying a large state militia, full of Black troops with guns. Historian George Rable explained why: "Conservatives accused Ames of attempting to goad whites to retaliatory violence, thereby providing a pretext for federal intervention. Armed Black banditti, editorialists claimed, would scour the state, break into homes, and assault innocent citizens. Furthermore, such a force would require vast expenditures and would place almost unlimited power in the hands of the governor and his black followers."[11]

Preventing Ames from arming a state militia would take as much time and creative energy over the next nine months for the Democrats as ensuring that Grant would remain neutral.

Years before he eulogized Senator Charles Sumner, L. Q. C. Lamar had identified the requirement for returning his home state to white control—keeping the federal government out of Mississippi—and the way to accomplish it: by assuring Northerners that the South would never undo that which the North had fought for. In early January, soon after Grant had intervened in the Vicksburg riots, the editor of the *New York Herald* gave Lamar space on the editorial page to respond to a series of questions, including one about the social and political ramifications "if the Federal government ceased to interfere in the affairs of the state and leave Mississippi alone to govern itself." Lamar was ready and cynically offered the appropriate assurances: "As to political rights, I presume your question points to those rights which the Northern people have insisted upon being secured to the black race—to wit, the rights of suffrage, of service on juries, and legal eligibility to office. I do not believe that any serious movement would be made in my state to injure or abridge any of those rights."[12]

A few weeks later, the newspaper in Brandon reminded its readers that Ames was the problem and drew the line between the white governor and white voters: "We seldom pick up an exchange from any of the negro counties in this state that does not contain one or two accounts of murders, assassinations, robberies or gin-house burnings by negroes and yet Adelbert Ames, our nigger equality governor, continues to pardon the scoundrels almost as fast as they are convicted."[13]

By the end of February, when it was becoming clear to Democrats in the Legislature that substantial property tax reform was hopeless, they called a meeting for March 3 to begin planning for the fall elections. Tishomingo state senator John M. Stone, a rising star in the party—and a future governor—was elected chairman of the group. They set May 17 as the next meeting and August 3 as the date for a statewide Democratic convention.[14]

A few days later, at the invitation of Democrats in Nashua, New Hampshire, Lamar, whose national reputation had only grown since his Sumner eulogy, spoke for two hours, criticizing Ames, asking for Mississippi to be left alone, urging the delegates to avoid the "color-line," and offering his usual guarantees about future Southern behavior: "It has been represented to you, fellow citizens of New Hampshire, that upon the part of the native white population of the South, there is a determined scheme to obtain supremacy and control, if necessary, by organized fraud, violence, murder, for the purpose of subjecting the newly enfranchised race of that section to a servitude something akin to their former bondage, and to defeat the results which you have achieved by the war that you closed in 1865. If you will give me your attention, I think I can satisfy you that no such purpose exists."[15]

When the Legislature adjourned and left town at the end of March, they had appropriated a small amount of money for and given Ames the authority to organize two militia regiments while doing little to satisfy the white Democrats clamoring for substantive tax relief. The battle lines were drawn.[16]

Frustration among the editors of the *Raymond Gazette* was uncontrollable when they titled an editorial "The Dirty Despotism on Earth" and wrote, "Radicalism in the hands of Ames and his Negroes has swept away every vestige of republican government in Mississippi. . . . If our fathers threw off the British yoke (which was less humiliating and barbarous than the yoke which has been placed on our necks by Ames and his negroes), should we not make a powerful effort to throw off the yoke which now bears us to the earth?"[17] The *Times* in Greenville reported on a May meeting of Washington County Democrats where they committed themselves to the campaign: "Whereas, it is a truth, which no thinking, well-informed man can deny, that the role of the Republican Party, in this State, has been one of oppression, destructive to our material interests, degrading to us as a people, subversive of civil liberty . . . and whereas the time has arrived when, in our judgment, by earnest, manly effort, thorough organization and increasing vigilance, we can attain its overthrow."[18]

Two days later, white Democrats met in Jackson to formalize their party name, organization, and timetable. They chose to call themselves the

Democratic-Conservative Party of Mississippi, targeted Ames specifically by publishing a list of complaints against his administration, set August 3 for a statewide party convention, invited Lamar to be the convention's keynote speaker, and encouraged the formation of county party organizations to elect delegates to the state convention and recruit candidates for the legislative and local offices that would be approved at the August convention to appear on the November ballot.[19]

Once it became known that Lamar would be the speaker, a leader of the new party, former US Senator Albert Gallatin Brown wrote to Ethelbert Barksdale, editor of the *Clarion* newspaper in Jackson and a fellow Democratic leader, concurring with the wisdom of choosing Lamar: "By making him our leader we make these expressions our own and thus disarm our Northern slanderers."[20]

Charles Nordhoff, a reporter for the *New York Herald*, happened to be in Mississippi at the time as part of a tour of the Southern states in the spring and summer months of 1875. After spending two months in Arkansas and Louisiana, he landed in Mississippi in May and after a few weeks posted the following observation. It was a reminder that what Lamar, editors, and other campaign leaders said and wrote for public consumption was not the underlying motive for their campaign.

> In Arkansas and Louisiana, I do not remember having once heard of the negro except as a part of the body politic . . . a good worker, and, as was often said to me by Democrats, "not to be blamed that he went wrong under bad advice." But in Mississippi, the commonest topic of discussion is the "damned nigger." A dozen times, at least, prominent Democrats told me he was a peculiar being, not possessing the virtues of the Caucasian race, and not fit by nature to vote, or to sit on a jury, or to bear witness— a creature admirably fitted to make cotton.[21]

By the beginning of summer, the November ballot had expanded in size and importance. First, the state treasurer elected with Ames in 1873, George Holland, had died earlier in the year. Both parties would therefore be nominating candidates to replace him, which meant a statewide office would be on the ticket in every county. Second, all six of Mississippi's congressional seats would be on the ballot. Under normal circumstances, those positions would have been filled in 1874, but because of a quirk in its official calendar that year, Congress would not be holding its first official session until December 1875. As a cost-saving measure, Mississippi was permitted to add its congressional elections to the November 1875 ballot, indirectly upping the stakes for both parties. The excitement generated by the legislative campaign would carry over to the congressional elections. While running a campaign to win power at the State Capitol, the Democrats could, at the same time, gain control of Mississippi's congressional delegation.[22]

Huge public outdoor rallies were the vehicle of choice for candidates to motivate voters and deliver campaign messages. A typical one took place in L. Q. C. Lamar's congressional district on July 12 in Tippah County, at Falkner's Station. Lamar's biographer reported that special trains were used to help pack the fairground with close to 3,000 people, and "these hardy partisans who braved ninety-degree temperatures did not go away disappointed. Lamar harangued against Ames and the Republicans for three torrid hours, blaming them for creating the deplorable color line and for the perversion of white-Negro relations."[23]

By this time, newspapers across the state were covering local meetings and rallies of Democrats and their candidates. In the meantime, Governor Ames had left Mississippi for his summer vacation, at the home of his wife's family in Massachusetts. Blanche Ames and their children remained in Massachusetts after Ames returned to Mississippi, but his almost daily letters to her in the ensuing months have been preserved and represent a deeply personal accounting of the events in Mississippi from Ames's perspective.

On his return to Mississippi in late July, Ames stopped at Long Branch, New Jersey, for a visit with President Grant, at his summer home. On July 24, Ames wrote to Blanche that Grant "shows his old interest in me." Perhaps judging this "interest" more optimistically than he should have, Ames left the meeting expecting he would receive military aid from Grant if needed.[24]

August 3 served as the official kickoff of the fall campaign when the Democratic-Conservative Party of Mississippi held its state convention in the House Chamber of the State Capitol in Jackson. The gathering represented the culmination of months of planning and years of pent-up frustration at the course of events in Mississippi since the War. Newspaper reports and contemporary accounts of the gathering make clear that the white men attending the special occasion felt the movement of history was finally on their side and that the November elections were their opportunity to wrest control of the state from the Republicans.[25]

Virtually everyone associated with Democrats in Mississippi over the previous fifteen years was there, including former US Senator Albert Gallatin Brown and former congressman Wiley P. Harris, former governors Benjamin Humphreys and Charles Clark, future governors John M. Stone and Robert Lowry, future US Senators Anselm J. McLaurin, Edward Walthall, and

Hernando D. Money, and future congressmen Pat Henry and Charles Hooker. After he was officially named party chairman and campaign manager, J. Z. George recognized his broader audience when he implored his members to "discharge our duties as American citizens, insisting in equality of benefits. ... Our statesmanship must embrace the whole country, seeking to advance the common interests, the common happiness, and the general welfare of the American people."[26]

From contemporary reports, Lamar's keynote address took all of three hours. He too recognized his national audience and used his time to excoriate Ames and to urge all in attendance to welcome any and all people to their cause.

About a third of the way through the speech, though, Lamar couldn't contain the way he really felt about Black Mississippians. Speaking about the "four million liberated slaves" and how they "cannot but endanger the nation's life," he asserted, "The Southern people ... knew the capabilities of the negro and his fitness to vote, and believed that to clothe him with these attributes, even with freedom's ballot and the incentive of freedom's blessings before him, would be a great wrong."[27]

Before adjourning, the convention adopted a platform to appeal to the larger national audience, promising "civil and political equality of all men," favoring "the education of all the children of the State in public schools," "economy in the administration of the government," "the encouragement of agriculture," and "cordially invit[ing] the voters of all the people of both races to unite vigorously with us."[28]

A Jackson newspaper the next day applauded Lamar's speech as "massive in argument, irresistible in logic, statesmanlike in the policy it advocated and eloquent."[29]

Governor Ames saw through the ploy, as he explained in an August 4 letter to his wife, Blanche: "The true sentiment of the assembly was 'color-line' though the platform says nothing about it. The understanding evidently is that each locality can act as it chooses, but the state convention put forth a platform for Northern consumption."[30]

The editor of the Hinds County newspaper echoed the Democratic talking points soon after the convention, when he wrote the election "will be an uprising of the taxpaying people to assert their rights as American citizens, and to indict before the world the illegal acts of Adelbert Ames and his party of imbeciles, corruptionists, and plunderers."[31]

Four days later, Lamar posted a letter to his friend Charles Reemelin, making clear his justification for avoiding the "color-line" in his speeches was to keep the federal government out of the state: "The negro race, which has no idea of a principle of government or of society beyond that of obedience to the mandate of a master, sees in [the federal government] the only embodiment of authority (mastership) in the country. We could, by forming the 'color line'. . . overcome the stolid, inert, and illiterate majority; but such a victory will bring about conflicts and race passions and collisions with Federal power. Our only deliverance is in a change of Federal policy toward us."[32]

The challenge facing George and the white Democrats was daunting indeed, especially when you consider their ultimate goal was not to gain a majority but to open the 1876 Legislature with a two-thirds supermajority in both houses. To end Reconstruction in Mississippi once and for all, Governor Ames, Black Republican Lieutenant Governor A. K. Davis, and Black Republican Superintendent of Education Thomas W. Cardozo had to be impeached, convicted, and removed from office. To accomplish that would require a two-thirds vote in the House to impeach and a two-thirds vote in the Senate to convict. To get there in the House, George would need to keep all thirty-eight of his Democratic incumbents and win half of the seventy-seven seats held by Republicans. For the Senate, he had to keep his twelve Democratic incumbents and win half of the twenty-five districts represented by Republicans. Considering that all of the Democratic incumbents represented majority-white counties, taking seats away from Republicans meant venturing into Mississippi's majority-Black counties.[33]

There was no Republican in a majority-Black county, white or Black, more noteworthy and more despised among whites than Albert T. Morgan, a Union Army veteran, farmer, and businessman from Wisconsin who moved to Yazoo County after the War, married a Black woman, established a school for Black children, and in short order established himself as the leader of the county, getting elected first to the board of supervisors and then sheriff, all the while organizing his own armed Black militia.[34] At a meeting on September 1 of local Republicans, convened by Morgan, a small group of armed Democrats showed up, and not unexpectedly, an argument soon deteriorated into a shooting match. Given how rumors take hold in a heated campaign, skirmishes between armed companies of Blacks and whites followed, based on whatever rumor individuals wanted to believe, culminating in random assassinations and an armed takeover of the county government by a mob of more than 800 white men. Morgan, fearing for his life, hid at a friend's house while sending a handwritten message to Ames:

> I am in great danger of losing my life. Not only that, all the leading Republicans, who have not run away, are in danger. The town is so strongly

guarded . . . and armed men . . . patrol the streets at night. . . . The [white] league here have adopted a new policy, which is to kill the leaders and spare the colored people unless they rise. . . . My friend, I fought four years; was wounded several times; suffered in hospitals, and as a prisoner; was in twenty-seven different engagements to free the slave and save our glorious Union—to save such a country as this! I have some love left for my country, but what is a country without it protecting its defenders?

A few days later, Morgan abandoned the county and made his way to the Governor's Mansion.[35]

Then there was Charles Caldwell, an enslaved blacksmith in Clinton before the War, who had rapidly become a recognized leader in the Black community. A member of the 1868 Constitutional Convention, he was one of the original five Black members elected to the Senate in 1869. In his early book on Reconstruction in Mississippi, even white Democrat sympathizer James Garner recognized Caldwell's abilities when he described him as "a courageous and dangerous negro." As Caldwell was helping to organize and lead a large and boisterous Republican rally in Clinton on September 4, armed whites showed up. Who fired the first shot remains a mystery, though, like the situation in Yazoo, rumors spread throughout Hinds County. By nightfall, after Clinton's mayor had dispatched telegrams warning of a Black takeover, special trains arrived with armed white men from Vicksburg and other nearby towns. The slaughter commenced at daylight. Over the next two days, more than thirty Blacks were murdered at random. A well-known white Republican was killed in front of his family by a mob for the simple reason he was a "friend of the nigger." George quickly appointed his own special committee to investigate and not surprisingly developed the findings into a campaign document called "In Exoneration of the White People of Clinton." It referred to the affair as a "premeditated massacre of the whites" to encourage federal participation.[36]

In his 2006 book on the 1875 election, Nicholas Lemann ended his description of the "Clinton Riot" with this succinct observation: "Back in the spring of 1863, Grant's Army had bloodily battled its way through this area on its way from Jackson to Vicksburg. Many of the whites who were gathering now had been Confederate soldiers then, and here was their chance to fight again for the same home ground, with a better result."[37]

The director of the Hinds County Democratic Campaign remembered: "During the next few days there was anarchy in our county. . . . The question which presented itself then to the people of Hinds County was whether or not the negroes . . . should rule the county. The terrible ordeal through which we passed on that eventful fourth of September fired a determination in the minds of the white people to overthrow the negro rule at any cost. Throughout the countryside, for several days the negro leadership, some white and some black were hunted down and killed."[38]

Ames described what he had heard about the riot in his daily letter to Blanche:

> There were present at a Republican barbecue about fifteen hundred colored people, men, women, and children. Seeking the opportunity white men, fully prepared, fired into the crowd. Two women were reported killed, also two children. . . . Last night, this morning, and today squads of white men are scouring the country killing Negroes. . . . Yesterday, the Negroes, though unarmed and unprepared, fought bravely and killed four of the ring-leaders. They know we have a majority of some thirty thousand and to overcome it they are resorting to intimidation and murder. The Mansion has been crowded all day long with Republican friends and Negroes from the field of battle.[39]

Here, at the onset of the fall campaign, was George's great challenge. The Democratic leader no doubt knew that if Grant wanted to help Ames with federal troops, the deadly riots in Clinton and Yazoo, extensively covered by the press, provided the justifiable excuse. On September 8, Ames put into play his ace: he issued a proclamation for the white private militias to disband and simultaneously sent a telegram to the White House with a formal request for federal troops.[40] The moment had arrived. Over the next five weeks, the ninety years of Mississippi history that would follow, along with the future of the new Black citizens of the state, would be resolved.

With Grant away from Washington for the summer, his new attorney general, Edwards Pierrepont, a conservative New York corporate lawyer, received the request from Ames. Two days later, in Grant's absence, Pierrepont responded to Ames by asking for more information and specifically requesting "what the state had done to suppress the disorders." He ended his telegram, though, with a ray of hope: "Forces had been put in readiness if the governor could demonstrate that an insurrection actually existed."[41]

It was then that Ames's failure to spend the summer and fall building a Republican election organization caught up with him. Unlike the energetic campaign he waged for governor in 1873, Ames was largely absent from the hustings in 1875. After spending the summer vacationing out of state, Ames rarely left the Governor's Mansion that fall. He admitted as much during his testimony to the congressional committee investigating the election. When a skeptical Pierrepont gave Ames one more chance to describe all that he had done to wage a credible campaign against the Democrats, as well as to deter violence and intimidation, Ames had nothing substantive or reassuring to offer in his reply the following day. Historian Brooke Simpson concluded that "Ames's increasing apathy about his job frittered away the party's position . . . [Grant] had lost interest in helping southern Republicans who did not help themselves . . . To protect their political interests, Grant wanted to make sure Ames was doing all he could do."[42]

At this particular time, those "political interests" involved an election in Ohio, specifically an election for governor of Ohio, along with other statewide and legislative officials, set for October 12 of that year. Pierrepont, Republican party leaders in Washington, and Republican officials in Ohio believed federal government intervention in Mississippi might deliver the Ohio statehouse to the Democrats. Protecting the rights of America's newest Black citizens, and their Republican backers in the South, had become more and more unpopular across the country. Moreover, as historian Charles Calhoun observed, "Many Republicans thought that Mississippi, which would cast only eight electoral votes in 1876, was a small price to pay for the swing state of Ohio with its 22 electoral votes."[43]

Within a few days, Northern newspapers had the telegrams and were weighing in with their own opinions, which almost uniformly consisted of pleas to stay out of Mississippi. The *New York Daily Herald* ridiculed Ames with the observation that "it looks a little as though Governor Ames has been firing a hole through his own hat." Those sentiments were given support from Mississippi when former senator Pease, Attorney General Harris, and former United States attorney Wells sent their telegrams to Pierrepont, urging him to ignore Ames, that the "problems had subsided," and that federal intervention would "only tend to aggravate existing difficulties."[44]

After surveying the Cabinet and finding little to no backing for Ames, Pierrepont accumulated all of the letters and telegrams and on September 13 forwarded them to Grant with his own recommendation to refrain from intervention. Ron Chernow, Grant's biographer, describes the president as "on a knife edge, torn between popular revulsion against Reconstruction and his fervent wish to aid threatened Blacks. He admitted to being 'perplexed' as to the ideal course of action." In the end, while Grant wrote a long letter to his attorney general that leaned toward sending federal troops, arguing that "I do not see how we are to evade the call of the governor if made strictly within the Constitution," he left the final decision to his attorney general. [45]

Pierrepont received Grant's decision and decided to make a few unauthorized changes in his telegram back to Ames. It was the key moment in the fall campaign, and was described by Chernow: "His letter written, Grant departed for a veterans' reunion in Utica, New York, leaving the matter to Pierrepoint, who sent Ames a message that substituted his own conservative judgment for the president's, while pretending he and Grant acted in unison. . . . He chastised the Mississippi governor for not having proven the existence of an insurrection . . . or taken sufficient steps to stop the violence on his own, a rebuke that left Ames feeling 'disgusted.'"[46]

Within a few days, state and national newspapers had Pierrepont's message disguised as Grant's message: Ames was on his own.[47]

Grant never overruled his Attorney General. The following year, Grant confided to Mississippi Congressman John Lynch, "If I had believed that any effort on my part would have saved Mississippi, I would have made it, even if I had been convinced that it would have resulted in the loss of Ohio. . . . But I was satisfied then, as I am now, that Mississippi could not have been saved to the party in any event and I wanted to avoid the responsibility of the loss of Ohio." George was, for the time being, in the clear. But his excitement at his lucky break was short lived, for Ames then resorted to his last remaining option: he issued official calls to organize the small militia force the Legislature had earlier authorized. And if George's worst nightmare—the governor's use of armed Blacks participating in Black militia squadrons—wasn't bleak enough, Ames chose Charles Caldwell to lead one of the companies.[48]

That being said, George's biographer made an insightful observation about the challenge the Democratic leader was facing: "George was caught between two difficult positions with no good choices. He could not let Black troops incite whites to riot, for fear of encouraging the use of federal troops, but on the other hand, the more Ames talked of black troops, the more white Republicans sided with the Democrats."[49]

Nevertheless, George could ill afford a race war. Within a few days, newspapers across the state were raising the ante. The *Weekly Clarion* in Jackson wrote alarmingly, "Ames is organizing a war of the races with all its attendant horrors, in our otherwise peaceful state. The time has arrived when the companies that have been organized for protective and defensive purposes should come to the front," while one of the newspapers in Copiah County was not to be outdone: "Much discussion is being had over the militia question; whether the white people shall muster or not. The organization of the militia by Gov. Ames is a great calamity, but as he has decided upon this course, let's meet the issue like men."[50]

Ames directed Caldwell to march from Jackson with a cache of arms and ammunition to Edwards to equip a separate militia unit. Since Caldwell and his troops were on foot, the journey took several days and was closely followed by newspapers—"the scent of blood is in the air. Ames is organizing murder, civil war, rapine, a war of races"—and by George, who worked day and night to convince his white supporters to avoid the bait and let Caldwell march. As the leader of Hinds County Democrats wrote years later, "While on this march, messenger after messenger came to the executive committee at Raymond from companies of white men who had hastily gotten together, asking for permission to attack the negro companies on their way to Edwards. It was all we could do to keep them from doing it."[51]

Democrats began holding huge rallies and parades across the state to counter Ames. The newspaper in Crystal Springs, for example, carried the announcement of a "Grand Democratic Rally" that would begin at a local park and then march through the town.[52]

About the same time in early October that three leading Black leaders— Blanche Bruce, Charles Caldwell, and Secretary of State Jim Hill—distributed a letter to all Black voters statewide urging a Republican vote in November, the Jackson *Weekly Clarion* announced it would go to a daily printing schedule for the remainder of the election.[53]

Realizing that events in Mississippi could soon spiral out of control, Pierrepont dispatched a friend and fellow New York lawyer, George K. Chase, to Mississippi to follow the election, report to him on critical developments, and try to avoid a bloody escalation. Chase arrived in Mississippi in early October and took up residence at the Governor's Mansion. He soon developed a network of "agents" in key counties around the state to report on developments, but, in a critical moment in the campaign, orchestrated one of the most improbable—and consequential—events in the annals of Mississippi campaign history: George and Ames met at the Governor's Mansion. Over time, it came to be known as the "Peace Meeting."[54]

It only took a few days on the ground in Mississippi for Chase to realize that passions among whites and Blacks had the potential to lead to the kind of widespread violence that Grant and Pierrepont surely wanted to avoid. So, after private discussions with a number of parties, he convinced Ames and George to meet in person to determine if an agreement could be reached to avoid bloodshed and ensure a fair election.[55]

Ames mentioned it in an October 12 letter to his wife: "The militia question is agitating the 'White-Liners' very much. . . . The leaders have asked me for an interview, which will take place tomorrow. . . . We began too late to organize and have too little means to accomplish much with the militia. . . . I understand they are willing to promise almost anything if I will cease with my militia movements."[56]

Of the years covered by this historical narrative, there are only three physical places attached to Reconstruction that one can visit today: the Verandah-Curlee House in Corinth where, in May of 1863, the Union Army's Adjutant General, Lorenzo Thomas, stood before hundreds of Black men and announced President Lincoln's new policy of allowing them to serve in the army; the Old State Capitol where the 1868 Constitution was written and where newly enfranchised Black citizens served in the Legislature; and the "West Parlor" room in the Governor's Mansion where the Ames/George meeting took place. Walk through the front door of the Mansion into the foyer, take a left into the parlor, and you are there.

The meeting took place on the morning of Wednesday, October 13, reportedly lasted a couple of hours, and resulted in an agreement between the two principals: Ames would call back the militia and George would commit to a fair election.[57]

Ames knew it was the end. In a letter to his wife two days later, he described how he had disbanded the militia companies, incurred the "indignation" of members of his party, but felt secure that "by and by they will thank me for it." A few days later, he confided to Blanche, "I am inclined to resign the very first day I can do so honorably. It is folly to expect anything but murder and violence till the State becomes Democratic." Ames had given up. George must have sensed it when he wrote, "We have a fair chance to relieve ourselves now. If we let the opportunity pass, another may never come."[58]

On the other hand, the day before, some 800 miles to the north in Ohio, The Republican candidate for governor prevailed in the election, though by a mere 5,544 votes out of 590,090 cast. His name was Rutherford B. Hayes, the future nineteenth president of the United States.[59]

Chase reported that the peace "continued so for several days, then the outrages began again." His agent in Yazoo County reported "that it would be impossible for a Republican to vote there." Responding to marches of Black Republicans in Madison County, the *Yazoo Democrat* editorialized, "Try the rope on such characters. It acts finely on such characters here."

Democrats soon held a parade in downtown Jackson, hitched a cannon up to four mules, and paraded it through Jackson. As they were passing the Governor's Mansion several in the crowd took out their pistols and shot at the mansion. As Chase once wrote, "The marks are in the mansion and can be seen there."

In response to Republican activity in Tallahatchie County, the *Vicksburg Herald* declared, "The Negroes in North Mississippi need a little killing." On Monday before the election, an ad in the Aberdeen newspaper included a pledge signed by 190 prominent businessmen and farmers to discriminate in making labor contracts against those who should vote for the Republican ticket. Similar ads showed up in papers in Lowndes, Chickasaw, and Noxubee Counties. An outspoken Black leader in Clay County was told after a speech by a white Democrat, "I am one of ten that has agreed to hang you if you ever make another such a speech." Another remembered Black farm hands telling him that their white farm owners had declared, "If you colored people vote, if you vote the Republican ticket this time if you do, you will never come from the election."

A parade and rally of several thousand Blacks in Port Gibson were attacked, with whites plowing through the parade with "sticks aiming for the heads of the marchers." At a Republican rally outside of Aberdeen, white Democrats had formed "an artillery company that had recently organized. . . . They had a 24-pound cannon, a caisson, several keys of powder, and several bags of buckshot." In Columbus, buildings in downtown Columbus were set on fire, at least four Blacks were murdered, and many Black families were ordered by armed groups of whites to leave their houses during the night.

In rural Kemper County, a Republican campaigner was followed by fifteen to twenty whites "armed with double-barrel shot-guns, rifles, and one thing or another." A Black leader was warned before a speech that whites "may kill a buck that day." Republicans in Holmes County refused to hold pre-election day meetings due to threats of violent reprisals, while the chair of the county Republican Executive Committee was threatened at the courthouse: "You have been here circulating your lying documents long enough, and you had better go away. . . . It is going to be too hot for you here, and the sooner you go away the better." Democrats in Durant lynched a local Black man a few days before the election. Armed men in Chickasaw County began patrolling the areas where Blacks would gather, warning them not to vote. One of the county's wealthiest planters told anyone who would listen, "We calculated to carry the election. We expected to carry it. It had got to be carried. If men had got to be killed, they had to be killed. We could not submit to this nigger rule any longer."

Cannons were dragged along roads and fired in the vicinity of Republican meetings. Blacks who campaigned for the Republicans had their names listed in "dead books." The *Weekly Clarion* reported on October 27 that 1500 had marched and rallied in Hinds County while over 3000 in Grenada rallied for the Democratic cause. On the Thursday before the Tuesday election, the

Brookhaven Ledger implored, "White men of Mississippi, are you ready for the contest on Tuesday when the question will be decided whether intelligence and honesty or ignorance and corruption shall rule the state? You who have negroes working for you can do more to control their votes than all the public speakers in the state."[60]

A week before the election, Chase informed the attorney general: "I deem it my duty to give you the facts relative to the situation in Mississippi today. It is impossible to have a fair election on November 2nd without the aid of U.S. troops."[61] Like Ames, Chase had given up.

When the congressional committee issued its report in August of 1876, one of its findings focused on the "Peace Meeting" and determined that "the stipulation on the part of the governor was faithfully kept, but the promise made by George was systematically disregarded by the Democrats in the larger portion of the state."[62]

Two prominent Democrats active in the 1875 campaign and authors of an early history of the state agreed: "From that date the Radical ranks were broken, the leaders on the run, and a Democratic victory almost achieved.[63]

THE OUTCOME

For the only statewide position on the ballot, the Democratic candidate for treasurer prevailed with 98,715 votes compared to 67,171 for the Republican. The Republican tally was only 2,699 less than the Ames 1873 vote for Governor while the Democratic count represented an unprecedented 48,225 more votes than the Alcorn 1873 total. In fact, the Republican vote in 1875 would have been sufficient to win any of the previous five contests, including the 1868 "no" vote on the constitution, then the highwater mark for Democratic turnout.[64]

Five of the state's six congressional districts went Democratic, a pick-up of four seats. Only Republican John R. Lynch from Natchez would return to Congress.

But, it was with the legislative races that the final tally loomed large. Of the 115-member House of Representatives, Democrats increased their margin a staggering 150 percent, from 38 seats to 95. The Republicans ended up winning just 20 districts. As for the 37-member Senate, the Democrats' share went from 12 to 27, leaving the Republicans with only 10 seats. Taking into consideration that the four-year Senate terms were staggered and that 12 districts were not even on the ballot, the actual results are even more breathtaking. Of the 25 Senate seats on the ballot, Democrats won 22.[65]

Impeachment and removal from office for Ames, Davis, and Cardozo was a foregone conclusion.

Only by examining the individual county returns can one discern not only the sweep of the victory but also the winning strategy. In the state's thirty-eight majority-white counties, where the legislative seats were already represented by Democrats, the Democratic vote for treasurer was 71 percent, compared to 64 percent two years earlier for governor. While the Democratic turnout was higher in these thirty-eight counties, so was the Republican vote. Since George could assume these counties would safely return Democrats to the Legislature, neither turnout figure was outside the norm.

For Democrats to gain seats in the Legislature, the party had to take them from the thirty-five majority-Black counties. For the 1873 election for governor, those thirty-five counties had produced 56,454 Republican votes and a paltry 24,983 Democratic votes. George would have to drastically alter that imbalance. In the end, that's what he did. When the final county tallies were publicly released, those thirty-five counties had produced 50,081 Republican votes and 56,566 Democratic votes, a stunning 126 percent turnaround for the Democrats.[66]

Given that recorded votes for Republicans were in line with the 1873 totals, despite unprecedented levels of violence, threats, and intimidation, it was the Democratic turnout that was the surprise of the election. Black men generally ignored threats of violence and intimidation and voted, an achievement contrary to the perception left by many accounts of the campaign. In the end, the successful Democratic initiative relied instead on manipulating precinct returns to generate thousands of fraudulent votes for their legislative candidates. What follows is an explanation of how that happened.[67]

THE ANALYSIS

To identify fraudulent Democratic votes, an estimate of white and Black men twenty-one years of age and older, by county, was developed for an analysis of voter turnout for the 1875 election.[68]

For those thirty-five majority-Black counties, the number of eligible white men came to 46,600, nearly 10,000 less than the number of actual Democratic votes. In virtually all of the majority-Black counties where Democrats picked up legislative seats, the Democratic vote exceeded the number of eligible white men, from a high of 289 percent in Clay County and 239 percent in Yazoo County to the more typical of 125 percent in Monroe County, 145 percent in

Panola County, or 116 percent in Claiborne County.[69] By and large, Democrats stole the election by fabricating votes during the balloting on election day or in the counting of the ballots afterward. George and his party officials could manufacture Democratic votes, or "stuff" the ballot boxes, because of the way people voted during this time in the nation's history.

First, there was no state government oversight or control of elections and voting. Those responsibilities were left to each county government. Each county was required by state law to establish an "independent" three-person Board of Registrars. That board was responsible for registering men to vote, staffing the precincts with workers to receive and count the ballots, and reporting the results to state officials. The sheriff appointed one member, as did the circuit judge and the chancery judge.[70] By 1875, Ames and his party had lost the support of many of the Boards of Registrars by the way the judges were originally appointed and re-appointed. When Mississippi emerged from military control, all of the judicial positions were vacant, so Governor Alcorn was given the unprecedented opportunity to fill every position. Those appointments generated the first signs of friction between Ames and Alcorn as they were all white and all friends of Alcorn. They would eventually become the more conservative Alcorn wing of the Republican Party.[71] By 1875, many of those white men, conservative to begin with, were primed to follow Alcorn to the Democratic Party after he lost the 1873 gubernatorial election to Ames.[72]

Second, there was no state or county official printed ballot. Each voter brought his ballot to the polling place. While voters were allowed to even bring handwritten ballots, by the late 1860s and into the 1870s, voters typically used a preprinted ballot that had been produced by either the Democratic Party or the Republican Party. Voters either cut the ballot out of the local newspaper, which had been placed as an advertisement, or made use of sample ballots printed by the local parties, often in different colors, and handed out at the polls. As a result, there were ample opportunities for precinct officials to alter the ballot count by swapping Republican ballots for Democratic ballots or simply adding or "stuffing" Democratic ballots into the boxes, either during the day or at the end of the day.[73]

For those majority-Black counties that elected white Democratic legislators, the extent to which the white judges, sheriffs, and their board members conspired with local white Democratic officials to deliver control of the vote-counting process to the Democrats or whether the Democrats took control through terror or a combination went unexamined by the 1876 Congressional Committee. Moreover, precinct clerks were given two days to deliver the results to the Board of Registrars. The Board would then tabulate the results and mail them to state officials in Jackson. The opportunities for adding and removing ballots, or simply changing the numbers along the way, were too easy and too numerous. In his speech on the Senate floor in favor of the investigation, Senator Blanche Bruce specifically highlighted the role of the registrars: "The evidence in hand and accessible will show . . . that in many parts of the state corrupt and violent influences were brought to bear upon the registrars of voters, thus materially affecting the character of the voting or poll lists; upon the inspectors of election, prejudicially and unfairly thereby changing the number of votes cast."[74]

Given the actual vote totals reported to state officials, the outcome of the election did not hinge on using violence and terror to deter Blacks from voting; the returns indicate they voted, despite the threats and intimidation. The outcome of the election, instead, was largely determined by white Democrats gaining control, either through terror or cooperation with sympathetic Boards of Registrars, of the ballot counting process and manipulating it to generate victories for their legislative candidates. To win, Democrats had to steal the election. The historical evidence gives us two clues to support this conclusion:

First, there would have been no need to inflate and manipulate votes in the majority-Black counties if terrorized Blacks were not showing up at the polls. It is for this very reason that the returns from the majority-white counties were within the estimates of eligible white and Black men. Democrats didn't need to manufacture votes in the majority-white counties because those were already safe seats for legislators of their party. In the majority-Black counties, if Blacks were not turning out in heavily Black precincts, and whites were, then the legitimate white votes, within the range of eligible white males, would have carried the day. But, that is not what happened.

Second, notwithstanding the state law that gave precinct workers two days to deliver the ballot boxes to the Board of Registrars, who then had the statutory responsibility to tabulate the voters for the entire county and mail the results to Jackson, George began receiving telegrams the night of the election from his contacts throughout the state with the actual returns—straight from the precinct to George's campaign headquarters in Jackson. Those telegrams became public when the congressional committee that investigated the Mississippi election used its subpoena power to obtain all of George's telegrams and include them in the printed report. The list consumed forty pages of fine print. At one point in the evening, George telegraphed J. B. Chesman in Brookhaven: "The news is certain. We will carry Hinds, Yazoo, Carroll, Grenada, Panola, Marshall, and Chickasaw. News good from all quarters. How about Lincoln?" By the end of election day, George's hubris got the better of him and he sent a telegram to the newspaper in Memphis: "Reports from all parts of the state indicate a sweeping Democratic victory. We have carried every doubtful county." George knew of the victory because his people were in charge of counting the ballots.[75]

When Julia Kendel wrote the history of Reconstruction in Lafayette County in 1913, she interviewed people still alive from the 1875 election and reported, "One of the chief means of fraud resorted to by the Democrats was the stuffing of ballot boxes. Sometimes the Democratic election officer would have Democratic tickets concealed up his sleeve and would substitute them for Republican tickets. At one election at the College Hill box, the Democrats had 150 majority, though there were only 45 white voters and 200 negroes in that precinct. This was due to the stuffing of the ballot box."[76]

On the other hand, just a few weeks after the election, an irate J. R. Ford, a Democratic official at one of the polling places in Noxubee County, wrote a letter to the editor of the *Macon Beacon* complaining about a scurrilous report circulating in the county that he had voted the Republican ticket. Ford used his letter to explain the misunderstanding that may have occurred over the assistance he provided to Black voters when they were at his precinct. After helping them cast their ballots, and unbeknownst to anyone at the time, after the voters had left, "I always scratched and put the Democratic nominees instead." Ford went on to justify his actions: "I did what I thought was my duty and every other man's duty who had his country at heart."[77]

Nevertheless, given the voter fraud that occurred throughout many of the majority-Black counties, that should not detract from nor minimize the threats and violence that white Democrats deployed to try to influence the election in their favor. The testimony from eyewitnesses revealed myriad ways whites tried to sway Black voting behavior, from threats of actual violence to terminating employment contracts to ending lease agreements on houses.

Yazoo County was a prime example of the use of terror by white Democrats, who by force took control of the courthouse and managed the election unimpeded. The actual result unashamedly reported to officials was 4,044 votes for the Democratic treasurer and seven for the Republican. The county was 26 percent white. The Democratic vote went from 617 in 1873 to the outlandish number of 4,044 just two years later, a turnout that was 239 percent of the eligible white men living in the county. The Republican vote for Ames just two years earlier was 2,409. Yazoo County sent three new Democratic representatives to Jackson, though its one senator remained a Republican because he had been elected in 1873 and thus was not on the ballot in 1875.[78]

Clay County, then known as Colfax County, after Grant's first vice president, set the record for reporting a total number of Democratic votes that exceeded the number of eligible white men: an astounding 289 percent. In 1873, the county produced 179 Democratic votes; two years later, that number had mushroomed to 1,737. The Republican vote declined from 1,556 to 659. The 1880 Census put the white population at 30 percent. Given that a significant number of Blacks were recorded as voting, either the Democratic vote was "adjusted" by switching other Black votes or it was simply inflated with bogus tickets "stuffed" into the ballot boxes. However the local Democrats manipulated the turnout, the county sent a new representative and a new senator to the Legislature, both white Democrats.[79]

Claiborne County was also home to a violent white takeover. A county that was only 24 percent white went from 179 Democratic votes in 1873 to 1,049 in 1875. While the overall turnout in the county was roughly the same, the GOP vote fell from 1,844 to 496. The Democratic vote was 116 percent of the estimate of the white men twenty-one years and older. As a result, a white farmer and a white lawyer, both Democrats, would be representing a majority-Black county in the state House of Representatives. As with Yazoo, Claiborne County's Republican senator was not on the ballot, having won his campaign in 1873.[80]

For the state's thirty-eight majority-white counties, the Democratic turnout exceeded the eligible white male vote in only one county (Newton). On the other hand, for the state's thirty-five majority-Black counties, the Democratic turnout exceeded the eligible number of white men in all but thirteen, and it was in those counties where Republicans won their state legislative seats. More importantly, from the perspective of Black turnout, in the thirty-five majority-Black counties, the Republican turnout in 1875 was 80 percent or higher than the 1873 turnout in all but ten counties. In fifteen counties, Republicans actually increased their vote over 1873 but lost half of them because of the ability of Democrats to inflate their returns beyond the Republican turnout. Republicans in Tallahatchie County, for example, increased their vote from 1873 to 1875 by 119 percent. Democrats, on the other hand, reported a 222 percent increase in their vote, which represented 131 percent of the eligible white male population in the county.[81]

Even if the Republicans had hit their high-water mark of 83,588 from the 1871 statewide election, they still would have lost in 1875. By and large, Black Republicans ignored the threats and voted. Because federal troops were not at the precincts to monitor the counting, Democrats were able to manipulate the results.

In March of the following year, when the Senate was debating the resolution to create the special committee, Senator Blanche Bruce urged his colleagues to support it by honoring his Black constituents who had exercised their right to vote even in the face of terror and intimidation.

> There was nothing in the character of the issues nor in the method of the canvass that would produce such an overwhelming revolution in the sentiments of the colored voters of the State as is implied in this pretended democratic success. The truth of the allegations relative to fraud and violence is strongly suggested by the very success claimed by the [Democrats]. It will not accord with the laws of history to brand the colored people as a race of cowards. On more than a historical field, beginning in 1776 and coming down to this centennial year of the Republic, they have attested in blood their courage as well as a love of liberty. I ask Senators to believe that no consideration of fear or personal danger has kept us quiet and forbearing under the provocations and wrongs that have so sorely tried our souls.[82]

Unfortunately, the committee established by the US Senate to investigate the 1875 election did not pursue fraudulent ballot-counting practices. Nor did the Senators investigate the extent to which the white judges, sheriffs, and their appointed boards of registrars conspired with local white officials to deliver control of the vote-counting process to the Democrats or whether Democrats took control through terror or a combination. The failure to investigate fraud was not by accident.

The preamble to the original legislation creating the committee, as introduced by Indiana Senator Oliver Morton, focused more on ballot fraud than acts of violence. In his floor speech, Morton enumerated the methods used by Democrats to prevail in the election, including "appointment of registrars and officers of the election who would carry out their plan," "false" and "counterfeit" tickets, "ballot-boxes stuffed," and "spurious tickets imposed upon voters." Morton told the Senate, "The result ... was that in several counties more votes were counted than there were ballots cast and the general returns of the elections ... show such an increase in the popular vote as cannot be accounted for by any rational theory of registered voters or actual immigration since the last state election in 1873."

Nevertheless, during the Senate floor debate, Morton accepted an amendment by Michigan Senator Isaac Christiancy to delete "ballot box manipulation" from the congressional inquiry. Morton apparently believed the watered-down resolution was the only one that would pass, though it would change the entire focus of the investigation. Christiancy admitted in his explanation of the amendment that he was sympathetic to southerners, or as he explained, "to make more allowance for their prejudices, their habits, and occasional outbreaks of passion." Consequently, a full contemporaneous accounting of the 1875 election has been lost to history.[83]

In closing, the reader might ask: "If white Democrats could repeat the lesson of 1868 in 1875, why would they not have asserted their power in any of the earlier elections in 1871 or 1873 and ended Reconstruction sooner?" The answer is timing. Before the Ames/Alcorn split, the Mississippi Republican Party enjoyed significant white support. Before the Panic of 1873, and President Grant's response to the Panic, the nation's economy was recovering from the effects of the Civil War, Republicans controlled Congress, and national support for Reconstruction policies in the South had not evaporated. And before 1874, Ames was not governor. He not only failed to build a competitive party organization, he failed to ensure his allies were in charge of key voting precincts. As the official responsible for managing the 1869 elections, he implemented safeguards at the precincts that year to prevent the Democrats from manipulating the vote tallies. Six years later, by neglecting that most basic campaign requirement, Ames all but guaranteed his own impeachment.

When Massachusetts Senator George Boutwell, the chair of the Senate committee charged with investigating the Mississippi election, submitted his report in August of 1876, the two thousand pages of testimony and exhibits demonstrated an election rife with election day violence, voter intimidation, and inexplicable returns. "One of the darkest chapters in American history" is how Boutwell characterized the 1875 election.[84] By then, though, Democrats were in charge of the House of Representatives and even many Senate Republicans were weary of Mississippi. The report was printed, released, ignored, and forgotten.

On Christmas Day, 1875, Charles Caldwell was assassinated, not far from his home in Clinton. Betrayed by someone he knew, lured to an out-of-the-way establishment for a drink, Caldwell was wounded by the shooter's first bullet. Confronted by three white men, all with guns, Caldwell stood up and said defiantly, "Remember when you kill me you kill a gentleman and a brave man. Never say you killed a coward. I want you to remember it when I am gone."[85]

THE REELECTION OF CONGRESSMAN JOHN R. LYNCH

Mississippi's Sixth Congressional District encompassed the southwest corner of the state, anchored by Natchez and Adams County along with the sparsely populated counties along the Gulf Coast and in southeast Mississippi. Republican John R. Lynch was first elected to that seat in 1872, winning with 64 percent of the vote, and was up for reelection in 1875. It was a heavily Black district that included the vote-rich counties of Wilkinson, Amite, Jefferson, Claiborne, and Pike.

Returns for the other five congressional districts, composed of either majority-white counties or Black majority counties under the control of local Democrats, came in relatively quickly after Election Day and showed strong margins of victory for the candidates supported by the Democratic Party. That was not the case with the Sixth District. Lynch's influence in rural majority-Black counties like Wilkinson, Jefferson, Amite, Pike, and, of course, Adams was too strong for Democrats to overcome. The outcome was close and vote counting was slow. The extent to which Democrats could manipulate the final tally in friendly counties was demonstrated by the way Lynch recorded his win in his personal history of the Reconstruction era, *The Facts of Reconstruction*:

> [My] election, it was afterwards developed, was due in all probability to a miscalculation on the part of some of the Democratic managers. Their purpose was to have a solid delegation . . . but in my district the plan miscarried.
>
> In one of the counties, there were two conflicting reports as to what the Democratic majority was. According to one report, it was two hundred and fifty. According to the other, it was five hundred. The report giving two hundred and fifty was no doubt the correct one, but the other no doubt would have been accepted had it been believed at the time to be necessary to insure the election of the Democratic candidate. . . . The election took place on Tuesday, but the count [in Adams County] was not finished until the following Friday evening. Hence the result for members of Congress could not be definitely ascertained until Friday night.
>
> The Democratic managers at the state capital were eager to know as soon as possible what the Republican majority in Adams County would be for the congressman; hence, on Wednesday evening the editor of the local Democratic paper received a telegram from the Secretary of the Democratic State Committee, requesting to be informed, immediately,

John R. Lynch, circa 1870. Courtesy of the Archives and Records Services Division, Mississippi Department of Archives and History.

about what the Republican majority for Congressman would be in Adams County. The editor read the telegram to me and asked what, in my opinion, would be my majority in that county. My reply was that I did not think it would exceed twelve hundred; whereupon he sent in the following report: "Lynch's majority in Adams will not exceed twelve hundred."

Upon receipt of this telegram, the majority of two hundred and fifty instead of five hundred was deemed sufficient from the county heretofore referred to. If the Republican majority in Adams would not exceed twelve hundred, the success of the Democratic congressional candidate by a small but safe majority was assured.

Several days later, when Adams County finally reported its totals, the margin was, surprisingly, much larger: 1,834 votes. Congressman Lynch received 2,626 votes to 792 for his Democratic opponent. Thereby, Lynch won reelection in the district by a mere 231 votes—13,741 to 13,510.[86]

As he remembered some thirty-eight years later, and you know he had to be smiling a little bit when he wrote this entry in his memoir: "The disappointment and chagrin on the part of the Democratic managers can better be imagined than described."[87]

CHAPTER 12

1876–1877
The Loss of Freedom

All the colored men wanted and demanded was a voice in the government under which they lived and to the support of which they contributed.
—JOHN R. LYNCH[1]

The word slavery will, of course, be wiped from the statute book, but the ancient relation can be just as well maintained by cunningly devised laws.
—JAMES McCUNE SMITH[2]

Nine months after his election as governor of Ohio, Rutherford B. Hayes received his party's nomination for president at the June 1876 Republican National Convention in Cincinnati. In addition to Hayes, three other men who have made cameo appearances in this narrative vied for the nomination: James Blaine from Maine, who presided as Speaker of the House of Representatives when L. Q. C. Lamar delivered his Sumner eulogy; Roscoe Conkling from New York, Blanche Bruce's escort to the well of the Senate; and Oliver Morton from Indiana, the author of the resolution to investigate the 1875 election in Mississippi. The Democrats nominated New York Governor Samuel Tilden as their candidate.

By the time the field was set for the 1876 presidential election, white Democrats in Mississippi had consolidated their power at the State Capitol, revised the voter registration laws to make it more difficult for Blacks to cast a ballot, redrawn the congressional district lines to prevent John R. Lynch from gaining reelection, dramatically cut funding for the public school system, and elevated L. Q. C. Lamar to the position of United States senator.

THE 1876 LEGISLATURE AND IMPEACHMENT

The new Legislature convened at noon in Jackson on Tuesday, January 4, 1876, and given that both chambers had white Democrats constituting more than two-thirds of the membership they wasted little time in invoking the provisions of Article IV of the Constitution to initiate impeachment proceedings. By February 17, the House had adopted and sent to the Senate five articles of impeachment against Lieutenant Governor Alexander Davis. On March 9, twelve articles were approved affecting Superintendent of Public Education Thomas Cardozo, and a mere four days later, the House referred twenty-one articles against Governor Ames to the Senate. Since the Constitution authorized impeachment for any "high crime or misdemeanor," the Democrats included virtually any wrong they could remotely argue would qualify as legitimate "high crimes." Moreover, if twenty-one reasons to impeach Ames were insufficient for anyone, the House Democrats added two more on March 25.[3]

By then, Davis had been convicted in the Senate and relieved of his office, Cardozo had resigned rather than face a trial, and a deal was in the works for the House to pull back the impeachment articles if Ames would consent to leave quietly. The agreement was consummated on March 29 when Ames submitted his letter of resignation early that afternoon. By 5:30, legislators were hurriedly gathering in the House chamber to witness John M. Stone, the president pro-tempore of the Senate, and a merchant from the northeast Mississippi county of Tishomingo, take the oath of office as governor. A few minutes later, as recorded in the *House Journal* for that day, "The Speaker of the House then announced and proclaimed that Honorable J. M. Stone, having taken the oath of office, is now the constitutional and legal Governor of the state of Mississippi." Reconstruction was thus given an ignominious burial four months after its death on election day, November 2, 1875.[4]

Not content to rid themselves of Ames, Davis, and Cardozo, Democrats then rushed through legislation that reallocated the counties among the state's six congressional districts in order to create one that was impossible for John Lynch to prevail in his reelection campaign later that year. Lynch's new district included every county along the entire stretch of the Mississippi River, from Tunica to Wilkinson. Only four counties from his old congressional district were included in the new map. The election margin later in November wasn't even close, with the incumbent Lynch garnering only 44 percent of the vote.[5]

With Stone in the governor's office, Democrats in the Legislature could be assured he would approve of a reorganization of the voter registration and

balloting procedures for the state. Sure enough, on April 7, he signed legislation that effectively put the Democrats in charge of appointing new election
officials for all counties. Every county would be assigned a five-member board
appointed by the State Board of Registration. On the state board would sit the
governor, the president pro-tempore of the Senate, and the secretary of state.
The local boards, hand-picked by the Democratic governor and Democratic
Senate leader would, in turn, be responsible for registering all voters, staffing
all of the voting precincts, and counting the ballots. These new procedures
would be in place by the date of the presidential election later that year. Fraud
would now be legal.[6]

Late in the session, after Ames, Davis, Cardozo, and Lynch were history or
soon-to-be history, the white Democrats cut property taxes, imposed substantial reductions in spending for the public education system, and reduced the
size and scope of the court system.[7]

Amidst this public policy debacle, the few Republicans remaining in
the Legislature did avail themselves of an opportunity to poke fun at the
Democrats.

On January 18, Robert Allen, a white planter from Lee County and a newly
elected senator, rose before his colleagues to nominate L. Q. C. Lamar for
the United States Senate seat that would soon be vacated by James Alcorn,
whose term would expire in early March of 1877. Hearing no one else nominated, the clerk closed the nominations and proceeded to call the roll in
alphabetical order. After Allen, being first, announced his vote for Lamar,
the clerk recognized George Albright, a Black farmer from Marshall County
and one of the handful of Republican senators still in the chamber by virtue
of being a member of the class elected in 1873. Albright responded: "I vote
blank." Somewhat flustered, the presiding officer declared the rules required
senators to vote for a named person. So, Albright came back with: "I vote
for Mr. Blank." Other Republicans joined in the fun. By the end of the roll
call, L. Q. C. Lamar had twenty-two votes; Mr. Blank had four votes; and Mr.
L. Q. C. Blank had two votes.

Over in the House, Lamar was approved for the United States Senate when
he received 92 votes, but not before Mr. Blank pulled in 16 votes from the few
Republicans who were lucky to win their election the previous November.[8] So,
the official tabulation sent to Washington from Mississippi, to be read into the
record, showed Mr. L. Q. C. Lamar with 114 votes, Mr. Blank with 20 votes, and
Mr. L. Q. C. Blank with 2 votes.[8]

THE 1876 PRESIDENTIAL ELECTION

A year later, with new election laws on the books, white Democrats showed even less restraint to ensure Mississippi's electoral votes were delivered to Samuel Tilden, the Democratic nominee for president.

In a state where 42 percent of the voting age population was white, the official results furnished Tilden with a winning margin of 68 percent, or 112,173 votes to 52,603 for Republican Rutherford B. Hayes. In a state with 35 majority-Black counties, only half a dozen went for Hayes. Tilden's vote represented 116 percent of the eligible white male population in the state and was nothing less than a demonstration of power and supremacy on the part of the Democrats.[9]

In six of the counties carried by Tilden, his vote totals exceeded by 200 percent the eligible white male population; in three of those counties, all majority-Black, the reported turnout for the Democrat was more than 300 percent. Leflore County, a major cotton-producing county in the Delta region of the state, had an estimated 645 white men twenty-one years or older living in the county in 1876. On election day, Tilden received 1,360 votes from Leflore (in addition to the 698 votes reported for the Republican candidate). Either Blacks who came to the polls and submitted tickets for the Republican had their votes switched during the counting process or Democratic officials simply manufactured the final number, or both.[10]

In the Delta county of Washington, with a 14 percent white population, officials there reported 2,901 votes for Tilden and 1,598 votes for Hayes, or a 64 percent win margin for the Democrat. The Republican vote was virtually the same in 1876 as the 1,638 recorded in 1875. No change there. Instead, the Tilden vote represented 301 percent of the eligible white male population. Given that there was no change in Black turnout, white officials simply fabricated votes for their candidate.

And then there was Yazoo. In 1875, that county reported seven votes for the Republican candidate for treasurer. A year later the election officials, apparently embarrassed at giving the Republican too many votes the previous year, reported two votes for Hayes. The margin in that majority-Black county was 3,672 to 2. Two other majority-Black counties replicated the Yazoo model: Tallahatchie reported one vote for Hayes (1,144 to 1) and Lowndes, which showed a final result of 2,073 for Tilden and 2 votes for the Republican.

And, as was the case in 1875, the United States Senate, still under Republican control, empowered a committee to investigate the election. The final report, released in early 1877, included testimony and exhibits covering more than

1,000 pages. As with the congressional report from the previous year, it was printed, distributed, ignored, and forgotten.[11]

Nationwide, the three Southern states where federal troops were still stationed—Louisiana, Florida, and South Carolina—delivered disputed state returns to the Electoral College. Given that without those three states, neither Tilden nor Hayes could reach a majority of electoral votes, and given that the members of the Electoral College were split down the middle, with half favoring the Democrat and half favoring the Republican, the country found itself in a constitutional crisis. With a presidential inauguration date of March 5, 1877, getting closer and closer on the calendar, and with no one approved to take the oath of office, Congress resolved the matter by creating a special one-time Federal Electoral Commission, composed of members from the House, Senate, and Supreme Court, to investigate the conflicting results from the three Southern states, plus one electoral college vote from Oregon, and determine the winner. Even though Tilden had won the national popular vote by 51 to 48 percent, the commission threw out the results that favored Tilden from the Southern states and, together with the lone Oregon vote, awarded the White House to Hayes.

While the House, which the Democrats continued to control, could have blocked the implementation of the Commission's recommendations, the party leadership chose not to in return for Hayes agreeing to remove all federal troops from the remaining Southern states and, most importantly, allowing white Democrats in all the Southern states to govern their states, unimpeded, without Republican oversight or involvement. It became known as the Compromise of 1877.

While the actual facts surrounding the "Compromise," remain in question among historians to this day, a few weeks after his inauguration, Hayes removed the last of the federal troops from Louisiana and South Carolina. James Z. George applauded the Republican president: "The wise and just constitutional policy of President Hayes in respect to our section, being in exact accordance with the principles of the Democratic Party, completes the restoration of the South to its place in the Union. We are now Americans, with no brand of inferiority upon us." Historian Richard White offered a more accurate view: "Hayes, like Grant before him, appeased his enemies and disappointed his friends. . . . After 1877, federal troops would for the rest of the nineteenth century never be deployed to protect the constitutional rights of black citizens."[12]

Back in Mississippi, Tilden's record number of votes in the state would stand for more than fifty years. Not until 1928, when Mississippi Democrats delivered 124,539 votes for Al Smith against Herbert Hoover, would the 1876 record turnout be eclipsed. Of course, by then, the number of eligible voters had doubled with the passage of the Nineteenth Amendment giving women the right to vote. Not until 1964 would Mississippians give their electoral college votes to a Republican, a span of almost ninety years. Historian Eric Foner summed up the status of Reconstruction following the Hayes inauguration: "Among other things, 1877 marked a decisive retreat from the idea, born in the Civil War, of a powerful national state protecting the fundamental rights of American citizens. Yet the federal government was not rendered impotent in all matters—only those concerning blacks."[13]

THE CONSEQUENTIAL ELECTION

The 1875 election was the state's most consequential election because its effects lasted for ninety years, and then some. Not until the enactment of the federal Civil Rights Act of 1964 and the Voting Rights Act of 1965 were the promises of the Fourteenth and Fifteenth Amendments restored. Not until the resolution of multiple school desegregation lawsuits in 1969 was the promise of an equitable public school system restored. Finally, it would take another ten years for the United States Supreme Court to enforce the Voting Rights Act and restore the promise of full representation in the Legislature for Black voters and still another three years for a federal district court judge to restore the promise of full representation in Congress for Black voters. Only then would Black Mississippians regain many of the freedoms they lost during the intervening ninety-plus years.

The most disturbing aspect of the ninety-year relentless move by white Democrats to undo the freedoms Black Mississippians began to enjoy during the short period of Reconstruction is not that white Mississippians did it, but that the rest of the nation let them do it. Given what we know about the core beliefs of white Mississippi in 1875, it was almost certain they would, over time, begin to enact harsh laws that separated Blacks from whites in schools and universities, public transportation, restaurants, entertainment and sporting venues, and public bathrooms. Many jobs would become off-limits for Blacks, as would most areas of the state for the purchase of a house or land to farm. The most fundamental democratic right—to vote in elections—would be virtually extinguished.

That this happened in Mississippi, while disheartening and tragic, is not surprising. What is demoralizing is that the United States Supreme Court, the

United States Congress, the national media, and people who didn't live in the South let it happen.

The Supreme Court is the greatest embarrassment. Notwithstanding the early decisions of the Court in the 1870s to significantly weaken the application of congressional legislation and the Fourteenth Amendment to discriminatory practices in the South, the 1896 *Plessy v. Ferguson* decision that held racial segregation did not violate the Constitution, the 1898 *Williams v. Mississippi* decision that upheld the provisions of the new Mississippi 1890 Constitution designed to disfranchise Black voters, the 1903 *Giles v. Harris* decision that upheld similar provisions in the Alabama Constitution, and the 1935 *Grovey v. Townsend* decision that allowed Southern states to continue excluding Black voters from primary elections gave Congress the legal standing to do nothing and gave white Southern politicians the legal standing to do whatever they wanted to do.[14]

Consequently, white Democrats spent the better part of the twenty-five years following the impeachment of Ames, Davis, and Cardozo putting in place a brutal system of laws and constitutional provisions that effectively removed Black Mississippians from participation in the affairs of the state. Schools were the first to get the "separate but equal" treatment from the Legislature. Less than three years after the 1875 election, the Legislature prohibited the teaching of "white and colored pupils" in the same schools.[15] Passenger rail cars were the next to be affected. In a bill euphemistically titled "An Act to promote the comfort of passengers on railroad transportation," the Legislature required all trains traveling through the state to provide "equal but separate accommodations for the white and colored races."[16]

Then came the Constitution of 1890. Delegates to the convention that year enacted a variety of provisions such as poll taxes and tests to determine a potential voter's eligibility to register that effectively removed the Black Mississippian from the voting booth. James Z. George, by then a United States senator, having been elected by the Legislature to replace Blanche Bruce, chaired the committee that drafted the sections on the franchise. Never bashful about making clear his position, George told a group the previous year, "Our chief duty when we meet in convention is to devise such measures . . . as will enable us to maintain a home government, under the control of the white people of the state." Unlike the framers of the 1869 Constitution, the 133 white men who wrote the 1890 document refused to submit it to the people for approval. They simply willed it into existence, a move that was affirmed by the Mississippi Supreme Court in 1892. Later that year, in the presidential election, the Republican vote in Mississippi dropped by 95 percent to 1,398, the lowest recorded vote for the Republican nominee among the states for that election.[17]

Nothing changed in Mississippi until 1964 and 1965.

THE AFTERMATH

March 10, 1884, was a day of much fanfare and excitement in Jackson: an old, unrepentant soldier returned to the State Capitol. Before a joint session of the Legislature, assembled in the House chamber, the seventy-six-year-old former president of the Confederate States of America was there to deliver a farewell address. Jefferson Davis was introduced as "Mississippi's most distinguished son."

After thanking everyone and reflecting on his life since his capture and imprisonment at the end of the War, Davis sought to clear the air about his position on their most important cause:

> It has been said that I should apply to the United States for a pardon, but repentance must precede the right of pardon, and I have not repented. Remembering as I must all which has been suffered, all which has been lost, disappointed hopes and crushed aspirations, yet I deliberately say, if it were to do over again, I would again do just as I did in 1861. . . . But never question or teach your children to desecrate the memory of the dead by admitting that their brothers were wrong in the effort to maintain the sovereignty, freedom, and independence that was their inalienable birthright.[18]

Apparently, Davis would willingly sacrifice another 620,000 American lives on behalf of the same cause. He would die five years later unrepentant and unapologetic.

There is in Washington, at the nation's Capital, the National Statuary Hall Collection. Enacted by Congress in 1864, each state Legislature was authorized to choose two individuals who were "illustrious for their historic renown or for distinguished civic or military services such as each State may deem to be worthy of this national commemoration" and to create life-size statues of those individuals. Some of the statues reside in the National Statuary Hall, a large ornate room in the United States Capitol while others are displayed in other areas of the Capitol building.

On June 2, 1931, the entire state's delegation to Congress, plus hundreds of other officials and dignitaries, unveiled the two statutes chosen for this high honor by the Mississippi Legislature: Jefferson Davis and James Z. George.

Pat Harrison, one of Mississippi's United States senators, opened his remarks about Davis: "The mighty figure represented in that beautiful bronze statue is today as much the idol of his people as he was their leader through the tragic days of his eventful career . . . Few men in the history of the Nation rendered more signal service for the country in peace and in war than did Mr. Davis."

Hubert Stephens, the state's other senator, offered accolades for George: "Measured by any standard, he was truly a great man; great in intellect, in character, in influence, in achievement. . . . A vital force pledged to the cause of all that was noble, generous, and good was lost to the people when he died. . . . In 1875, conditions became unbearable. . . . In all his heroic proportions of soul and courage [George] stood forth to save the State."[19]

Today, the state of Mississippi is still represented by the Davis statue in the main Statuary Hall. The George statue is located in the Capitol Visitor Center.

Over the years, the Legislature created new counties to honor William Sharkey, Benjamin Humphreys, James Z. George, Jefferson Davis, John Stone, and L. Q. C. Lamar, while Colfax County, named after Grant's first vice president, was changed to Clay, and Sumner County, notwithstanding Lamar's eulogy, quietly became Webster County.

THE VERDICT

Following the Reconstruction era, and as part and parcel of the move to demote the status of Mississippi's new Black citizens, it became commonplace among historians and politicians to belittle them in their capacities as voters and as elected officials. Claiming Black men were unfit to govern was the excuse white Democrats needed to justify their actions during the election of 1875 and in the enactment of a segregated Mississippi over the ensuing ninety years.

Jackson newspaper editor Ethelbert Barksdale led the chorus to write a new constitution in 1890 when he complained that "Every male person of legal age, resident in the state, including negroes who and were totally ignorant of the responsibilities of citizenship, were authorized to vote for the [1869 Constitution]."[20]

In their late nineteenth-century history of Mississippi, Robert Lowry and William H. McCardle echoed Barksdale in their section on Reconstruction: "In selecting delegates to that [1868 Constitutional] Convention a large number of the most intelligent white citizens in the State were excluded from participation . . . while the negroes, ignorant and unscrupulous, knowing nothing of the responsibility attaching to the elective franchise, were made the docile instruments of an equally ignorant and more corrupt and worthless class of white men than ever cursed a free country."[21]

J. S. McNeily's history of Reconstruction was published in 1916 by the Mississippi Historical Society. He could hardly contain himself in describing the enfranchisement of Black Mississippians: "Several hundred thousand of the negro race, unfitted for political equality with the white race, have been turned loose upon society."[22]

Even as late as 1959, in a Mississippi school textbook, the author offered this closing summary to her young readers in the chapter on Reconstruction: "We have already considered some of the unfortunate features of . . . reconstruction in Mississippi. We have learned that many of the most intelligent citizens were denied any part in the reconstruction program because they had been leaders in the Confederate cause. We have seen the result of the tremendous Negro majority among the voters. These things were bad, for they took the power from the hands of able men and put it in the hands of people who were incompetent and uneducated."[23]

Statements by historians that denigrated the new Black citizens of 1870 only have substantive meaning, and can only be evaluated, when put in context and compared against the record of white Democrats when they were in control of state government. Mississippians were told relentlessly that Reconstruction was an abject failure because the government was managed by Republican "carpetbaggers" and "ignorant" Blacks. Only when the "intelligent white citizens" intervened in 1875, as the line went, was the future of the state preserved.

So, what was the record of white Democrats?

By the time the 1970 Census data had been released, white Democrats had created a state with the lowest per capita income and lowest family median income in the country. On the other hand, Mississippi had the highest number of families living in poverty and the nation's highest infant mortality rate. Its per-pupil spending was the lowest in the country, as were the salaries schools were paying their teachers. Only 8 percent of its population had completed four years of college, and other than South Carolina, no other state had fewer people employed in white-collar occupations. Only 44 percent of the state's housing units had the full complement of indoor plumbing facilities; again, the lowest ranking in the country. Consequently, population growth had declined so substantially relative to the other states that Mississippi had lost three congressional districts by 1970.[24]

Early into the decade of the 1960s, when the political handwriting was on the wall, when the practice of segregation was becoming more and more indefensible for many in the South, white Mississippians nevertheless waged a vicious and unrelenting war against the demands of the Civil Rights Movement. When the Kennedy administration dispatched federal troops to the campus of the University of Mississippi in the fall of 1962, it was an admission that nothing had changed since federal troops were required in the state to ensure a fair election in 1867 and to restore order in Vicksburg in late 1874.

The Black and white Republicans who controlled state and local government in the latter years of Reconstruction certainly could not have done any worse, and, by all accounts, would have done much better.

Historical Memory
The Dunning Era, JFK, and Mississippi Textbooks

As a reader, you know you are in for a wild ride when the title of a formal paper in a prestigious journal of history is "The Dark and Bloody Ground of Reconstruction Historiography."[1]

Historiography is the study of the writing of history, and it is generally accepted among professional historians that the narrative about Reconstruction that was produced by members of their profession in the decades following 1877 and into much of the twentieth century was not only not accurate but was slanted by ideology and prejudice. That was the case made by Bernard Weisberger, the author of the "Dark and Bloody Ground" article. He ended with a plea for a more balanced approach by acknowledging the obvious: "Underlying the problem is the fact that Reconstruction confronts American writers of history with things which they prefer, like other Americans, to ignore—brute power and its manipulation, class conflict, race antagonism."

Writing a few years earlier, Howard Beale posed similar questions in his critique of what had passed for credible histories of Reconstruction: "Is it not time that we studied the history of Reconstruction without first assuming, at least subconsciously, that carpetbaggers and Southern white Republicans were wicked, that Negroes were illiterate incompetents, and that the whole white South owes a debt of gratitude to the restorers of 'white supremacy?'"[2]

What Weisberger and Beale were criticizing was the prevailing historical theme of the Reconstruction era as told by authors associated with what has come to be known as the "Dunning School." While none of these themes persist today among professional historians, nevertheless, much of the information in this volume of the Heritage of Mississippi Series was withheld from white and Black Mississippians, and especially from students, for 100 years following the end of Reconstruction.

WILLIAM A. DUNNING

Born on the New Jersey side of New York City in 1857, William Dunning finished first in his high school class and enrolled in what was then the city's Columbia College, later to become Columbia University. By the time he received his PhD in 1885, Dunning had identified Reconstruction as his subject of choice, writing his dissertation on the influence of the Civil War and Reconstruction on the United States Constitution. As one of his biographers noted, "In the early decades of the twentieth century, William Dunning emerged as the most influential historian of the post–Civil War period." Not only did he write articles and books that set the tone for understanding that period, but Dunning supervised several graduate students who turned their dissertations describing Reconstruction in Southern states into popular books. James W. Garner, who published *Reconstruction in Mississippi* in 1901, was one of Dunning's students.[3]

For Dunning, his students, and the popular authors and other professional historians who relied on Dunning's interpretation of the events following the War, it was the way they diminished the new Black citizens that gave sustenance to the contemporaneous movement by white Democrats all across the South who were enacting legislation to segregate Blacks from whites, to bar Blacks from the voting booth, and to restrict economic opportunities for the region's Black workers.

In 1907, when Dunning, a professional historian working at one of the country's most prestigious universities, published his book on Reconstruction, his justification of the Black Codes would resonate with whites for generations: "In justifying the Black Code legislation adopted by many of the Southern states in the fall of 1865, in its general principle it corresponded very closely to the actual facts of the situation. The freedmen were not, and in the nature of the case could not for generations be, on the same social, moral, and intellectual plane with the whites; and this fact was recognized by constituting them a separate class in the civil order."[4] In the same book, Dunning gave white Democrats in Mississippi the moral defense they needed for their actions in the election of 1875: "The negro had no pride of race and no aspiration or ideals save to be like the whites. With civil rights and political power, not won, but almost forced upon him, he came gradually to understand and crave those more elusive privileges that constitute social equality. . . . But every form and suggestion of social equality was resented and resisted by the whites with the energy of despair. The dread of it justified in their eyes modes of lawlessness which were wholly subversive of civilization."[5]

Forty years later, in 1947, the editors of the respected History of the South series, all professional historians at major universities, published Volume 8 of their series—*The South During Reconstruction, 1865–1877*, by Merton Coulter, a professor of history at the University of Georgia. Not much had changed in the profession to offer a different, or more accurate, perspective. This is from Coulter:

> Negroes were wronged by Reconstruction as much as the whites. . . .
> Policies were dictated not by what the Negroes were but by what the
> conquerors thought they ought to be. Slavery had not been an unmixed
> evil for the Negroes; it had brought them from barbarism and sometimes
> slavery in Africa to America and subjected them to the white man's civi-
> lization, the product of a thousand years of freedom.
>
>   Nor did the whites come out of the war with resentment and ill will
> toward the Negroes. They knew that Negroes had not won their free-
> dom, that they had not conspicuously asked for it, and that some had
> actually not wanted it.[6]

While it is easy to read "slavery had not been an unmixed evil" or "some had actually not wanted it" and think that this was just some crackpot, this viewpoint was given credence by professional historians and thus generally accepted by the public at large for decades.

By far the best-selling book to appear during the time was *The Tragic Era* by Charles G. Bowers. First published in 1929, it took all the Dunning School had written, exaggerated it, and turned the decade of Reconstruction into a fast-paced narrative of rescue from Republican ruin by white Democrats that captured the popular imagination. What follows are two selections to give you a flavor of the book: "We must have the background of the wreckage wrought by the alien rule of Governor Adelbert Ames. Whatever may have been the intent of this deadly dull army officer, he lacked the courage or capacity to cope with the criminals around him. His own election had drawn the color line; the blacks were more powerful than ever and more exacting with the car-petbaggers. They controlled the Legislature, one of the most grotesque bodies that ever assembled." And if white Democrats needed political cover for what their political ancestors did in the 1875 election strategy, Bowers provided it to them: "Thus was notice served on Mississippi that negroes would rule the State, and the worst element immediately demonstrated its ability to domi-nate the flabby Ames. The darkest days of Mississippi had dawned, and soon, to be driven to desperate resolves, we shall find her people in a revolutionary mood making stern preparations for the elections of the next year."[7] I could go on for pages, citing more examples from Dunning, Bowers, and Coulter, plus many other historians who set the tone for the public's understanding of Reconstruction for much of the twentieth century.

The most insidious aspect of their approach, however, was to follow in the footsteps of L. Q. C. Lamar and separate Black men and women from the life of the state and the task of rebuilding, to treat them as a problem rather than as an equal partner. When Dunning wrote, "If the problem of adjusting the blacks to a useful place and function in the Southern economy was the first that demanded a solution, the problem of civil government in each state was not far behind in importance," he was relegating the Black population to the same status as the flooding of the Mississippi River, the absence of railroads, or pests in the cotton fields.[8]

Coulter reinforced the view that the new Black citizens were incapable of independent action or thought and were, instead, one of many "problems" to be addressed by the white leaders: "The Negro as a slave had been property; he had no rights, civil or political. The mere act of setting him free still left him without these rights; he was still not a citizen. It was a problem of the first importance to nurse him into the responsibilities of a free citizenship among a population which had always been free."[9]

Coulter wrote his history of Reconstruction some seventy-three years after Lamar's eulogy of Sumner, but the echoes of that deceptive and cynical address on the floor of the House of Representatives showed up in Coulter's writing. Lamar had been successful in making the reunion of the North and South about the reunion of white people: "The surrender was a term early used by Southerners to mark the end of their efforts to set up a new nation. . . . Southerners were of the same race and language as the rest of the United States, and they had a common heritage. They were now ready to resume their position in the old government, and it is a remarkable fact that not one Southerner thereafter took up arms against the United States."[10] "Of the same race and language"—Lamar would have been pleased. It was irrelevant that those same Southerners had, in fact, "took up arms" against the Black population.

There are a variety of ways to demonstrate the breadth and depth of the influence of these writers, but one popular example is the publication of John F. Kennedy's *Profiles in Courage*. In the 1955 book, Kennedy selected individuals in public life to "profile" because of their "political courage in the face of constituent pressures." Chapter 7 was consumed with L. Q. C. Lamar and his Sumner eulogy. Notwithstanding that Kennedy, and his ghostwriter and future presidential speechwriter Ted Sorenson, missed—or ignored—the nuances of Lamar's speech and mistakenly took his alleged sincerity for the real thing, in providing a Mississippi context for the time of Lamar's eulogy, Kennedy parroted Dunning and Bowers: "No state suffered more from carpetbag rule than Mississippi. Adelbert Ames, first Senator and then Governor, was a native of Maine. . . . He was chosen Governor by a majority composed of freed slaves and radical Republicans, sustained and nourished by Federal bayonets."[11] Of course, there were no "Federal bayonets" while the deteriorating price of cotton and the Panic of 1873 were the principal causes of the "suffering." In his short list of "Additional References" for the chapter on Lamar, Kennedy included *The Tragic Era* by Charles G. Bowers.

MISSISSIPPI MEMORY

The life stories of Blacks and whites responding to the new social and economic order, as documented in the archives of the Freedmen's Bureau and in other contemporaneous accounts, stand in sharp contrast to the record created by whites in the decades after Reconstruction. The history of the ten years following the Civil War was willfully distorted by whites who owned the newspapers and by whites who wrote the textbooks and journal articles depicting Reconstruction in Mississippi. To compare the daily struggles of Blacks and whites as recounted in the Freedmen Bureau's documents with the editorials and the later articles and books of history is to bear witness to two different worlds—one real and one made up.[12]

James Garner, a Dunning graduate student, wrote the first book-length history of Reconstruction in Mississippi in 1901 and offered this observation about the work habits of Blacks: "The failure, however, was not due solely to unfavorable seasons, but in great measure to the unreliable character of negro labor. Even now, the negro is not a model of industry, frugality, and foresight. He was much farther from it in 1866. His undertakings nearly always resulted in failure. He was peculiarly unfitted to the cultivation of the cotton crop, which requires careful attention to the greater part of the entire year."[13] The creation of the Mississippi Department of Archives and History in 1902 and the work of its first director, Dunbar Rowland, was focused, in part, on preserving this specific point of view about Reconstruction and the need to defend the segregation culture that followed. As one historian remarked, "Neither the Mississippi Legislature that created the Department of Archives and History during the early years of segregation, nor Rowland who directly led it, was interested in the participation of the whole Mississippi population in the understanding of history."[14]

Rowland went beyond the Dunning School authors and simply fabricated "facts" to fit his ideological point of view, as in this description of Ku Klux Klan activities during Reconstruction:

> Undoubtedly, the Ku Klux Klan did summarily put a curb upon acts committed by ignorant and arrogant white and black Republicans which were unbearable to the pride and traditions of Southern whites, but neither that organization nor the real leaders of the South deliberately planned to set race against race; that was the scheme of radical Republicans in the North and political adventurers in the South. The special cause of the disorders of 1871, as they appeared in Mississippi, was not due to any campaign on the part of any Southern organization or combination to keep from the freedmen their right to legal protection.[15]

Or, in this case, when Rowland put his official stamp of approval on the outcome of the 1875 election: "Under stress of violent excitement, there were undoubtedly cases of intimidation both by Democrats and Republicans; but it was nearer the standard of a fair election than the State had witnessed for six years."[16]

The influence of Rowland and others was felt deep into the twentieth century. The way their version of history affected the outlook of white Mississippians, especially during the Civil Rights era, was once described by historian Charles Reagan Wilson: "Reconstruction thus became synonymous in the southern white memory with the assertion of African American rights. It also become synonymous with the idea of outside intervention, of northerners and the federal government trying to change southern civilization."[17]

SCHOOL TEXTBOOKS

While Dunning, Bowers, Coulter, Rowland, and others like them were read by adults, their themes and distortions of the facts easily made their way into the textbooks provided to generations of Mississippi school children, both Black and white.

As late as 1964, the pivotal year of the Civil Rights Movement, the Mississippi History textbook by John K. Bettersworth used in public schools opened the chapter on Reconstruction with this preface: "The war was over, but the fighting was not; reconstruction was a worse battle than the war had ever been. Slavery was gone, but the problem of the free former slaves was not. . . . The struggle of the state to free itself in the war was hardly more difficult than the struggle to free itself during Reconstruction. Yet, by 1875, the old political order had returned, and white and black people set about the task of getting along together in the 'New South' as they had in the 'Old.'" The worst was: "getting along together in the New South as they had in the Old." One could write an entire book picking apart the author's description of Reconstruction, but the author's bias becomes clear in the section where the Freedmen's Bureau is introduced: "The bureau provided for Negro education and medical care, and it also took steps to provide ways by which the freed Negroes could support themselves." He then followed with the putdown: "Some of the Negroes even thought it was a magical piece of furniture."

After the author introduced the topic of military occupation of the state, he sought compassion for people who looked like him: "The fortunes of Mississippi white men were at their lowest level." In describing the outcome of the 1875 election, the author neglected to include the reaction of a majority of the state: "Election day, November 3 [sic], passed with only minor disturbances, except to Carpetbag morale."[18]

The 1959 textbook ended the section on Reconstruction with, "After 1875, the old bitterness began to wane. Mississippi was back under the control of the white people, the Redeemers."[19] For the teacher's guide that accompanied the textbook, the author gave a series of "topics for discussion" under the chapter on Reconstruction. Among them were the ever-present, "Explain the problems of dealing with the freedmen after the war ended," and "Describe the extravagance and waste of the Reconstruction governments."[20]

Going back even further, the *Teacher's Handbook of Mississippi History* that Franklin L. Riley wrote in 1910 included this ominous "thought question"— "Would you have voted for the abolition of slavery if you had been in the Convention of 1865?" Leaving his students with the impression that a negative answer would have been acceptable, Riley then instructed them to "Give reasons for answer."[21]

The ninety years that followed the election of 1875 were defined by not only the actual practice of Jim Crow, but also by the use of ideology and propaganda by state politicians, education officials, and professional historians. Given a span of time as long as ninety years, the school textbooks and popular history books that relentlessly imparted a fictionalized account of the lives of Black Mississippians wielded an enormous influence on the political, economic, and social life of the state. Examining the way textbooks were used to sustain the white supremacy ideology by Mississippi politicians for an article in the *Journal of Mississippi History*, Rebecca Miller Davis concluded, "This warped view of history had a profound psychological impact on all students, black and white."[22]

Even as late as the 1975, the Bettersworth textbook continued to perpetuate the myth that the new Black citizens were both a "problem" to be resolved and were incapable of independent thought or independent action, that someone had to do that for them. This passage is taken from the section on Reconstruction: "The problem of what to do with the former slaves, or freed blacks, was critical. . . . The blacks had to adjust to a whole new way of life. Then some visitors arrived—Carpetbaggers. They were Northerners—some good and some bad—who came in to lead the free blacks. Finally, in 1875, the Southern whites, or Redeemers, regained control."[23]

In 2014, historian James W. Loewen wrote a fascinating piece for the online History News Network in which he described in some detail the influence of the author of many of these public school history textbooks, John K. Bettersworth. At one point in his career, Loewen was a professor at Tougaloo College, a historically Black private college in Jackson, Mississippi. What follows is his encounter with first-year students in January 1969:

> I asked them, "What was Reconstruction? What images come to your mind about that era?" Sixteen of my seventeen students told me, "Reconstruction was that time, right after the Civil War, when African Americans took over the governing of the Southern states, including Mississippi, but they were too soon out of slavery, so they messed up, and reigned corruptly, and whites had to take back control." That was straight Bettersworth.[24]

The tragedy is not that white politicians told lies about Reconstruction—that Black men, women, and children had failed to meet the demands of freedom; that Republicans, both Black and white, had failed at governing; and that white Democrats were justified in using fraud and violence to regain control of state governments. This you would expect from the politicians of the day. The tragedy is that those lies were affirmed by professional historians and incorporated into textbooks by professional educators that informed the thinking of generations of students.

Notes

PREFACE AND ACKNOWLEDGMENTS

1. William C. Harris, *Presidential Reconstruction in Mississippi* (Baton Rouge: Louisiana State University Press, 1967) and William C. Harris, *The Day of the Carpetbagger: Republican Reconstruction in Mississippi* (Baton Rouge: Louisiana State University Press, 1979). Harris is professor emeritus of history at North Carolina State University.

2. In the last ten years alone, since I began work on this volume, five comprehensive accounts of Reconstruction have been published, each of which seeks to provide a fresh examination of this time in our nation's history. Three of the books even have the same subtitle, "A New History of Reconstruction." Allen C. Guelzo, *Fateful Lightning: A New History of the Civil War and Reconstruction* (New York: Oxford University Press, 2012); Douglas R. Egerton, *The Wars of Reconstruction: The Brief, Violent History of America's Most Progressive Era* (New York: Bloomsbury, 2014); Mark Wahlgren Summers, *The Ordeal of the Reunion: A New History of Reconstruction* (Chapel Hill: University of North Carolina Press, 2014); John Patrick Daly, *The War After the War: A New History of Reconstruction* (Athens: University of Georgia Press, 2022); and Manisha Sinha, *The Rise and Fall of the Second American Republic: Reconstruction, 1860–1920* (New York: Liveright, 2024).

3. The six volumes in the series *Freedom: A Documentary History of Emancipation, 1861–1867*, published between 1982 and 2013, are included in the Bibliography. The first three were published by Cambridge University Press while the University of North Carolina press released the last three. The quote appears at the beginning of the Introduction to each of the volumes in the series.

4. DeeDee Baldwin, Against All Odds: The First Black Legislators in Mississippi, https:// much-ado.net/legislators/; Eric Foner, *Freedom's Lawmakers: A Directory of Black Officeholders During Reconstruction*, rev. ed. (1993; repr., Baton Rouge: Louisiana State University Press, 1996).

INTRODUCTION

1. Stephanie McCurry, *Confederate Reckoning: Power and Politics in the Civil War South* (Cambridge, MA: Harvard University Press, 2010), 1.

2. Leon F. Litwack, *Been in the Storm So Long: The Aftermath of Slavery* (New York: Alfred A. Knopf, 1979), xii.

3. The white and enslaved numbers come from the 1860 Census. As for "free" Blacks, the 1860 Census could identify only 773 in Mississippi, with a third of them residing in Adams County and another fourth living in the three Gulf Coast counties. Obviously the numbers were different five years later at the end of the war, though, given the nature of

the disruption and the near total absence of civilian government, I doubt accurate numbers would be knowable.

4. Erik Mathisen, *The Loyal Republic: Traitors, Slaves, and the Remaking of Citizenship in Civil War America* (Chapel Hill: University of North Carolina Press, 2018), 7.

5. *Congressional Globe*, March 31, 1876 (44th Cong., 1st Sess., Vol. 4, Pt. 3), 2103.

6. See, for example: Eric Foner, *The Second Founding: How the Civil War and Reconstruction Remade the Constitution* (New York: W. W. Norton, 2019), xxi–xxv.

7. Robert Lowry and William H. McCardle, *A History of Mississippi* (Jackson, MS: R. H. Henry, 1891), 373.

8. E. Merton Coulter, *The South During Reconstruction, 1865–1877* (Baton Rouge: Louisiana State University Press, 1947), 47–48.

9. John K. Bettersworth, *Mississippi: Yesterday and Today* (Austin: Steck-Vaughn, 1964), 222 –38.

CHAPTER 1. 1862–1864: THE BEGINNING OF FREEDOM

1. Brooks D. Simpson, *Let Us Have Peace: Ulysses S. Grant and the Politics of War and Reconstruction, 1861–1868* (Chapel Hill: University of North Carolina Press, 1991), 27.

2. Philip S. Foner, ed., *The Life and Writings of Frederick Douglass*, vol. 3 (1950), 13, 94.

3. This chapter is primarily focused on the transition of Blacks from slavery to freedom that took place in the years during the Civil War. For those readers interested in other aspects of life in the state during the war, see Timothy B. Smith, *Mississippi in the Civil War: The Home Front* (Jackson: University Press of Mississippi, 2010); Jarret Ruminski, *The Limits of Loyalty: Ordinary People in Civil War Mississippi* (Jackson: University Press of Mississippi, 2017); Noralee Frankel, *Freedom's Women: Black Women and Families in Civil War Era Mississippi* (Bloomington: Indiana University Press, 1999); and James L. Roark, *Masters Without Slaves: Southern Planters in the Civil War and Reconstruction* (New York: W. W. Norton, 1977), esp. ch. 2.

4. Keith S. Hebert, *Cornerstone of the Confederacy: Alexander Stephens and the Speech That Defined the Lost Cause* (Knoxville: University of Tennessee Press, 2021), 223.

5. Bell Irvin Wiley, *Southern Negroes, 1861–1865*, 2d ed. (1938; repr., New Haven, CT: Yale University Press, 1965), 18. (C. Vann Woodward wrote in a foreword to the new edition that "the first myth to fall before Wiley's scrutiny was one of the South's most beloved and celebrated—the myth of the loyal slave, faithfully laboring in support of the Confederate master. The evidence destroys the legend of the Negro's indifference to freedom."); see also David M. Oshinsky, *Worse than Slavery: Parchman Farm and the Ordeal of Jim Crow Justice* (New York: Simon & Schuster, 1996), 19–20; Roark, *Masters Without Slaves*, 70–73, 80–82; Smith, *Mississippi: The Home Front*, 147; Litwack, *Been in the Storm So Long*, 14–17, 59.

6. John Cimprich, *Navigating Liberty: Black Refugees and Antislavery Reformers in the Civil War South* (Baton Rouge: Louisiana State University Press, 2023), 1–6; Edward L. Pierce, "The Contrabands at Fortress Monroe," *Atlantic Monthly* (November 1861); Michael Perman, *Emancipation and Reconstruction*, 2d ed. (Wheeling, IL: Harlan Davidson, 2003), 6–7; Steven Hahn, *A Nation Under Our Feet*, 68–70; Ira Berlin et al., eds., *Freedom: A Documentary History of Emancipation, 1861–1867*, 1st ser., vol. 1, *The Destruction of Slavery* (Cambridge: Cambridge University Press, 1985), 14–18; Dale Kretz, *Administering Freedom: The State of Emancipation After the Freedmen's Bureau* (Chapel Hill: University of North Carolina Press, 2022), 15–19; and James M. McPherson, *Battle Cry of Freedom: The Civil War Era* (New York: Oxford University Press, 1988), 354–56.

7. Eric Foner, *The Fiery Trial: Abraham Lincoln and American Slavery* (New York: W.W. Norton, 2010), 220; Gregory P. Downs, "The Southern Nations, 1860–1880," in W. Fitzhugh Brundage, ed., *A New History of the American South* (Chapel Hill: University of North Carolina

Press, 2023), 263–65; Timothy B. Smith, *Corinth 1862: Siege, Battle, Occupation* (Lawrence: University Press of Kansas, 2012), 288–90; Simpson, *Let Us Have Peace*, 30; Wiley, *Southern Negroes*, 176; Berlin et al., *Destruction of Slavery*, 249.

8. "An Act to Confiscate Property used for Insurrectionary Purposes" (First Confiscation Act) adopted on August 6, 1861, at *Statutes at Large, Treaties, and Proclamations of the United States of America*, vol.12 (Boston: Little, Brown, 1863), 319; "An Act to Make an Additional Article of War" (Prohibiting the Return of the Slaves) adopted on March 13, 1862, at *US Statutes at Large*, 354; see also Perman, *Emancipation and Reconstruction*, 7; Hahn, *A Nation Under Our Feet*, 71–73; Foner, *Reconstruction*, 5–8; for coverage of the time from Butler's decision in Virginia to the spring of 1862, including the activities in Congress as well as on the ground in the fields of battle, see Berlin et al., *Destruction of Slavery*, 16–26 and David P. Currie, "The Civil War Congress," *University of Chicago Law Review* 73 (Fall 2006).

9. According to the 1860 Census, there were 22,436 "slaves" in the four counties (Tishomingo, Tippah, Itawamba, and Pontotoc) that made up the northeast corner of Mississippi. The other four counties of that area of the state, Alcorn, Lee, Prentiss, and Union, were created after the War. Corinth was not on the list of municipalities the Census provided population data for in 1860, being too small and too young. Alcorn County, of which Corinth became the county seat, was not created until 1870. At the time, Corinth was in Tishomingo County, which had an 1860 population of 19,159 whites, 9 free Blacks, and 4,981 slaves. Of the 3,209 families recorded in the county by the 1860 Census, 707 were slaveholders.

10. McPherson, *Battle Cry of Freedom*, 416–17; Smith, *Corinth 1862*, xi–xii, 6–8; the large maps, narrative, and supporting documentation at the Civil War Interpretive Center in Corinth make this point very clear; north-south and east-west trains still run through the center of the town, and there is a depot and small museum where the old depot was located.

11. For information about the siege and battle of Corinth see Michael B. Ballard, *The Civil War in Mississippi: Major Campaigns and Battles* (Jackson: University Press of Mississippi, 2011) and Smith, *Corinth 1862*.

12. Simpson, *Let Us Have Peace*, 27–29; Berlin et al., *Destruction of Slavery*, 291. "An Act to Suppress Insurrection, to Punish Treason and Rebellion, to Seize and Confiscate the Property of Rebels, and for Other Purposes" (Second Confiscation Act), adopted July 17, 1862, *US Statutes at Large*, 589.

13. Cam Walker, "Corinth: The Story of a Contraband Camp," *Civil War History* (March 20, 1974), 6–7; "Letter of Chaplain J. B. Rogers to the Secretary of War," dated September 19, 1862, in Berlin et al., *The Lower South*, 667–70.

14. Simpson, *Let Us Have Peace*, 29–30; Berlin et al., *Destruction of Slavery*, 252.

15. "First Inaugural Address," *A Compilation of the Messages and Papers of the Presidents, 1789–1897*, vol. 6 (Washington: Government Printing Office, 1897), 5.

16. The proposed proclamation, dated September 22, 1862, is found at *US Statutes at Large*, 1267; Allen C. Guelzo, *Lincoln's Emancipation Proclamation: The End of Slavery in America* (New York: Simon & Schuster, 2004), 117–24; Foner, *The Fiery Trial*, 240–47; Ira Berlin et al., eds., *Freedom: A Documentary History of Emancipation, 1861–1867*, 1st ser., vol. 3, *The Wartime Genesis of Free Labor: The Lower South* (Cambridge: Cambridge University Press, 1990), 630; McPherson, *Battle Cry of Freedom*, 557–59.

17. Perman, *Emancipation and Reconstruction*, 12–13; Egerton, *Wars of Reconstruction*, 32–34; Foner, *Reconstruction*, 4; Currie, "Civil War Congress," 1147–52; examples of the shift towards the abolitionist point of view include the congressional end of slavery in the District of Columbia on April 16, 1862, and the congressional end of slavery in the territories on June 19, 1862 (*US Statutes at Large*, 376, 432); for a discussion and explanation of the legal issues surrounding the issuance of the Emancipation Proclamation, see Currie, "The Civil War Congress," 1157–63.

18. Ballard, *Mississippi in the Civil War*, 103.

19. Simpson, *Let Us Have Peace*, 30; John Eaton, *Grant, Lincoln and the Freedmen: Reminiscences of the Civil War* (New York: Longmans, Green, 1907), 2–3.

20. "Order by the Commander of the Department of Tennessee and 13th Army Corps," dated November 14, 1862, in Berlin et al., *The Lower South*, 670–71; Eaton, *Grant, Lincoln and the Freedmen*, 11–13; U. S. Grant, *Personal Memoirs*, vol. 1 (New York: Charles L. Webster, 1885), 425.

21. Ballard, *Mississippi in the Civil War*, 106–9.

22. See footnote accompanying Grant's November 15, 1862, letter to Halleck in John Y. Simon, ed., *The Papers of Ulysses S. Grant*, vol. 6, 315–17; Eaton, *Grant, Lincoln and the Freedmen*, 26–28; Walker, "Corinth: The Story," 7. John C. Rodrigue, *Freedom's Crescent: The Civil War and the Destruction of Slavery in the Lower Mississippi Valley* (New York: Cambridge University Press, 2023), 94–95.

23. "Governor's Message," *House Journal* (December Session of 1862), 9–13.

24. *House Journal* (December Session of 1862), 39; Ballard, *Mississippi in the Civil War*, 118; William J. Cooper Jr., *Jefferson Davis, American* (New York: Alfred A. Knopf, 2000), 418–19; Ruminski, *The Limits of Loyalty*, 3.

25. The Emancipation Proclamation, dated January 1, 1863, is at *US Statutes at Large*, 1268; Joseph P. Reidy, *Illusions of Emancipation: The Pursuit of Freedom and Equality in the Twilight of Slavery* (Chapel Hill: University of North Carolina Press, 2019), 28–33; Foner, *Reconstruction*, 1–2; and Perman, *Emancipation and Reconstruction*, 15.

26. Berlin et al., *The Lower South*, 647.

27. Berlin et al., *The Lower South*, 626; for example, "General Superintendent of Contrabands in the Department of Tennessee to the Headquarters of the Department," dated April 29, 1863, at 684–98; see "Commander of an Iowa Regiment to the HQ of the Department of the Tennessee," dated March 26, 1863, in Berlin et al., *Destruction of Slavery*, as an example of contrabands and the wartime intelligence they provided to the Union; Eaton, *Grant, Lincoln and the Freedmen*, 20–23; Walker, "Corinth: The Story," 8–12; Joseph E. Brent, "Occupied Corinth: The Contraband Camp and the First Alabama Regiment of African Descent, 1862–1864," Paper Prepared for the City of Corinth, Mississippi and The Siege and Battle of Corinth Commission, (February 1995), 9–11; Smith, *Corinth 1862*, 289–93.

28. Walker, "Corinth: The Story," 7–11; Thomas W. Knox, *Camp-Fire and Cotton-Field: A "New York Herald" Correspondent's View of the American Civil War* (1865; repr., London: Leonaur, 2008), 145–47; McPherson, *Battle Cry of Freedom*, 496–97; see "Testimony by a Mississippi Freedman before the Southern Claims Commission," dated August 17, 1863, and "Testimony by a Mississippi Freedman before the Southern Claims Commission," dated February 23, 1878, both in Berlin et al., *The Lower South*, at 722, for examples of Union soldiers stealing from former slaves; for examples of derogatory comments made by Union soldiers about the contrabands, see Paul S. Pardue, "In Search of the 1st Regiment of African Descent and the Contraband Camp of Corinth, Mississippi" (Corinth, MS: Corinth Civil War Interpretative Center Archives, September 2000), 10–12; for an example of the failure of the Union Army to timely pay the contrabands, see James E. Yeatman, *A Report on the Condition of the Freedmen of the Mississippi, Presented to the Western Sanitary Commission, December 17, 1863* (Saint Louis: Western Sanitary Commission Rooms, 1864), 4; Michael Wayne, *The Reshaping of Plantation Society: The Natchez District, 1860–1880* (Baton Rouge: Louisiana State University Press, 1983), 39. The Natchez story, from the journal of Annie E. Harper, at the Mississippi Department of Archives and History, and the Vicksburg story, from a letter from John Eaton to Levi Coffin, at the National Archives, are both referenced in William Leon Woods, "The Travail of Freedom: Mississippi Blacks, 1862–1870" (PhD Dissertation, Princeton University, 1979), 7–9; the letter from the Union soldier, Enoch Baker, to his wife is in the manuscript collection of the Historical Society of Pennsylvania in Woods, "The Travail of Freedom," at 18–19; David Slay, "Abraham

Lincoln and the United States Colored Troops of Mississippi," *Journal of Mississippi History* 70 (Spring 2008), 77. See also Chandra Manning, *Troubled Refuge: Struggling for Freedom in the Civil War* (New York: Alfred A. Knopf, 2016), 114–18.

29. Eaton, *Grant, Lincoln, and the Freedmen*, 22, 33–34, 105. For the popularly held belief about slavery, see Nancy D. Bercaw, *Gendered Freedoms: Race, Rights, and the Politics of Household in the Delta, 1861–1875* (Gainesville: University of Florida Press, 2004), 26. For more on Eaton's attitudes towards the newly freed slaves, see Simpson, *Let Us Have Peace*, 32.

30. Eaton, *Grant, Lincoln, and the Freedmen*, 207.

31. Walker, "Corinth: The Story," 9; Eaton's quotation is from his answer to Interrogatory 20 contained in his report to the Headquarters of the Department of Tennessee in Berlin et al., *The Lower South*, at 696; Smith, *Corinth 1862*, 291–92; Slay, "Abraham Lincoln," 68–70; and Reidy, *Illusions of Emancipation*, 73.

32. Foner, *Reconstruction*, 8; Walker, "Corinth: The Story," 9, 15; Ballard, *Mississippi in the Civil War*, 275; the higher figure comes from Bercaw, *Gendered Freedoms*, at 14 where she writes: "More than twenty thousand black men qualified to serve in the United States military in the Delta"; Berlin et al., *The Lower South*, 684–706; see esp. Eaton's May 18, 1863, letter to the corresponding secretary of the American Missionary Association at 703; Brian T. Corrigan, "Contraband Camps: The Cultural and Political Meeting Grounds of the Civil War" (Master's Thesis, Boston College, 2005), 57; Gaines M. Foster, "The Limitations of Federal Health Care for Freedmen, 1862–1868," *Journal of Southern History* 48 (August 1982), 351–52; Ira Berlin, Joseph P. Reidy, and Leslie S. Rowland, *Freedom: A Documentary History of Emancipation, 1861–1867*, 2d ser., *The Black Military Experience* (Cambridge: Cambridge University Press, 1982), 520; and Smith, *Corinth 1862*, 292–93.

33. Walker, "Corinth: The Story," 12–13; John Polk Thompson, "The American Missionary Association in Mississippi, 1865–1877" (Master's Thesis, Mississippi State University, 1978), 25–28; Joe M. Richardson, *Christian Reconstruction: The American Missionary Association and Southern Blacks, 1861–1890* (Tuscaloosa: University of Alabama Press, 1986), 25–53; James T. Currie, *Enclave: Vicksburg and Her Plantations, 1863–1870* (Jackson: University Press of Mississippi, 1980), 40–42.

34. These data were taken from the 1860 Census. The north-south railroad running through the middle of the state was used to divide the eastern counties from the western counties. According to the 1860 Census, there were 316 slaveholders in Mississippi who owned more than 100 slaves. Of that number, 259 were in the western counties, or 82 percent.

35. Wiley, *Southern Negroes*, 38; Cimprich, *Navigating Liberty*, 60–62; Smith, *Mississippi: The Home Front*, 146–57; Foner, *Reconstruction*, 3, 47; Ballard, *Mississippi in the Civil War*, 149; Donald L. Miller, *Vicksburg: Grant's Campaign That Broke the Confederacy* (New York: Simon & Schuster, 2019), 207–11; Timothy B. Smith, *The Siege of Vicksburg: Climax of the Campaign to Open the Mississippi River, May 23–July 4, 1863* (Lawrence: University Press of Kansas, 2021), 20–23; see also "General Superintendent of Contrabands in the Department of Tennessee to the Headquarters of the Department" in Berlin et al., *The Lower South*, 677–98; Justin Behrend, *Reconstructing Democracy: Grassroots Black Politics in the Deep South After the Civil War* (Athens: University of Georgia Press, 2017), 52–54; Litwack, *Been in the Storm So Long*, 28; Currie, *Enclave*, xxii, 46–49; and Bercaw, *Gendered Freedoms*, 19.

36. Berlin et al., *Destruction of Slavery*, 259–62; Berlin et al., *The Lower South*, 621–22; Smith, *Mississippi: The Home Front*, 40–41.

37. "Affidavit of a Mississippi Former Slaveholder, and Affidavits of Two of His Former Slaves," Berlin et al., *The Lower South*, 671–73; Berlin et al., 621–623; Egerton, *Wars of Reconstruction*, 66; Wiley, *Southern Negroes*, 4–6, 11–37; Roark, *Masters Without Slaves*, 74; "Catch the Runaway," *The Tri-Weekly Citizen*, Canton, Mississippi (February 5, 1864) in Corrigan, "Contraband Camps"); Litwack, *Been in the Storm*, 31–33, 138; for an example of what happened to one

fugitive slave turned scout, see Woods, *The Travail of Freedom*, 23; for reports of what life was like for the fugitive slaves in and around Vicksburg after its surrender, see Currie, *Enclave*, 33–54.

38. *Laws of Mississippi*, Ch. 30 (November 1863), 147.

39. Berlin et al., *The Lower South*, 628–47; also esp. "Provost Marshal of Freedmen in the Department of the Tennessee to the Adjutant General of the Army," dated June 15, 1864, therein; Foner, *Reconstruction*, 57; "Army Surgeon to the Secretary of War," July 27, 1863 in Berlin et al., *The Lower South*, 715; Wiley, *Southern Negroes*, 222–29; for an example of a slaveholder paying his slaves toward the end of the war, see Thomas D. Cockrell, "Meadow Woods, 1839–1989: A Mississippi Plantation" (PhD Dissertation, Mississippi State University, 1989), 101; Martha M. Bigelow, "Plantation Lease Problems in 1864," *Journal of Southern History* 27 (August 1961), 354–67; for detailed discussions of the impact of the leasing program on Black families during this time, see Frankel, *Freedom's Women*, 47–55 and Bercaw, *Gendered Freedoms*, 33–40; see also Lawrence N. Powell, *New Masters: Northern Planters During the Civil War and Reconstruction* (New Haven, CT: Yale University Press, 1980), 10–34.

40. Berlin et al., *The Lower South*, 628–47; Wiley, *Southern Negroes*, 222–29; Currie, *Enclave*, 62–68; Bercaw, *Gendered Freedoms*, 39–40; Powell, *New Masters*, 10–34; Amy Murrell Taylor, *Embattled Freedom: Journeys Through the Civil War's Slave Refugee Camps* (Chapel Hill: University of North Carolina Press, 2018), 130.

41. Walker, "Corinth: The Story," 18–19; Currie, *Enclave*, 37; Ballard, *Mississippi in the Civil War*, 270; the Sherman quote is from his February 29, 1864, letter to General Halleck in Frankel, *Freedom's Women*, 32.

42. Egerton, *Wars of Reconstruction*, 61–63; Foner, *Reconstruction*, 36, 60–67; Currie, *The Civil War Congress*, 1212–19.

43. Roark, *Masters Without Slaves*, 70–77.

CHAPTER 2. 1865: MISSISSIPPI AT THE END OF THE WAR

1. Gregory P. Downs, "The Southern Nations, 1860–1880" in *A New History of American South*, W. Fitzhugh Brundage, ed., 276.

2. Stephen V. Ash, *A Year in the South: Four Lives in 1865* (New York: Palgrave Macmillan, 2002), 80–81. Ash is quoting from a journal of Samuel Agnew, a Tippah County, Mississippi, farmer and minister.

3. J. T. Trowbridge, *The South: A Tour of its Battlefields and Ruined Cities: A Journey Through the Desolated States and Talks with the People* (Hartford, CT: L. Stebbins, 1866). The Corinth section of the book begins at 293. See also Whitelaw Reid, *After the War: A Southern Tour, May 1, 1865 to May 1, 1866* (New York: Moore, Wilstach & Baldwin, 1866); Percy Roberts, "The Southern Cotton Crop—Mississippi," *Debow's Review* 2 (August 1866); John Richard Dennett *The South as It Is: 1865–1866* (New York: Viking, 1965).

4. Trowbridge, *The South*, 296.

5. *1870 Census of Population and Housing*, 10. Mississippi was the seventh wealthiest state in the country in 1860, using true value of real and personal estate as the guide. By 1870, it had declined to number twenty-six (out of thirty-seven states). The major decline: personal estate declined from $351,636,175 in 1860 to $59,000,430 (which reflected the loss of the value of the slaves). See also Guelzo, *Fateful Lightning*, 35. Per capita calculations for 1860 were based on total population.

6. *1860 Census of Population and Housing: Agriculture of the United States in 1860*, 185; James L. Watkins, *King Cotton: A Historical and Statistical Review, 1790–1908* (New York: James L. Watkins & Sons, 1908), 176–85.

7. Smith, *Mississippi: The Home Front*, 68; George Kline Shank Jr., "Meridian: A Mississippi City at Birth During the Civil War and in Reconstruction," *Journal of Mississippi History* 26 (November 1964), 275–77.

8. *Official Records*, 1st ser., vol. 32, pt. 2, 176.

9. Reid, *After the War*, 390.

10. Harris, *Presidential Reconstruction*, 18; Reid, *After the War*, 423, found "solitary chimneys and shattered ruins" still in the state capital; the letter is dated June 1, 1865, ran in the *New Orleans Times*, and was reprinted in the *New York Times* on June 18, 1865.

11. Smith, *Mississippi: The Home Front*, 84–87. See also John Hebron Moore, "Economic Conditions in Mississippi on the Eve of the Civil War," *Journal of Mississippi History* 22 (1960), 175.

12. Cockrell, "Meadow Woods," 104.

13. Smith, *Mississippi: The Home Front*, 6, 69; Robert L. Brandfon, *Cotton Kingdom of the New South: A History of the Yazoo Mississippi Delta from Reconstruction to the Twentieth Century* (Cambridge, MA: Harvard University Press, 1967), 35–36. The following books also contain summaries of what Mississippi looked like at the end of the War: Garner, *Reconstruction in Mississippi*, 10–17, 38–43, 122–24, 140–45; Harris, *Presidential Reconstruction*, 18–36; and William Charles Sallis, "The Color Line in Mississippi Politics, 1865–1915" (PhD Dissertation, University of Kentucky, 1965), 4–20. Smith, *Mississippi: The Home Front*, at 50–87 describes the damages to the infrastructure. For most of the 400 pages of his dissertation at Duke University, Ross H. Moore described in great detail virtually all of the aspects of living in Mississippi following the War: Ross H. Moore, "Social and Economic Conditions in Mississippi During Reconstruction" (PhD Dissertation, Duke University, 1937).

14. George C. Osborn, "The Life of a Southern Plantation Owner During Reconstruction as Revealed in the Clay Sharkey Papers," *Journal of Mississippi History* 6 (April 1944), 106; Smith, *Mississippi: The Home Front*, 191–92; Moore, "Conditions in Mississippi," 152–55.

15. *Jackson Daily Mississippian* on August 29, 1865, in Moore, "Conditions in Mississippi," 153–54; Garner, *Reconstruction*, 139–41.

16. Moore, "Conditions in Mississippi," 332–47.

17. *Letter of the Secretary of War, Communicating, in Compliance with a Resolution of the Senate of March 2, 1867* (40th Cong., 1st Sess., Senate Ex. Doc. No. 1, Serial 1308; 1867), 5–9.

18. 1860 Census; King, *Southern States*, 313; Mississippi would not get its full complement of 82 counties until Humphreys was established in 1918; as of the publication of this book, the state has over 350 incorporated cities and towns.

19. Willis, *Forgotten Time*, 1–3.

20. Moore, "Conditions in Mississippi," 9, 77–130, 351–60; Harris, *Presidential Reconstruction*, 6–8; Smith, *Mississippi: The Home Front*, 47–48; Ash, *Four Lives*, 144–45; *Message of the President of the United States, Communicating, in Compliance with a Resolution of the Senate of the 12th Instant, Information in Relation to the States of the Union Lately in Rebellion, Accompanied by a Report of Carl Schurz* (39th Cong., 1st Sess., Senate Ex. Doc. No. 2, Serial 1237; 1865) 3–21.

21. Moore, "Social and Economic Conditions," 105–10; author calculations from 1870 Census; Smith, *Mississippi: The Home Front*, 68–69, 72–73.

22. Frederic A. Bancroft, *A Sketch of The Negro in Politics, Especially in South Carolina and Mississippi* (New York: J. F. Pearson, 1885), 39.

23. *Message of the President of the United States, Communicating, in Compliance with a Resolution of the Senate of the 12th Instant*; letter is at 68 and is dated September 17, 1865, from Colonel Charles H. Gilchrist, writing to Schurz, from the Headquarters Sub-District of Jackson.

24. Author calculations from the 1860 Census; Harris, *Presidential Reconstruction*, at 20, refers to a relevant 1868 US Secretary of Agriculture report.

25. George C. Osborn, "The Life of a Southern Plantation Owner During Reconstruction as Revealed in the Clay Sharkey Papers," *Journal of Mississippi History* 6 (April 1944), 105.

26. Ballard, *Civil War in Mississippi*, 11; (Garner, *Reconstruction*, at 19 cites 78,000); according to a reference to the 1860 Census in Garner at 19, there were 70,295 white males in the state between the ages of 18–45. See also Ben Wynne, *Mississippi's Civil War: A Narrative History* (Macon, GA: Mercer University Press, 2006), 178.

27. 1860 Census; Smith, *Mississippi: The Home Front*, 103.

28. Caroline E. Janney, *Ends of War: The Unfinished Fight of Lee's Army After Appomattox* (Chapel Hill: University of North Carolina Press, 2021), 247–48; Gregory P. Downs, *After Appomattox: Military Occupation and the Ends of War* (Cambridge, MA: Harvard University Press, 2015), 55.

29. Willis, *Forgotten Time*, 6.

30. Commander of the Mississippi Squadron to the Adjutant General of the Army, dated October 21, 1863, in Berlin et al., *The Lower South*, 746; see also in same volume Affidavit of a Mississippi or Louisiana Freedman, dated March 3, 1864, at 790, which describes a plantation lessee refusing to pay his workers; Ballard, *Mississippi in the Civil War*, 179.

31. Trowbridge, *The South*, 332.

32. Dennett, *South as It Is*, 352.

33. *Report of the Joint Committee on Reconstruction* (39th Cong., 1st Sess., House of Representatives Report No. 30, Serial 1273; 1866), 544–65; Moore, "Conditions in Mississippi," 357–58.

34. Reid, *After the War*, 290, 481.

35. Moore, "Conditions in Mississippi," 76–86, 143–45; Smith, *Mississippi: The Home Front*, 197; Harris, *Presidential Reconstruction*, 25–26.

36. Harris, *Presidential Reconstruction*, 4.

37. David G. Sansing, "The Failure of Johnsonian Reconstruction in Mississippi, 1865–1866," *Journal of Mississippi History* 34 (November 1972), 373; Ruminski, *The Limits of Loyalty*, 73–106.

38. Garner, *Reconstruction*, at 24–25, and Harris, *Presidential Reconstruction*, at 11, both cite Official Records, ser. 1.

39. These conflicts of Confederate soldiers as well as residents back home, between maintaining loyalty to the Confederacy or returning home to try to salvage a life is well documented by Harris in *Presidential Reconstruction*, 3–17; Garner, *Reconstruction*, 29–63; Smith, *Mississippi: The Home Front*, 125–43; Reid, *After the War*, 290.

40. Ruminski, *The Limits of Loyalty*, 85; Foner, *Reconstruction*, 14.

41. *Jackson Daily Mississippian*; reprinted in the *New York Times*, February 15, 1863.

CHAPTER 3. 1865–1866: THE EXPERIENCE OF FREEDOM

1. Henry Louis Gates Jr., *Stony the Road: Reconstruction, White Supremacy, and the Rise of Jim Crow* (New York: Penguin, 2019), 20.

2. *Dred Scott v. Sandford*, 60 US 393 (1857).

3. Leonard L. Richards, *Who Freed the Slaves?: The Fight Over the Thirteenth Amendment* (Chicago: University of Chicago Press, 2015), 7–9, 187–251; Foner, *The Second Founding*, 21–54; Harold Holzer and Sara Vaughn Gabbard, eds., *Lincoln and Freedom: Slavery, Emancipation, and the Thirteenth Amendment* (Carbondale: Southern Illinois University Press, 2007), 161–91.

4. Steven Hahn et al., eds., *Freedom: A Documentary History of Emancipation, 1861–1867*, 3d ser., vol. 1, *Land and Labor, 1865* (Chapel Hill: University of North Carolina Press, 2008), 4–20; Foner, *Reconstruction*, 78–80; Litwack, *Been in the Storm*, 292–335.

5. Michael Perman, *Reunion Without Compromise: The South and Reconstruction, 1865–1868* (Cambridge: Cambridge University Press, 1973), 16–17. See also Summers, *The Ordeal of the Reunion*, 46–52.

6. Many of these observations can be found in a long July 4, 1865, letter from a chaplain to the Freedmen's Bureau assistant commissioner in Mississippi, in Hahn et al., *Land and Labor, 1865*, 110–28; Foner, *Reconstruction*, 77–78.

7. Perman, *Reunion Without Compromise*, 18; Ruminski, *The Limits of Loyalty*, 143–45.

8. *Message of the President . . . Accompanied by a Report of Carl Schurz*, 21; throughout the report are numerous examples under the headings "Opinions of the Whites" and "General Ideas and Schemes of Whites Concerning the Freedmen."

9. Reid, *After the War*, 417–18.

10. Roark, *Masters Without Slaves*, 111; Hahn et al., *Land and Labor, 1865*, 74; and Willis, *Forgotten Time*, 16–18.

11. Foner, *Reconstruction*, 129–33; July 8, 1862, editorial in New Orleans *Picayune* in W. E. B. DuBois, *Black Reconstruction* (New York: Russell & Russell, 1935), 129.

12. Foner, *Reconstruction*,132.

13. Douglas A. Blackmon, *Slavery by Another Name* (New York: Anchor Books, 2008), 41.

14. *US Statutes at Large*, vol. 12, 1866, chap. 90, 507–9; Dale Kretz, *Administering Freedom*, 24–40; Paul A. Cimbala, *The Freedmen's Bureau: Reconstructing the American South After the Civil War* (Malabar, Florida: Krieger, 2005), 6–8; George R. Bentley, *A History of the Freedmen's Bureau* (Philadelphia: University of Pennsylvania Press, 1955), 46–49; Fawn M. Brodie, *Thaddeus Stevens: Scourge of the South* (New York: W. W. Norton, 1959), 236.

15. Cimbala, *Freedmen's Bureau*, 8; Clifton L. Garrus Jr., "The Freedmen's Bureau in Mississippi" (PhD Dissertation, Tulane University, 1953), 79–81.

16. Cimbala, *Freedmen's Bureau*, 10.

17. Garrus, *Freedmen's Bureau*, x; Kretz, *Administering Freedom*, 26.

18. Ronald L. F. Davis, *Good and Faithful Labor: From Slavery to Sharecropping in the Natchez District, 1860–1890* (Westport, CT: Greenwood, 1982), 74–75.

19. Author estimates from 1870 Census schedules and relevant data.

20. Eric Foner, *Nothing but Freedom: Emancipation and Its Legacy* (Baton Rouge: Louisiana State University Press, 1983), 6.

21. Garrus, *Freedmen's Bureau*, 26–27.

22. Garrus, *Freedmen's Bureau*, 101–2, 146–47, 334.

23. Garrus, *Freedmen's Bureau*, 39.

24. See, for example, the July 4, 1865, letter to the Mississippi Freedmen's Bureau assistance commissioner from a chaplain who had been tasked to visit central and north Mississippi and report his findings in *Land and Labor, 1865*, 110–28.

25. Garrus, *Freedmen's Bureau*, 101–2, 229; Blackmon, *Slavery by Another Name*, 27.

26. John W. Kyle, "Reconstruction in Panola County," *Publications of the Mississippi Historical Society* 13 (1913), 49.

27. *Hinds County Gazette*, November 18, 1868, in Garrus, *Freedmen's Bureau*, at 368; Vicksburg *Daily Times*, October 20, 1866, in Garrus, *Freedmen's Bureau*, at 368.

28. Moore, "Social and Economic Conditions," 54.

29. *Land and Labor, 1865*, 4, 23; Regosin and Shaffer, *Voices of Emancipation*, 87.

30. *Land and Labor, 1865*, 113; July 4, 1865, letter of Chaplain of a Black Regiment to the Mississippi Freedmen's Bureau Assistant Commissioner; see also Dale Edwyna Smith, *The Slaves of Liberty: Freedom in Amite County, Mississippi, 1820–1868* (New York: Garland, 1999), 146–47 and Egerton, *Wars of Reconstruction*, 154–58.

31. *Land and Labor, 1865*, 150–51.

32. *Land and Labor, 1865*, 150–51.

33. Reid, *After the War*, 34; see also example of whipping Blacks in Roark, *Masters Without Slaves*, 147–48.

34. *Land and Labor, 1865*, 39–40.

35. This narrative is informed by the following sources: Michael L. Lanza, *Agrarianism and Reconstruction Politics: The Southern Homestead Act* (Baton Rouge: Louisiana State University Press, 1990), 5–52; Hahn et al., *Land and Labor, 1865*, 398–99; Foner, *Reconstruction*, 153–75; Gates, *Stony the Road*, 29; Behrend, *Reconstructing Democracy*, 102–109; LaWanda Cox, "The Promise of Land for the Freemen," *The Mississippi Valley Historical Review* 45 (December 1958), 413–40; Guelzo, *Fateful Lightning*, 494–96; Egerton, *Wars of Reconstruction*, 104–8; George D. Humphrey, "The Failure of the Mississippi Freedmen's Bureau in Black Labor Relations, 1865–1867," *Journal of Mississippi History* 45 (February 1983), 23; Walter L. Fleming, "Forty Acres and a Mule," *North American Review* 182 (May 1906), 721–37; Martin Abbott, "Free Land, Free Labor, and the Freedmen's Bureau," *Agricultural History*, 30 (October 1956), 150–56; and Henry Louis Gates Jr.'s blog article titled "The Truth Behind 40 Acres and a Mule," accessed November 13, 2016, at www.theroot.com.

36. Roark, *Masters Without Slaves*, 142–43; DuBois, *Black Reconstruction*, 7–8. See also Ruminski, *The Limits of Loyalty*, 147–48 and Mark Wahlgren Summers, *The Ordeal of the Reunion*, 298–99.

37. Both quotes are from Cox, *The Promise of Land for the Freedmen*, 432.

38. Wharton quoted in Jay R. Mandle, *Not Slave, Not Free: The African American Economic Experience Since the Civil War* (Durham, NC: Duke University Press, 1992), 14.

39. *US Statutes at Large*, vol. 13, chap. 90, 507–9. The land provision of the Freedmen's Bureau Act was in effect until July 16, 1866, when the Freedmen's Bureau legislation was reenacted over the veto of President Johnson (*US Statutes at Large*, vol. 14, chap. 200, 173–77). The section dealing with land was not included in the new Bureau legislation but was instead incorporated into new legislation: "An Act for the Disposal of the Public Lands for Homestead Actual Settlement in the States of Alabama, Mississippi, Louisiana, Arkansas, and Florida." It was otherwise known as the Southern Homestead Act and became law on June 21, 1866 (*US Statutes at Large*, vol. 14, chap. 127, 66–67). For a variety of reasons, the Southern Homestead Act failed at providing land in any significant quantities to Freedpeople, either in Mississippi or throughout the South (Lanza, *Agrarianism and Reconstruction Politics*, 125–35). For a discussion of the Savannah, Georgia, meeting, see, for example, Bennett Parten, *Somewhere Toward Freedom: Sherman's March and the Story of America's Largest Emancipation* (New York: Simon & Schuster, 2025), 150–57.

40. *Land and Labor, 1865*, 433–35

41. Garrus, *Freedmen's Bureau*, 84–86.

42. Foner, *Reconstruction*, 164; see also: Mathisen, *The Loyal Republic*, 146–48.

43. Commander of the 15th Army Corps to the Commander of the 17th Army Corps, dated September 1, 1863, in Berlin et al., *The Lower South*, 720; in the same volume, Eaton's report, dated January 31, 1865, is at 871.

44. A typical contract can be found between a Bolivar County planter and his former slaves in Hahn et al., *Land and Labor, 1865*, 344–46; see also Paul A. Cimbala and Randall M. Miller, eds., *The Freedmen's Bureau and Reconstruction: Reconsiderations* (New York: Fordham University Press, 1999), x; and Egerton, *Wars of Reconstruction*, 115–17.

45. Davis, *Good and Faithful Labor*, 74–76; Hahn et al., *Land and Labor, 1865*, 26; Mathisen, *The Loyal Republic*, 161.

46. July 19, 1865, letter from Assistant Commissioner Samuel Thomas to John R. Baird, Acting Provost Marshall of Freedmen in Washington County: *Records of the Field Offices for the State of Mississippi Bureau of Refugees, Freedmen, and Abandoned Lands 1865–1869* (National

Archives Microfilm Publication M1907, roll 1); Records of the Bureau of Refugees, Freedmen and Abandoned Lands, Record Group 105; National Archives Building, Washington, DC.

47. *Message of the President . . . Accompanied by a Report of Carl Schurz,*16–18; Currie, *Enclave,* 146–47.

48. Roark, *Masters Without Slaves,* 139–40; Garrus, *Freedmen's Bureau,* 191.

49. Hahn et al., *Land and Labor, 1865,* 29.

50. *Message of the President . . . Accompanied by a Report of Carl Schurz,* 19.

51. Hahn et al., *Land and Labor, 1865,* 152–53.

52. Hahn et al., *Land and Labor, 1865,* 32; Perman, *Reunion Without Compromise,* 8–9.

53. Hahn et al., *Land and Labor, 1865,* 513–14; another report at 588–89; Willis, *Forgotten Time,* 27–28.

54. Garrus, *Freedmen's Bureau,* 550–52.

55. Davis, *Good and Faithful Labor,* 78.

56. Davis, *Good and Faithful Labor,* 78.

57. Hahn et al., *Land and Labor, 1865,* 35–37.

58. Roark, *Masters Without Slaves,* 139; Litwack, *Been in the Storm,* 344–45.

59. Berlin et al., *The Lower South,* at 692–93.

60. Eric Foner, "The Meaning of Freedom in the Age of Emancipation," *Journal of American History* 81 (September 1994), 453–54.

CHAPTER 4. 1865–1866: THE BLACK CODE

1. Trowbridge, *The South,* 392.

2. Harris, *Presidential Reconstruction,* 3.

3. Guelzo, *Fateful Lightning,* 463–64; Kenneth M. Stampp, *The Era of Reconstruction: America After the Civil War, 1865–1877* (London: Eyre & Spottiswoode, 1965), 50–52; James E. Sefton, *The United States Army and Reconstruction, 1865–1877* (Baton Rouge: Louisiana State University Press, 1967), 12–14; Foner, *Reconstruction,* 176–80.

4. Donald Hubert Breese, "Politics in the Lower South During Presidential Reconstruction, April to November 1865," (PhD Dissertation, University of California, Los Angeles, 1964), 123–24; Foner, *Reconstruction,* 185–90.

5. See William Yerger's speech to the 1865 Constitutional Convention on Monday, August 21, 1865, printed in *Journal of the Proceedings and Debates in the Constitutional Convention of the State of Mississippi* (August 1865), 140–48; Harris, *Presidential Reconstruction,* 3–5, 39–50; Garner, *Reconstruction,* 58–62; L. Marshall Hall, "William L Sharkey and Reconstruction, 1866–1873," *Journal of Mississippi History* 27 (February 1965), 1.

6. Proclamation No. 39, issued June 13, 1865, *US Statutes at Large, Treaties, and Proclamations of the United States of America,* 761–62. The proclamation providing for amnesty and the oaths was No. 37 at 758 issued on May 29, 1865.

7. Winbourne Magruder Drake, "The Mississippi Reconstruction Convention of 1865," *Journal of Mississippi History* 21 (October 1959), 226–27; Buford Satcher, "Blacks in Mississippi Politics, 1865–1900" (PhD Dissertation, Oklahoma State University, 1976), 4–5; Harris, *Presidential Reconstruction,* 41–43.

8. Harris, *Presidential Reconstruction,* 47–48; Donald Hubert Bresse, "Politics in the Lower South During Presidential Reconstruction, April to November, 1865," (PhD Dissertation, University of California at Los Angeles, 1964), 393–96.

9. David G. Sansing, "The Failure of Johnsonian Reconstruction in Mississippi, 1865–1866," *Journal of Mississippi History* 34 (November 1972), 373–76.

10. Sansing, "Failure," 377; *Friars Point Coahomian*, September 27, 1865, given as a footnote in the Sansing article.

11. Paul H. Bergeron, *Andrew Johnson's Civil War and Reconstruction* (Knoxville: University of Tennessee Press, 2011), 76–77.

12. Steven Hahn, *A Nation Without Borders: The United States and Its World in an Age of Civil Wars, 1830–1910* (New York: Viking, 2016), 306–7. See also Stampp, *Era of Reconstruction*, 54, 62–70; Foner, *Reconstruction*, 176–84.

13. "The Progress of Reconstruction," *New York Times*, August 18, 1865; Sansing, "The Failure," 232; Garner, *Reconstruction*, 83–84; Theodore Brantner Wilson, *The Black Codes of the South* (Birmingham: University of Alabama Press, 1965), 63. Rodrigue, *Freedom's Crescent*, 426–27.

14. Wilson, *Black Codes*, 235–36.

15. Wharton, *Negro in Mississippi*, 140; Perman, *Reunion Without Compromise*, 77–78.

16. *1865 Convention Journal*, 48–52.

17. *1865 Convention Journal*, 386.

18. Breese, "Politics in the Lower South," 138–39; Sallis, "Color Line," 19.

19. *1865 Convention Journal*, 141.

20. *1865 Convention Journal*, 146.

21. *1865 Convention Journal* at 53 for the vote on Potter's substitute and at 164–65 for the August 21 vote on final adoption of the provision; see also Garner, *Reconstruction*, 85–90 and *New York Times*, August 23, 1865.

22. *1865 Convention Journal*, 178–81; Drake, "Convention," 242–46; and Garner, *Reconstruction*, 91–93.

23. Drake, "Convention," 251; "Important Dispatch from President Johnson," *New York Times*, August 26, 1865.

24. *Joint Committee on Reconstruction*, 134; Harris, *Presidential Reconstruction*, 57; *New York Times*, August 27, 1865.

25. Sallis, "Color Line," 39.

26. Sallis, "Color Line," 36; Wilson, *Black Codes*, 64–65.

27. Harris, *Presidential Reconstruction*, 104.

28. Wharton, *Negro in Mississippi*, 81.

29. Harris, *Presidential Reconstruction*, 124.

30. Harris, *Presidential Reconstruction*, has an exhaustive review of the candidates and their campaigns at 104–16; J. S. McNeily, "From Organization to Overthrow of Mississippi's Provisional Government," *Publications of the Mississippi Historical Society*, Centenary Series 1 (1916), 12.

31. *House Journal* (1865), 15–18; Humphreys's speech was printed in the October 28, 1865, *New York Times*.

32. Sansing, "Failure," 380; Wilson, *Black Codes*, 65–67.

33. Harris, *Presidential Reconstruction*, 132.

34. Egerton, *Wars of Reconstruction*, 178–82.

35. Harris, *Presidential Reconstruction*, 133; "President Johnson's Dispatch to Gov. Humphreys," *New York Times*, November 27, 1865.

36. Message from Governor Humphreys to the Legislature on November 20, 1865, at 44–46 of the Appendix to the *House Journal* (1865).

37. *Laws of 1865*, Ch. 4 (An Act to Confer), passed the House on November 21 by 58–31 (page 284 in the *House Journal*) and on November 24 in the Senate by 16–13 (page 232 in the *Senate Journal*); Roderick Van Daniel, *Unjustifiably Oppressed: Black Codes of Mississippi* (Memphis: Van Daniel Marketing, 2018); *Laws of 1865*, Ch. 48 (Supplemental to the act to confer civil rights), signed December 2, 1865; Wharton, *Negro in Mississippi*, 86–90.

38. McNeily, "From Organization," 37; Wharton, *Negro in Mississippi,* 87.

39. *Laws of 1865,* Ch. 5 (An Act to Regulate the Relation of "Master" and Apprentice); Wharton, *Negro in Mississippi,* 84.

40. *Laws of 1865,* Ch. 6 (An Act to Amend the Vagrant Laws of the State); Wharton, *Negro in Mississippi,* 84–86.

41. *Laws of 1865,* Ch. 6 (Section 6, at page 92).

42. *Report of the Committee Approved by the Constitutional Convention to Report to the Legislature Such Laws That Would Be Necessary to Regulate the Freedmen* (Appendix to the *House Journal,* October, November and December Session of 1865), 13; Harris, *Presidential Reconstruction,* 125.

43. McNeily, "From Organization," 45.

44. *Laws of 1865,* Ch. 79 (railroads); Ch. 23 (guns); Ch. 23 (speech).

45. *Laws of 1865,* Ch. 23 (Sect. 4); Wharton, *Negro in Mississippi,* 89.

46. *Laws of 1865,* Ch. 2; McNeily, "From Organization," 19–20. The Joint Committee established to developed legislation remarked that "crime, lawlessness and demoralization now prevalent in most localities resulting from the war and consequent on sudden emancipation" called for a more "speedy and rigid enforcement of law than ordinary tribunals afford."

47. Foner, *Reconstruction,* 198; Harris, *Presidential Reconstruction,* 139.

48. *Laws of 1865,* Ch. 16 (artificial legs); Ch. 35 (Confederate taxes); Ch. 65 (misdemeanors); Ch. 14 (20 percent).

49. *Laws of 1865,* Ch. 8.

50. Harris, *Presidential Reconstruction,* 142.

51. *Laws of 1865,* Ch. 108; "Report of the Joint Standing Committee on State and Federal Relations in the Legislature of the State of Mississippi on the Proposed Amendment to the Constitution of the United States as Article XIII."

52. Richards, *Who Freed the Slaves?,* 239.

53. *Senate Journal* (1865), 297.

54. The report was approved by the House on Monday, November 27 by a vote of 45–25 (p. 336 of the *House Journal*) and by the Senate on Saturday, December 2, by a vote of 20–4. (p. 298 of the *Senate Journal*). It was enrolled on December 4 and presented to the governor, who signed it on that date. The House actually voted against approving just Section 1, on an amendment proposed by the Speaker, which failed 21 to 50 (p. 334 of the *House Journal*). The amendment on the Senate floor removing "respectfully" is found on page 297. See also Richards, *Who Freed the Slaves?,* at 239–40.

55. December 1 editorial; see Harris, *Presidential Reconstruction,* 141.

56. "What the South Has Done and Left Undone," *Bedford Inquirer,* December 22, 1865; Satcher, "Blacks in Mississippi Politics," 19. See also the Cleveland (Ohio) *Leader,* December 9, 1865, and Foner, *Reconstruction,* 200.

57. "The Act of the Legislature Concerning Freedmen Annulled by the President," *New York Times,* December 18, 1865; Harris, *Presidential Reconstruction,* 147; Sallis, "Color Line," 46; Wilson, *Black Codes,* 70.

58. *Vicksburg Herald,* December 4, 1865.

59. Sansing, "Failure," 385.

60. Sansing, "Failure," 384.

61. Sallis, "Color Line," 49; see also, Guelzo, *Fateful Lightning,* 490–92.

62. Harris, *Presidential Reconstruction,* 48.

63. *Laws of 1865,* Ch. 108; "Report of the Joint Standing Committee on State and Federal Relations in the Legislature of the State of Mississippi on the Proposed Amendment to the Constitution of the United States as Article XIII."

64. *Congressional Globe* (39th Cong., 1st Sess.), 1–39.

65. Perman, *Reunion Without Compromise*, 145; *Congressional Globe* (39th Cong., 1st Sess.); Sharkey's credentials and Alcorn's credentials were presented in the Senate on December 5; were laid on the table, 7; Michael Les Benedict, *A Compromise of Principle: Congressional Republicans and Reconstruction, 1863–1869* (New York: W. W. Norton, 1974), 134–35.

CHAPTER 5. 1866–1867: CONGRESSIONAL REPUBLICANS TAKE CHARGE

1. Stampp, *Era of Reconstruction*, 127; Foner, *Reconstruction*, 235–36.

2. McNeily, "From Organization," 83.

3. The actual language is as follows: "Representatives and direct Taxes shall be apportioned among the several States which may be included within this Union, according to their respective Numbers, which shall be determined by adding to the whole Number of free Persons, including those bound to Service for a Term of Years, and excluding Indians not taxed, three fifths of all other Persons." For a discussion of the three-fifths provision, see Akhil Reed Amar, *America's Constitution: A Biography* (New York: Random House, 2005), 87–98.

4. Laura F. Edwards, *A Legal History of the Civil War and Reconstruction: A Nation of Rights* (New York: Cambridge University Press, 2015), 107.

5. Historians have generally divided the years following the Civil War into Presidential Reconstruction (1865–1867), governed mainly by President Johnson, and Congressional Reconstruction (1867–1871), when "Radical" Republicans in Congress asserted control over the process. The literature on Republicans in Congress during this time, the battles with President Johnson, enactment of military control, and passage of the Fourteenth and Fifteenth Amendments is vast. In addition to biographies of the major subjects, coverage of Congress by the comprehensive histories of Reconstruction, and countless law review articles, recent books that focus on Congress, Republicans, and the amendments include: Jeffery A. Jenkins and Justin Peck, *Congress and the First Civil Rights Era, 1861–1918* (Chicago: University of Chicago Press, 2021); Michael A. Bellesiles, *Inventing Equality: Reconstructing the Constitution in the Aftermath of the Civil War* (New York: St. Martin's, 2020); Laura F. Edwards, *A Legal History of the Civil War and Reconstruction* (New York: Cambridge University Press, 2015); Heather Cox Richardson, *To Make Men Free: A History of the Republican Party* (New York: Basic Books, 2014); Michael Les Benedict, *Preserving the Constitution* (New York: Fordham University Press, 2006); Foner, *The Second Founding*; Herman Belz, *A New Birth of Freedom: The Republican Party and Freedmen's Rights, 1861–1866* (New York: Fordham University Press, 2000).

6. Foner, *Reconstruction*, 228–30.

7. Stampp, *Era of Reconstruction*, 87–88.

8. *Natchez Democrat* editorial of January 6, 1866, found in Sallis, "Color Line," 60.

9. Dunbar Rowland, *History of Mississippi: The Heart of the South*, vol. 2 (Chicago-Jackson: S. J. Clarke, 1925), 105.

10. Stampp, *Era of Reconstruction*, 14–15; see also Garrett Epps, "The Undiscovered Country: Northern Views of the Defeated South and the Political Background of the Fourteenth Amendment," *Temple Political and Civil Rights Law Review* 411 (Spring 2004), 423–26.

11. Michael Perman, *Emancipation and Reconstruction*, 50; Foner, *Reconstruction*, 237–38; and Rene Hayden et al., eds., *Freedom: A Documentary History of Emancipation, 1861–1867*, 3d ser., vol. 2, *Land and Labor, 1866–1867* (Chapel Hill: University of North Carolina Press, 2013), 10–11.

12. Eric L. McKitrick, *Andrew Johnson and Reconstruction* (Chicago: University of Chicago Press, 1960), 10–11; Perman, *Emancipation and Reconstruction*, 50; Stampp, *Era of Reconstruction*, 76.

13. In *Presidential Reconstruction*, William Harris includes very informative chapters on Agricultural Recovery (9), Levee Reconstruction (10), Restoration of the Railroads (11), and Revitalization of Towns and Businesses (12).

14. Hahn et al., *Land and Labor, 1866–1867*, 61–80; describing complaint among planters about Freedpeople refusing to contract, "strange and idle rumors having filled their ears, concerning great donations from the Gov't they expected to receive." Hahn et al., *Land and Labor, 1865*, 898.

15. Circular No. 2, dated January 2, 1866, from Mississippi Freedmen's Bureau Assistant Commissioner, Hahn et al., *Land and Labor, 1866–1867*, 86–88.

16. Letter from M. Howard to Col. Thomas, January 25, 1866, in Hahn et al., *Land and Labor, 1866–1867*, 105–6.

17. Freedmen's Bureau Subcommissioner at Jackson, Mississippi, to the Mayor of Clinton; and the Mayor's reply, February 3 and 6, 1866, *Land and Labor, 1866–1867*, 107–9.

18. Freedmen's Bureau Subcommissioner for the District of Jackson, Mississippi to the HQ for the Mississippi Freedmen's Bureau Assistant Commissioner, August 31, 1866; Affidavit of Three Mississippi Freedmen; Affidavit of a Mississippi Overseer; and Affidavit of a Mississippi Freedwoman, February 1, 1866; Freedman's Bureau Officer in Mississippi to the HQ of the Mississippi Freedmen's Bureau Assistant Commissioner, April 9, 1866; Hahn et al., *Land and Labor, 1866–1867*, 152–54, 391–97, 407–12. See also 525–28, 570–75, 813–16, 821–24, 844–47, 864–65, 899–900, 922–23, 941–42.

19. Freedmen's Bureau Subcommissioner at Grenada, Mississippi to the Freedmen's Bureau Acting Assistance Commissioner for the Northern District of Mississippi, January 10, 1866, *Land and Labor, 1866–1867*, 570–75.

20. Hahn et al., *Land and Labor, 1866–1867*, 55.

21. Hahn et al., *Land and Labor, 1866–1867*, 2–3; see also Harris, *Presidential Reconstruction*, 102–3.

22. From the *Vicksburg Herald* in McNeily, "From Organization," 223–24.

23. *Joint Committee on Reconstruction*; Stampp, *Era of Reconstruction*, 110–12; Foner, *Reconstruction*, 239–40.

24. McNeily, "From Organization," 74.

25. *Joint Committee on Reconstruction*, vii–xxi.

26. Egerton, *Wars of Reconstruction*, 171–84; Stampp, *Era of Reconstruction*, 123; Sallis, "Color Line," 61–65.

27. *Joint Committee on Reconstruction*, pt. 3, Testimony of W. A. P. Dillingham, March 1, 1866, 116–17.

28. *Joint Committee on Reconstruction*, pt. 3, Testimony of Major General Clinton B. Fish, January 30, 1866, 31.

29. *Joint Committee on Reconstruction*, pt. 3, Testimony of Captain J. H. Matthews, March 10, 1866, 141–42.

30. Don H. Thompson, *Stennis: Plowing a Straight Furrow* (Oxford, MS: Triton, 2015), 140.

31. *Joint Committee on Reconstruction*, pt. 3, Testimony of former governor William L. Sharkey, March 8, 1866, 132–36.

32. Stampp, *Era of Reconstruction*, 109.

33. Hahn et al., *Land and Labor, 1866–1867*, 19; Foner, *Reconstruction*, 243; Stampp, *Era of Reconstruction*, 131.

34. Egerton, *Wars of Reconstruction*, 123–25; Stampp, *Era of Reconstruction*, 135; Foner, *Reconstruction*, 69. The initial bill to reauthorize the Freedmen's Bureau passed the Senate on January 25 and the House on February 6. It was vetoed on February 19, and that veto was sustained in the Senate on February 21. A compromise Freedmen's Bill was passed in early summer, vetoed again by President Johnson, and this time that veto was overridden on July 16.

35. Summers, *The Ordeal of the Reunion*, 88–90; Stampp, *Era of Reconstruction*, 83–90; Perman, *Emancipation and Reconstruction*, 52–56.

36. Johnson's veto message can be found at *Congressional Globe*, February 19, 1866 (39th Cong., 1st Sess.), 915–17; Egerton, *Wars of Reconstruction*, 126–28; Foner, *Reconstruction*, 247.

37. Freedmen's Bureau legislation is at *US Statutes at Large*, vol. 14, chapter 200, 173–177 (became law on July 16, 1866, when the veto was overridden); Civil Rights legislation is at *US Statutes at Large*, vol. 14, chapter 31, 27–29 (became law on April 9, 1866, when the veto was overridden).

38. Egerton, *Wars of Reconstruction*, 201–3; Foner, *Reconstruction*, 244; James G. Rhodes, *History of the United States*, vol. 6, 65–66.

39. Joseph A. Ranney, *In the Wake of Slavery: Civil War, Civil Rights, and the Reconstruction of Southern Law* (Westport, CT: Praeger, 2006), 50–51; Edwards, *Legal History*, 100–101; Stampp, *Era of Reconstruction*, 135.

40. Johnson's veto message can be found: *Congressional Globe*, March 27, 1866 (39th Cong., 1st Sess.), 1679–81. The vote on the 1866 Civil Rights bill took place in the Senate on February 2 and in the House on March 13. It was vetoed on March 27. The veto override vote took place in the Senate on April 6 and then in the House on April 9; Edwards, *Legal History*, 102.

41. David S. Bogen, "The Transformation of the Fourteenth Amendment," *Maryland Law Review* 44 (1985), 992, 1005; Stampp, *Era of Reconstruction*, 136–38.

42. Edwards, *Legal History*, 105–7; Thomas H. Burrell, "Justice Stephen Field's Expansion of the Fourteenth Amendment," *Gonzaga Law Review* 43, 86; Bogen, "Transformation," 1001; Stampp, *Era of Reconstruction*, 138.

43. Paul Finkelman, "Original Intent and the Fourteenth Amendment: Into the Black Hole of Constitutional Law," *Chicago-Kent Law Review* 89 (June 2014), 1020–22.

44. Edwards, *Legal History*, 103–6; Foner, *Reconstruction*, 251–61; George S. Boutwell, "Reconstruction Its True Basis," Speech at Weymouth, MA, July 4, 1865.

45. Summers, *The Ordeal of the Reunion*, 89–92; William Gillette, *Retreat from Reconstruction, 1869–1879* (Baton Rouge: Louisiana State University Press, 1979), 4–5; Michael W. Fitzgerald and Mark Bohnhorst, "Reconstruction, Racial Terror, and the Electoral College," *Journal of the Civil War Era* 14 (March 2024), 33–34; Foner, *Reconstruction*, 252–53.

46. McNeily, "From Organization," 235; Epps, "The Undiscovered Country," 415.

47. Harris, *Presidential Reconstruction*, 231–32.

48. Harris, *Presidential Reconstruction*, 232–36; Sallis, "Color Line," 66–92.

49. Sallis, "Color Line," 67–70.

50. *Vicksburg Herald* in McNeily, "From Organization," 247.

51. *House Journal*, 1866 Called Legislative Session, October 16, 1866, 7–9.

52. *House Journal*, 1866 Called Legislative Session, January 25, 1867, 201; *Senate Journal*, 1866 Called Legislative Session, January 25, 1867, 196; Sallis, "Color Line," 71–74; Harris, *Presidential Reconstruction*, 150–52, 235–37.

53. Sallis, "Color Line," 74.

54. Foner, *Reconstruction*, 260.

55. Stampp, *Era of Reconstruction*, 117.

56. Gillette, *Retreat*, 6–7; Stampp, *Era of Reconstruction*, 118.

57. Stampp, *Era of Reconstruction*, 111–18, first two ellipses original; Gillette, *Retreat*, 5.

58. Foner, *Reconstruction*, 215–16

59. Guelzo, *Fateful Lightning*, 496–97; Stampp, *Era of Reconstruction*, 144; Gillette, *Retreat*, 6; Foner, *Reconstruction*, 271–74.

60. *US Statutes at Large*, 39th Cong., Ch. 153, March 2, 1867 (vetoed and overridden on the same day Johnson sent it to Congress); 40th Cong., Ch. 6, March 23, 1867 (vetoed and overridden on the same day); 40th Cong., Ch. 30, July 19, 1867 (vetoed and overridden on the same day); 40th Cong., Ch. 25, March 11, 1868 (became law without Johnson's signature); Summers, *The Ordeal of the Reunion*, 102–5; Stampp, *Era of Reconstruction*, 144; Foner, *Reconstruction*, 275–77.

61. Johnson's veto message is at *Congressional Globe*, March 2, 1867 (39th Cong., 2d Sess.), 1969–1972.

62. Foner, *Reconstruction*, 273–78; Guelzo, *Fateful Lightning*, 496–499; Egerton, *Wars of Reconstruction*, 220–22.

63. *Mississippi v. Johnson* 71 US 475 (1867); McNeily, "From Organization," 279–81, 291; Frank Johnston, "Suffrage and Reconstruction in Mississippi," *Publications of the Mississippi Historical Society* 6 (1902), 183–85.

64. Reid, *After the War*, 29.

65. Guelzo, *Fateful Lightning*, 499–502; Stampp, *Era of Reconstruction*, 148–50; Gillette, *Retreat*, 12–13.

66. Stampp, *Era of Reconstruction*, 126–30; Egerton, *Wars of Reconstruction*, 105.

67. Foner, *Reconstruction*, 236–37; Stampp, *Era of Reconstruction*, 128–29.

68. Gillette, *Retreat*, 8–10; see also Stampp, *Era of Reconstruction*, at 88.

69. Foner, *Reconstruction*, 237, 278; Gillette, *Retreat*, 6.

70. Egerton, *Wars of Reconstruction*, 107.

71. Stampp, *Era of Reconstruction*, 129–30.

72. Harris, *Presidential Reconstruction*, 180–86; Watkins, *King Cotton*, 182–85.

CHAPTER 6. 1868–1869: A NEW CONSTITUTION: BLACK AND WHITE REPUBLICANS ASSERT THEIR POWER

1. J. L. Power, "The Black and Tan Convention," *Publications of the Mississippi Historical Society*, III (1901), 80.

2. Albert T. Morgan, *Yazoo: On the Picket Line of Freedom in the South, A Personal Narrative* (1884; repr., Columbia: University of South Carolina Press, 2000), 205.

3. Copies of the four constitutions as originally adopted are at the State Law Library of Mississippi. The 1890 provision requiring segregated schools is in Section 207 and the restriction on Blacks and whites marrying is in Section 263. Section 16 of Article VI of the 1817 Constitution and Section 14 of Article VII of the 1832 Constitution both contain the same language that is the only mention of education in either constitution: "schools, and the means of education, shall forever be encouraged in this state." For reviews of Mississippi's constitutions, see David Sansing, "Mississippi's Four Constitutions," *Mississippi Law Journal* 56 (1986); John W. Winkle III, "The History of the Mississippi Constitution," *Oxford Commentaries on the State Constitutions of the United States* (2014); Walter Gerald Howell, "An Appraisal of the 1868 Mississippi Constitutional Convention, and Its Negro Delegates" (Master's Thesis, Mississippi College, 1964); Winbourne Magruder Drake, "The Mississippi Constitutional Convention of 1832," *Journal of Southern History* 13 (August 1957); J. L. Power, "The Black and Tan Convention," 73–85; Richard L. Hume and Jerry B. Gough, *Blacks, Carpetbaggers, and Scalawags: The Constitutional Conventions of Radical Reconstruction* (Baton Rouge: Louisiana State University Press, 2008).

4. Ord named on March 11, 1867, by *General Orders No. 10* (Microfilm roll 2585, MDAH, Records of the War Department, United States Army Commands, Army Headquarters in Washington, DC, 4th Military District); Gregory P. Downs, *After Appomattox*, 187–219.

5. *General Orders No. 1* and *No. 2* issued on March 26, 1867, dealt with assuming command in Vicksburg; *No. 3* divided the Fourth District into subdistricts and assigned A. C. Gillem command of Mississippi; *No. 4* required the Freedmen's Bureau to submit circulars and orders to HQ (these are *General Orders* from the Headquarters of the Fourth Military District in Vicksburg, which originated in the War Department Headquarters in Washington, DC); Harris, *Carpetbagger*, 2–3; Garner, *Reconstruction*, 161.

6. *General Orders No. 5*, Fourth Military District, Vicksburg HQ, 1867; Harris, *Carpetbagger*, 6–19; Currie, *Enclave*, 268.

7. Harris, *Carpetbagger*, 3–6; *General Orders No. 9* issued on May 16, 1867, on horse stealing; *No. 12* issued on June 12, 1867, on illegal whiskey; *No. 15* on June 27, 1867, on poll taxes; and *No. 39* on December 5, 1867, on stolen goods and a black market. See also Currie, *Enclave*, 270.

8. Harris, *Carpetbagger*, 22–24; *General Orders No. 19* issued on August 13, 1867, instructing agents to investigate and *General Orders No. 22* issued on November 30, 1867, establishing boards of arbitration; Michael Brian Connolly, "Reconstruction in Kemper County" (Master's Thesis, Old Dominion University, 1989), 42–44.

9. *General Orders No. 16* on June 29, 1867, Fourth Military District, Vicksburg HQ; Harris, *Carpetbagger*, 67–77; Currie, *Enclave*, 272.

10. Sallis, "Color Line," 59–60, 67.

11. Sallis, "Color Line," 68.

12. Sallis, "Color Line," 69.

13. Sallis, "Color Line," 74; Reid, *After the War*, 288; Harris, *Carpetbagger*, 4–6.

14. Sallis, "Color Line," 77.

15. Harris, *Carpetbagger*, 77–90; Wharton, *Negro in Mississippi*, 141–43; Sallis, "Color Line," 79–82.

16. Wharton, *Negro in Mississippi*, 144.

17. Foner, *Reconstruction*, 281.

18. Michael William Fitzgerald, "The Union League Movement in Alabama and Mississippi" (PhD Dissertation, University of California at Los Angeles, 1986), 33–41; Foner, *Reconstruction*, 283–85; Litwack, *Been in the Storm*, 470–71; Sallis, "Color Line," 87–91; Hahn, *A Nation Under Our Feet*, 166–67, 183–84, 246–48 (the Lynch quote is at 178); George A. Sewell and Margaret L. Dwight, *Mississippi Black History Makers* (Jackson: University Press of Mississippi, 1984), 38–39.

19. Fitzgerald, "Union League Movement," 14–22, 79–81; Harris, *Carpetbagger*, 91–104; Foner, *Reconstruction*, 281–83; Hahn, *A Nation Under Our Feet*, 177–79 (Freedmen's Bureau quote is at 203).

20. Fitzgerald, "Union League Movement," 34–41, 79–85, 152, 168; Foner, *Reconstruction*, 283–85, 293.

21. Fitzgerald, "Union League Movement," 87–88, 171; Wharton, *Negro in Mississippi*, 145; Hahn, *A Nation Under our Feet*, 177–81.

22. Foner, *Reconstruction*, 291.

23. Foner, *Reconstruction*, 291.

24. Harris, *Carpetbagger*, has these numbers at 76; he rightly points out that a number of others who have written about Reconstruction in Mississippi, James Garner and Vernon Lane Wharton, for example, gave lower numbers because they failed to take into account the supplemental registration that was undertaken by Ord prior to the election. Howell, "Appraisal," 6 also uses the lower (incorrect) numbers, as does Sallis, "Color Line"; James T. Currie, "The

Beginnings of Congressional Reconstruction in Mississippi," *Journal of Mississippi History* 35 (August 1973) uses the correct numbers at 275–77.

25. Circular No. 1, issued on May 13, 1867, "Instructions for Use and Guidance of Boards of Registration, Vicksburg Headquarters; Elizabeth A. Regosin and Donald R. Shaffer, eds., *Voices of Emancipation: Understanding Slavery, the Civil War and Reconstruction Through the U.S. Pension Bureau Files* (New York: New York University Press, 2008), 2–4, 33–36; Harris, *Carpetbagger*, 71, 74; *Natchez Weekly Democrat*, October 11, 1871, in Harris at 74; *Condition of Affairs in Mississippi: Evidence Taken by the Committee on Reconstruction* (40th Cong. 3d Sess., House of Representatives Mis. Doc. No. 53, Serial 1385; 1869), 116.

26. Estimates calculated by author; refer to chapter 11, note 68 for details.

27. *General Orders No. 31*, issued on September 26, 1867, Fourth Military District, Vicksburg HQ. Several later white historians (cf: Garner, *Reconstruction*, 187) argued that Ord stacked the convention delegates in a way that would favor the Republicans and Freedmen. But, as Howell demonstrated, the ratio of delegates from majority-Black counties to majority-white counties mirrored the ratio of the Black population to the white population (see Howell, "Appraisal," at 4–6); Harris, *Carpetbagger*, at 77–80.

28. Howell, "Appraisal," 6–7; Wharton, *Negro in Mississippi*, 146.

29. Wharton, *Negro in Mississippi*, 145.

30. Sallis, "Color Line," 81–87; Harris, *Carpetbagger*, 77–80.

31. Wharton, *Negro in Mississippi*, 145; Harris, *Carpetbagger*, 103–6.

32. *General Orders No. 42* issued on December 16, 1867, Fourth Military District, Vicksburg, HQ; Howell, "Appraisal," 7; Sallis, "Color Line," 91–93. The "scene" quote came from Litwack, *Been in the Storm*, 502.

33. *Natchez Tri-Weekly Democrat*, November 7, 1867, in Sallis, "Color Line," 93.

34. *Natchez Tri-Weekly Democrat*, November 9, 1867, in Harris, *Carpetbagger*, 109.

35. *General Orders No. 37* issued on December 5, 1867, Fourth Military District, Vicksburg, HQ; *General Orders No. 42* convened the convention.

36. Harris, *Carpetbagger*, 26–32.

37. 1868 *Convention Journal*, 85–86.

38. 1868 *Convention Journal*, 223–24.

39. 1868 *Convention Journal*, 224–28.

40. *General Orders No. 104* issued on December 28, 1867, Washington, DC, named Major General A. C. Gillem. Later orders specified that "Major General Irvin McDowell will proceed to Vicksburg and relieve General Gillem in command of the Fourth Military District."

41. 1868 *Convention Journal*, 225–26.

42. Sallis, "Color Line," 95.

43. During the 1867 campaign, 100 delegates were elected. According to Hume and Gough, *Blacks, Carpetbaggers*, four of the white delegates never attended the convention. According to the journal record of the first day, eighty-four delegates answered their names to the roll call, including the seventeen Black delegates. During the next day's votes for officers, ninety delegates participated in those decisions. The first legislative session in the State Capitol was held in 1839. That building, at the intersection of Capitol Street and North State Street in downtown Jackson, is now the Old Capitol Museum. The entire building, as well as the floor of the House Chamber, has been restored to look like it did in the 1860s.

44. On the morning of January 7, 1861, 98 of the 100 delegates answered to the roll call.

45. Address by Alston Mygatt in the *Journal of the Constitutional Convention of the State of Mississippi* (January 7, 1868), 3; Harris, *Carpetbagger*, provides biographical information on Mygatt at 101–2.

46. 1868 *Convention Journal*, 4.

47. This demographic description and breakdown of the convention delegates is based on Hume and Gough, *Blacks, Carpetbaggers*, 97–113. The authors did an enormous amount of research into all the Reconstruction conventions and provided tables of individual delegates with detailed biographical and demographic data. They identified seventeen Black delegates, as did Garner, *Reconstruction*, at 187 and Currie, "The Beginnings of Congressional Reconstruction" at 282. Howell and Sallis put the number at sixteen while Harris, *Carpetbagger*, referenced eighteen Black delegates at 115. According to Hume and Gough, four of the delegates never made it to Jackson to serve, with which Currie agrees at 280. Moreover, Hume and Gough could not find any relevant demographic data on four of the white delegates, which is two less than Currie at 280. Harris at 115 indicated that there were twenty-three "carpetbaggers"; Howell found twenty-four, Sallis identified twenty-six while Hume and Gough classified just twenty-one as Northern whites. Garner at 187 wrote, "The so-called 'carpet-bag' element had twenty odd representatives." Harris identified seventeen conservative whites; Howell found sixteen; Sallis classified nineteen as "white conservatives" as did Garner at 187. Garner at 187 wrote, "There twenty-nine native white Republicans, derisively called 'Scalawags.'" Harris provided a wealth of biographical information about many of the delegates at 115–29.

48. *Hinds County Gazette*, June 3, 1868, in Charles Madison Bacon, "A History of Hinds County, Mississippi During Reconstruction, 1865–1875," (Master's Thesis, Mississippi College, 1959), 36.

49. 1868 *Convention Journal*, 7; Hume and Gough, *Blacks, Carpetbaggers*, identified fourteen former Union soldiers; Harris, *Carpetbagger*, at 115 found nineteen; Sallis, "Color Line," 99; Howell, "Appraisal," 12.

50. 1868 *Convention Journal*, 398–99; reply on January 18, 1868; Sallis, "Color Line," 103. There's a floor plan of the Old Capitol building in Timothy B. Smith, *The Mississippi Secession Convention* (Jackson: University Press of Mississippi, 2014), 48; "limbo" quote is from William A. Russ Jr., "Registration and Disfranchisement Under Radical Reconstruction," *Mississippi Valley Historical Review* 21 (September 1934), 163.

51. Sallis, "Color Line," 118; Foner, *Reconstruction*, 294–97.

52. 1868 *Convention Journal*, 209; see also Sallis, "Color Line," 114–15; Howell, "Appraisal," 38. Stricklin later apologized at 209–11 of the Journal, but then resigned in March at 411 of the Journal; Harris, *Carpetbagger*, 93–97. The Democrat/scalawag quote is from David H. Donald, "The Scalawag in Mississippi Reconstruction," *Journal of Southern History* 10 (November 1944), 451. For information about carpetbaggers and scalawags, see Allen W. Trelease, "Who were the Scalawags?" *Journal of Southern History* 29 (November 1963); Warren A. Ellem, "Who Were the Mississippi Scalawags?" *Journal of Southern History* 38 (May 1972); William C. Harris, "The Creed of the Carpetbagger: The Case of Mississippi," *Journal of Southern History* 40 (May 1974); and Richard L. Hume, "Carpetbaggers in the Reconstruction South," *Journal of American History* 64 (September 1977).

53. There's a small map of Jackson in Smith, *The Mississippi Secession Convention*, 47. See also Walter McClusky Hurns, "Post-Reconstruction Municipal Politics in Jackson, Mississippi" (PhD Dissertation, Kansas State University, 1989), 57–59; Harris, *Carpetbagger*, 133.

54. Howell, "Appraisal," 13–14; *Natchez Tri-Weekly Democrat*, January 11, 1868, in Sallis, "Color Line," 98.

55. Sallis, "Color Line," 113–18; Howell, "Appraisal," 14–18, 42; Harris, *Carpetbagger*, 131–32.

56. 1868 *Convention Journal*, 18; Howell, "Appraisal," 14.

57. 1868 *Convention Journal*, 396–97, 578–79; Howell, "Appraisal," 22–23; Sallis, "Color Line," 103–4.

58. Sallis, "Color Line," 116–119; Harris, *Carpetbagger*, provides exhausting detail on the Democratic convention and the delegates at 160–72; "Organization of the Conservatives in Mississippi," *New York Times*, January 28, 1868.

59. Howell, "Appraisal," 31.

60. See page 190 of the 1868 *Convention Journal* for problems with collecting the taxes to fund the convention. At one point, the treasurer of the convention indicated the only way to make people pay the taxes would be for the military to force them. Like many of the white historians that followed his 1901 book on Reconstruction in Mississippi, Garner spent the overwhelming part of his examination of the 1868 Convention on the cost and expense (188–94, 197–200, 203–4); Howell, "Appraisal," 58.

61. Sallis, "Color Line," 106.

62. Marriage was legally authorized for "any free white persons within" the state, per Ch. 40, Sect. 1, Art. I, *The Revised Code of the Statute Laws of the State of Mississippi, 1857* (Jackson: E. Barksdale, State Printer), 331–32.

63. 1868 *Convention Journal*, 199, 211–12; Howell, "Appraisal," 47–48 (pp. 11–12 for information on Stringer); Hume and Gough, *Blacks, Carpetbaggers*, at 110; Sallis, "Color Line," 109; Wharton, *Negro in Mississippi*, 149; C. B. Waldrip, "Sex, Social Equality, and Yankee Values: White Men's Attitudes toward Miscegenation During Mississippi's Reconstruction," *Journal of Mississippi History* 64 (2002), 125–31.

64. 1868 *Convention Journal*, 255–56; Hume and Gough, *Blacks, Carpetbaggers*, 110; Sallis, "Color Line," 107–8.

65. Richardson, *Christian Reconstruction*, 27–41; Christopher M. Span, "I Must Learn Now or Not at All: Social and Cultural Capital in the Educational Initiatives of Formerly Enslaved African-Americans in Mississippi, 1862–1869," *Journal of African American History* 87 (Spring 2002), 198; DuBois, *Black Reconstruction*, 637–50.

66. *Woodville Republican*, December 22, 1832, in Aubrey Keith Lucas, "Education in Mississippi from Statehood to the Civil War," *A History of Mississippi*, vol. 1 (Hattiesburg: University & College Press of Mississippi, 1973), 375. For the state laws, refer to Chapter 33 (Slaves, Free Negroes and Mulattoes), Section 8 and Section 10, *The Revised Code of the Statute Laws of the State of Mississippi, 1857* (Jackson, MS: E. Barksdale, State Printer).

67. DuBois, *Black Reconstruction*, 641–45; Christopher M. Span, *From Cotton Field to Schoolhouse: African American Education in Mississippi, 1862–1875* (Chapel Hill: University of North Carolina Press, 2009), 10.

68. 1868 *Convention Journal*, 47, 315–25, 364; Jackson *Clarion*, March 9, 1868, in Sallis, "Color Line," 108–9; Howell, "Appraisal," 46; Hume and Gough, *Blacks, Carpetbaggers*, 110–11; Compton's amendment failed on March 9, 1868, at p. 318 of the *Convention Journal*; March 16, 1868, vote to establish a state agricultural college is at page 364 of the *Convention Journal*.

69. 1868 *Convention Journal*, 409–10, 632–34.

70. 1868 *Convention Journal*, 28–29, 739; Hume and Gough, *Blacks, Carpetbaggers*, 110; Sallis, "Color Line," 109–11; Howell, "Appraisal," 48–50. Quotes are from Garner, *Reconstruction*, 201.

71. 1868 *Convention Journal*, 323, 382–83; Hume and Gough, *Blacks, Carpetbaggers*, at 112–13; Sallis, "Color Line," 111.

72. 1868 *Convention Journal*, 491, 499, 518–19; Hume and Gough, *Blacks, Carpetbaggers*, 113; Garner, *Reconstruction*, 202.

73. 1868 *Convention Journal*, 519–20; Howell, "Appraisal," 38–40.

74. Hume and Gough, *Blacks, Carpetbaggers*, 113.

75. McNeily, "From Organization," 371.

CHAPTER 7. 1868–1869: A NEW CONSTITUTION: WHITE DEMOCRATS ASSERT THEIR POWER

1. Dunbar Rowland, "The Rise and Fall of Negro Rule in Mississippi," *Publications of the Mississippi Historical Society* 2 (1899), 189–200.

2. Hume and Gough, *Constitutional Conventions of Radical Reconstruction*, 74–76, 94. While the ratification vote in Alabama in early February produced a sizeable majority in favor of the new constitution, the total vote was less than the majority of all registered voters that was required by the 1867 Reconstruction Acts. Consequently, Congress enacted the fourth of the Reconstruction Acts on March 11, 1868, removing the majority requirement and accepting the Alabama results (Hume and Gough at 93). See also "The Recent Election—The Charges of Fraud and Intimidation," *New York Times*, July 16, 1868.

3. 1868 *Convention Journal*, 40; Sallis, "Color Line," 107–9; Harris, *Carpetbagger*, 157–59; 177, 197–98; Garner, *Reconstruction*, 211; Garner at 223 also refers to Watson's testimony about the disqualifying provisions of the constitution before the Congressional Committee on Reconstruction.

4. "Are You Ready for the Question," Jackson *Daily Clarion*, May 13, 1868; Brooks D. Simpson, *The Reconstruction Presidents* (Lawrence: University Press of Kansas, 1998), 128; *General Orders No. 19*, issued on May 19, 1868, Fourth Military District, Vicksburg HQ; acknowledged the adoption of the new constitution and set the election for June 22, 1868, with voter registration to begin fourteen days before the election.

5. Circular No. 6, issued on May 28, 1868, Fourth Military District, Vicksburg HQ, set out the state and legislative officials to be on the ballot with the constitution. See also McNeily, "From Organization," 383; Sallis, "Color Line," 119–20; and Harris, *Carpetbagger*, 178–79.

6. *General Orders No. 104*, issued December 28, 1867, Washington, DC, named Major General A. C. Gillem; Peter Maslowski, *Treason Must Be Made Odious: Military Occupation and Wartime Reconstruction in Nashville, Tennessee, 1862–65* (Millwood, New York: KTO, 1978), 40–41; Bernarr Cresap, *Appomattox Commander: The Story of General E. O. C. Ord* (New York: A. S. Barnes, 1981), 260–61; Simpson, *Let Us Have Peace*, 185, 250; Paul H. Bergeron, *Andrew Johnson's Civil War and Reconstruction* (Knoxville: University of Tennessee Press, 2011), 51, 236; *General Orders No. 20*, issued by Gillen on May 20, 1868, provided for the appointment of three registrars for each county: "Registrars shall constitute the Board of Registration for the purpose of conducting the ensuing election upon the question of the ratification of the Constitution."

7. Harris, *Carpetbagger,* 178–81, 188.

8. "The Proposed Mongrel Constitution," Jackson *Daily Clarion*, May 22, 1868; "Defeat the Constitution," *Vicksburg Herald*, May 29, 1868.

9. *Natchez Tri-Weekly Democrat*, June 13, 1868, at Sallis, "Color Line," 121.

10. Fitzgerald, "Union League Movement," 34–41, 62–64, 79–85; Foner, *Reconstruction*, 285; Harris, *Carpetbagger*, 186–90.

11. The registered voters by county for the 1868 election are found in Addenda to *General Orders No. 50*, Series of 1869, General Orders and Circulars, Headquarters Fourth Military District.

12. Harris, *Carpetbagger*, 190–96.

13. *The Papers of Ulysses S. Grant*, vol. 18, October 1, 1867, to June 30, 1868, 279–81. *General Orders No. 21*, issued on May 27, 1868, relieved Ames from his duty as acting assistant inspector general of the district and ordered him to report to the commanding office for Mississippi; *General Orders No. 22*, issued on June 4, acknowledged that General McDowell assumed command of the 4th military district; *General Orders No. 23*, issued on June 15, appointed Major General Adelbert Ames as provisional governor of Mississippi, vice Benjamin G. Humphreys,

hereby removed, and Captain Jasper Myers appointed attorney general, vice C. E. Hooker, hereby removed. Hooker was the candidate for attorney general on the Democratic ticket. On July 4, 1868, McDowell was transferred to another state and Gillem resumed command of Mississippi (*General Orders No. 27* and *No. 28*).

14. "Off With His Head," *Grenada Sentinel*, June 20, 1868; "To the People of Mississippi," *Natchez Democrat*, June 23, 1868.

15. Howell, "Appraisal," 63; "The Mississippi Election," *Natchez Democrat*, July 30, 1868.

16. *Natchez Democrat*, July 18, 1868; *Meridian Mercury* in Sallis, "Color Line," 127.

17. The registered voters by county for the 1868 election are found in Addenda to *General Orders No. 50*, Series of 1869, General Orders and Circulars, Headquarters Fourth Military District. The 1868 election results by county are found in *Message of the President of the United States and Accompanying Documents to the Two Houses of Congress, Report of the Secretary of War*, 40th Cong., 3d Sess., House of Representatives Ex. Doc. No. 1, at 590–92; Ruth Watkins, "Reconstruction in Newton County," *Proceedings of the Mississippi Historical Society* 11 (1910), 213.

18. *Condition of Affairs in Mississippi*, 20, 24, 26, 53, 55, 56, 94, 97, 115, 137, 139, 140–43, 274, 277; the Yazoo report is at 139; Jackson *Clarion*, July 3, 1868.

19. In 1871, a law was passed that adopted what had been tradition at the polling place: the official at the polling place was to "receive and fold the ballot, if not before folded (announcing the name of the voter), examine the certificate and compare with the duplicate register [of voters] and poll-book the name therein, and check both certificate and poll-book as 'voted' and then deposit the ballot, folded, in the ballot-box." See Chapter 6, *Laws of 1871*, Section 371.

20. Spencer D. Albright, *The American Ballot* (Washington, DC: American Council on Public Affairs, 1942), 21–30.

21. Simpson, *Let us Have Peace*, 249–50.

22. Garner, *Reconstruction*, 216–18; Harris, *Carpetbagger*, 196–206. *General Orders No. 33*, issued on June 30, 1868, McDowell is relieved from the command of the district and Alvan C. Gillem is assigned command of the district. *General Orders No. 28*, issued on July 4, 1868, Alvan C. Gillem assumed command of the Fourth Military District. General Orders No. 55, issued on July 28, 1868, indicated that the Fourth Military District consisted only of Mississippi and will be commanded by Gillem. In the interim, Arkansas, the other member state of this district, resumed its representation in Congress.

23. Harris, *Carpetbagger*, 199.

24. Gillette, *Retreat*, 8–10.

25. Foner, *Reconstruction*, 333–45; Bruce Ackerman, *We the People: Transformations* (Cambridge, MA: Belknap Press of Harvard University Press, 1998), 234.

26. Harris, *Carpetbagger*, 206–7; Ackerman, *We the People*, 238; Wharton, *Negro in Mississippi*, 153.

27. "Grant's Great Triumph," *New York Times*, November 4, 1868.

28. Ackerman, *We the People*, 236.

29. *US Statutes at Large*, vol. 15, 1869, 346, adopted February 27, 1869; David Herbert Donald, Jean Harvey Baker, and Michael F. Holt, *The Civil War and Reconstruction* (New York: W.W. Norton, 2001), 575–76; David P. Currie, "The Reconstruction Congress," *University of Chicago Law Review* 75 (2008), 33–34; Foner, *Reconstruction*, 447; Gillette, *Retreat*, 17–20.

30. *US Statutes at Large*, vol. 15, 1869, 711, issued December 25, 1868.

31. Harris, *Carpetbagger*, 199–212; Garner, *Reconstruction*, 222–26.

32. Garner at 229; *General Orders No. 10*, issued on March 5, 1869 (Washington, DC, Headquarters) directed Gillem to turn over the command of the district to the next senior officer; *General Orders No. 14*, issued on March 17, 1869, Vicksburg Headquarters, in which Ames assumed command of the military district of Mississippi.

33. Blanche Ames, *Adelbert Ames: 1835–1933* (New York: Argosy-Antiquarian,1964), 1–61.

34. Brooks D. Simpson, *The Reconstruction Presidents*, 140; Charles W. Calhoun, *The Presidency of Ulysses S. Grant* (Lawrence: University Press of Kansas, 2017), 97; *A Compilation of the Messages and Papers of the Presidents*, 7:11–12 and 7:16–18 (entry dated April 7, 1869); *The Papers of Ulysses S. Grant*, vol. 19, July 1, 1868 to October 31, 1869, 164.

35. HR 405; *Congressional Globe*, 41st Cong., 1st Sess., 620, 633–35, 656, 661–62, 699–700; *US Statutes at Large*, Ch. 16, Ch. 17 (April 10, 1869), 40–41; "General Grant on Reconstruction," *New York Herald*, April 9, 1869; Harris, *Carpetbagger*, 199–217, 224–57; Garner, *Reconstruction*, 225–30.

36. Grant Proclamation, dated July 13, 1896, *The Papers of Ulysses S. Grant*, vol. 19, July 1, 1868, to October 31, 1869, 204–8; *General Orders No. 67*, issued on September 10, 1869, Jackson Headquarters, contained the proclamation of the President, referenced the act of Congress approved April 10, 1869, and designated November 30, 1869, as the date for the constitutional election that had been adopted in 1868. Separate votes would be submitted on: Article VII, Section 3 and Section 5 and Article XII, Section 5 and Section 26; it further provided that Sections 4, 5, 6, 7, 8, 9, 10, 11, 12, 13, 14, and 15 of Article XIII, under the head of Ordinance, are considered as forming no part of the said constitution; *General Orders No. 55*, issued October 14, 1869, Washington Headquarters, indicated that Wednesday, December 1, was added as an additional day for voting, added the election of state offices called for by the constitution as well as congressional officers; Boards of Registration were mandated to revise the registration rolls from November. 16 for the ensuing five days; Garner, *Reconstruction*, 237–40.

37. Harris, *Carpetbagger*, 206–7.

38. Harris, *Carpetbagger*, 218–27; Wharton, *Negro in Mississippi*, 154–55; Sallis, "Color Line," 1365; Garner, *Reconstruction*, 237–43.

39. Alcorn speech about opposing the disqualifying provisions in the *Mississippi Pilot*, November 27, 1869; the Republican Party Platform in the *Natchez Weekly Democrat*, October 14, 1869; Sallis, "Color Line," 136; Wharton, *Negro in Mississippi*, 154–55. Harris, *Carpetbagger*, 228–32, 242–45.

40. Wharton, *Negro in Mississippi*, 154; Ames, 280–82.

41. Harris, *Carpetbagger*, 234–36.

42. Grant letter to Lewis Dent, dated August 1, 1869, *The Papers of Ulysses S. Grant*, vol. 19, July 1, 1868, to October 31, 1869, 221–23; Harris, *Carpetbagger*, 240–41; Garner, *Reconstruction*, 241–42.

43. Harris, *Carpetbagger*, 248–59; Garner, *Reconstruction*, 228–37, 244–46.

44. *General Orders No. 60*, issued on December 20, 1869, Jackson Headquarters, declared the constitution ratified; the author analyzed the turnout by county using the returns published as an Addenda to *General Orders No. 60*.

45. Harris, *Carpetbagger*, 216–17.

46. *Forest Register*, December 4, 1869, in Harris, *Carpetbagger*, 259 and *Meridian Mercury*, December 18, 1869, in Harris at 260.

47. *General Orders No. 25*, issued February 26, 1870, Washington, DC, Headquarters: "The Senators and Representatives from the State of Mississippi having been admitted to their respective houses of Congress, the command known as the Fourth Military District has ceased to exist." Virginia rejoined the Union on January 26, 1870; February 23, 1870, was the date for Mississippi; Texas was readmitted on March 30, 1870. Georgia had earlier been readmitted, then was sent packing again because of decisions by the Legislature; it was finally readmitted again on July 15, 1870.

48. Foner, *Reconstruction*, 449

49. Howell, "Appraisal," 62.

CHAPTER 8. 1870–1872: BLACK OFFICIALS, PUBLIC SCHOOLS, AND TERRORISM

1. Eaton, *Grant, Lincoln, and the Freedmen*, 208.

2. DuBois, *Black Reconstruction*, 638.

3. *General Orders No. 25*, issued February 26, 1870, Washington, DC, Headquarters: "The Senators and Representatives from the State of Mississippi having been admitted to their respective houses of Congress, the command known as the Fourth Military District has ceased to exist"; *An Act to Admit the State of Mississippi to Representation in the Congress of the United States*, signed into law on February 23, 1870, by President Grant (41st Cong., 2d Sess., Ch. 19, 16 Stat. 67). The last sentence in that new law: "Third, That the constitution of Mississippi shall never be so amended or changed as to deprive any citizen or class of citizens of the United States of the school rights and privileges secured by the constitution of said State."

4. *Journal of the State Convention and Ordinances and Resolutions*, January 1861 (Jackson, MS: E. Barksdale, State Printer, 1861), Ordinance of Secession, adopted by a vote of 84-15, on January 9, 1861, on page 16. The ordinance itself is at pages 119–21.

5. *Texas v. White*, 74 US 700, at 725–26.

6. The Reconstruction Acts included this admission language: "said State shall be declared entitled to representation in Congress, and senators and representatives shall be admitted therefrom on their taking the oath prescribed by law." Adopted March 2, 1867 (Ch. 153, 15 Stat. 428).

7. *Senate Journal*, Tuesday, January 11, 1870, pages 3–7; Powers spoke on January 13 on page 7.

8. Using DeeDee Baldwin's website Against All Odds: The First Black Legislators in Mississippi and Eric Foner's *Freedom's Lawmakers: A Directory of Black Officeholders During Reconstruction*, I was able to identify each of the Black legislators who were elected in 1869 and who served in the 1870 Regular Legislative Session. I compared the individuals identified by Baldwin and Foner with attendance tabulations in the 1870 and 1871 House and Senate Journals and also with the lists of early legislators first published in the state of Mississippi's Official and Statistical Register (1904 and 1906 editions). Article XI of the 1869 Constitution prescribed a House of Representatives with 107 members and a Senate with 33 members. An additional Black representative was elected from Panola County but died before he could take the oath of office. Sallis, "Color Line," at 144 had 82 Republicans in the House and 28 in the Senate. Wharton, *Negro in Mississippi*, at 172 also had 82 Republicans in the House and 28 in the Senate. Harris, *Carpetbagger*, at 264 had 109 Republicans. A former House Speaker, H. M. Street, writing in the July 11, 1896, issue of the *Meridian Semi-Weekly*, "Scenes of the Carpet Bag Reign in Mississippi," remembered that the Democrats had seven senators and twenty-four representatives. Frank Montgomery, a white Democrat, who wrote a 1901 well-read memoir, *Reminiscences of a Mississippian in Peace and War*, claimed the 1870 Legislature was "two-thirds Negro."

9. *Senate Journal* (Saturday, January 15), 19 (the Fourteenth Amendment was approved 24-2 (Hardy and Striklin voting NO) while the Fifteenth was approved 28-0); *House Journal* (Saturday, January 15), 19-21 (the House vote on the Fourteenth was 87-6 (Curry, Collins, Hartfield, Maxey, McLeod, and Street voting NO) and the Fifteenth was approved 93-1 (McLeod the lone NO vote). Then on Monday, January 17, the House concurred in the Senate resolution approving the Fourteenth Amendment by a vote of 76-2 (Collins and Greer the NO votes) and the Fifteenth by a unanimous vote of 77-0 (25-27).

10. *Senate Journal* (Tuesday, January 18, 1870), 26-42. The Senate elected Alcorn without any opposition and then elected Ames 22 to 5 over Robert Lowry (Duncan, Hardy, Johnson, Seal, and Stricklin voting NO) and with 1 for Horace Greeley (Gibbs); Harris, *Carpetbagger*, at 265–66, explains in some detail the reasons behind the selection of Alcorn and Ames.

11. Harris, *Carpetbagger*, 265–67; John R. Lynch, *The Facts of Reconstruction*, ed. William C. Harris (1913; repr., Indianapolis: Bobs-Merrill, 1970), 45.

12. Lynch, *Facts*, 44–46; Wharton, *Negro in Mississippi*, 159–61; Harris, *Carpetbagger*, 266–67; John Roy Lynch, *Reminiscences of an Active Life* (Chicago: University of Chicago Press, 1970 [this edition was edited by John Hope Franklin]), 75–80.

13. Julius Eric Thompson, "Hiram R. Revels, 1827–1901: A Biography," (PhD Dissertation, Princeton University, 1973), 1–57; Philip Dray, *Capitol Men: The Epic Story of Reconstruction Through the Lives of the First Black Congressmen* (New York: Houghton Mifflin, 2008), 59–62.

14. *An Act to Admit the State of Mississippi to Representation in the Congress of the United States*, signed into law on February 23, 1870 (41st Cong., 2d Sess., Ch. 19, 16 Stat. 67); Senate vote on HR 1096 was on p. 1366; *Congressional Globe*, 41st Cong., 2d Sess., Pt. 2; House vote was on February 3 on p. 1014.

15. Billy W. Libby, "Senator Hiram Revels of Mississippi Takes His Seat, January, February, 1870," *Journal of Mississippi History* (November 1975), 383–90; Harris, *Carpetbagger*, 71–76; *Congressional Globe*, 1870 (41st Cong., 2d Sess., Pt. 2), 1503–4, 1542–43, 1566–68; "Congress: The Colored Member Admitted to His Seat in the Senate," *New York Times*, February 26, 1870; David Donald, *Charles Sumner and the Rights of Man* (New York: Alfred A. Knopf, 1970), 426–27. See also Egerton, *Wars of Reconstruction*, 279.

16. *Congressional Globe*, 1870 (41st Cong., 2d Sess., Pt. 2), 2349. Ames was approved by a vote of 40-12 with nineteen absent. The five members from Mississippi elected to the US were George E. Harris (Tupelo), George C. McKee (Jackson), Legrand W. Perce (Natchez), Joseph Morphis (Pontotoc), and Henry W. Barry (Columbus). They were all Republicans.

17. Sallis, "Color Line," 146.

18. *Senate Journal* (March 8, 1870), 42.

19. *Laws of 1870*, Ch. 1, 1–19.

20. Pereyra, *Alcorn*, 25–58.

21. Pereyra, *Alcorn*, 121–30; Harris, *Carpetbagger*, 312–18; Wharton, *Negro in Mississippi*, 172–78.

22. Alcorn's message on education is in the Appendix to the 1870 *House Journal*, at Document C, 12–20.

23. The broader narrative of this section on education was informed by the following: Span, *From Cotton Field to Schoolhouse*, 5–26, 118; James D. Anderson, *The Education of Blacks in the South: 1860–1935* (Chapel Hill: University of North Carolina Press, 1988), 4–31; Ronald E. Butchart, *Schooling the Freed People: Teaching, Learning, and the Struggle for Black Freedom, 1861–1876* (Chapel Hill: University of North Carolina Press, 2010), 2–21; Harris, *Carpetbagger*, 311–25; Sallis, "Color Line," 151–52.

24. *House Journal* (June 10, 1870), 464. The substitute amendment lost 36-41 with twenty-six absent and then the original amendment to prohibit any integrated classrooms lost 24-52, with twenty-six absent.

25. *House Journal* (June 21, 1870), 497. The substitute amendment was tabled 42-30 with twenty-nine absent.

26. *House Journal* (June 21, 1870), 499–502. That amendment passed 40-38 with twenty-four absent.

27. *Senate Journal* (1870), 417–46. The Powers speech is at 436–40; Harris, *Carpetbagger*, 430–31.

28. Lynch, *Facts*, 52–53; Pereyra, *Alcorn*, 121–24; Harris, *Carpetbagger*, 347–48; Justin Behrend, *Reconstructing Democracy*, 129–30; Sallis, "Color Line," 152–53; Robert L. Jenkins, "The Development of Black Higher Education in Mississippi (1865–1920)," *Journal of Mississippi History* 45 (November 1983), 272; *Senate Journal* (1871), 589–90; *House Journal* (1871), 931–33.

29. The narrative in this section is informed by the following sources: Elaine Frantz Parsons, *Ku-Klux: The Birth of the Klan During Reconstruction* (Chapel Hill: University of North

Carolina, 2015), 5–26 and 161–65; Michael Newton, *The Ku Klux Klan in Mississippi: A History* (Jefferson, NC: McFarland, 2010), 11–45; Fergus M. Bordewich, *Klan War: Ulysses S. Grant and the Battle to Save Reconstruction* (New York: Alfred A. Knopf, 2023), 251–77; John Patrick Daly, *The War After the War*, 115–25; Kidada E. Williams, *I Saw Death Coming: A History of Terror and Survival in the War Against Reconstruction* (New York: Bloomsbury, 2023), 37–52; Stephen Budiansky, *The Bloody Shirt: Terror After the Civil War* (New York: Plume/Penguin Group, 2008), 28–47; Eric Foner, *Reconstruction: America's Unfinished Revolution, 1863–1877* (1988; repr., New York: HarperCollins, 2005), 425–59; George C. Rable, *But There Was No Peace: The Role of Violence in the Politics of Reconstruction* (Athens: University of Georgia Press, 1984), 94–116; Allen W. Trelease, *White Terror: The Ku Klux Klan Conspiracy and Southern Reconstruction* (New York: Harper & Row, 1971), 275–78, 287–301; Harris, *Carpetbagger*, 371–405; William Charles Sallis, "The Color Line in Mississippi Politics: 1865–1915" (PhD Dissertation, University of Kentucky, 1967), 148–61; and *Joint Select Committee to Inquire into the Condition of Affairs in the Late Insurrectionary States* (42d Cong., 2d Sess., House of Representatives Report No. 22, Serial 1539; 1872) 23–455 (published in the spring of 1872 in thirteen large and dense volumes).

30. Parsons, *Ku-Klux*, 1. The Meridian lawyer quote is in Robert Somers, *The Southern States Since the War: 1870–1871* (Tuscaloosa: University of Alabama Press, 1965), 152.

31. William T. Blain, "Challenge to the Lawless: The Mississippi Secret Service, 1870–1871," *Journal of Mississippi History* 40 (May 1978), 122–23.

32. A. J. Brown, *History of Newton County, Mississippi from 1834–1894* (Jackson: Clarion-Ledger Printing Company, 1894), 173.

33. *Affairs in the Late Insurrectionary States*, 325–34.

34. *Affairs in the Late Insurrectionary States*, 270–71.

35. E. F. Puckett, "Reconstruction in Monroe County," *Publications of the Mississippi Historical Society* 11 (1910), 128–30.

36. Bordewich, *Klan War*, 262; Newton, *Ku Klux Klan in Mississippi*, 28–29; Forrest Cooper, "Reconstruction in Scott County," *Publications of the Mississippi Historical Society* 13 (1913), 139.

37. *Affairs in the Late Insurrectionary States*, 223–38.

38. Julia Kendel, "Reconstruction in Lafayette County," *Publications of the Mississippi Historical Society* 13 (1913), 242.

39. Timberlake, "Public Schools?," 87–88. See also Bordewich, *Klan War*, 262–64.

40. Blain, "Challenge to the Lawless," 119–31; *An Act to Prevent and Punish Certain Crimes*, approved July 21, 1870, Ch. 17, *Laws of Mississippi*, 1870, 89–92; *An Act Appropriating Fifty Thousand Dollars to the Executive Contingent Fund*, approved April 6, 1870, Ch. 276, *Laws of Mississippi*, 1870, 607.

41. Jeffrey A. Jenkins and Justin Peck, *Congress and the First Civil Rights Era: 1861–1918* (Chicago: University of Chicago Press, 2021), 133–46; Foner, *Reconstruction*, 454–56; Ron Chernow, *Grant* (New York: Penguin, 2017), 704–6; *First Enforcement Act*, signed into law on May 31, 1870 (41st Cong., 2d Sess., Ch. 114, 16 Stat. 140); *Second Enforcement Act*, signed into law on February 28, 1871 (41st Cong., 3d Sess., Ch. 99, 16 Stat. 433); *Third Enforcement Act*, signed into law on April 20, 1871 (42d Cong., 1st Sess., Ch. 22, 17 Stat. 13). The act creating the Department of Justice was signed on June 22, 1870 (41st Cong., 2d Sess., Ch. 150, 16 Stat. 162).

42. *Third Enforcement Act*, signed into law on April 20, 1871 (42d Cong., 1st Sess., Ch. 22, 17 Stat. 13), 13; Newton, *Ku Klux Klan in Mississippi*, 32; Daly, *The War After the War*, 96–97; Harris, *Carpetbagger*, 396.

43. Daly, *The War After the War*, 95–98; Parsons, *Ku Klux*, 146; Newton, *Ku Klux Klan in Mississippi*, 32–35; Harris, *Carpetbagger*, 395–402; Jean Edward Smith, *Grant* (New York: Simon & Schuster, 2001), 545–47.

44. Foner, *Reconstruction*, 457; Bordewich, *Klan War*, 292–93; Parsons, *Ku Klux*, 184–86; Harris, *Carpetbagger*, 404–5; Stephen Cresswell, "Enforcing the Enforcement Acts: The Department of Justice in Northern Mississippi, 1870–1890," *Journal of Southern History* 53 (August 1987), 422–40; Everette Swinney, "Enforcing the Fifteenth Amendment, 1870–1877," *Journal of Southern History* 28 (May 1962), 202–18.

45. Foner, *Reconstruction*, 458. See also Guy Gugliotta, *Grant's Enforcer: Taking Down the Klan* (Athens: University of Georgia Press, 2025), 222–23.

46. Foner, *Reconstruction*, 455; Morgan, *Yazoo*, 313.

47. Chernow, *Grant*, 709–10.

48. *Annual Report of the Superintendent of Public Education*, Appendix to the *House Journal*, Session of 1872, 134–35; *Annual Report of the Superintendent of Public Education*, Appendix to the *Senate Journal*, Session of 1874, 717–20.

49. Harris, *Carpetbagger*, 426–27; Newton, *Ku Klux Klan in Mississippi*, 37.

50. Berlin et al., *The Lower South*, 331–38.

51. Who was not related to John R. Lynch.

52. The biographical sketch of Lynch's life is taken from William C. Harris, "James Lynch: Black Leader in Southern Reconstruction," *Historian* 34 (November 1971), 40–61. See also Charles B. Gordon, "Curious Story of the Long Ago," Jackson *Clarion-Ledger* (April 7, 1974) and Peter Barr Miazza, *Voices Heard from the Grave: Lives and Stories of People Buried in Greenwood Cemetery* (Saline, MI: McNaughton & Gunn, 2018), 179–93.

53. *Laws of 1900*, Ch. 130; HB 452 introduced in the House on January 15, 1900, *House Journal*, 1900 Regular Sess., 461. See also Jerry Mitchell, "Radar Helps Find Casket of Official," Jackson *Clarion-Ledger* (October 28, 1995) and Buford Satcher, "Blacks in Mississippi Politics, 1865–1900" (PhD Dissertation, Oklahoma State University, 1976), 77–78.

54. 43d Cong., 1st Sess., Ch. 11, 17 Stat. 222, approved February 2, 1872.

CHAPTER 9. 1873: COTTON, ECONOMICS, AND POLITICS

1. Sven Beckert, *Empire of Cotton: A Global History* (New York: Alfred A. Knopf, 2014), 246.

2. Beckert, *Empire of Cotton*, 242–43; Walter Johnson, *River of Dark Dreams: Slavery and Empire in the Cotton Kingdom* (Cambridge, MA: Belknap Press of Harvard University Press, 2013), 10–11; Kris Manjapra, *Black Ghost of Empire: The Long Death of Slavery and the Failure of Emancipation* (New York: Scribner, 2022), 121.

3. Watkins, *King Cotton*, 30–31, 174–78.

4. Donald, Baker, and Holt, *The Civil War and Reconstruction*, 317–19; McPherson, *Battle Cry of Freedom*, 383–86; Mark Thornton and Robert B. Ekelund Jr., *Tariffs, Blockades, and Inflation: The Economics of the Civil War* (Wilmington, DE: Scholarly Resources, 2004), 30–31; Johnson, *River of Dark Dreams*, 11, 257. The quote comes from Roark, *Masters Without Slaves*, 29.

5. *Congressional Globe*, March 4, 1858, (35th Cong., 1st Sess.), 961.

6. Donald, Baker, and Holt, *Civil War and Reconstruction*, 317–19; McPherson, *Battle Cry of Freedom*, 369–79; Beckert, *Empire of Cotton*, 245–46; James L. Watkins, "Production and Price of Cotton for One Hundred Years," US Department of Agriculture (Miscellaneous Series, Bulletin No. 9, 1895), 10–12; Roark, *Masters Without Slaves*, 38–41.

7. Donald, Baker, and Holt, *Civil War and Reconstruction*, 317–19.

8. Kevin Dougherty, *Strangling the Confederacy: Coastal Operations of the American Civil War* (Havertown, PA: Casemate, 2010), 32–36, 184–85; McPherson, *Battle Cry of Freedom*, 380–82; Norman A. Graebner, "Northern Diplomacy and European Neutrality," in David Donald, ed., *Why the North Won the Civil War* (Baton Rouge: Louisiana State University Press,

1960), 54–60; Johnson, *River of Dark Dreams*, 6–10; Guelzo, *Fateful Lightning*, 312; Cooper, *Jefferson Davis*, 330. See also Christopher J. Olsen, *The American Civil War: A Hands-On History* (New York: Hill & Wang, 2006), 181–84.

9. Aaron D. Anderson, *Builders of a New South: Merchants, Capital, and the Remaking of Natchez, 1865–1914* (Jackson: University Press of Mississippi, 2013), 215.

10. Guelzo, *Fateful Lightning*, 517; McPherson, *Battle Cry of Freedom*, 383–86; Beckert, *Empire of Cotton*, 255–59; Roger Lowenstein, *Ways and Means: Lincoln and His Cabinet and the Financing of the Civil War* (New York: Penguin, 2022), 180; John Christopher Schwab, *The Confederate States of America: A Financial and Industrial History of the South During the Civil War* (New York: Charles Scribner's Sons, 1901), 236; Hahn, *Nation Without Borders*, 329–30.

11. Beckert, *Empire of Cotton*, 245–46; Lowenstein, *Ways and Means*, 214; Emory Q. Hawk, *Economic History of the South* (New York: Prentice-Hall, 1934), 415.

12. Author's analysis of 1870 US Census schedules.

13. 1870 US Census; *The State of Mississippi: Resources, Condition, and Wants*, Compiled by the State Board of Immigration and Agriculture (1879), 10–11; Erin Stewart Mauldin, *Unredeemed Land: An Environmental History of Civil War and Emancipation in the Cotton South* (New York: Oxford University Press, 2018), 106.

14. Gilbert C. Fite, *Cotton Fields No More: Southern Agriculture, 1865–1980* (Lexington: University Press of Kentucky, 1984), 9–10; Gavin Wright, *Old South, New South: Revolutions in the Southern Economy Since the Civil War* (New York: Basic Books, 1986), 34.

15. Mauldin, *Unredeemed Land*, 134; Watkins, *King Cotton*, p. 20–31.

16. Mauldin, *Unredeemed Land*, 134–35; Watkins, "Production and Price of Cotton," 10–12.

17. Watkins, *King Cotton*, 176–80. For 1870, for example, Mississippi produced 504,938 bales of cotton, the most of any state that year (per the 1870 Census).

18. Mauldin, *Unredeemed Land*, p. 138–44; Fite, *Cotton Fields No More*, 72–95; Harris, *Carpetbagger*, 481–83; Robert L. Brandfon, *Cotton Kingdom of the New South: A History of the Yazoo Mississippi Delta from Reconstruction to the Twentieth Century* (Cambridge, MA: Harvard University Press, 1967), 18; Richard Griggs, *Annual Report of the Commissioner of Immigration* (Appendix to the 1874 House Journal), 538.

19. Harold D. Woodman, *King Cotton and His Retainers* (Lexington: University of Kentucky Press, 1968), 249–50.

20. The coverage of this topic in the popular and academic literature is extensive. For purposes of this section, the following sources were used: Mark Wahlgren Summers, *The Ordeal of the Reunion*, 300–303; Howard Rabinowitz, *The First New South, 1865–1920* (Arlington Heights, IL: Harlan Davidson, 1992), 7–28; Richard Sutch and Roger Ransom, "Sharecropping: Market Response or Mechanism of Race Control?" in *What Was Freedom's Price* (Jackson: University Press of Mississippi, 1978), 51–92; Brandfon, *Cotton Kingdom of the New South*, 19; Willis, *Forgotten Time*, 7–47; Ronald L. F. Davis, *Good and Faithful Labor: From Slavery to Sharecropping in the Natchez District, 1860–1890* (Westport, CT: Greenwood, 1982), 89–174; Roark, *Masters Without Slaves*, 171–76; Michael Wayne, *The Reshaping of Plantation Society: The Natchez District, 1860–1880* (Baton Rouge: Louisiana State University Press, 1983), 127; Anderson, *Builders of a New South*, 72–86; Mauldin, *Unredeemed Land*, 19–106; Fite, *Cotton Fields No More*, 1–28; Edward E. Baptist, *The Half Has Never Been Told: Slavery and the Making of American Capitalism* (New York: Basic Books, 2014), 407–11; Woodman, *King Cotton*, 249–98; Wright, *Old South, New South*, 84–123.

21. Other terms, such as Redeemer, Bourbon, Whig, and Scalawag have fallen out of common use.

22. Foner, *Reconstruction*, 405.

23. Davis, *Good and Faithful Labor*, 95.

24. Ted Ownby, *American Dreams in Mississippi: Consumers, Poverty & Culture, 1830–1998* (Chapel Hill: University of North Carolina Press, 1999), 63–68.

25. Sutch and Ransom, "Sharecropping," 57.

26. Reprinted in Bradley G. Bond, *Mississippi: A Documentary History* (Jackson: University Press of Mississippi, 2003), 128–29. See also, for example: Eugene M. Lerner, "Southern Output and Agricultural Income, 1860–1880," *Agricultural History* 33 (July 1959), 120–21.

27. While the 1870 Census did not include ownership information about the farms, the 1880 Census did. In Mississippi, for the 14,456 farms under 20 acres, 84 percent were rented to sharecroppers.

28. The 1870 Census reported 68,023 farms, up from 42,840 in 1860. That number of farms was close to the Census figure of 77,102 farmers. In addition to those farmers, the Census reported 181,523 agricultural laborers. The total agricultural workers reported by the Census for 1870 was 259,199, out of a total working population of 318,850.

29. A detailed description of how the credit system operated can be found at Woodman, *King Cotton and His Retainers*, 297–98, though most of the sources used for this narrative include a discussion of the debt cycle and the role of the crop-lien laws in contributing to the never-ending debt of the sharecroppers.

30. Beckert, *Empire of Cotton*, 286.

31. This narrative about Davis Bend is taken from Thavolia Glymph, "The Second Middle Passage: The Transition from Slavery to Freedom at Davis Bend, Mississippi" (PhD Dissertation, Purdue University, 1994); Janet Sharp Hermann, *The Pursuit of a Dream* (New York: Oxford University Press, 1981); Frank E. Everett Jr., *Brierfield: Plantation Home of Jefferson Davis* (Hattiesburg: University & College Press of Mississippi, 1971); Currie, *Enclave*, 83–144; Martha Mitchell Bigelow, "Vicksburg: Experiment in Freedom," *Journal of Mississippi History* 26 (February, 1964), 28–44; Foner, *Reconstruction*, 58–60; Cooper, *Jefferson Davis*, 404, 574.

32. November 12, 1864, correspondence from Vicksburg printed in the December 4, 1864, issue of the *New York Times*.

33. Hermann, *Pursuit of a Dream*, 96.

34. *Land and Labor, 1866–1867*, 946–47.

35. Currie, *Enclave*, 142.

36. Wharton, *Negro in Mississippi*, 41.

37. The narrative for this section is informed by the following sources: Michael J. Megelsh, *Adelbert Ames, the Civil War, and the Creation of Modern American* (Kent, OH: Kent State University Press, 2024), 167–211; Harris, *Carpetbagger*, 459–80; Blanche Ames, *Adelbert Ames*, 370–90; Sallis, "Color Line," 170–81; Pereyra, *Alcorn*, 121–163; Lynch, *Facts*, 70–86; Harry King Benson, "The Public Career of Adelbert Ames, 1861–1876" (PhD Dissertation, University of Virginia, 1975); Garner, *Reconstruction*, 290–301; and Wharton, *Negro in Mississippi*, 156–80.

38. Wharton, *The Negro in Mississippi*, 158.

39. Pereyra, *Alcorn*, 135.

40. *Congressional Globe*, March 21, 1871 (42d Cong., 1st Sess., Pt. 1), 194–98.

41. *Congressional Globe*, May 20, 1872 (42d Cong., 2d Sess., Pt. 1, Appendix), 393–409 and *Congressional Globe*, May 21, 1872 (42d Cong., 2d Sess., Pt. 5), 3701–4.

42. Blanche Ames, *Adelbert Ames*, 368.

43. Lynch, *Facts*, 73–75.

44. Blanche Ames, *Adelbert Ames*, 380.

45. Pereyra, *Alcorn*, 145.

46. These vote totals were submitted to the Congressional Committee investigating the 1875 election by James Hill, the secretary of state, at 138 (Mississippi in 1875, Documentary Evidence,

Pt. 3). The Hill submission was taken from the county returns, and statewide tabulation, reported in the 1874 *House Journal* on January 22, 1874, at 26–27.

47. Harris, *Carpetbagger*, 479; Garner, *Reconstruction*, 294; Wharton, *Negro in Mississippi*, 176. Garner and Wharton agree on the numbers; Harris differs by two.

48. Using DeeDee Baldwin's website at Mississippi State University, Against All Odds: The First Black Legislators in Mississippi, and Eric Foner's *Freedom's Lawmakers: A Directory of Black Officeholders During Reconstruction*, I was able to identify each of the Black legislators who were elected in 1873 and who served in the 1874 Regular Legislative Session. I compared the individuals identified by Baldwin and Foner with attendance tabulations in the 1874 and 1875 House and Senate Journals and also with the lists of early legislators first published in the state of Mississippi's Official and Statistical Register (1904 and 1906 editions). Following the 1870 Census, the Legislature took advantage of Article XI of the 1869 Constitution and expanded the size of the Legislature to 152 members at the same time it redrew district lines to account for population changes and the additional counties that it had created; see Edward H. Hobbs, *Legislative Apportionment in Mississippi* (University, MS: Bureau of Public Administration, 1956), 12. The party affiliations came from Harris, *Carpetbagger*, 479; Garner, *Reconstruction*, 294; and Wharton, *Negro in Mississippi*, 176. Garner and Wharton agree on the numbers; Harris differs by two.

49. The population figures were calculated by the author using individual county data from the 1870 Census.

50. Summers, *The Ordeal of the Reunion*, 350.

CHAPTER 10. 1874: THE BEGINNING OF THE END

1. Lynch, *Facts*, 113.

2. These are 1875 estimates by the author of Mississippi Black and white males twenty-one years of age and older.

3. Nicolas Barreyre, *Gold and Freedom: The Political Economy of Reconstruction* (Charlottesville: University of Virginia Press, 2015), 202; Richard White, *The Republic for Which It Stands: The United States During Reconstruction and the Gilded Age, 1865–1896* (New York: Oxford University Press, 2017), 261–68; Chernow, *Grant*, 777. See also Harold James, *Seven Crashes: The Economic Crises that Shaped Globalization* (New Haven, CT: Yale University Press, 2023), 59–67.

4. Chernow, *Grant*, 777–78; Irwin Unger, *The Greenback Era: A Social History and Political History of American Finance, 1865–1879* (Princeton, NJ: Princeton University Press, 1964), 213; Barreyre, *Gold and Freedom*, 202; White, *The Republic*, 266–67.

5. Harris, *Carpetbagger*, 605–6; *Annual Report of Auditor of Public Accounts for 1873 Fiscal Year*, dated January 1, 1874, Appendix to 1874 *Senate Journal*, 179.

6. *Annual Report of Auditor of Public Accounts for 1874 Fiscal Year*, starting on page 40 of the 1875 *House Journal*. The auditor wrote, "These figures are so appalling in their magnitude as to occasion serious concern for the future."

7. For mentioning the "slave tax," tip of the hat to J. Mills Thornton III, "Fiscal Policy and the Failure of Radical Reconstruction in the Lower South," in *Region, Race and Reconstruction: Essays in Honor of C. Vann Woodward*, J. Morgan Kousser and James M. McPherson, eds. (New York: Oxford University Press, 1982), 349. The percentage of revenue generated by the "slave tax" was calculated by the author from the Auditor's Report dated November 7, 1859, found in the 1859 *House Journal* (75–298) and Section 3 (Of the Assessment of Taxes) of Chapter 3 of the *Revised Code of the Statute Laws of the State of Mississippi* (1857), 70–89.

8. *Annual Report of Auditor of Public Accounts for 1873 Fiscal Year*, dated January 1, 1874, Appendix to 1874 *Senate Journal*, 179.

9. *House Journal*, 1874 Regular Session, 31–32.

10. "Special Message on Finances," dated February 7, 1874, at 151–53, *House Journal*, 1874 Regular Session.

11. Spending in 1871 was $1,729,000. For 1874, it was $1,319,000. Financial detail contained in annual auditor reports to the Legislature, Appendix to 1874 *Senate Journal*, 179; auditor's report, 1875 *House Journal*, 36; and governor's report to the Legislature, 1874 *Senate Journal*, 16.

12. Charles Hillman Brough, "History of Taxation in Mississippi," *Proceedings of the Mississippi Historical Society* 2 (1899), 113–24. See also M. C. Rhodes, *History of Taxation in Mississippi (1798–1929)* (Nashville: George Peabody College for Teachers, 1930).

13. William Bland Whitley, "Precious Memories: Narratives of the Democracy in Mississippi, 1865–1915" (PhD Dissertation, University of Florida, 2004), 56–57.

14. Harris, *Carpetbagger*, 623.

15. The sources for this narrative section include Donald, Baker, and Holt, *The Civil War and Reconstruction*, 623–32; Barreyre, *Gold and Freedom*, 202; White, *The Republic for Which it Stands*, 261–68; Chernow, *Grant*, 77; Foner, *Reconstruction*, 512–24.

16. Chernow, *Grant*, 778.

17. Jean Edward Smith, *Grant*, 575–82; William S. McFeely, *Grant: A Biography* (1981; repr., Norwalk, CT: Easton, 1987), 392–97; Chernow, *Grant*, 777–81.

18. White, *The Republic*, 274; see also Chernow, *Grant*, 783.

19. David W. Blight, *Race and Reunion: The Civil War in American Memory* (Cambridge, MA: Harvard University Press, 2001), 130; Donald, Baker, and Holt, *The Civil War and Reconstruction*, 623–32; James M. McPherson, *Ordeal by Fire: The Civil War and Reconstruction* (New York: McGraw-Hill, 1982), 591–95; White, *Republic for Which it Stands*, 278–87; and Chernow, *Grant*, 783–85. In his history of Reconstruction, Eric Foner devoted nearly thirty pages to documenting how, during this time, Northern voters and, hence Northern officials, lost interest in the South and in maintaining Republicans in power in Southern governments, at *Reconstruction: America's Unfinished Revolution*, 524–53.

20. McPherson, *Ordeal by Fire*, 593; Henry Louis Gates Jr., *Stony the Road*, 11.

21. Chernow, *Grant*, 794; Donald, Baker, and Holt, *The Civil War and Reconstruction*, 625–26.

22. Geoffrey Perret, *Ulysses S. Grant: Soldier and President* (New York: Random House, 1997), 421.

23. The narrative for this section is based on the following sources: *Vicksburgh [sic] Troubles: Testimony Taken by the Select Committee to Visit Vicksburgh* (43d Cong., 2d Sess., House of Representatives Report No. 265, Serial 1659; 1875), Harris, *Carpetbagger*, 623–49; Wharton, *Negro in Mississippi*, 189–93; Garner, *Reconstruction*, 332–37; Gillette, *Retreat*, 150–53; Foner, *Reconstruction*, 557–63; Sallis, "Color Line," 184–95; and Chernow, *Grant*, 149–53.

24. Chernow, *Grant*, 788–89; Gillette, *Retreat*, 152.

25. Chernow, *Grant*, 790.

26. Gillette, *Retreat*, 152.

27. *House Journal*, March 13, 1874, 402–13; *Senate Journal*, March 13, 1874, 322–36.

28. SB 54, introduced on January 31, 1874, was originally drafted to respond to requests from voters in that part of the state for their own county. As originally introduced, SB 54 would have created Ames County. But, it was changed to Sumner County after the senator died, and was signed into law on April 6, 1874 (Ch. 112, *Laws of 1874*). The 1882 Legislature changed the name to Webster (Ch. 132, *Laws of 1882*).

29. Edward Mayes, *Lucius Q. C. Lamar: His Life, Times, and Speeches, 1825–1893* (1896; repr., New York: AMS, 1974); James B. Murphy, *L. Q. C. Lamar: Pragmatic Patriot* (Baton Rouge:

Louisiana State University Press, 1973); Wirt Armistead Cate, *Lucius Q. C. Lamar: Secession and Reunion* (Chapel Hill: University of North Carolina Press, 1935). See also the chapter on Lamar in Dean Faulkner Wells and Hunter Cole, eds., *Mississippi Heroes* (Jackson: University of Mississippi Press, 1980) and Allen J. Going, "Review, James B. Murphy, *L. Q. C. Lamar: Pragmatic Patriot*," *Journal of Southern History* 39 (November 1973), 602–4.

30. The quote is from Smith, *Mississippi Secession Convention*, 5.

31. Mayes, *Lamar*, 170, 182.

32. Mayes, *Lamar*, 170–71.

33. Mayes, *Lamar*, 177.

34. *Congressional Globe*, April 28, 1874 (44th Cong., 1st Sess.), 2105; (43d Cong., 1st Sess.), 3410–11.

35. Mayes, *Lamar*, 188.

36. Mayes, *Lamar*, 191–92.

37. Mayes, *Lamar*, 198.

38. Mayes, *Lamar*, 212.

39. Murphy, *L. Q. C. Lamar: Pragmatic Patriot*, 116.

40. James G. Blaine, *Twenty Years of Congress* (Norwich, CT: Henry Bill, 1886), 196.

41. *Mississippi's Greatest Hour*, Mississippi Civil War Centennial, 6. See also Matthew Reonas, "Served Up on a Silver Platter: Ross Barnett, the Tourism Industry, and Mississippi's Civil War Centennial," *Journal of Mississippi History* 72 (Summer 2010), 123–62.

42. "New Old Capitol, with Museum, Opens on Tuesday," Jackson *Clarion-Ledger*, March 19, 1961; "27 Mixers Jailed on Arrival Here," Jackson *Clarion-Ledger*, May 25, 1961.

43. Approved in a joint session on Tuesday, Feb. 3 by a vote of 74-30 for Robert Lowry.

44. The biographical information is taken from the following: Lawrence Otis Graham, *The Senator and The Socialite: The True Story of America's First Black Dynasty* (New York: HarperCollins, 2006); Philip Dray, *Capitol Men: The Epic Story of Reconstruction Through the Lives of the First Black Congressmen* (New York: Houghton Mifflin Co., 2008), 204–11; and David W. Blight, *Frederick Douglass: Prophet of Freedom* (New York: Simon & Shuster, 2018), 648–51. The Conkling story is also in Melvin I. Urofsky, "Blanche K. Bruce: United States Senator, 1875–1881," *Journal of Mississippi History* 29 (May 1967), 118–42 and Kenneth Eugene Mann, "Blanche Kelso Bruce: United States Senator Without a Constituency," *Journal of Mississippi History* 38 (1976), 183–98.

45. Graham, *The Senator and the Socialite*, 1–5. See also *Congressional Globe* (44th Cong., Special Sess.). Your author has used this anecdote in speeches, especially to students, to demonstrate the power of what one person, ignoring the pressure to conform, can do for someone else, who may be different.

CHAPTER 11. 1875: THE END: WHITE DEMOCRATS REASSERT THEIR POWER

1. Mayes, *Lamar*, 229. Mayes was one of Lamar's biographers, and this sentence came from his introduction to the chapter on the 1875 election.

2. Dunbar Rowland was director of the Mississippi Department of Archives and History from 1902 until his death in 1937. This quote is taken from the *Official and Statistical Register*, State of Mississippi, 195 and 203.

3. Constitution of 1869: Article IV, Section 2 prescribes two-year house terms; Article IV, Section 4 prescribes four-year senate terms; Article IV, Section 36 divides the initial senate into two classes, chosen by lot, with the first class to serve only two years, thus creating the overlapping terms; Article V, Section 1 prescribed a four-year term for governor. Election day would be the first Tuesday after the first Monday in November, per Section 7 of Article IV of the 1869 Constitution.

4. These are 1875 estimates by the author of Mississippi Black and white males twenty-one years of age and older: 109,465 Black vs. 96,369 white, or a difference of 13,096. (See note chapter 11, note 86.) Harris in *Carpetbagger* at page 658 suggested Black voters had a registered majority of "about 20,000." We know from the 1869 registration of voters that the Black majority then was 24,575.

5. Timothy B. Smith, *James Z. George: Mississippi's Great Commoner* (Jackson: University Press of Mississippi, 2012), 96–101.

6. For this chapter, the following sources were used: Nicholas Lemann, *Redemption: The Last Battle of the Civil War* (New York: Farrar, Straus, & Giroux, 2006), 101–209; Behrend, *Reconstructing Democracy*, 210–16; Daly, *The War After the War*, 119–26; Hahn, *A Nation Under Our Feet*, 298–302; Harris, *Carpetbagger*, 650–75; Sallis, "Color Line," 200–254; Smith, *James Z. George*, 95–113; Mayes, *Lamar*, 220–64; Chernow, *Grant*, 788–818; Lynch, *Facts*, 100–127; Rable, *But There Was No Peace*, 150–62; Wharton, *Negro in Mississippi*, 180–201; Garner, *Reconstruction*, 372–409; Gillette, *Retreat*, 150–65; Foner, *Reconstruction*, 557–63; Budiansky, *The Bloody Shirt*, 192–217; Morgan, *Yazoo*, 431–71; Charles Nordhoff, *The Cotton States in the Spring and Summer of 1875* (New York: D. Appleton, 1876), 74–84; and Blanche Ames, *Adelbert Ames*, 370–90. The Senate and House Legislative Journals from the 1875 Regular and Special Sessions were also used, along with the 1876 report of the Congressional Committee that investigated the election, the various publications of the Mississippi Historical Society from 1898 to 1916 (refer to Bibliography), and various national and Mississippi newspapers.

7. William L. Coker, "The United States Senate Investigation of the Mississippi Election of 1875," *Journal of Mississippi History* 37 (May 1975), 143–63. The Senate Report is *Mississippi in 1875: Report of the Select Committee to Inquire into the Mississippi Election of 1875, with the Testimony and Documentary Evidence* (44th Cong., 1st Sess., Senate Report No. 527, Serials 1669 and 1670; 1876). After the 1876 presidential election, a separate congressional committee produced another report: *Mississippi: Testimony as to Denial of Elective Franchise in Mississippi at the Elections of 1875 and 1876* (44th Cong., 2d Sess., Senate Misc. Doc. No. 45, Serial 1725; 1877).

8. Both David Donald and Warren Ellem make the case that by the 1875 elections, those Southern whites who had supported the Republican Party at the outset of Reconstruction had abandoned the party. David H. Donald, "The Scalawag in Mississippi Reconstruction," *Journal of Southern History* 10 (November 1944), 453–54; Warren A. Ellem, "Who Were the Mississippi Scalawags?" *Journal of Southern History* 38 (May 1972), 226–27. There is testimony in *Mississippi in 1875* that indicates the "schism" in the Republican Party hurt their prospects in the fall election. See, for example, the testimony of J. H. Estell at 326.

9. Mayes, *Lamar*, 231; Sallis, "Color Line," 209.

10. *House Journal* (January 5, 1875), Ames's message is at pages 5–14. The reference to a state police force is on page 11.

11. Rable, *But There Was No Peace*, 150–51.

12. "Congressman Lamar on Mississippi Government," *New York Herald*, January 16, 1875.

13. *Brandon Republican*, February 18, 1875.

14. "Reorganization," *Star of Pascagoula*, March 20, 1875; "Democratic Meeting," *Newton Weekly Ledger*, March 11, 1875.

15. Mayes, *Lamar*, 219.

16. Harris, *Carpetbagger*, 632–33, 650–51; "The Wrongs of the Taxpayers and the Ultimate Remedy," *The Weekly Clarion*, March 31, 1875.

17. *Raymond Gazette*, March 31, 1875, as reprinted in the April 24, 1875, *Canton Mail*.

18. *Greenville Times*, May 15, 1875, reporting on the May 12 meeting.

19. *Weekly Clarion*, May 19, 1875; "The Fall Election," *Newton Weekly Ledger*, May 27, 1875.

20. Letter dated May 26 at Mayes, *Lamar*, 248.

21. Nordhoff, *Cotton States*, 76.

22. Ch. 336, 43rd Congress, 1st Sess., June 20, 1874; *The Daily Clarion*, February 16, 1875; "The Vacant Treasurer's Office," *The Weekly Clarion*, February 25, 1875.

23. Murphy, *Pragmatic Patriot*, 151.

24. Blanche Ames, *Adelbert Ames*, 416–17.

25. "The Convention," Jackson *Weekly Clarion*, August 4, 1875; *Canton Mail*, August 7, 1875; "The Primary Election," Vicksburg *Daily Herald*, August 11, 1875.

26. Smith, *James Z. George*, 99–100.

27. Mayes, *Lamar*, 252–54.

28. Mayes, *Lamar*, 255–56. Platform in *Appleton's Annual Cyclopaedia*, 514.

29. "Hon. L. Q. C. Lamar's Speech," Jackson *Weekly Clarion*, August 4, 1875.

30. Harris, *Carpetbagger*, 655.

31. *Hinds County Gazette*, August 21, 1875, at Harris, *Carpetbagger*, 657.

32. Mayes, *Lamar*, 258–59; letter dated August 25, 1875.

33. Author's analysis of the membership of the 1875 Legislature and the House and Senate districts the members represented.

34. Lemann, *Redemption*, 101–2.

35. Budiansky, *The Bloody Shirt*, 198–99; Blanche Ames, *Adelbert Ames*, 418–22; Morgan, *Yazoo*, 458–73.

36. One of the most written about events of the 1875 election, the "Clinton Riot" is included in almost all of the works cited in the earlier endnote, including *Mississippi in 1875*, Lemann, Budiansky, and Harris. George's campaign document was reprinted in a number of newspapers.

37. Lemann, *Redemption*, 113.

38. W. Calvin Wells, "Reconstruction and Its Destruction in Hinds County," *Publications of the Mississippi Historical Society* 9 (1906), 100.

39. Blanche Ames, *Adelbert Ames*, 419: letter dated September 4; Budiansky, *Bloody Shirt*, 196–97.

40. "The Mississippi Riots," *New York Times*, September 9, 1875; "Governor Ames Calls for Troops," *New York Herald*, September 10, 1875.

41. "Attorney General Awaiting a Reply," *New York Times*, September 11, 1875.

42. *Mississippi in 1875*, 31 (In response to a question, Ames admitted he had attended no meetings.); unlike 1873, the local newspapers contain few, if any, articles that reference an Ames's public speech, and in Ames's letters to his wife, there is no mention of meetings outside the Governor's Mansion. Simpson, *The Reconstruction Presidents*, 184–88.

43. Elyria [Ohio] *Weekly Republican*, October 9, 1875; the *Cleveland Leader*, October 15, 1875; Calhoun, *The Presidency of Ulysses S. Grant*, 2017), 509.

44. "Is There an Insurrection in Mississippi," *New York Herald*, September 11, 1875; Harris, *Carpetbagger*, 663–66; Rable, *But There Was No Peace*, 156; Budiansky, *Bloody Shirt*, 197–203; Lemann, *Redemption*, 121–23; and Gillett, *Retreat from Reconstruction*, 155.

45. Chernow, *Grant*, 814.

46. Chernow, *Grant*, 814. Calhoun, *Grant*, 506–9. See also Gillette, *Retreat from Reconstruction*, 155–60. Gillette's book has extensive notes and references a variety of letters between Pierrepont and Grant, and between Pierrepont and others, to describe the ways Pierrepont altered Grant's letter to Pierrepont and that Pierrepont finally sent to Ames. He also documented independent reports from other government officials to Pierrepont, describing why only federal military intervention could ensure a fair election. "For Pierrepont," Gillette wrote, "reports opposing intervention were probably unimportant, for Attorney General Edwards Pierrepoint opposed federal intervention from the beginning. Pierrepont acted on the advice that supported his original intentions" (Notes 41–46 on p. 400).

47. "He Takes the Odium," New York *Tribune*, September 21, 1875; "Mississippi Affairs," *New York Times*, September 17, 1875; "The Mississippi Affair," *New York Herald*, September 17, 1875.

48. Lynch, *Facts*, 147–55. See also Simpson, *The Reconstruction Presidents*, 184; Lemann, *Redemption*, 135–37; Chernow, *Grant*, 818–20; and Keith Ian Polakoff, *The Politics of Inertia: The Election of 1876 and the End of Reconstruction* (Baton Rouge: Louisiana State University Press, 1973), 179–81; *New York Herald*, September 17, 1875; "Ames' Warlike Operation," *The Weekly Clarion*, October 13, 1875; Blanche Ames, *Adelbert Ames*, 433–36; Lemann, *Redemption*, 124–29.

49. Smith, *James Z. George*, 103.

50. Jackson *Weekly Clarion*, October 13, 1875; Hazlehurst *Mississippi Democrat*, October 13, 1875.

51. Wells, "Reconstruction and Its Destruction in Hinds County," 105.

52. *Crystal Springs Monitor*, October 7, 1875. Harris, *Carpetbagger*, at 677–79 includes descriptions of similar rallies attended by thousands of Democrats.

53. *The Daily Clarion*, October 11, 1875; *The Weekly Clarion*, October 13, 1875.

54. Frank Johnston, "The Conference of October 15th, 1875, Between General George and Governor Ames," *Publications of the Mississippi Historical Society* 6 (1902), 65–77. Johnston, who was in the meeting, gives the date of the meeting as October 15, which was off by two days, and takes issue with the role Chase played in arranging the meeting, which is taken from Chase's testimony to the Congressional committee (*Mississippi in 1875*, 1803–1819), Ames's letters, and Grant's biographies and papers. See also Lemann, *Redemption*, 130–36 and Smith, *James Z. George*, 104–6.

55. *Mississippi in 1875*, Pt. 1, xii.

56. Blanche Ames, *Adelbert Ames*, 433.

57. *Mississippi in 1875*, Pt.1, xii.

58. Blanche Ames, *Adelbert Ames*, 439–42; Smith, *James K. George*, 104.

59. Deborah Kalb, *Guide to US Elections* (Washington, DC: CQ Press, 1976), 1721; "The Ohio Election," *New York Times*, October 16, 1875.

60. Examples in the previous paragraphs taken from: Blanche Ames, *Adelbert Ames*, 442–448; Garner, *Reconstruction*, 393; *Mississippi in 1875*, Pt.1, 126–28, 168, 221–28, 573, 584, 757, 790, 1022–30; Sallis, "Color Line," 212–14; Jackson *Weekly Clarion*, October 27, 1875; the Brookhaven *Ledger*, October 28, 1875.

61. Blanche Ames, *Adelbert Ames*, 444.

62. *Mississippi in 1875*, Pt. 1, xii–xiii

63. Robert Lowry and William H. McCardle, *A History of Mississippi* (Jackson, MS: R. H. Henry, 1891), 403.

64. These vote totals were submitted to the Congressional Committee investigating the 1875 election by James Hill, the secretary of state, at 137–45 (*Mississippi in 1875*, Documentary Evidence, Pt. 3). The Hill submission was taken from the county returns, and statewide tabulation, reported in the 1876 *House Journal* on January 5, 1876, at 19–22. The total of 67,171 for the Republican treasurer agrees with the sum total of the county returns. The total of 98,715 for the Democratic treasurer differs from the total of 99,005 when the individual county totals are summed. During Ames's testimony to the Committee, he submitted his own tabulation, at 36–38, which differed in minor ways from that of the Secretary of State. Ames had a total of 97,922 for the Democratic treasurer and 67,000 for the Republican treasurer. The 1873 returns for the Ames/Alcorn gubernatorial election were also submitted to the congressional committee by Hill at 138, which were taken from the returns reported in the 1874 *House Journal* on January 22, 1874, at 26–27.

65. For the members of the 1876 Legislature, the names, party affiliations, race, home counties, and occupations are provided in appendices to the 1876 Legislative Journals. The list of representatives is found in the *House Journal* at 678–82 and the list of senators is found in the *Senate Journal* at 690–92. Since similar lists for earlier legislative memberships were not

included in the journals, I relied on the following sources to develop information about the membership of the 1875 Legislature: Harris, *Carpetbagger*, 479; James W. Garner, *Reconstruction in Mississippi* (New York: MacMillan, 1901), 294; Wharton, *The Negro in Mississippi*, 176; Foner, *Freedom's Lawmakers: A Directory of Black Officeholders During Reconstruction*; and the website maintained by Baldwin at Mississippi State University, *Against All Odds: The First Black Legislators in Mississippi*. See also *Mississippi in 1875*, "Present Legislature of Mississippi" (June 19, 1876), Pt. 4, Documentary Evidence, submitted by James Hill, secretary of state, 146–48. The staggered Senate terms and the changes in legislative membership from 1875 to 1876 were developed from comparing and analyzing the aforementioned sources.

66. For the 1875 election, Mississippi had seventy-three counties. The majority-Black and majority-white county designations were based on the 1870 and 1880 Census counts for each county.

67. For a discussion of how most historical accounts ignore the role of fraud in the 1875 campaign and instead incorrectly assert that Black voters were deterred by white violence and intimidation, see Jere Nash, "The End of Reconstruction in Mississippi: The Fraudulent Election of 1875," *Journal of Mississippi History* (Spring/Summer 2025), 1–24.

68. For this analysis, estimates were made of white and Black men twenty-one years of age and older for the 1875 election, by county, by using (1) 1860, 1870, and 1880 Census returns, (2) 1867, 1868, and 1869 tabulation of registered Black and white voters by the military, and (3) reported returns for the 1867, 1868, 1869, 1871, 1872, 1873, 1875, and 1876 elections. The military registered voter figures by county and by race and the election turnout figures by county (except for 1871) were obtained from the reports, messages, and memoranda that were ultimately filed with Congress or that were included in congressional reports. An Excel spreadsheet was built with columns for those lists and rows for each county (and, of course, the number of counties changed with each election). The 1870 and 1880 Censuses gave individual county totals for men of voting age, the three Censuses gave individual county totals for Black and white men, and the 1870 and 1880 Censuses gave the statewide totals of Black men twenty-one years of age and over and white men twenty-one years of age and over. An Excel program was written to generate an estimate of the 1875 individual Black and white county totals of eligible male voters that, when summed, would generate the applicable known statewide totals, that would be in line with the known county racial breakdown for men, applicable for each election, and that would be in line with the 1867, 1868, and 1869 tabulations, in addition to the individual county returns for relevant elections. The 1876 Senate report, *Mississippi in 1875*, does not contain county or statewide tabulations of registered voters. During the course of my research, I could not find registered voter data for 1875 printed in local newspapers or in the relevant files of the Mississippi Department of Archives and History. An article in the October 2, 1875, issue of *The Weekly Pilot* in Jackson, for example, informed its readers that Hinds County had "about 4500 black voters and 1500 white voters." This appears reasonably accurate, given the Hinds County vote in 1873: 3,480 votes for Ames and 1,246 for Alcorn. Nevertheless, the 1875 returns for Hinds County failed to conform to the published number of registered voters: 2,321 votes for the Republican candidate for Treasurer and 3,836 votes for the Democratic candidate.

69. There were certainly cases where the Democratic turnout included Blacks who felt threatened and cast a Democratic ballot. Still, the county-by-county review of Democratic and Republican turnout shows a substantial number of Republican votes being counted at the same time Democratic votes are being inflated. Only in a county like Yazoo, where virtually no Republican votes were recorded, could someone claim every Black man in the county had come to the polls with a Democratic ballot (and we know from the evidence that whites made clear Blacks were not welcome at the precincts on election day). By and large, though, writers who have claimed Republicans lost the 1875 election through the terror tactics of white Democrats argue Blacks were deterred from even showing up to vote.

70. *Laws of 1875* (Special Session), Ch. 1; *Laws of 1873* (Regular Session), Ch. 68; *Laws of 1871* (Regular Session), Chs. 5 and 6. For multicounty districts, such as senator, and for House districts, the board of each county was directed to send the returns to the secretary of state, who would then open them, along with the governor, to tabulate the results (*Laws of 1871*, Ch. 6, Sect. 378). Statewide officer tabulations were directed to the secretary of state, who would then deliver them to the Speaker of the House for counting in the next regular session of the Legislature. The Senate would be invited to join in the counting (Sect. 383). Prior to the 1873 law, the appointing authorities for the Board of Registrars were the sheriff, president of the board of supervisors, and the chancery clerk.

71. David G. Sansing, "The Role of the Scalawag in Mississippi Reconstruction" (PhD Dissertation, University of Southern Mississippi, 1969), 156–59.

72. While Ames would appoint some judges during his tenure as governor, he was limited to lawyers, and in some cases simply reappointed those who were originally chosen by Alcorn. See, for example, Ames's testimony to the Congressional Committee, *Mississippi in 1875*, at 29.

73. Spencer D. Albright, *The American Ballot* (Washington, DC: American Council on Public Affairs, 1942), 21–30. In the United States, the way in which we vote today was imported from Australia, was known as the "Australian ballot" and had four components: (a) an official ballot was printed at public expense, (b) names of the nominated candidates of all parties were printed on the official ballot, (c) ballots were distributed only at the polling place, and (d) ballots were marked in secret. In the United States, most states had moved to secret ballots soon after the presidential election of 1884. After Kentucky became the last state to adopt a secret ballot, the first presidential election conducted completely under the Australian ballot was the Grover Cleveland campaign in 1892. State law in 1875 required the official in charge of the polling place to "receive and fold the ballot, if not before folded (announcing the name of the voter), examine the certificate and compare with the duplicate register [of voters] and poll-book the name therein, and check both certificate and poll-book as 'voted' and then deposit the ballot, folded, in the ballot-box." See: *Laws of 1871*, Ch. 6, Sect. 371.

74. *Congressional Globe*, 44th Cong. 1st Sess., Vol. 4, 2100–2104 on March 31, 1876.

75. *Mississippi in 1875*, 378–420; the telegraph to Chesman is at 399; "A Sweeping Majority Claimed by the Democrats," *New York Times*, November 3, 1875. The *New York Times* article read: "Memphis, Tenn., Nov. 2—Gen. J. Z. George, Chairman Democratic State Executive Committee at Jackson, Miss., telegraphs to the Appeal: 'Reports from all parts of the State indicate a sweeping Democratic victory. We have carried every doubtful county.'" The telegrams, dated November 2, 1875, to the Memphis newspaper, are at 403.

76. Julia Kendel, "Reconstruction in Lafayette County," *Publications of the Mississippi Historical Society* 13 (1913), 250–52.

77. Macon, *Beacon*, November 20, 1875.

78. Budiansky, *The Bloody Shirt*, 198–200; Albert T. Morgan, *Yazoo; Or, on the Picket Line of Freedom in the South: A Personal Narrative* (1884; repr., Columbia: University of South Carolina Press, 2000), 453–70; Daly, *War After the War*, 124–25; Rable, *But There Was No Peace*, 154–56; and *Mississippi in 1875*, 1647–1784 (the testimony from Yazoo County consumed nearly 140 pages, from both Democratic and Republican participants). The Ames testimony about Yazoo is at 9–12.

79. *Mississippi in 1875*, 220–59. Three Black Clay County Republican voters and two white Democrats testified at the congressional committee hearing. All three Black witnesses offered specific examples of intimidation, threats, and other scare tactics. The two whites claimed the election was peaceful and denied hearing about any threats.

80. *Mississippi in 1875*, 158–219; Lemann, *Redemption*, 149–50.

81. County vote totals were taken from the tabulation submitted to the Congressional Committee investigating the 1875 election by James Hill, the secretary of state, at 137–45 (*Mississippi in 1875*, Documentary Evidence, Pt. 3). The majority-Black and majority-white county designations were based on the 1870 and 1880 Census counts for each county.

82. *Congressional Globe*, March 31, 1876 (44th Cong., 1st Sess., Vol. 4, Pt. 3), 2101.

83. *Congressional Globe*, 44th Cong. 1st Sess., Vol. 4, 233–34 on December 16, 1875; 1968–1969 on March 27, 1876; 2100–2120 on March 31, 1876. Following the 1874 elections, when Democrats made broad gains across the country, Michigan was no exception. In 1875, the new Michigan Legislature replaced the state's three-term Senator, Radical Republican Zachariah Chandler, with the more moderate Christiancy.

84. *Mississippi in 1875*, xxvi.

85. Herbert Aptheker, "Mississippi Reconstruction and the Negro Leader Charles Caldwell," *Science and Society* (Fall 1947), 169; Daly, *War After the War*, 119–20.

86. These vote totals came from the report submitted to the Congressional committee by the Secretary of State, *Mississippi in 1875*, 144–45 (Documentary Evidence). The following counties in the district had Democratic majorities of 250 votes: Greene, Hancock, and Marion.

87. Lynch, *Facts*, 143–45 (This is from the 1970 edition published by The Bobbs-Merrill Company and edited by William C. Harris). See also John Roy Lynch, *Reminiscences of an Active Life*, 168–69.

CHAPTER 12. 1876–1877: THE LOSS OF FREEDOM

1. Lynch, *Reminiscences*, 142.

2. Black abolitionist James McCune Smith in Perman, *Emancipation and Reconstruction*, 20.

3. Sections 27 and 28 of Article IV of the 1869 Mississippi Constitution governed impeachment proceedings. The Articles of Impeachment against Lt. Governor Davis are at *House Journal* (February 17, 1876), 281–84. The Articles of Impeachment against Superintendent of Public Education Cardozo are at *House Journal* (March 9, 1876), 395–408. The Articles of Impeachment against Governor Ames are at *House Journal* (March 13, 1876), 424–49 and *House Journal* (March 25, 1876), 516–18.

4. Notice of Davis conviction is at *House Journal* (March 23, 1876), 500. The resignation letter and House approval for Cardozo is at *House Journal* (March 21, 1876), 486 and at *House Journal* (March 22, 1876), 492. The Ames resignation is at *House Journal* (March 29, 1876), 530–31. The Stone inauguration is at *Senate Journal* (March 29, 1876), 544–46.

5. *Laws of 1876*, Chapter 7, effective March 18, 1876. The new sixth district included the counties of Tunica, Coahoma, Bolivar, Washington, Issaquena, Yazoo, Warren, Claiborne, Jefferson, Adams, and Wilkinson.

6. *Laws of 1876*, Chapter 67, effective April 7, 1876.

7. *Laws of 1876*: Chapter 73 reduced the state millage rate; Chapter 113 cut funding for public education; and Chapter 134 scaled back the judiciary.

8. *Senate Journal* (January 18, 1876), 97–99; *House Journal* (January 18, 1876), 98–99.

9. The Mississippi statewide and county vote totals for the 1876 presidential election come from W. Dean Burnham, *Presidential Ballots, 1836–1892* (Baltimore: Johns Hopkins University Press, 1955), 552–71. A list of county returns and the statewide tabulation for the 1876 election can also be found in *Mississippi: Testimony as to Denial of Elective Franchise in Mississippi*, Serial 1725, 813. The voting age population statistics and county racial population were derived from 1870 and 1880 census data.

10. To be fair to the Democrats, they might argue that the increase in votes for the Democrat came from Black voters, since the overall turnout for Leflore was less than the total eligible male population for the county. But, if that was the case, if Black voters in those numbers had suddenly, in less than a year, become willing Democrats, then one would see similar results in majority-Black counties all over the state, and that didn't happen. In fact, in Leflore's neighboring counties of Sunflower and Carroll, the Tilden vote represented 97 percent and 105 percent respectively of eligible white male voters.

11. *Mississippi: Testimony as to Denial of Elective Franchise in Mississippi*, Serial 1725.

12. White, *Republic for Which it Stands*, 334–36. Keith Ian Polakoff, *The Politics of Inertia: The Election of 1876 and the End of Reconstruction* (Baton Rouge: Louisiana State University Press, 1973), 233–313; Foner, *Reconstruction*, 575–82; See Michael F. Holt, *By One Vote: The Disputed Presidential Election of 1876* (Lawrence: University Press of Kansas, 2008), at 175–243, with a different take on the ultimate results. It was C. Vann Woodward in *Reunion and Reaction: The Compromise of 1877 and the End of Reconstruction* (Boston: Little, Brown, 1951) who popularized the "compromise." A critical review of Woodward is Michael Les Benedict, "Southern Democrats in the Crisis of 1876–1877: A Reconsideration of Reunion and Reaction," *Journal of Southern History* 46 (November 1980), 489–524. See also Allan Peskin, "Was There a Compromise of 1877," *Journal of American History* 60 (June 1973), 63–75. The George quote is from Mayes, *Lamar*, 319.

13. Foner, *Reconstruction*, 382–83.

14. The early decisions included: *Slaughter-House Cases*, 83 U.S. (16 Wall.) 36 (1873); *United States v. Cruikshank*, 92 US 542 (1876); and the *Civil Rights Cases*, 109 U.S. 3 (1883). *Plessy v. Ferguson*, 163 U.S. 537 (1896); *Williams v. Mississippi*, 170 US 213 (1898); *Giles v. Harris*, 189 US 475 (1903); *Grovey v. Townsend*, 295 US 45 (1935).

15. *Laws of 1878*, Ch. 14, Sect. 35.

16. *Laws of 1888*, Ch. 27.

17. *Sproule v. Fredericks*, 69 Miss. 898 (1892) was the Mississippi Supreme Court decision. The George address was covered by a Jackson newspaper and included in James P. Coleman, "The Origin of the Constitution of 1890," *Journal of Mississippi History* 19 (April 1957), 69–92. While the poll tax and understanding provisions also affected many poor and uneducated whites, local election officials, all white, gradually relaxed the applicability of the provisions for white voters.

18. Speech reprinted in the March 17, 1884, issue of the *New York Times*.

19. *Acceptance and Unveiling of the Statues of Jefferson Davis and James Z. George*, Proceedings in the Congress and in Statuary Hall, United States Capitol, June 2, 1931 (72d Cong., 1st Sess., Senate Doc. No. 103).

20. Ethelbert Barksdale, "Reconstruction in Mississippi," in Hilary A. Herbert, *Why the Solid South* (Baltimore: R. H. Woodward, 1890), 327, 343.

21. Robert Lowry and William H. McCardle, *A History of Mississippi* (Jackson, MS: R. H. Henry, 1891), 373.

22. J. S. McNeily, "From Organization to Overthrown of Mississippi's Provisional Government," Publications of the Mississippi Historical Society, Centenary Series, I (1916), 96.

23. Pearl Vivian Guyton, *Our Mississippi, Revised Edition* (Austin, TX: The Steck Company, 1959), 198–99.

24. 1961 Statistical Abstract of the United States, United States Department of Commerce; 1960 Census, Census of Housing, vol. 1, pt. 1, United States Summary; 1970 Census of Population, vol. 1, pt. 1.

EPILOGUE. HISTORICAL MEMORY:
THE DUNNING ERA, JFK, AND MISSISSIPPI TEXTBOOKS

1. Bernard A. Weisberger, "The Dark and Bloody Ground of Reconstruction Historiography," *Journal of Southern History* 25 (November 1959), 427–47.

2. Howard K. Beale, "On Rewriting Reconstruction History," *American Historical Review* 45 (July 1940), 808.

3. John David Smith and J. Vincent Lowery, *The Dunning School: Historians, Race and the Meaning of Reconstruction* (Lexington: University of Kentucky Press, 2013); Donald Yacovone,

Teaching White Supremacy (New York: Pantheon Books, 2022), 174–76. See Eric Foner's forward, at ix–xii, and the James S. Humphrey article on William Dunning, at 77–106. The book also contains a chapter on James W. Garner.

4. Dunning, *Reconstruction*, 58.

5. Dunning, *Reconstruction*, 214.

6. E. Merton Coulter, *The South During Reconstruction, 1865–1877* (Baton Rouge: Louisiana State University Press, 1947), 47–48.

7. Claude G. Bowers, *The Tragic Era: The Revolution After Lincoln* (1929; repr., Boston: Houghton Mifflin Co., Sentry Edition, 1957), 448, 414.

8. Dunning, *Reconstruction*, 13.

9. Coulter, *The South During Reconstruction*, 38.

10. Coulter, *The South During Reconstruction*, 24.

11. John F. Kennedy, *Profiles in Courage: Decisive Moments in the Lives of Celebrated Americans* (New York: Harper & Brothers, 1955), 160–61. As part of the same Ames paragraph, Kennedy writes: "One Cardoza, under indictment for larceny in New York, was placed at the head of the public schools and two former slaves held the offices of Lieutenant Governor and Secretary of State." That is virtually identical to a what Charles Bowers wrote on page 414 of his book about the Ames administration. In his book *Redemption*, Nicholas Lemann has a wonderful vignette at pages 205–9 on the effort made by Ames's daughter to have then President Kennedy make a correction to his book to more accurately reflect her father's role in Mississippi.

12. See Eugene R. Mechelke, "Some Observations on Mississippi's Reconstruction Historiography," *Journal of Mississippi History* 33 (February 1971), 21–38; Thomas S. Edwards, "Reconstructing Reconstruction: Changing Historical Paradigms in Mississippi," *Journal of Mississippi History* 51 (August 1989), 165–80; John Hope Franklin, "Mirror for Americans: A Century of Reconstruction History," *American Historical Review* 85 (February 1980), 1–14; Eric Foner, "Reconstruction Revisited," *Reviews in American History* 10 (December 1982), 82–100.

13. James Wilford Garner, *Reconstruction in Mississippi* (1901; repr., Gloucester, MA: Peter Smith, 1964), 137–38.

14. Patricia Galloway, "Archives, Power, and History: Dunbar Rowland and the Beginning of the State Archives of Mississippi (1902–1936)," *The American Archivist* 69 (Spring/Summer 2006), 83.

15. Dunbar Rowland, *History of Mississippi: The Heart of the South* (Chicago-Jackson: S. J. Clarke, 1925), 168.

16. Rowland, *History of Mississippi*, 200.

17. Charles Reagan Wilson, *The Southern Way of Life: Meanings of Culture and Civilization in the American South* (Chapel Hill: University of North Carolina Press, 2022), 51.

18. John K. Bettersworth, *Mississippi: Yesterday and Today* (Austin: Steck-Vaughn, 1964), 222–38.

19. John K. Bettersworth, *Mississippi: A History* (Austin: Steck, 1959), 333.

20. *Teacher's Manual for Mississippi: A History*, 20.

21. Franklin L. Riley, *Teacher's Handbook of Mississippi History* (Richmond: B. F. Johnson, 1910), 41.

22. Rebecca Miller Davis, "The Three R's—Reading, 'Riting, and Race: The Evolution of Race in Mississippi History Textbooks," *Journal of Mississippi History* 72 (Spring 2010), 1–46. For a fascinating account of how one history textbook tried to challenge the narrative orthodoxy, see Charles W. Eagles, *Civil Rights, Culture Wars: The Fight Over a Mississippi Textbook* (Chapel Hill: University of North Carolina Press, 2017).

23. John K. Bettersworth, *Your Mississippi* (Austin: Steck-Vaughn, 1975), 223.

24. James W. Loewen, "How Two Historians Responded to Racism in Mississippi," *History News Network* (December 7, 2014), 14.

Bibliography and Sources

The two-volume history of Reconstruction in Mississippi by William C. Harris is the only fair, comprehensive history of the decade following the Civil War in our state that has appeared to date. Two others on the topic have also been published. Vernon Lane Wharton's 1947 account provides a wealth of information and perspective, especially about Black Mississippians, for the nearly fifty-year period following the War, but by the nature of Wharton's approach, he did not cover many key aspects of the Reconstruction period. Even though James W. Garner's 1901 book is called *Reconstruction in Mississippi*, he ignores the contributions of the new Black citizens of the state, serves as a cheerleader for white Democrats, and generally blames whatever ills Reconstruction brought to Mississippi on the former newly enfranchised Black voters of the state.

James W. Garner, *Reconstruction in Mississippi* (New York: MacMillan, 1901).
William C. Harris, *Presidential Reconstruction in Mississippi* (Baton Rouge: Louisiana State University Press, 1967).
William C. Harris, *The Day of the Carpetbagger: Republican Reconstruction in Mississippi* (Baton Rouge: Louisiana State University Press, 1979).
Vernon Lane Wharton, *The Negro in Mississippi, 1865–1890* (New York: Harper & Row, 1947).

Two different approaches to chronicling Mississippi history more generally are found in the comprehensive two-volume set by Richard A. McLemore, ed., *A History of Mississippi*, a project that was funded by the state in connection with the celebration of the American Revolution Bicentennial, and the much more recent one-volume history by Dennis Mitchell that the University Press of Mississippi published. Each of these resources contains two chapters on the Reconstruction era.

William C. Harris, "The Reconstruction of the Commonwealth, 1865–1870," in Richard Aubrey McLemore, ed., *A History of Mississippi*, vol. 1 (Hattiesburg: University & College Press of Mississippi, 1973).
David G. Sansing, "Congressional Reconstruction," in Richard Aubrey McLemore, ed., *A History of Mississippi*, vol. 1 (Hattiesburg: University & College Press of Mississippi, 1973).
Dennis J. Mitchell, *Mississippi: A New History* (Jackson: University Press of Mississippi, 2014), chaps. 7 and 8.

Three previously published books of the Heritage of Mississippi Series that bookend the period covered by this volume were always helpful:

Michael B. Ballard, *The Civil War in Mississippi: Major Campaigns and Battles* (Jackson: University Press of Mississippi, 2011).

Stephen Cresswell, *Rednecks, Redeemers, and Race: Mississippi After Reconstruction, 1877–1917* (Jackson: University Press of Mississippi, 2006).

Timothy B. Smith, *Mississippi in the Civil War: The Home Front* (Jackson: University Press of Mississippi, 2010).

Other books that are generally Mississippi-specific and that served as valuable resources include the following:

Nancy D. Bercaw, *Gendered Freedoms: Race, Rights, and the Politics of Household in the Delta, 1861–1875* (Gainesville: University Press of Florida, 2003).

Bradley G. Bond, *Mississippi: A Documentary History* (Jackson: University Press of Mississippi, 2003).

Bradley G. Bond, *Political Culture in the Nineteenth-Century South: Mississippi, 1830–1900* (Baton Rouge: LSU Press, 1995).

James C. Cobb, *The Most Southern Place on Earth: The Mississippi Delta and the Roots of Regional Identity* (New York: Oxford University Press, 1992).

Noralee Frankel, *Freedom's Women: Black Women and Families in Civil War Era Mississippi* (Bloomington: Indiana University Press, 1999).

Meredith Lang, *Defender of the Faith: The High Court of Mississippi, 1817–1875* (Jackson: University Press of Mississippi, 1977).

Nicholas Lemann, *Redemption: The Last Battle of the Civil War* (New York: Farrar, Straus and Giroux, 2006).

John R. Lynch, *The Facts of Reconstruction* (New York: Neale, 1913). I used the 1970 reprint edition published by The Bobbs-Merrill Company and edited by William C. Harris.

John Roy Lynch, *Reminiscences of an Active Life*, John Hope Franklin, ed. (Chicago: University of Chicago Press, 1970).

Kathryn B. McKee, *Reading Reconstruction: Sherwood Bonner and the Literature of the Post-Civil War South* (Baton Rouge: Louisiana State University Press, 2019)

David M. Oshinsky, *Worse than Slavery: Parchman Farm and the Ordeal of Jim Crow Justice* (New York: Free Press Paperbacks/Simon & Schuster, 1996).

Ted Ownby, *American Dreams in Mississippi: Consumers, Poverty and Culture, 1830–1998* (Chapel Hill: University of North Carolina Press, 1999).

Jarret Ruminski, *The Limits of Loyalty: Ordinary People in Civil War Mississippi* (Jackson: University Press of Mississippi, 2017).

Julius Thompson, *The Black Press in Mississippi, 1865–1985* (Gainesville: University Press of Florida, 1993).

Julius E. Thompson, *Black Life in Mississippi: Essays on Political, Social and Cultural Studies in a Deep South State* (New York: University Press of America, 2001).

As mentioned in the Preface, what follows are the publications of the Freedmen and Southern Society Project, housed in the University of Maryland History Department. Simply put, an enormous resource.

Ira Berlin, Barbara J. Fields, Thavolia Glymph, Joseph P. Reidy, and Leslie S. Rowland, eds., *Freedom: A Documentary History of Emancipation, 1861–1867*, 1st ser., vol. 1, *The Destruction of Slavery* (Cambridge: Cambridge University Press, 1985).

Ira Berlin, Steven F. Miller, Joseph P. Reidy, and Leslie S. Rowland, eds., *Freedom: A Documentary History of Emancipation, 1861–1867*, 1st ser., vol. 2, *The Wartime Genesis of Free Labor: The Upper South* (Cambridge: Cambridge University Press, 1988).

Ira Berlin, Barbara J. Fields, Thavolia Glymph, Steven F. Miller, Joseph P. Reidy, Leslie S. Rowland, and Julie Saville, eds., *Freedom: A Documentary History of Emancipation,*

1861–1867, 1st ser., vol. 3, *The Wartime Genesis of Free Labor: The Lower South* (Cambridge: Cambridge University Press, 1990).

Ira Berlin, Joseph P. Reidy, and Leslie S. Rowland, eds., *Freedom: A Documentary History of Emancipation, 1861–1867*, 2d ser., *The Black Military Experience* (London: Cambridge University Press, 1982).

Steven Hahn, Steven F. Miller, Susan E. O'Donovan, John C. Rodrigue, and Leslie S. Rowland, eds., *Freedom: A Documentary History of Emancipation, 1861–1867*, 3d ser., vol. 1, *Land and Labor, 1865* (Chapel Hill: University of North Carolina Press, 2008).

Rene Hayden, Anthony E. Kaye, Kate Masur, Steven F. Miller, Susan E. O'Donovan, Leslie S. Rowland, and Stephen A. West eds., *Freedom: A Documentary History of Emancipation, 1861–1867*, 3d ser., vol. 2, *Land and Labor, 1866–1867* (Chapel Hill: University of North Carolina Press, 2013).

Ira Berlin, Barbara J. Fields, Steven F. Miller, Joseph P. Reidy, and Leslie S. Rowland, *Slaves No More: Three Essays on Emancipation and the Civil War* (Cambridge: Cambridge University Press, 1992).

Ira Berlin, Barbara J. Fields, Steven F. Miller, Joseph P. Reidy, and Leslie S. Rowland, eds., *Free at Last: A Documentary History of Slavery, Freedom, and the Civil War* (New York: New Press, 1992).

Congress sent their committees and staff to Mississippi to conduct investigations throughout the decade of Reconstruction. When those reports are combined with the letters and memoranda dealing with Mississippi from the War Department during the military occupation of the state, one is virtually overwhelmed with the enormous number of pages of witness testimony and evidentiary material. Much like the documents from the Freedmen's Bureau, these materials offer a researcher a window back through time.

Report of the Secretary of War: Preliminary Report Touching the Condition and Management of Emancipated Refugees, Made to the Secretary of War by the American Freedman's Inquiry Commission, June 30, 1863 (38th Cong., 1st Sess., Senate Ex. Doc. No. 53, Serial 1176; 1864).

Message of the President of the United States, Communicating, In Compliance with a Resolution of the Senate of the 12th Instant, Information in Relation to the States of the Union Lately in Rebellion, Accompanied by a Report of Carl Schurz on the States of South Carolina, Georgia, Alabama, Mississippi, and Louisiana; Also a Report of Lieutenant General Grant, on the Same Subject (39th Cong., 1st Sess., Senate Ex. Doc. No. 2, Serial 1237; 1865).

Message from the President of the United States, Communicating, Correspondence with Provisional Governors (39th Cong., 1st Sess., Senate Ex. Doc. No. 26, Serial 1237; 1866).

Message from the President of the United States, Communicating, Reports of the Assistant Commissioners of the Freedmen's Bureau Made Since December 1, 1865 (39th Cong., 1st Sess., Senate Ex. Doc. No. 27, Serial 1238; 1866).

Message from the President of the United States, Transmitting, Report of the Commissioner of the Bureau of Refugees, Freedmen, and Abandoned Lands (39th Cong., 1st Sess., House of Representatives Ex. Doc. No. 11, Serial 1255; 1866).

Letter from the Secretary of War, in Answer to a Resolution of the House of March 8, Transmitting Report by the Commissioner of the Freedmen's Bureau, of All Orders Issued by Him or Any Assistant Commissioner (39th Cong., 1st Sess., House of Representatives Ex. Doc. No. 70, Serial 1256; 1866).

Report of the Joint Committee on Reconstruction (39th Cong., 1st Sess., House of Representatives Report No. 30, Serial 1273; 1866).

Letter of the Secretary of War, Communicating, in Compliance with a Resolution of the Senate of December 17, 1866, Reports of the Assistant Commissioners of Freedmen, and Synopsis of Laws Respecting Persons of Color in the Late Slave States (39th Cong., 2d Sess., Senate Ex. Doc. No. 6, Serial 1276; 1866).

Letter of the Secretary of War, Communicating, In Compliance with a Resolution of the Senate of March 2, 1867, a Report of Major General Howard, Commissioner of Freedmen, Respecting Extreme Want and Danger of Starvation in Several of the Southern States (40th Cong., 1st Sess., Senate Ex. Doc. No. 1, Serial 1308; 1867).

Message of the President of the United States, and Accompanying Documents, to the Two Houses of Congress at the Commencement of the Third Session of the Fortieth Congress, Report of the Secretary of War (40th Cong., 3d Sess., House of Representatives Ex. Doc. No. 1, Serial 1367; 1868).

Condition of Affairs in Mississippi: Evidence Taken by the Committee on Reconstruction (40th Cong., 3d Sess., House of Representatives Mis. Doc. No. 53, Serial 1385; 1869).

"Return of Ballots Cast in the State Elections of 1869 in Mississippi," Entry 409, *Preliminary Inventory of the Records of the United States Army Continental Commands, 1821–1920*, vol. 1, Record Group 393, National Archives Building, Washington, DC.

Affairs in the Late Insurrectionary States (42d Cong., 2d Sess., House of Representatives Report No. 22, Serials 1529, 1539, and 1540; 1872).

Vicksburgh [sic] Troubles: Testimony Taken by the Select Committee to Visit Vicksburgh (43d Cong., 2d Sess., House of Representatives Report No. 265, Serial 1659; 1875).

Message from the President of the United States, Communicating, In Answer to a Senate Resolution of July 20, 1876, Information in Relation to the Slaughter of American Citizens at Hamburgh, S.C. (44th Cong., 1st Sess., Senate Ex. Doc. No. 85, Serial 1664; 1876).

Mississippi in 1875: Report of the Select Committee to Inquire into the Mississippi Election of 1875, with the Testimony and Documentary Evidence (44th Cong., 1st Sess., Senate Report No. 527, Serials 1669 and 1670; 1876).

Mississippi: Testimony as to Denial of Elective Franchise in Mississippi at the Elections of 1875 and 1876 (44th Cong., 2d Sess., Senate Misc. Doc. No. 45, Serial 1725; 1877).

Various scholarly publications, such as the *Journal of Mississippi History* and the *Journal of Southern History*, have published a number of articles about Reconstruction in Mississippi. I used the following. Others appear below in the subject matter listings.

Thomas B. Alexander, "Persistent Whiggery in the Confederate South," *Journal of Southern History* 27 (August 1961).

E. H. Anderson, "A Memoir on Reconstruction in Yazoo City," *Journal of Mississippi History* 4 (October 1942).

John D. Barnhart, "Reconstruction on the Lower Mississippi," *Mississippi Valley Historical Review* 21 (December 1934).

William T. Blain, "Banner Unionism in Mississippi: Choctaw County, 1861–1869," *Mississippi Quarterly* 29 (Spring 1976).

William T. Blain, "Challenge to the Lawless: The Mississippi Secret Service, 1870–1871," *Journal of Mississippi History* 40 (1978).

Jacob S. Clawson, "Militias, Manhood, and Citizenship in Reconstruction Mississippi," *Journal of Mississippi History* 76 (Fall/Winter 2014).

William L. Coker, "The United States Senate Investigation of the Mississippi Election of 1875," *Journal of Mississippi History* 37 (May 1975).

James T. Currie, "The Beginnings of Congressional Reconstruction in Mississippi," *Journal of Mississippi History* 35 (August 1973).

David H. Donald, "The Scalawag in Mississippi Reconstruction," *Journal of Southern History* 10 (November 1944).

Winbourne Magruder Drake, "The Mississippi Reconstruction Convention of 1865," *Journal of Mississippi History* 21 (October 1959).

Warren A. Ellem, "The Overthrow of Reconstruction in Mississippi," *Journal of Mississippi History* 54 (May 1992).

Warren A. Ellem, "Who Were the Mississippi Scalawags?" *Journal of Southern History* 38 (May 1972).

Sever L. Eubank, "The McCardle Case: A Challenge to Radical Reconstruction," *Journal of Mississippi History* 18 (1956).

Claude E. Fike, ed., "Diary of James Oliver Hazard Perry Sessions of Rokeby Plantation, on the Yazoo: January 1, 1862 to June 1872," *Journal of Mississippi History* 39 (September 1977).

John E. Gonzales, "Henry Stuart Foote in Exile: 1865," *Journal of Mississippi History* 15 (1953).

L. Marshall Hall, "William L. Sharkey and Reconstruction, 1866–1875," *Journal of Mississippi History* 27 (February 1965).

Willie D. Halsell, "Democratic Dissensions in Mississippi, 1878–1882," *Journal of Mississippi History* 2 (July 1940).

William C. Harris, "The Creed of the Carpetbagger," *Journal of Southern History* 40 (May 1974).

William C. Harris, "Formulation of the First Mississippi Plan: The Black Code of 1865," *Journal of Mississippi History* 29 (April 1967).

William C. Harris, "A Mississippi Whig and the Ascension of Rutherford B. Hayes to the Presidency," *Journal of Mississippi History* 30 (August 1968).

William C. Harris, "A Reconsideration of the Mississippi Scalawag," *Journal of Mississippi History* 32 (February 1970).

William B. Hesseltine and Larry Gara, "Mississippi's Confederate Leaders After the War," *Journal of Mississippi History* 13 (April 1951).

Richard L. Hume, "Carpetbaggers in the Reconstruction South," *Journal of American History* 64 (September 1977).

Andrew F. Lang, "Republicanism, Race, and Reconstruction: The Ethos of Military Occupation in Civil War America," *Journal of the Civil War Era* 4 (December 2014).

Nicholas Lemann, "Lecture on the History of the History of Reconstruction on February 7, 2017," *Journal of Mississippi History* 83 (Spring/Summer 2021).

William Alexander Mabry, "Disfranchisement of the Negro in Mississippi," *Journal of Southern History* 4 (August 1938).

Neil R. McMillen, "Reconstruction and Its Aftermath: Mississippi History, 1865–1890," *Journal of American History* 77 (June 1990).

Irvin C. Mollison, "Negro Lawyers in Mississippi," *Journal of Negro History* 15 (January 1930).

James Tice Moore, "Redeemers Reconsidered: Change and Continuity in the Democratic South, 1870–1900," *Journal of Southern History* 44 (August 1978).

George C. Osborn, "The Life of a Southern Plantation Owner During Reconstruction as Revealed in the Clay Sharkey Papers," *Journal of Mississippi History* 6 (April 1944).

Lawrence N. Powell, "Correcting for Fraud: A Quantitative Reassessment of the Mississippi Ratification Election of 1868," *Journal of Southern History* 55 (November 1989).

William A. Russ Jr., "The Negro and White Disfranchisement During Radical Reconstruction," *Journal of Negro History* 19 (April 1934).

William A. Russ Jr., "Registration and Disfranchisement Under Radical Reconstruction," *Mississippi Valley Historical Review* 21 (September 1934).

David G. Sansing, "The Failure of Johnsonian Reconstruction in Mississippi, 1865–1866," *Journal of Mississippi History* 34 (November 1972).

George Kline Shank Jr., "Meridian: A Mississippi City at Birth, During the Civil War, and in Reconstruction," *Journal of Mississippi History* 26 (November 1964).

L. Moody Simms Jr., "In the Gloomy Macrocosm of Lucifer: A Mississippian Comments on the Beginnings of Reconstruction," *Journal of Mississippi History* 30 (1968).

James L. Sledge III, "The Chisholm Massacre: Politics and Violence in East Mississippi," *Journal of Mississippi History* 55 (August 1993).

David L. Smiley, "Cassius M. Clay and the Mississippi Election of 1875," *Journal of Mississippi History* 19 (October 1957).

Alfred Holt Stone, "The Basis of White Political Control in Mississippi," *Journal of Mississippi History* 6 (October 1944).

Alfred Holt Stone, "A Mississippian's View of Civil Rights, States Rights, and the Reconstruction Background," *Journal of Mississippi History* 10 (1948).

Alfred Holt Stone, "Post Bellum Reconstruction: An American Experience," *Journal of Mississippi History* 3 (1941).

Allen W. Trelease, "Who Were the Scalawags?" *Journal of Southern History* 29 (November 1963).

William W. White, "Mississippi Confederate Veterans in Public Office: 1875–1900," *Journal of Mississippi History* 20 (1958).

William F. Winter, "Mississippi's Civil War Governors," *Journal of Mississippi History* 51 (1989).

What follows are the graduate theses and dissertations that were consulted, with the first four used as constant sources of reference:

Ross H. Moore, "Social and Economic Conditions in Mississippi During Reconstruction" (PhD Dissertation, Duke University, 1937).

William Charles Sallis, "The Color Line in Mississippi Politics, 1865–1915" (PhD Dissertation, University of Kentucky, 1967).

Buford Satcher, "Blacks in Mississippi Politics, 1865–1900" (PhD Dissertation, Oklahoma State University, 1976).

William Whitley, "Precious Memories: Narratives of the Democracy in Mississippi, 1865–1915" (PhD Dissertation; University of Florida, 2003).

* * *

Charles Bacon, "A History of Hinds County, Mississippi During Reconstruction, 1865–1875" (Master's Thesis, Mississippi College, 1959).

Donald Breese, "Politics in the Lower South During Presidential Reconstruction" (PhD Dissertation, UCLA, 1964).

Euline Brock, "Black Political Leadership During Reconstruction" (PhD Dissertation, North Texas State University, 1974).

Paul William Burch, "How Are You Going to Keep Them Down on the Farm?: A Legislative and Judicial Survey of the Mississippi Enticement Laws: 1865–1917" (Master's Thesis, University of Mississippi, 1979).

Elizabeth Caldwell, "Reconstruction in Yazoo County, Mississippi" (Master's Thesis, University of North Carolina, 1931).

Shaan Jehangir Chilukuri, "Sharecropping, Shackles, Sugar, and Shipyards: Tracing and Contrasting Rural and Urban Black Labor in Louisiana During and After Radical Reconstruction, 1867–90" (Master's Thesis, George Washington University, 2023).

Michael Connolly, "Reconstruction in Kemper County, Mississippi" (Master's Thesis, Old Dominion University, 1989).

James T. Currie, "Vicksburg, 1863–1870: The Promise and the Reality of Reconstruction in Mississippi (PhD Dissertation, University of Virginia, 1975).

Michael Fitzgerald, "The Union League Movement in Alabama and Mississippi: Politics and Agricultural Change" (PhD Dissertation, UCLA, 1986).

Walter Gerald Howell, "An Appraisal of the 1868 Mississippi Constitutional Convention and its Negro Delegates," (Master's Thesis; Mississippi College, 1964).

Richard L. Hume, "The Black and Tan Constitutional Conventions of 1867–1869 in Ten Former Confederate States: A Study of Their Membership," (PhD Dissertation, University of Washington, 1969).

DeVin Johnson, "Reconstruction in Georgia and Legal Precedent" (Master's Thesis, San Diego State University, 2023).

Sally McWhite, "Echoes of the Lost Cause: Civil War Reverberations in Mississippi from 1865 to 2001" (PhD Dissertation, University of Mississippi, 2002).

Mary Lou Peyton, "The Mississippi Whigs" (Master's Thesis, University of Alabama, 1932).

Lawrence Powell, "New Masters: Northern Planters During the Civil War and Reconstruction" (PhD Dissertation, Yale University, 1976).

David G. Sansing, "The Role of the Scalawag in Mississippi Reconstruction" (PhD Dissertation, University of Southern Mississippi, 1969).

Irene Shurden, "A History of Washington County, Mississippi to 1900" (Master's Thesis, Mississippi College, 1963).

Dorothy Vick Smith, "Black Reconstruction in Mississippi, 1862–1870" (PhD Dissertation, University of Kansas, 1985).

John Polk Thompson, "The American Missionary Association in Mississippi, 1865–1877" (Master's Thesis, Mississippi State University, 1978).

Michael Wayne, "Ante-Bellum Planters in the Post-Bellum South: The Natchez District, 1860–1880" (PhD Dissertation, Yale University, 1979).

James Levon Williams, "Civil War and Reconstruction in the Yazoo Mississippi Delta, 1863–1875" (PhD Dissertation, University of Arizona, 1992).

Keith Andrew Winsell, "Black Identity: The Southern Negro, 1830–1895" (PhD Dissertation, UCLA, 1971).

William Leon Woods, "The Travail of Freedom: Mississippi Blacks, 1862–1870" (PhD Dissertation, Princeton University, 1979).

GeColby J. Youngblood, "Hiram R. Revels, Founder and First President of Alcorn State University: A Political History of Reconstruction, Republicanism, and Redemption in Mississippi, 1865–1875" (Master's Thesis, North Carolina Central University, 2023).

Throughout the decade following the end of the War, there was a cottage industry of journalists and reporters who toured all or parts of the South and published dispatches as they went with their home newspapers or magazines. Those dispatches were then compiled and published as books. Here's a list of the ones I found helpful:

Frederic A. Bancroft, *A Sketch of the Negro in Politics, Especially in South Carolina and Mississippi* (New York: J. F. Pearson, 1885).

Randy Bishop, *Marching for Union: A Civil War Soldier's Walk Across Reconstruction South* (Guilford, CT: Stackpole Books, 2021).

John Richard Dennett, *The South as It Is, 1865–1866* (1866; repr., Athens: University of Georgia Press, 1986).

Arthur James Lyon Fremantle, *Three Months in the Southern States, April–June, 1863* (London: William Blackwood & Sons, 1863) BiblioLife reprint.

J. Matthew Gallman, ed., *A Tour of Reconstruction: Anna Dickinson, Travel Letters of 1875* (Lexington: University Press of Kentucky, 2011).

Edward King, *The Southern States of North America: A Record of Journeys* (London: Blackie & Son, 1875) Nabu Public Domain Reprint.

Edward King, "The Great South," *Scribner's Monthly* 8 (September 1874).

Thomas W. Knox, *Camp-Fire and Cotton-Field: A "New York Herald" Correspondent's View of the American Civil War* (London: Leonaur, 2008). This is a Leonaur reprint of the book originally published in 1865 under the title *Camp-Fire and Cotton-Field: Southern Adventure in Time of War*.

Charles Nordhoff, *The Cotton States in the Spring and Summer of 1875* (New York: D. Appleton, 1876).

Whitelaw Reid, *After the War: A Southern Tour, May 1, 1865 to May 1, 1866* (New York: Moore, Wilstach & Baldwin, 1866).

Robert Somers, *The Southern States Since the War, 1870–1871* (1871; repr., Tuscaloosa: University of Alabama Press, 1965).

J. T. Trowbridge, *The South: A Tour of Its Battlefields and Ruined Cities: A Journey Through the Desolated States and Talks with the People* (Hartford, CT: L. Stebbins, 1866) Nabu Public Domain Reprint.

Ernst von Hesse-Wartegg, *Travels on the Lower Mississippi: 1879–1880* (Columbia: University of Missouri Press, 1990).

From 1898 to 1914, the newly organized Mississippi Historical Society published an annual collection of articles covering state history topics, including a number of county-specific histories of reconstruction. The Mississippi Historical Society separately published three long articles from 1912 to 1916 by journalist J. S. McNeily. All of the Mississippi Historical Society papers gave the unvarnished white Democratic perspective, and while much of what those authors wrote is unashamedly slanted toward that view, there are times, especially when they are describing KKK activities or electioneering, that what they wrote is believable because it comes off more as bragging about what they were able to accomplish than embellishment. Taking into consideration that more than thirty years had passed since the fateful 1875 election, and what they did was celebrated by whites throughout the South, these writers were proud to lay claim to their achievements.

Robert Bowman, "Reconstruction in Yazoo County," *Publications of the Mississippi Historical Society* 7 (1903).

W. H. Braden, "Reconstruction in Lee County," *Publications of the Mississippi Historical Society* 10 (1909).

F. Z. Browne, "Reconstruction in Oktibbeha County," *Publications of the Mississippi Historical Society* 13 (1914).

Charles Hillman Brough, "The Clinton Riot," *Publications of the Mississippi Historical Society* 6 (1902).

Charles Hillman Brough, "History of Taxation in Mississippi," *Publications of the Mississippi Historical Society* 2 (1989).

S. S. Calhoun, "The Causes and Events That Led to the Calling of the Constitutional Convention of 1890," *Publications of the Mississippi Historical Society* 6 (1902).

Josie Frazee Cappleman, "Importance of the Local History of the Civil War," *Publications of the Mississippi Historical Society* 3 (1900).

W. H. Hardy, "Recollections of Reconstruction in East and Southeast Mississippi," *Publications of the Mississippi Historical Society* 4 (1901).

W. H. Hardy, "Recollections of Reconstruction in East and Southeast Mississippi," *Publications of the Mississippi Historical Society* 8 (1904).

Frank Johnson, "The Conference of October 15, 1875, Between General George and Governor Ames," *Publications of the Mississippi Historical Society* 6 (1902).

Frank Johnson, "Suffrage and Reconstruction in Mississippi," *Publications of the Mississippi Historical Society* 6 (1902).

J. H. Jones, "Reconstruction in Wilkinson County," *Publications of the Mississippi Historical Society* 8 (1904).

Julia Kendel, "Reconstruction in Lafayette County," *Publications of the Mississippi Historical Society* 13 (1914).

George J. Leftwich, "Reconstruction in Monroe County," *Publications of the Mississippi Historical Society* 9 (1906).

J. S. McNeily, "Climax and Collapse of Reconstruction in Mississippi, 1874–1876," *Publications of the Mississippi Historical Society* 12 (1912).

J. S. McNeily, "From Organization to Overthrow of Mississippi's Provisional Government, 1865–1868," *Publications of the Mississippi Historical Society*, Centenary Series 1 (1916).

J. S. McNeily, "War and Reconstruction in Mississippi, 1863–1890," *Publications of the Mississippi Historical Society*, Centenary Series 2 (1918).

Irby C. Nichols, "Reconstruction in DeSoto County," *Publications of the Mississippi Historical Society* 11 (1910).

J. L. Power, "The Black and Tan Convention," *Publications of the Mississippi Historical Society* 3 (1900).

Dunbar Rowland, "The Rise and Fall of Negro Rule in Mississippi," *Publications of the Mississippi Historical Society* 2 (1899).

Alfred Holt Stone, "Mississippi's Constitution and Statutes in Reference to Freedmen and Their Alleged Relation to the Reconstruction Acts and War Amendments," *Publications of the Mississippi Historical Society* 4 (1901).

Ruth Watkins, "Reconstruction in Marshall County," *Publications of the Mississippi Historical Society* 12 (1912).

Ruth Watkins, "Reconstruction in Newton County," *Publications of the Mississippi Historical Society* 11 (1910).

W. Calvin Wells, "Reconstruction and its Destruction in Hinds County," *Publications of the Mississippi Historical Society* 9 (1906).

Fred M. Witty, "Reconstruction in Carroll and Montgomery Counties," *Publications of the Mississippi Historical Society* 10 (1909).

These are books and articles written generally about Reconstruction in America that either had significant sections on the Mississippi experience or provided regional or national context for what was happening in the state. The first group includes the ones I used most often:

Justin Behrend, *Reconstructing Democracy: Grassroots Black Politics in the Deep South After the Civil War* (Athens: University of Georgia Press, 2017).

Herman Belz, *A New Birth of Freedom: The Republican Party and Freedmen's Rights, 1861–1866* (Westport, CT: Greenwood, 1976).

David W. Blight, *Race and Reunion: The Civil War in American Memory* (Boston: Harvard University Press, 2001).

David Herbert Donald, Jean Harvey Baker, and Michael F. Holt, *The Civil War and Reconstruction* (New York: W. W. Norton, 2001).

W. E. B. DuBois, *Black Reconstruction in America* (New York: Russell & Russell, 1935).

Douglas R. Egerton, *The Wars of Reconstruction: The Brief, Violent History of America's Most Progressive Era* (New York: Bloomsbury, 2014).

Eric Foner, *Reconstruction: America's Unfinished Revolution, 1863–1877* (New York: HarperCollins, 1988).

Henry Louis Gates Jr., *Stony the Road: Reconstruction, White Supremacy, and the Rise of Jim Crow* (New York: Penguin, 2019).

William Gillette, *Retreat from Reconstruction: 1869–1879* (Baton Rouge: Louisiana State University Press, 1979).

Allen C. Guelzo, *Fateful Lightning: A New History of the Civil War and Reconstruction* (New York: Oxford University Press, 2012).

Steven Hahn, *A Nation Under Our Feet: Black Political Struggles in the Rural South from Slavery to the Great Migration* (Cambridge, MA: Harvard University Press, 2003).

Richard L. Hume and Jerry B. Gough, *Blacks, Carpetbaggers, and Scalawags: The Constitutional Conventions of Radical Reconstruction* (Baton Rouge: Louisiana State University Press, 2008).

Erik Mathisen, *The Loyal Republic: Traitors, Slaves, and the Remaking of Citizenship in Civil War America* (Chapel Hill: University of North Carolina Press, 2018).

Stephanie McCurry, *Confederate Reckoning: Power and Politics in the Civil War South* (Cambridge, MA: Harvard University Press, 2010).

James M. McPherson, *Battle Cry of Freedom: The Civil War Era* (New York: Oxford University Press, 1988).

James M. McPherson, *Ordeal by Fire: The Civil War and Reconstruction* (New York: McGraw-Hill, 1982).

Michael Perman, *Reunion Without Compromise: The South and Reconstruction, 1965–1868* (Cambridge, MA: Harvard University Press, 1973).

Michael Perman, *The Road to Redemption: Southern Politics, 1869–1879* (Chapel Hill: University of North Carolina Press, 1984).

Heather Cox Richardson, *The Death of Reconstruction: Race, Labor, and Politics in the Post-Civil War North, 1865–1901* (Cambridge, MA: Harvard University Press, 2001).

Kenneth M. Stampp, *The Era of Reconstruction: America After the Civil War, 1865–1877* (New York: Alfred A. Knopf, 1965).

Richard White, *The Republic for White It Stands: The United States During Reconstruction and the Gilded Age, 1865–1896* (New York: Oxford University Press, 2017).

*   *   *

Eric Anderson and Alfred A. Moss Jr., eds., *The Facts of Reconstruction: Essays in Honor of John Hope Franklin* (Baton Rouge: Louisiana State University Press, 1991).

Edward L. Ayres, *The Promise of the New South: Life After Reconstruction* (New York: Oxford University Press, 1992).

Bruce E. Baker, *What Reconstruction Meant: Historical Memory in the American South* (Charlottesville: University of Virginia Press, 2007).

Lerone Bennett Jr., *Black Power U.S.A.: The Human Side of Reconstruction, 1867–1877* (Chicago: Johnson, 1967).

Douglas A. Blackmon, *Slavery by Another Name: The Re-Enslavement of Black Americans from the Civil War to World War II* (New York: Anchor Books/Random House, 2008).

Thomas J. Brown, ed., *Reconstructions: New Perspectives on the Postbellum United States* (Oxford: Oxford University Press, 2006).

W. Fitzhugh Brundage, ed., *A New History of the American South* (Chapel Hill: University of North Carolina Press, 2023).

Dan T. Carter, *When the War Was Over: The Failure of Self-Reconstruction in the South, 1865–1867* (Baton Rouge: Louisiana State University Press, 1985).

Hodding Carter, *The Angry Scar: The Story of Reconstruction* (New York: Doubleday, 1959).

Paul A. Cimbala and Randall M. Miller, eds., *The Great Task Before Us: Reconstruction as America's Continuing Civil War* (New York: Fordham University Press, 2010).

LaWanda Cox and John H. Cox, eds., *Reconstruction, the Negro, and the New South* (Columbia: University of South Carolina Press, 1973).

Richard Nelson Current, *Those Terrible Carpetbaggers: A Reinterpretation* (New York: Oxford University Press, 1988).

Robert Cruden, *The Negro in Reconstruction* (Englewood Cliffs: Prentice-Hall, 1969).

John Patrick Daly, *The War After the War: A New History of Reconstruction* (Athens: University of Georgia Press, 2022).

Luis-Alejandro Dinnella-Borrego, *The Risen Phoenix: Black Politics in the Post-Civil War Sound* (Charlottesville: University of Virginia Press, 2016).

David Donald, *The Nation in Crisis, 1861–1877* (New York: Appleton-Century Crofts, 1969).

David Donald, *The Politics of Reconstruction, 1863–1867* (Nashville: Parthenon, 1965).

Frederick Douglass, "Reconstruction," *Atlantic Monthly* (December 1866).

Gregory P. Downs, *Declarations of Dependence: The Long Reconstruction of Popular Politics in the South, 1861–1908* (Chapel Hill: University of North Carolina Press, 2011).

Michael J. Dubin, *United States Congressional Elections, 1788–1997* (London: McFarland,, 1998).

W. E. B. DuBois, "Reconstruction and its Benefits," *American Historical Review* (July 1910).

Carol Faulkner, *Women's Radical Reconstruction: The Freedmen's Aid Movement* (Philadelphia: University of Pennsylvania Press, 2004).

Michael W. Fitzgerald, *Splendid Failure: Postwar Reconstruction in the American South* (Chicago: Ivan R. Dee, 2007).

Walter L. Fleming, *Documentary History of Reconstruction: Political, Military, Social, Religious, Educational, and Industrial 1865 to the Present Time* (Cleveland, OH: Arthur H. Clark, 1907).

Lacy K. Ford, ed., *A Companion to The Civil War and Reconstruction* (Malden, MA: Blackwell, 2005).

Gaines M. Foster, *Moral Reconstruction: Christian Lobbyists and the Federal Legislation of Morality, 1865–1920* (Chapel Hill: University of North Carolina Press, 2002).

John Hope Franklin, *Race, and History: Selected Essays, 1938–1988* (Baton Rouge: Louisiana State University Press, 1989).

John Hope Franklin, *Reconstruction After the Civil War* (Chicago: University of Chicago Press, 1961).

Jon Grinspan, *The Age of Acrimony: How Americans Fought to Fix Their Democracy, 1865–1915* (New York: Bloomsbury, 2021).

William E. Gienapp, ed., *The Civil War and Reconstruction: A Documentary Collection* (New York: W. W. Norton, 2001).

Michael Goldfield, *The Color of Politics: Race and the Mainsprings of American Politics* (New York: New Press, 1997).

Allen C. Guelzo, *The Crisis of the American Republic: A History of the Civil War and Reconstruction Era* (New York: St. Martin's, 1995).

Steven Hahn, *A Nation Without Borders: The United States and Its World in an Age of Civil Wars, 1830–1910* (New York: Viking, 2016).

David Hardin, *The Lives and Images of Major Civil War Figures After the Shooting Stopped* (Chicago: Ivan R. Dee, 2010).

Robert Harrison, *Washington During Civil War and Reconstruction: Race and Radicalism* (Cambridge: Cambridge University Press, 2011).

Michel F. Holt, *By One Vote: The Disputed Presidential Election of 1876* (Lawrence: University Press of Kansas, 2008).

Peter Kolchin, *A Sphinx on the American Land: The Nineteenth-Century South in Comparative Perspective* (Baton Rouge: Louisiana State University Press, 2003).

J. Morgan Kousser and James M. McPherson, *Region, Race, and Reconstruction: Essays in Honor of C. Vann Woodward* (New York: Oxford University Press, 1982).

Charles Lane, *The Day Freedom Died: The Colfax Massacre, the Supreme Court, and the Betrayal of Reconstruction* (New York: Henry Holt, 2008).

John R. Lynch, "Some Historical Errors of James Ford Rhodes," *Journal of Negro History* 2 (October 1917).

Kris Manjapra, *Black Ghost of Empire: The Long Death of Slavery and the Failure of Emancipation* (New York: Scribner, 2022).

August Meier, *Negro Thought in America, 1880–1915: Racial Ideologies in the Age of Booker T. Washington* (Ann Arbor: University of Michigan Press, 1969).

A. B. Moore, "One Hundred Years of Reconstruction of the South," *Journal of Southern History* 9 (May 1943).

Jack Noe, *Contesting Commemoration: The 1876 Centennial, Independence Day, and the Reconstruction-Era South* (Baton Rouge: Louisiana State University Press, 2021).

Otto H. Olsen, ed., *Reconstruction and Redemption in the South* (Baton Rouge: Louisiana State University Press, 1980).

Michael Perman, *Pursuit of Unity: A Political History of the American South* (Chapel Hill: University of North Carolina Press, 2009).

Keith Ian Polakoff, *The Politics of Inertia: The Election of 1876 and the End of Reconstruction* (Baton Rouge: Louisiana State University Press, 1973).

K. Stephen Prince, *Radical Reconstruction: A Brief History with Documents* (New York: Bedford/St. Martin's, 2016).

Howard N. Rabinowitz, "From Exclusion to Segregation: Southern Race Relations, 1865–1890," *Journal of American History* 63 (September 1976).

Elizabeth A. Regosin and Donald R. Shaffer, *Voices of Emancipation: Understanding Slavery, the Civil War, and Reconstruction Through the U.S. Pension Bureau Files* (New York: New York University Press, 2008).

Heather Cox Richardson, *West from Appomattox: The Reconstruction of America After the Civil War* (New Haven, CT: Yale University Press, 2007).

Patrick W. Riddleberger, "The Radicals' Abandonment of the Negro During Reconstruction," *Journal of Negro History* 45 (April 1960).

David G. Sansing, ed., *What Was Freedom's Price* (Jackson: University Press of Mississippi, 1978).

James P. Shenton, *The Reconstruction: A Documentary History of the South After the War, 1865–1877* (New York: G. P. Putnam's Sons, 1963).

Francis Butler Simkins, *A History of the South* (New York: Alfred A. Knopf, 1956).

Brooks D. Simpson, ed., *Reconstruction: Voices from America's First Great Struggle for Racial Equality* (New York: Library of America, 2018).

Manisha Sinha, *The Rise and Fall of the Second American Republic: Reconstruction, 1860–1920* (New York: Liveright, 2024).

John David Smith, ed., *Reconstruction: Interpreting American History* (Kent, OH: Kent State University Press, 2016).

Mitchell Snay, *Fenians, Freedmen, and Southern Whites: Race and Nationality in the Era of Reconstruction* (Baton Rouge: Louisiana State University Press, 2007).

Mark Wahlgren Summers, *The Ordeal of the Reunion: A New History of Reconstruction* (Chapel Hill: University of North Carolina Press, 2014).

Charles Sumner, "Our Domestic Relations: Or, How to Treat the Rebel States," *Atlantic Monthly* (October 1863).

E. P. Whipple, "Reconstruction and Negro Suffrage," *Atlantic Monthly* (August 1865).

Brenda Wineapple, *Ecstatic Nation: Confidence, Crisis, and Panic, 1848–1877* (New York: HarperCollins, 2013).

C. Vann Woodward, "Books Considered: The Confederate Nation by Emory N. Thomas," *New Republic* (March 17, 1979).

PUBLIC POLICY TOPICS AND SPECIFIC ISSUES RELATED TO MISSISSIPPI RECONSTRUCTION

Agriculture, Cotton, and the Economy

Aaron Dale Anderson, *Builders of A New South: Merchants, Capital, and the Remaking of Natchez, 1865–1914* (Jackson: University Press of Mississippi, 2013).

George L. Anderson, "The South and Problems of Post-Civil War Finance," *Journal of Southern History* 9 (May 1943).

Bruce E. Baker and Brian Kelly, eds., *After Slavery: Race, Labor, and Citizenship in the Reconstruction South* (Gainesville: University Press of Florida, 2013).

Edward E. Baptist, *The Half Has Never Been Told: Slavery and the Making of American Capitalism* (New York: Basic Books, 2014).

Nicolas Barreyre, *Gold and Freedom: The Political Economy of Reconstruction* (Charlottesville: University of Virginia Press, 2015).

Sven Beckert, *Empire of Cotton: A Global History* (New York: Alfred A. Knopf, 2014).

Justin Behrend, "Freedpeople's Democracy: African-American Politics and Community in Postemancipation Natchez" (PhD Dissertation, Northwestern University, 2006).

Robert L. Brandfon, *Cotton Kingdom of the New South: A History of the Yazoo Mississippi Delta from Reconstruction to the Twentieth Century* (Cambridge, MA: Harvard University Press, 1967).

D. Clayton Brown, *King Cotton in Modern America: A Cultural, Political, and Economic History Since 1945* (Jackson: University Press of Mississippi, 2011).

Thomas D. Cockrell, "Meadow Woods, 1839–1989: A Mississippi Plantation" (PhD Dissertation, Mississippi State University, 1989).

"The Cotton Crop of the South," *Debow's Review* 1 (May 1866).

James T. Currie, *Enclave: Vicksburg and Her Plantations, 1863–1870* (Jackson: University Press of Mississippi, 1980).

Gene Dattel, *Cotton and Race in the Making of America: The Human Costs of Economic Power* (Chicago: Ivan R. Dee, 2009).

Ronald L. F. Davis, *Good and Faithful Labor: From Slavery to Sharecropping in the Natchez District, 1860–1890* (Westport, CT: Greenwood, 1982).

Gregory P. Downs and Kate Masur, eds., *The World the War Made* (Chapel Hill: University of North Carolina Press, 2015).

James S. Ferguson, "The Grange and Farmer Education in Mississippi," *Journal of Southern History* 8 (November 1942).

Gilbert C. Fite, *Cotton Fields No More: Southern Agriculture, 1865–1980* (Lexington: University Press of Kentucky, 1984).

"The Great Cotton Question," *Debow's Review* 1 (April 1866).

Emory Q. Hawk, *Economic History of the South* (New York: Prentice-Hall, 1934).

"Immigration Convention at Jackson, Mississippi," *Debow's Review* 5 (April 1868).

"Industrial Association of Mississippi," *Debow's Review* 5 (January 1868).

D. Clayton James, "Mississippi Agriculture: 1861–1865," *Journal of Mississippi History* 24 (July 1962).

Harold James, *Seven Crashes: The Economic Crises that Shaped Globalization* (New Haven, CT: Yale University Press, 2023).

Walter Johnson, *River of Dark Dreams: Slavery and Empire in the Cotton Kingdom* (Cambridge, MA: Harvard University Press, 2013).

Michael L. Lanza, *Agrarianism and Reconstruction Politics: The Southern Homestead Act* (Baton Rouge: Louisiana State University Press, 1990).

Jay R. Mandle, *Not Slave, Not Free: The African American Economic Experience Since the Civil War* (Durham, NC: Duke University Press, 1992).

Erin Stewart Mauldin, "Freedom, Economic Autonomy, and Ecological Change in the Cotton South, 1865–1880," *Journal of the Civil War Era* 7 (September 2017).

Erin Stewart Mauldin, *Unredeemed Land: An Environmental History of Civil War and Emancipation in the Cotton South* (New York: Oxford University Press, 2018).

John Hebron Moore, *Agriculture in Ante-Bellum Mississippi* (Columbia: University of South Carolina Press, 2010 and 1958).

John Hebron Moore, "Economic Conditions in Mississippi on the Eve of the Civil War," *Journal of Mississippi History* 22 (1960).

National Bureau of Economic Research, *Trends in the American Economy in the Nineteenth Century: Studies in Income and Wealth* (Princeton, NJ: Princeton University Press, 1960).

William N. Parker, "The South in the National Economy, 1865–1970," Paper Presented to the Third Conference of US/USSR Historians held at the Academy of Sciences, Moscow, December 1–5, 1978.

Lawrence N. Powell, *New Masters: Northern Planters during the Civil War and Reconstruction* (New Haven, CT: Yale University Press, 1980).

Howard N. Rabinowitz, *The First New South, 1865–1920* (Arlington Heights, IL: Harlan Davidson, 1992).

Roger L. Ransom and Richard Sutch, *One Kind of Freedom: The Economic Consequences of Emancipation* (New York: Cambridge University Press, 1977).

James L. Roark, *Masters Without Slaves: Southern Planters in the Civil War and Reconstruction* (New York: W. W. Norton, 1977).

Percy Roberts, "The Southern Cotton Crop—Mississippi," *Debow's Review* 2 (August 1866).

Sellew Roberts, "The Federal Government and Confederate Cotton," *American Historical Review* 32 (January 1927).

Mikko Saikku, *This Delta, This Land: An Environmental History of the Yazoo-Mississippi Floodplain* (Athens: University of Georgia Press, 2005).

Dale Edwyna Smith, *The Slaves of Liberty: Freedom in Amite County, Mississippi, 1820–1868* (New York: Garland, 1999).

"Statistics of Cotton," *Debow's Review* 1 (January 1866).

Irwin Unger, *The Greenback Era: A Social and Political History of America Finance, 1865–1879* (Princeton, NJ: Princeton University Press, 1964).

US Census Bureau, "Agriculture of the United States in 1860," *1860 Census of Population and Housing.*

US Census Bureau, "Report on Cotton Production in the United States; Also Embracing Agriculture and Physico-geographical Descriptions of Several Cotton States and of California, Part I: Mississippi Valley and Southwestern States," *1880 Census of Population and Housing,* vols. 5 and 6.

US Census Bureau, "Report on the Productions of Agriculture Embracing General Statistics and Monographs," *1880 Census of Population and Housing,* vol. 3.

Melissa Walker and James C. Cobb, eds., "Agriculture and Industry," in *The New Encyclopedia of Southern Culture*, vol. 11 (Chapel Hill: University of North Carolina Press, 2008).

James L. Watkins, *King Cotton: A Historical and Statistical Review, 1790–1908* (New York: James L. Watkins & Sons, 1908).

Michael Wayne, *The Reshaping of Plantation Society: The Natchez District, 1860–1880* (Baton Rouge: Louisiana State University Press, 1983).

B. I. Wiley, "Vicissitudes of Early Reconstruction Farming in the Lower Mississippi Valley," *Journal of Southern History* 3 (November 1937).

John C. Willis, *Forgotten Time: The Yazoo-Mississippi Delta After the Civil War* (Charlottesville: University Press of Virginia, 2000).

Harold D. Woodman, *King Cotton and His Retainers: Financing and Marketing the Cotton Crop of the South, 1800–1925* (Lexington: University of Kentucky Press, 1968).

Gavin Wright, *Old South, New South: Revolutions in the Southern Economy Since the Civil War* (New York: Basic Books, 1986).

Gavin Wright, *The Political Economy of the Cotton South: Households, Markets, and Wealth in the Nineteenth Century* (New York: W. W. Norton, 1978).

Conditions in Mississippi During the Time

Stephen V. Ash, *A Year in the South: Four Lives in 1865* (New York: Palgrave MacMillan, 2002).

John D. Barnhart, "Reconstruction on the Lower Mississippi," *Mississippi Valley Historical Review* 21 (December 1934).

Bradley G. Bond, *Political Culture in the Nineteenth-Century South: Mississippi, 1830–1900* (Baton Rouge: Louisiana State University Press, 1995).

Edwin DeLeon, "The New South: Agricultural Aspect," *Harper's New Monthly Magazine* 48 (January 1874).

Edwin DeLeon, "The New South: Commerce and Navigation," *Harper's New Monthly Magazine* 49 (September 1874).

Edwin DeLeon, "The New South: Industrial, Manufacturing, and Material Progress," *Harper's New Monthly Magazine* 48 (February 1874).

Edwin DeLeon, "Ruin and Reconstruction of the Southern States: A Record of Two Tours in 1868 and 1873, Prefatory," *Southern Magazine* 7 (January 1874).

Edwin DeLeon, "Ruin and Reconstruction of the Southern States: A Record of Two Tours in 1868 and 1873, II" *Southern Magazine* 7 (March 1874).

Edwin DeLeon, "Ruin and Reconstruction of the Southern States: Political Reconstruction, Past and Present, III" *Southern Magazine* 7 (May 1874).Edwin DeLeon, "Ruin and Reconstruction of the Southern States: A Record of Two Tours in 1868 and 1873, IV," *Southern Magazine* 7 (June 1874).

Robert W. Dubay, "Mississippi Political, Civilian, and Military Realities of 1861: A Study in Frustration and Confusion," *Journal of Mississippi History* 36 (1974).

"Education of the Freedmen," *Debow's Review* 2 (September 1866).

"Education of the Freedmen," *Debow's Review* 3 (March 1867).

Richard Griggs, *Guide to Mississippi* (Jackson: Pilot, 1874) Archives and Special Collections, University of Mississippi Library, Oxford, Mississippi.

Jack W. Gunn, "Mississippi in 1860 As Reflected in the Activities of the Governor's Office," *Journal of Mississippi History* 22 (1960).

William A. Love, "Reminiscences of the Closing Days of the War of Secession," *Publications of the Mississippi Historical Society*, Centenary Series 4 (1921).

Dunbar Rowland, "Plantation Life in Mississippi Before the War," *Publications of the Mississippi Historical Society* 3 (1900).

James W. Silver, "The Breakdown of Morale in Central Mississippi in 1864: Letters of Judge
    Robert S. Hudson," *Journal of Mississippi History* 16 (1954).
E. G. Wall, *State of Mississippi: Resources, Condition and Wants* (Jackson: Clarion Steam
    Printing Establishment, 1879). Archives and Special Collections, University of Mississippi
    Library, Oxford, Mississippi.
Jesse Thomas Wallace, "A History of the Negroes of Mississippi from 1865 to 1890" (PhD
    Dissertation, Columbia University, 1927).

Congress, Constitution, Judiciary, Law, and the Amendments

Martin Abbott, *The Republican Party and the South, 1855–1877: The First Southern Strategy*
    (Chapel Hill: University of North Carolina Press, 1986).
Keith Aoki, "The Scholarship of Reconstruction and the Politics of Backlash," *Iowa Law Review*
    81 (July 1996).
David A. Bateman, Ira Katznelson, and John S. Lapinski, *Southern Nation: Congress and White
    Supremacy After Reconstruction* (Princeton, NJ: Princeton University Press, 2018).
Michael A. Bellesiles, *Inventing Equality: Reconstructing the Constitution in the Aftermath of the
    Civil War* (New York: St. Martin's, 2020).
Herman Belz, *Emancipation and Equal Rights: Politics and Constitutionalism in the Civil War
    Era* (New York: W. W. Norton, 1978).
Herman Belz, "Origins of Negro Suffrage During the Civil War," *Southern Studies* (Summer
    1978).
Herman Belz, *Reconstructing the Union: Theory and Policy During the Civil War* (Ithaca, New
    York: Cornell University Press, 1969).
Michael Les Benedict, *A Compromise of Principle: Congressional Republicans and
    Reconstruction, 1863–1869* (New York: W. W. Norton, 1974).
Michael Les Benedict, "Preserving the Constitution: The Conservative Basis of Radical
    Reconstruction," *Journal of American History* 61 (June 1974).
Michael Les Benedict, *Preserving the Constitution: Essays on Politics and the Constitution in the
    Reconstruction Era* (New York: Fordham University Press, 2006).
Michael Les Benedict, "Southern Democrats in the Crisis of 1876–1877: A Reconsideration of
    Reunion and Reaction," *Journal of Southern History* 46 (November 1980).
W. R. Brock, *An American Crisis: Congress and Reconstruction, 1865–1867* (New York:
    MacMillan, 1963).
Anthony Chase, "Historical Reconstruction in Poplar Legal and Political Culture," *Seton Hall
    Law Review* 24 (1994).
Gabriel J. Chin, "The Voting Rights Act of 1867: The Constitutionality of Federal Regulation of
    Suffrage During Reconstruction," *North Carolina Law Review* 82 (June 2004).
William Cohen, "Negro Involuntary Servitude in the South, 1865–1940: A Preliminary
    Analysis," *Journal of Southern History* 42 (February 1976).
David P. Currie, "The Civil War Congress," *University of Chicago Law Review* 73 (Fall 2006).
David P. Currie, "The Constitution in the Supreme Court: Civil War and Reconstruction,
    1865–1873," *University of Chicago Law Review* 51 (Winter, 1984).
David P. Currie, "The Reconstruction Congress," *University of Chicago Law Review* 75 (Winter
    2008).
Faye E. Dudden, *Fighting Chance: The Struggle over Woman Suffrage and Black Suffrage in
    Reconstruction America* (New York: Oxford University Press, 2011).
Laura F. Edwards, *A Legal History of the Civil War and Reconstruction: A Nation of Rights* (New
    York: Cambridge University Press, 2015).

Eric Foner, *The Second Founding: How the Civil War and Reconstruction Remade the Constitution* (New York: W. W. Norton, 2019).

Katherine M. Franke, "Becoming a Citizen: Reconstruction Era Regulation of African American Marriages," *Yale Journal of Law and the Humanities* 11 (Summer 1999).

Sally E. Hadden and Patricia Hagler Minter, eds., *Signposts: New Directions in Southern Legal History* (Athens: University of Georgia Press, 2013).

John Harrison, "The Lawfulness of the Reconstruction Amendments," *University of Chicago Law Review* 68 (Spring 2001).

Peter Charles Hoffer, *Uncivil Warriors: The Lawyers' Civil War* (New York: Oxford University Press, 2018).

Harold Holzer and Sara Vaughn Gabbard, eds., *Lincoln and Freedom: Slavery, Emancipation, and the Thirteenth Amendment* (Carbondale: Southern Illinois University Press, 2007).

Harold M. Hyman, *A More Perfect Union: The Impact of the Civil War and Reconstruction on the Constitution* (New York: Alfred A. Knopf, 1973).

Joseph B. James, *The Framing of the Fourteenth Amendment* (Urbana: University of Illinois Press, 1965).

Jeffery A. Jenkins and Justin Peck, *Congress and the First Civil Rights Era, 1861–1918* (Chicago: University of Chicago Press, 2021).

Robert J. Kaczorowski, "Federal Enforcement of Civil Rights During the First Reconstruction," *Fordham Urban Law Journal* 23 (1995).

Larry Kincaid, "Victims of Circumstance: An Interpretation of Changing Attitudes Toward Republican Policy Makers and Reconstruction," *Journal of American History* 57 (June 1970).

Earl M. Matz, "The Fourteenth Amendment as Political Compromise: Section One in the Joint Committee on Reconstruction," *Ohio State Law Journal* 45 (1984).

Donald G. Nieman, "From Slaves to Citizens: African-Americans, Rights Consciousness, and Reconstruction," *Cardozo Law Review* 17 (May 1996).

Dylan C. Penningroth, *Before the Movement: The Hidden History of Black Civil Rights* (New York: W. W. Norton, 2023).

Allan Peskin, "Was There a Compromise of 1877," *Journal of American History* 60 (June 1973).

Richard H. Pildes, "Democracy, Anti-Democracy, and the Canon," *Constitutional Commentary* 17 (Summer 2000).

David Prior, *Between Freedom and Progress: The Lost World of Reconstruction Politics* (Baton Rouge: Louisiana State University Press, 2019).

Joseph A. Ranney, *In the Wake of Slavery: Civil War, Civil Rights, and the Reconstruction of Southern Law* (Westport, CT: Praeger, 2006).

Leonard L. Richards, *Who Freed the Slaves?: The Fight over the Thirteenth Amendment* (Chicago: University of Chicago Press, 2015).

Heather Cox Richardson, *To Make Men Free: A History of the Republican Party* (New York: Basic Books, 2014).

Christopher W. Schmidt, "The Fourteenth Amendment and the Transformation of Civil Rights," *Journal of the Civil War Era* 10 (March 2020).

Everette Swinney, "Enforcing the Fifteenth Amendment, 1870–1877," *Journal of Southern History* 28 (May 1962).

Christopher Waldrep, "Black Access to Law in Reconstruction: The Case of Warren County, Mississippi," *Chicago-Kent Law Review* 70 (1994).

Christopher Waldrep and Lynne Curry, *The Constitution and the Nation: The Civil War and American Constitutionalism: 1830–1890* (New York: Peter Lang, 2003).

C. Vann Woodward, *Reunion, and Reaction: The Compromise of 1877 and the End of Reconstruction* (Boston: Little, Brown, 1951).

Emancipation, Labor, Land, Contrabands, Refugees, and the Freedman's Bureau

Martin Abbott, "Free Land, Free Labor, and the Freedmen's Bureau," *Agricultural History* 30 (October 1956).

Kevin Adams and Leonne M. Hudson, eds., *Democracy and the American Civil War: Race and African Americans in the Nineteenth Century* (Kent, OH: Kent State University Press, 2016).

Danielle Alexander, "Forty Acres and a Mule: The Ruined Hope of Reconstruction," *Humanities* 25 (January/February 2004).

Herbert Aptheker, "Notes on Slave Conspiracies in Confederate Mississippi," *Journal of Negro History* 29 (January 1944).

Ira Berlin, *The Long Emancipation: The Demise of Slavery in the United States* (Cambridge, MA: Harvard University Press, 2015).

Martha M. Bigelow, "Plantation Lease Problems in 1864," *Journal of Southern History* 27 (August 1961).

John W. Blassingame, ed., *Slave Testimony: Two Centuries of Letters, Speeches, Interviews, and Autobiographies* (Baton Rouge: Louisiana State University Press, 1977).

Joseph E. Brent, "Occupied Corinth: The Contraband Camp and the First Alabama Regiment of African Descent, 1862–1864," Paper Prepared for the City of Corinth, Mississippi and The Siege and Battle of Corinth Commission, (February 1995).

H. Clark Burkett, "Jefferson College, the Freedmen's Bureau and Union Occupation," *Journal of Mississippi History* 66 (Summer 2004).

Paul A. Cimbala, *The Freedmen's Bureau: Reconstructing the American South After the Civil War* (Malabar, FL: Krieger, 2005).

Paul A. Cimbala and Randall M. Miller, eds., *The Freedmen's Bureau and Reconstruction: Reconsiderations* (New York: Fordham University Press, 1999).

John Cimprich, *Navigating Liberty: Black Refugees and Antislavery Reformers in the Civil War South* (Baton Rouge, Louisiana State University Press, 2023).

William Cohen, *At Freedom's Edge: Black Mobility and the Southern White Quest for Racial Control, 1861–1915* (Baton Rouge: Louisiana State University Press, 1991).

Brian T. Corrigan, "Contraband Camps: The Cultural and Political Meeting Grounds of the Civil War" (Master's Thesis, Boston College, 2005).

LaWanda Cox, "The Promise of Land for the Freedmen," *Mississippi Valley Historical Review* 45 (December 1958).

Gregory Downs, *After Appomattox: Military Occupation and the Ends of War* (Cambridge, MA: Harvard University Press, 2015).

Jim Downs, *Sick from Freedom: African-American Illness and Suffering During the Civil War and Reconstruction* (New York: Oxford University Press, 2012).

W. E. B. DuBois, "The Freedmen's Bureau," *Atlantic Monthly* (March 1901).

John Eaton, *Grant, Lincoln, and the Freedmen: Reminiscences of the Civil War* (New York: Longmans, Green, 1907), Nabu Public Domain Reprint.

Paul D. Escott, *What Shall We Do With the Negro? Lincoln, White Racism, and Civil War America* (Charlottesville: University of Virginia Press, 2009).

Walter L. Fleming, "Forty Acres and a Mule," *North American Review* 182 (May 1906).

Richard Follett, Eric Foner and Walter Johnson, *Slavery's Ghost: The Problem of Freedom in the Age of Emancipation* (Baltimore: Johns Hopkins University Press, 2011).

Eric Foner, *Forever Free: The Story of Emancipation and Reconstruction* (New York: Vintage Books, 2005).

Eric Foner, "The Meaning of Freedom in the Age of Emancipation," *Journal of American History* 81 (September 1994).

Eric Foner, *Nothing but Freedom: Emancipation and Its Legacy* (Baton Rouge: Louisiana State University Press, 1983).

Lacy K. Ford, *Deliver Us from Evil: The Slavery Question in the Old South* (New York: Oxford University Press, 2009).

Gaines M. Foster, "The Limitations of Federal Health Care for Freedmen, 1862–1868," *Journal of Southern History* 48 (August 1982).

"The Freedmen's Story," *Atlantic Monthly* (February 1866 and March 1866).

Clifton Ganus, "The Freedmen's Bureau in Mississippi" (PhD Dissertation, Tulane University, 1953).

Paul Wallace Gates, "Federal Land Policy in the South, 1866–1888," *Journal of Southern History* 6 (August 1940).

Kenneth S. Greenberg, "The Civil War and the Redistribution of Land: Adams County, Mississippi, 1860–1870," *Agricultural History* 52 (April 1978).

Allen C. Guelzo, *Lincoln's Emancipation Proclamation: The End of Slavery in America* (New York: Simon & Schuster, 2004).

Herbert G. Gutman, *The Black Family in Slavery and Freedom, 1750–1925* (New York: Pantheon Books, 1976).

Steven Hahn, *The Political Worlds of Slavery and Freedom* (Cambridge, MA: Harvard University Press, 2009).

George D. Humphrey, "The Failure of Mississippi Freedmen's Bureau in Black Labor Relations, 1865–1867," *Journal of Mississippi History* 45 (February 1983).

Dale Kretz, *Administering Freedom: The State of Emancipation After the Freedmen's Bureau* (Chapel Hill: University of North Carolina Press, 2022).

Andrew F. Lang, *In the Wake of War: Military Occupation, Emancipation, and Civil War America* (Baton Rouge: Louisiana State University Press, 2017).

Leon F. Litwack, *Been in the Storm So Long: The Aftermath of Slavery* (New York: Alfred A. Knopf, 1979).

Ed. M. Main, *The Story of the Marches, Battles and Incidents of the Third United States Colored Cavalry* (Louisville, KY: Globe, 1980), Nabu Public Domain Reprint.

Chandra Manning, *Troubled Refuge: Struggling for Freedom in the Civil War* (New York: Alfred A. Knopf, 2016).

Chandra Manning, "Working for Citizenship in Civil War Contraband Camps," *Journal of the Civil War Era* 4 (June 2014).

William S. McFeely, *Yankee Stepfather: General O. O. Howard and the Freedmen* (New Haven, CT: Yale University Press, 1968).

James M. McPherson, *The Negro's Civil War: How American Negroes Felt and Acted During the War for the Union* (New York: Pantheon Books, 1965).

Donald G. Nieman, "Andrew Johnson, the Freedmen's Bureau, and the Problem of Equal Rights, 1865–1866," *Journal of Southern History* 44 (August 1978).

Donald G. Nieman, "The Freedmen's Bureau and the Mississippi Black Code," *Journal of Mississippi History* 40 (May 1978).

Paul S. Pardue, *In Search of the 1st Regiment of African Descent and the Contraband Camp of Corinth, Mississippi,* (Corinth, MS: Corinth Civil War Interpretative Center Archives, September 2000).

Bennett Parten, *Somewhere Toward Freedom: Sherman's March and the Story of America's Largest Emancipation* (New York: Simon & Schuster, 2025).

Michael Perman, *Emancipation and Reconstruction*, 2d ed., (Wheeling, IL: Harlan Davidson, 2003).

Edward L. Pierce, "The Contrabands at Fortress Monroe," *Atlantic Monthly* (November 1861).

Records of the Assistant Commissioner for the State of Mississippi Bureau of Refugees, Freedmen, and Abandoned Lands 1865–1869 (National Archives Microfilm Publication M826, roll 1 and roll 7); Records of the Bureau of Refugees, Freedmen and Abandoned Lands, Record Group 105; National Archives Building, Washington, DC.

Records of the Field Offices for the State of Mississippi Bureau of Refugees, Freedmen, and Abandoned Lands 1865–1869 (National Archives Microfilm Publication M1907, roll 1); Records of the Bureau of Refugees, Freedmen and Abandoned Lands, Record Group 105; National Archives Building, Washington, DC.

Joseph P. Reidy, Illusions of Emancipation: The Pursuit of Freedom and Equality in the Twilight of Slavery (Chapel Hill: University of North Carolina Press, 2019).

Joe M. Richardson, Christian Reconstruction: The American Missionary Association and Southern Blacks, 1861–1890 (Tuscaloosa: University of Alabama Press, 1986).

John C. Rodrigue, Freedom's Crescent: The Civil War and the Destruction of Slavery in the Lower Mississippi Valley (New York: Cambridge University Press, 2023).

Willie Lee Rose, Rehearsal for Reconstruction: The Port Royal Experiment (Athens: University of Georgia Press, 1999 edition).

James E. Sefton, The United States Army and Reconstruction, 1865–1877 (Baton Rouge: Louisiana State University Press, 1967).

David Slay, "Abraham Lincoln and the United States Colored Troops of Mississippi," Journal of Mississippi History 70 (Spring 2008).

Dorothy Sterling, ed., The Trouble They Seen: Black People Tell the Story of Reconstruction (New York: Doubleday, 1976).

Daniel E. Sutherland, "A Special Kind of Problem: The Response of Household Slaves and Their Masters to Freedom," Southern Studies 20 (Summer 1981).

Amy Murrell Taylor, Embattled Freedom: Journeys Through the Civil War's Slave Refugee Camps (Chapel Hill: University of North Carolina Press, 2018).

Cam Walker, "Corinth: The Story of a Contraband Camp," Civil War History 20 (March 1974).

Michelle Wartman, "Contraband, Runaways, Freemen: New Definitions of Reconstruction Created by the Civil War," International Social Science Review (Fall/Winter, 2001).

Kristy Armstrong White, "Life in Civil War Tishomingo County, Mississippi" (Master's Thesis, Mississippi State University, 1998).

Bell Irvin Wiley, Southern Negroes: 1861–1865 (Baton Rouge: Louisiana State University Press, 1938).

Davis Bend

Martha Mitchell Bigelow, "Vicksburg: Experiment in Freedom," Journal of Mississippi History 26 (February 1964).

James T. Currie, ed., "Freedmen at Davis Bend, April 1864," Journal of Mississippi History 46 (May 1984).

Frank E. Everett Jr., Brierfield: Plantation Home of Jefferson Davis (Hattiesburg: University & College Press of Mississippi, 1971).

Thavolia Glymph, "The Second Middle Passage: The Transition from Slavery to Freedom at Davis Bend, Mississippi" (PhD Dissertation, Purdue University, 1994).

Janet Sharp Hermann, The Pursuit of a Dream (New York: Oxford University Press, 1981).

Steven Joseph Ross, "Freed Soil, Freed Labor, Freed Men: John Eaton and the Davis Bend Experiment," Journal of Southern History 44 (May 1978).

Education

James D. Anderson, *The Education of Blacks in the South, 1860–1935* (Chapel Hill: University of North Carolina Press, 1988).

Charles C. Bolton, *The Hardest Deal of All: The Battle over School Integration in Mississippi, 1870–1980* (Jackson: University Press of Mississippi, 2005).

Ronald E. Butchart, *Schooling the Freed People: Teaching, Learning, and the Struggle for Black Freedom, 1861–1876* (Chapel Hill: University of North Carolina Press, 2010).

Alfred Benjamin Butts, "Public Education," chap. 2 in "Public Administration in Mississippi," *Publications of the Mississippi Historical Society*, Centenary Series 3 (1919).

Clarice T. Campbell and Oscar Allan Rogers Jr., *Mississippi: The View from Tougaloo* (Jackson: University Press of Mississippi, 1979).

Sarah L. Hyde, *Schooling in the Antebellum South: The Rise of Public and Private Education in Louisiana, Mississippi, and Alabama* (Baton Rouge: Louisiana State University Press, 2016).

Robert L. Jenkins, "The Development of Black Higher Education in Mississippi," *Journal of Mississippi History* 45 (November 1983).

Kenneth R. Johnson, "Legrand Winfield Perce: A Mississippi Carpetbagger and the Fight for Federal Aid to Education," *Journal of Mississippi History* 34 (November 1972).

Ward M. McAfee, *Religion, Race, and Reconstruction: The Public School in the Politics of the 1870s* (Albany: State University of New York Press, 1998).

"On Negro Schools," *Harper's New Monthly Magazine* 44 (September 1874).

Christopher M. Span, "Citizen or Laborer? The Social Purpose of Black Schooling in Reconstruction Mississippi" (PhD Dissertation, University of Illinois-Champaign, 2001).

Christopher M. Span, *From Cotton Field to Schoolhouse: African American Education in Mississippi, 1862–1875* (Chapel Hill: University of North Carolina Press, 2009).

Christopher M. Span, "I Must Learn Now or Not at All: Social and Cultural Capital in the Educational Initiatives of Formerly Enslaved African Americans in Mississippi, 1862–1869," *Journal of African American History* 87 (Spring 2002).

Randy J. Sparks, "The White People's Arms Are Longer than Ours: Blacks, Education, and the American Missionary Association in Reconstruction Mississippi," *Journal of Mississippi History* 54 (February 1992).

Elise Timberlake, "Did the Reconstruction Regime Give Mississippi Her Public Schools," *Publications of the Mississippi Historical Society* 12 (1912).

Ku Klux Klan, Terror, and Violence

William Bell, "The Ku Klux Klan in Mississippi, 1866–1872" (Master's Thesis, Mississippi State University, 1963).

Fergus M. Bordewich, *Klan War: Ulysses S. Grant and the Battle to Save Reconstruction* (New York: Alfred A. Knopf, 2023).

Stephen Budiansky, *The Bloody Shirt: Terror After the Civil War* (New York: Penguin Group, 2008).

Stephen Cresswell, "Enforcing the Enforcement Acts: The Department of Justice in Northern Mississippi, 1870–1890," *Journal of Southern History* 53 (August 1987).

Guy Gugliotta, *Grant's Enforcer: Taking Down the Klan* (Athens: University of Georgia Press, 2025).

Jack Hurst, *Nathan Bedford Forrest: A Biography* (New York: Alfred A. Knopf, 1994).

Clark Leonard Miller, "Let Us Die to Make Men Free: Political Terrorism in Post-Reconstruction Mississippi, 1877–1895" (PhD Dissertation, University of Minnesota, 1983).

Michael Newton, *The Ku Klux Klan in Mississippi: A History* (Jefferson, NC: McFarland, 2010).

Elaine Frantz Parsons, *Ku-Klux: The Birth of the Klan During Reconstruction* (Chapel Hill: University of North Carolina, 2015).

George C. Rable, *But There Was No Peace: The Role of Violence in the Politics of Reconstruction* (Athens: University of Georgia Press, 1984).

Campbell F. Scribner, "Surveying the Destruction of African American Schoolhouses in the South, 1864–1876," *Journal of the Civil War Era* 10 (December 2020).

Julius E. Thompson, *Lynchings in Mississippi: A History, 1865–1965* (Jefferson, NC: McFarland, 2007).

Alan W. Trelease, *White Terror: The Ku Klux Klan Conspiracy and Southern Reconstruction* (New York: Harper & Row, 1971).

Kidada E. Williams, *I Saw Death Coming: A History of Terror and Survival in the War Against Reconstruction* (New York: Bloomsbury Publishing, 2023).

Media and the Press

Richard H. Abbott, *For Free Press and Equal Rights: Republican Newspapers in the Reconstruction South* (Athens: University of Georgia Press, 2004).

Thomas B. Alexander, "Persistent Whiggery in Mississippi: The *Hinds County Gazette*," *Journal of Mississippi History* 23 (April 1961).

Hodding Carter, *Their Words Were Bullets: The Southern Press in War, Reconstruction, and Peace* (Athens: University of Georgia Press, 1969).

Patricia Freeman, "The Times of London and Reconstruction of the Southern States: 1865–1877" (PhD Dissertation, University of Washington, 1977).

Donald B. Kelley, "Intellectual Isolation: Gateway to Secession in Mississippi," *Journal of Mississippi History* 36 (1974).

August Meier, *Negro Thought in America, 1880–1915* (Ann Arbor: University of Michigan Press, 1969).

David L. Porter, "The Mississippi Press and the Election of 1860," *Journal of Mississippi History* 34 (1972).

Thomas Adams Upchurch, "Speaking on Behalf of the Vagabond Rebels: The Mississippi Press on Race and Reconstruction in 1865," *Journal of Mississippi History* 61 (Winter 1999).

Religion

John K. Bettersworth, "Mississippi Unionism: The Case of the Reverend James A. Lyon," *Journal of Mississippi History* 1 (October 1939).

Steve Longenecker, *Pulpits of the Lost Cause: The Faith and Politics of Former Confederate Chaplains During Reconstruction* (Tuscaloosa: University of Alabama Press, 2023).

Margaret DesChamps Moore, "Religion in Mississippi," *Journal of Mississippi History* 22 (1960).

George C. Rable, *God's Almost Chosen Peoples: A Religious History of the American Civil War* (Chapel Hill: University of North Carolina Press, 2010).

Randy J. Sparks, "Mississippi's Apostle of Slavery: James Smylie and the Biblical Defense of Slavery," *Journal of Mississippi History* 51 (1989).

Randy J. Sparks, *Religion in Mississippi* (Jackson: University Press of Mississippi, 2001).

John W. Storey, "Southern Baptists and the Racial Controversy in the Churches and Schools During Reconstruction," *Mississippi Quarterly* 31 (1977–1978).

Jemar Tisby, *The Color of Compromise: The Truth About the American Church's Complicity in Racism* (Grand Rapids, MI: Zondervan, 2019).

Charles Wilson, "Baptized in Blood: Southern Religion and the Cult of the Lost Cause, 1865–1920" (PhD Dissertation, University of Texas, 1977).

PERSONALITIES

Mississippi Officials Generally

Biographical and Historical Memoirs of Mississippi, vol. 2, pts. 1 and 2 (Gretna, LA: Firebird, reprinted 1999).

Robert Jenkins, "Black Voices in Reconstruction: The Senate Careers of Hiram R. Revels and Blanche K. Bruce" (Master's Thesis, Mississippi State University, 1975).

Howard N. Rabinowitz, ed., *Southern Black Leaders of the Reconstruction Era* (Chicago: University of Illinois Press, 1982).

Clayton Rand, *Men of Spine in Mississippi* (Gulfport, MS: Dixie, 1940).

Dunbar Rowland, ed., *Mississippi: Comprising Sketches of Counties, Towns, Events, Institutions, and Persons, Arranged in Cyclopedic Form* (Atlanta: Southern Historical Publishing Association, 1907).

Dunbar Rowland, ed., *The Official and Statistical Register, State of Mississippi* (Nashville: Press of the Brandon Printing Company, 1908).

George Alexander Sewell and Margaret L. Dwight, *Mississippi Black History Makers* (Jackson: University Press of Mississippi, 1984).

Cecil L. Sumners, *The Governors of Mississippi* (Gretna, LA: Pelican, 1998).

Dean Faulkner Wells and Hunter Cole, *Mississippi Heroes* (Jackson: University Press of Mississippi, 1980).

Mississippi Republicans

James Lusk Alcorn

Lillian A. Pereyra, *James Lusk Alcorn: Persistent Whig* (Baton Rouge: Louisiana State University Press, 1966).

Mary Fisher Robinson, "A Sketch of James Lusk Alcorn," *Journal of Mississippi History* 12 (1950).

P. L. Rainwater, "Letters of James Lusk Alcorn," *Journal of Southern History* 3 (May 1937).

Adelbert Ames

Blanche Ames, *Adelbert Ames: Broken Oaths and Reconstruction in Mississippi: 1835–1933* (New York: Argosy-Antiquarian, 1964).

Harry Benson, "The Public Career of Adelbert Ames, 1861–1876" (PhD Dissertation, University of Virginia, 1975).

S. David Buice II, "The Military and Civil Career of Adelbert Ames" (Master's Thesis, University of Southern Mississippi, 1963).

Michael J. Megelsh, *Adelbert Ames, the Civil War, and the Creation of Modern America* (Kent, OH: Kent State University Press, 2024).

Blanche K. Bruce

Lawrence Otis Graham, *The Senator and the Socialite: The True Story of America's First Black Dynasty* (New York: HarperCollins, 2006).

Kenneth Eugene Mann, "Blanche Kelso Bruce: United States Senator Without a Constituency," *Journal of Mississippi History* 38 (1976).

Nicholas Patler, "A Black Vice President in the Gilded Age? Senator Blanche Kelso Bruce and the
   National Republican Convention of 1860," *Journal of Mississippi History* 71 (Summer 2009).
Melvin I. Urofsky, "Blanche K. Bruce: United States Senator, 1875–1881," *Journal of Mississippi
   History* 29 (May 1967).

Charles Caldwell

Herbert Aptheker, "Mississippi Reconstruction and the Negro Leader Charles Caldwell,"
   Science and Society (Fall 1947).

Thomas Cardozo

Euline W. Brock, "Thomas W. Cardozo: Fallible Black Reconstruction Leader," *Journal of
   Southern History* 47 (May 1981).

James Lynch

William C. Harris, "James Lynch: Black Leader in Southern Reconstruction," *Historian* 34
   (November 1971).
Peter Barr Miazza, *Voices Heard From the Grave: Lives and Stories of People Buried in
   Greenwood Cemetery* (Saline, MI: McNaughton and Gunn, 2018).

John Roy Lynch

Frank C. Bell, "The Life and Times of John R. Lynch: A Case Study, 1847–1939," *Journal of
   Mississippi History* 38 (February 1976).
John Roy Lynch, *The Autobiography of John Roy Lynch: Reminiscences of an Active Life,* Negro
   American Biographies and Autobiographies, edited by John Hope Franklin (Chicago:
   University of Chicago Press, 1970).
James McLaughlin, "John R. Lynch: the Reconstruction Politician, A Historical Perspective"
   (PhD Dissertation, Ball State University, 1981).

Albert T. Morgan

Albert T. Morgan, *Yazoo: On the Picket Line of Freedom in the South, A Personal Narrative*
   (1884; repr., Columbia: University of South Carolina Press, 2000).

Hiram R. Revels

Billy W. Libby, "Senator Hiram Revels of Mississippi Takes His Seat, January-February, 1870,"
   Journal of Mississippi History 37 (November 1975).
Julius Thompson, "Hiram R. Revels, 1827–1901: A Biography" (PhD Dissertation, Princeton
   University, 1973).

Mississippi Democrats

Albert G. Brown

James Byrne Ranck, *Albert Gallatin Brown: Radical Southern Nationalist* (Philadelphia: Porcupine, 1974).

Jefferson Davis

Michael B. Ballard, *A Long Shadow: Jefferson Davis and the Final Days of the Confederacy* (Jackson: University Press of Mississippi, 1986).
William J. Cooper Jr., *Jefferson Davis, American* (New York: Alfred A. Knopf, 2000).
William J. Cooper Jr., ed., *Jefferson Davis: The Essential Writings* (New York: Modern Library, 2003).
William C. Davis, *Jefferson Davis: The Man and His Hour* (New York: HarperCollins, 1991).
Jordan Thomas, "Jefferson Davis," *Harper's New Monthly Magazine* 31 (October 1865).
W. Stuart Towns, "To Preserve the Traditions of Our Fathers: The Post-War Speaking Career of Jefferson Davis," *Journal of Mississippi History* 52 (1990).

James Z. George

James Z. George, *The Political History of Slavery in the United States* (New York: Neale, 1915).
Timothy B. Smith, *James Z. George: Mississippi's Great Commoner* (Jackson: University Press of Mississippi, 2012).

William Harris Hardy

Toney A. Hardy, *No Compromise with Principle: Autobiography and Biography of William Harris Hardy* (New York: Stratford, 1946).

Benjamin Humphreys

Lizzie George Henderson, "Private Letters of Mrs. Humphreys," *Publications of the Mississippi Historical Society* 3 (1900).
P. L. Rainwater, "The Autobiography of Benjamin Grubb Humphreys," *Mississippi Valley Historical Review* 21 (September 1934).

L. Q. C. Lamar

Wirt Armistead Cate, *Lucius Q. C. Lamar: Secession and Reunion* (New York: Russell & Russell, 1935).
Willie D. Halsell, "The Friendship of L. Q. C. Lamar and Jefferson Davis," *Journal of Mississippi History* 6 (1944).
Michael H. Hoffheimer, "L. Q. C. Lamar, 1825–1893," *Mississippi Law Journal* 63 (Fall 1993).
Edward Mayes, *Lucius Q. C. Lamar: His Life, Times, and Speeches* (Nashville: Publishing House of the Methodist Episcopal Church, South, 1896).
James B. Murphy, *L. Q. C. Lamar: Pragmatic Patriot* (Baton Rouge: Louisiana State University Press, 1973).
Frank E. Shanahan Jr., "L. Q. C. Lamar: An Evaluation," *Journal of Mississippi History* 26 (May 1964).

James H. Stone, ed., "L. Q. C. Lamar's Letters to Edward Donaldson Clark, 1868–1885, Part I: 1868–1873" *Journal of Mississippi History* 35 (1973).

James H. Stone, ed., "L. Q. C. Lamar's Letters to Edward Donaldson Clark, 1868–1885, Part II: 1874–1878" *Journal of Mississippi History* 37 (1975).

John Pettus

Robert W. Dubay, *John Jones Pettus, Mississippi Fire-Eater: His Life and Times, 1813–1867* (Jackson: University Press of Mississippi, 1975).

John Marshall Stone

Ben Earl Kitchens, *John Marshall Stone: Mississippi's Honorable and Longest Serving Governor* (Iuka, MS: Thornwood, 2014).

William Yerger

Sever Eubank, "The Yerger Case: A Side Light of Reconstruction" (Master's Thesis, Colorado College, 1950).

Members of Congress

Philip Avillo, "Slave State Republicans in Congress, 1861–1877" (PhD Dissertation, University of Arizona, 1975).

Michael J. Birkner, Randall M. Miller, and John W. Quist, *The Worlds of James Buchanan and Thaddeus Stevens* (Baton Rouge: Louisiana State University Press, 2019).

Jeffrey Boutwell, *Boutwell: Radical Republican and Champion of Democracy* (New York: W.W. Norton, 2025).

Fawn M. Brodie, *Thaddeus Stevens: Scourge of the South* (New York: W. W. Norton, 1959).

Alfred R. Conkling, *The Life and Letters of Roscoe Conkling* (New York: Charles L. Webster, 1889).

David Donald, *Charles Sumner and the Coming of the Civil War* (New York: Alfred A. Knopf, 1961).

David Donald, *Charles Sumner and the Rights of Man* (New York: Alfred A. Knopf, 1970).

Philip Dray, *Capitol Men: The Epic Story of Reconstruction Through the Lives of the First Black Congressmen* (Boston: Houghton Mifflin Company, 2008).

William James Hull Hoffer, *The Caning of Charles Sumner: Honor, Idealism, and the Origins of the Civil War*, (Baltimore: Johns Hopkins University Press, 2010).

Janice Hood, "Brotherly Hate: A Quantitative Study of Southern Reconstruction Congressmen" (PhD Dissertation, Washington State University, 1974).

David M. Jordan, *Roscoe Conkling of New York: Voice in the Senate*, (Ithaca, NY: Cornell University Press, 1971).

Ralph Korngold, *Thaddeus Stevens: A Being Darkly Wise and Rudely Great* (New York: Harcourt, Brace, 1955).

D. Laurence Rogers, *Apostles of Equality: The Birneys, the Republicans, and the Civil War* (East Lansing: Michigan State University Press, 2011).

Rebecca E. Zietlow, *The Forgotten Emancipator: James Mitchell Ashley and the Ideological Origins of Reconstruction* (New York: Cambridge University Press, 2018).

UNITED STATES PRESIDENTS

John Y. Simon, *The Union Forever: Lincoln, Grant, and the Civil War* (Lexington: University Press of Kentucky, 2012).

Brooks D. Simpson, *The Reconstruction Presidents* (Lawrence: University of Kansas Press, 1998).

Abraham Lincoln

David Herbert Donald, *Lincoln* (New York: Simon & Schuster, 1995).

Eric Foner, *The Fiery Trial: Abraham Lincoln and American Slavery* (New York: W. W. Norton, 2010).

William Lee Miller, *Lincoln's Virtues: An Ethical Biography* (New York: Alfred A. Knopf, 2002).

James Oakes, *The Radical and the Republican: Frederick Douglass, Abraham Lincoln, and the Triumph of Antislavery Politics* (New York: W. W. Norton, 2007).

Ronald C. White Jr., *A. Lincoln: A Biography* (New York: Random House, 2009).

Andrew Johnson

Howard K. Beale, *The Critical Years: A Study of Andrew Johnson and Reconstruction* (New York: Ungar, 1958).

Paul H. Bergeron, *Andrew Johnson's Civil War and Reconstruction*, (Knoxville: University of Tennessee Press, 2011).

Winbourne Magruder Drake, ed., "A Mississippian's Appraisal of Andrew Johnson: Letters of James T. Harrison, December 1865," *Journal of Mississippi History* 17 (1955).

Annette Gordon-Reed, *Andrew Johnson* (New York: Henry Holt, 2011).

Eric L. McKitrick, *Andrew Johnson and Reconstruction* (Chicago: University of Chicago Press, 1960).

David O. Stewart, *Impeached: The Trial of President Andrew Johnson and the Fight for Lincoln's Legacy* (New York: Simon & Schuster, 2009).

Brenda Wineapple, *The Impeachers: The Trial of Andrew Johnson and the Dream of a Just Nation* (New York: Random House, 2019).

Ulysses S. Grant

Josiah Bunting III, *Ulysses S. Grant* (New York: Henry Holt, 2004).

Charles W. Calhoun, *The Presidency of Ulysses S. Grant* (Lawrence: University Press of Kansas, 2017).

Ron Chernow, *Grant* (New York: Penguin, 2017).

William B. Hesseltine, *Ulysses S. Grant: Politician* (New York: Frederick Ungar, 1935).

John F. Marszalek, ed., *The Personal Memoirs of Ulysses S. Grant: The Complete Annotated Edition* (Cambridge, MA: Harvard University Press, 2017).

William S. McFeely, *Grant: A Biography* (Norwalk, CT: Easton, 1981).

Geoffrey Perret, *Ulysses S. Grant: Soldier and President* (New York: Random House, 1997).

John Reeves, *Soldier of Destiny: Slavery, Secession and the Redemption of Ulysses S. Grant* (New York: Pegasus Books, 2023).

Ryan P. Semmes, *Exporting Reconstruction: Ulysses S. Grant and a New Empire of Liberty* (Columbia: University of South Carolina Press, 2024).

John Y. Simon, ed., *The Papers of Ulysses S. Grant*, vols. 6–26 (Carbondale and Edwardsville: Southern Illinois University Press).

Brooks D. Simpson, *Let Us Have Peace: Ulysses S. Grant and the Politics of War and Peace, 1861–1868* (Chapel Hill: University of North Carolina Press, 1997).

Jean Edward Smith, *Grant* (New York: Simon & Schuster, 2001).

John Russell Young, *Around the World with General Grant*, abridged; edited and introduced by Michael Fellman (Baltimore: Johns Hopkins University Press, 2002).

Rutherford B. Hayes

Hans L. Trefousse, *Rutherford B. Hayes* (New York: Henry Holt, 2002).

OF RELEVANCE TO RECONSTRUCTION IN MISSISSIPPI

Civil War Era

Michael B. Ballard, *Civil War Mississippi: A Guide* (Jackson: University Press of Mississippi, 2000).

William J. Cooper Jr., *Approaching Civil War and Southern History* (Baton Rouge: Louisiana State University Press, 2019).

Bernarr Cresap, *Appomattox Commander: The Story of General E. O. C. Ord* (New York: A. S. Barnes, 1981).

Joseph G. Dawson III, *Army Generals and Reconstruction: Louisiana, 1862–1877* (Baton Rouge: Louisiana State University Press, 1982).

Charles B. Dew, *Apostles of Disunion: Southern Secession Commissioners and the Causes of the Civil War* (Charlottesville: University of Virginia Press, 2016 and 2001).

David Donald, ed., *Why the North Won the Civil War* (Baton Rouge: Louisiana State University Press, 1960).

Kevin Dougherty, *Strangling the Confederacy: Coastal Operations of the American Civil War* (Philadelphia: Casemate, 2010).

Robert W. Dubay, "Mississippi Political, Civilian, and Military Realities of 1861: A Study in Frustration and Confusion," *Journal of Mississippi History* 36 (1974).

Caroline E. Janney, *Ends of War: The Unfinished Fight of Lee's Army after Appomattox* (Chapel Hill: University of North Carolina Press, 2021).

Bruce Levine, *The Fall of the House of Dixie: The Civil War and the Social Revolution That Transformed the South* (New York: Random House, 2013).

William A. Love, "Reminiscences of the Closing Days of the War of Secession," *Publications of the Mississippi Historical Society*, Centenary Series 4 (1921).

Roger Lowenstein, *Ways and Means: Lincoln and His Cabinet and the Financing of the Civil War* (New York: Penguin, 2022).

M. Philip Lucas, "To Carry Out Great Fundamental Principles: The Antebellum Southern Political Culture," *Journal of Mississippi History* 52 (1990).

Peter Maslowski, *Treason Must Be Made Odious: Military Occupation and Wartime Reconstruction in Nashville, Tennessee, 1862–65* (Millwood, NY: KTO, 1978).

James M. McPherson, *This Mighty Scourge: Perspectives on the Civil War* (Oxford: Oxford University Press, 2007).

James McPherson, *The War That Forged a Nation: Why the Civil War Still Matters* (New York: Oxford University Press, 2015).

Donald L. Miller, *Vicksburg: Grant's Campaign That Broke the Confederacy* (New York: Simon & Schuster, 2019).

Michael O'Brien, *Intellectual Life and the American South, 1810–1860* (Chapel Hill: University of North Carolina Press, 2010).

Christopher J. Olsen, *The American Civil War: A Hands-On History* (New York: Hill & Wang, 2006).

Gerald R. Powell, Matthew C. Cordon, and J. Barto Arnold III, *Civil War Blockade-Runners* (College Station, TX: Institute of Nautical Archaeology, 2012).

James W. Silver, "The Breakdown of Morale in Central Mississippi in 1864: Letters of Judge Robert S. Hudson," *Journal of Mississippi History* 16 (1954).

James W. Silver, ed., *Mississippi in the Confederacy* (Baton Rouge: Louisiana State University Press, 1961).

Timothy B. Smith, *Corinth 1862: Siege, Battle, Occupation* (Lawrence: University Press of Kansas, 2012).

Timothy B. Smith, *The Siege of Vicksburg: Climax of the Campaign to Open the Mississippi River, May 23–July 4, 1863* (Lawrence: University Press of Kansas, 2021).

Mark Thornton and Robert B. Ekelund Jr., *Tariffs, Blockades, and Inflation: The Economics of the Civil War* (Wilmington, DE: Scholarly Resources, 2004).

Ben Wynne, *Mississippi's Civil War: A Narrative History* (Macon, GA: Mercer University Press, 2006).

Lost Cause, Monuments, and Memory

A good overview of this topic is Gaines M. Foster, *The Limits of the Lost Cause: Essays on Civil War Memory* (Baton Rouge: Louisiana State University Press, 2024).

Catherine Clinton, ed., *Confederate Statutes and Memorialization* (Athens: University of Georgia Press, 2019).

Karen L. Cox, *Dixie's Daughters: The United Daughters of the Confederacy and the Preservation of Confederate Culture* (Gainesville: University Press of Florida, 2003).

Karen L. Cox, *No Common Ground: Confederate Monuments and the Ongoing Fight for Racial Justice* (Chapel Hill: University of North Carolina Press, 2021).

Carole Emberton and Bruce E. Baker, eds., *Remembering Reconstruction: Struggles over the Meaning of America's Most Turbulent Era* (Baton Rouge: Louisiana State University Press, 2017).

Susan T. Falck, *Remembering Dixie: The Battle to Control Historical Memory in Natchez, Mississippi, 1865–1941* (Jackson: University Press of Mississippi, 2019).

Drew Gilpin Faust, *The Creation of Confederate Nationalism: Ideology and Identity in the Civil War South* (Baton Rouge: Louisiana State University Press, 1988).

Gaines M. Foster, *Ghosts of the Confederacy: Defeat, the Lost Cause, and the Emergence of the New South, 1865 to 1913* (New York: Oxford University Press, 1987).

Gaines M. Foster, *The Limits of the Lost Cause: Essays on Civil War Memory* (Baton Rouge, Louisiana State University Press, 2024).

Gary W. Gallagher and Alan T. Nolan, eds., *The Myth of the Lost Cause and Civil War History* (Bloomington: Indiana University Press, 2000).

Michael J. Goleman, *Your Heritage Will Still Remain: Racial Identity and Mississippi's Lost Cause* (Jackson: University Press of Mississippi, 2017).

Christopher Alan Graham, *Faith, Race, and the Lost Cause: Confessions of a Southern Church* (Charlottesville: University of Virginia Press, 2023).

Sheldon Hackney, *Magnolias Without Moonlight: The American South from Regional Confederacy to National Integration* (New Brunswick, NJ: Transaction, 2005).

Keith S. Hebert, *Cornerstone of the Confederacy: Alexander Stephens and the Speech That Defined the Lost Cause* (Knoxville: University of Tennessee Press, 2021).

Caroline E. Janney, *Remembering the Civil War: Reunion and the Limits of Reconciliation* (Chapel Hill: University of North Carolina Press, 2013).

James W. Loewen and Edward H. Sebesta, eds., *The Confederate and Neo-Confederate Reader: The "Great Truth" About the "Lost Cause"* (Jackson: University Press of Mississippi, 2010).

Edward A. Pollard, *The Lost Cause: A New Southern History of the War of the Confederates* (New York: E. B. Treat, 1867).

K. Stephen Prince, *Stories of the South: Race and Reconstruction of Southern Identity, 1865–1915* (Chapel Hill: University of North Carolina Press, 2014).

Charles Reagan Wilson, *Baptized in Blood: The Religion of the Lost Cause, 1865–1920* (Athens: University of Georgia Press, 1980).

Charles Reagan Wilson, *The Southern Way of Life: Meanings of Culture and Civilization in the American South* (Chapel Hill: University of North Carolina Press, 2022).

Kirk Savage, *Standing Soldiers, Kneeling Slaves: Race, War, and Monument in Nineteenth-Century America* (Princeton, NJ: Princeton University Press, 1997).

Ty Seidule, *Robert E. Lee and Me: A Southerner's Reckoning with the Myth of the Lost Cause* (New York: St. Martin's, 2020).

Donald Yacovone, *Teaching White Supremacy: America's Democratic Ordeal and the Forging of Our National Identity* (New York: Pantheon Books, 2022).

Howard Zinn, *The Southern Mystique* (New York: Alfred A. Knopf, 1970).

Secession

William L. Barney, *The Secessionist Impulse: Alabama and Mississippi in 1860* (Princeton, NJ: Princeton University Press, 1974).

Christopher J. Olsen, *Political Culture and Secession in Mississippi: Masculinity, Honor, and the Antiparty Tradition, 1830–1860* (Oxford: Oxford University Press, 2000).

Percy Lee Rainwater, *Mississippi: Storm Center of Secession, 1856–1861* (Baton Rouge: Otto Claitor, 1938).

Timothy B. Smith, *The Mississippi Secession Convention: Delegates and Deliberations in Politics and War, 1861–1865* (Jackson: University Press of Mississippi, 2014).

Thomas H. Woods, "A Sketch of the Mississippi Secession Convention of 1861—its Membership and Work," *Publications of the Mississippi Historical Society* 6 (1902).

Slavery

Ira Berlin, *Many Thousands Gone: The First Two Centuries of Slavery in North America* (Cambridge, MA: Harvard University Press, 1998).

David Brion Davis, *The Problem of Slavery in the Age of Emancipation* (New York: Alfred A. Knopf, 2014).

Peter Kolchin, *American Slavery: 1619–1877* (New York: Hill & Wang, 1993).

Michael P. Mills, "Slave Law in Mississippi from 1817–1861," *Mississippi Law Journal* 71 (Fall 2001).

Frederick Law Olmsted, *The Cotton Kingdom: A Traveler's Observations on Cotton and Slavery in the American Slave States, 1853–1861* (New York: DaCapo, 1996).

John C. Rodrigue, *Freedom's Crescent: The Civil War and the Destruction of Slavery in the Lower Mississippi Valley* (New York: Cambridge University Press, 2023).

Alfred H. Stone, "The Early Slave Laws of Mississippi," *Publications of the Mississippi Historical Society* 2 (1899).

Charles Sydnor, *Slavery in Mississippi* (Gloucester, MA: Peter Smith, 1965).

Sean Wilentz, *No Property in Man: Slavery and Antislavery at the Nation's Founding* (Cambridge, MA: Harvard University Press, 2018).

AFTER RECONSTRUCTION

Stephen Cresswell, *Multi-Party Politics in Mississippi, 1877–1902* (Jackson: University Press of Mississippi, 1995).

Willie D. Halsell, "The Bourbon Period in Mississippi Politics, 1875–1890," *Journal of Southern History* 11 (November 1945).

Albert D. Kirwan, *Revolt of the Rednecks: Mississippi Politics, 1876–1925* (New York: Harper & Row, 1951).

Dorothy Overstreet Pratt, *Sowing the Wind: The Mississippi Constitutional Convention of 1890* (Jackson: University Press of Mississippi, 2018).

John David Smith, ed., *When Did Southern Segregation Begin?* (New York: Bedford/St. Martin's, 2002).

C. Vann Woodward, *The Burden of Southern History* (Baton Rouge: Louisiana State University Press, 1960).

C. Vann Woodward, *Origins of the New South, 1877–1913* (Baton Rouge: Louisiana State University Press, 1951).

C. Vann Woodward, *The Strange Career of Jim Crow*, rev. ed. (New York: Oxford University Press, 1957).

THE DUNNING SCHOOL ERA AUTHORS

American and Mississippi Reconstruction Historiography

By and About the Dunning School Era

Claude G. Bowers, *The Tragic Era: The Revolution After Lincoln* (New York: Houghton Mifflin, 1929).

E. Merton Coulter, *The South During Reconstruction, 1865–1877* (Baton Rouge: Louisiana State University Press, 1947).

William Archibald Dunning, *Reconstruction: Political and Economic, 1865–1877* (New York: Harper & Row, 1907).

Walter L. Fleming, *Documentary History of Reconstruction: Political, Military, Social, Religious, Educational, and Industrial, 1865 to the Present Time* (Cleveland, OH: Arthur H. Clark, 1907).

Dunbar Rowland, *History of Mississippi: The Heart of the South* (Chicago: S. J. Clarke, 1925).

John David Smith and J. Vincent Lowery, *The Dunning School: Historians, Race, and the Meaning of Reconstruction* (Lexington: University Press of Kentucky, 2013).

Studies in Southern History and Politics (Port Washington, NY: Kennikat, 1964 and 1914) ("Inscribed to William Archibald Dunning by his former pupils the authors.")

Richard Taylor, *Destruction and Reconstruction: Personal Experiences of the Late War* (1877; repr., New York: Longmans, Green, 1955).

Mississippi Reconstruction Historiography

Rebecca Miller Davis, "The Three R's—Reading, 'Riting, and Race: The Evolution of Race in Mississippi History Textbooks," *Journal of Mississippi History* 72 (Spring 2010).

Thomas Edwards, "Reconstructing Reconstruction: Changing Historical Paradigms in Mississippi," *Journal of Mississippi History* 51 (August 1989).

Patricia Galloway, "Archives, Power, and History: Dunbar Rowland and the Beginning of the State Archives of Mississippi (1902–1936)," *American Archivist* 69 (Spring/Summer, 2006).

John Edmond Gonzales, "Some Further Observations on the Recent Writing of Mississippi History," *Journal of Mississippi History* 41 (1979).

Sanford W. Higginbotham, "The Writing of Mississippi History: A Brief Survey," *Journal of Mississippi History* 20 (1958).

William D. McCain, *Mississippiana for Public, High School, and Junior College Libraries* (self-published in Jackson, Mississippi by the author in 1941; copy at Mississippi Department of Archives and History).

Richard Aubrey McLemore and Nannie Pitts McLemore, "Histories of Mississippi," *Journal of Mississippi History* 9 (1947).

Neil R. McMillen, "Reconstruction and Its Aftermath: Mississippi History, 1865–1890," *Journal of American History* 77 (June 1990).

Eugene R. Mechelke, "Some Observations on Mississippi's Reconstruction Historiography," *Journal of Mississippi History* 33 (February 1971).

Charles S. Sydnor, "Historical Activities in Mississippi in the Nineteenth Century," *Journal of Southern History* 3 (1938).

Charles S. Sydnor, ed., "Letters from Franklin L. Riley to Herbert B. Adams, 1894–1901," *Journal of Mississippi History* 2 (1940).

Reconstruction Historiography Generally

Howard K. Beale, "On Rewriting Reconstruction History," *American Historical Review* 45 (July 1940).

Herman Belz, "The New Orthodoxy in Reconstruction Historiography," *Reviews in American History* 1 (March 1973).

LaWanda Cox and John H. Cox, "Negro Suffrage and Republican Politics: The Problem of Motivation in Reconstruction Historiography," *Journal of Southern History* 33 (August 1967).

W. E. B. DuBois, "Reconstruction and Its Benefits," *American Historical Review* 15 (July 1910).

Eric Foner, "Reconstruction Revisited," *Reviews in American History* 10 (December 1982).

John Hope Franklin, "Mirror for Americans: A Century of Reconstruction History," *American Historical Review* 85 (February 1980).

John Hope Franklin, "Whither Reconstruction Historiography?" *Journal of Negro Education* 17 (Autumn 1948).

Fletcher M. Green, "Walter Lynwood Fleming: Historian of Reconstruction," *Journal of Southern History* 2 (November 1936).

Robert Green, "Reconstruction Historiography: A Source of Teaching Ideas," *Social Studies* 82 (July/August 1991).

Larry Kincaid, "Victims of Circumstance: An Interpretation of Changing Attitudes Toward Republican Policy Makers During Reconstruction," *Journal of American History*, 57 (June 1970).

David A. Lincove, ed., *Reconstruction in the United States: An Annotated Bibliography* (Westport, CT: Greenwood, 2000).

John R. Lynch, "Some Historical Errors of James Ford Rhodes," *Journal of Negro History* 2 (October 1917).

August Meier, "An Epitaph for the Writing of Reconstruction History?" *Reviews in American History* 9 (March 1981).

Armstead L. Robinson, "Beyond the Realm of Social Consensus: New Meanings of Reconstruction for American History," *Journal of American History* 68 (September 1981).

Hannah Rosen, "Teaching Race and Reconstruction," *Journal of the Civil War Era* 7 (March 2017).

Francis B. Simkins, "New Viewpoints of Southern Reconstruction," *Journal of Southern History* 5 (February 1939).

Brooks D. Simpson, "Mission Impossible: Reconstruction Policy Reconsidered," *Journal of the Civil War Era* 6 (March 2016).

Bernard A. Weisberger, "The Dark and Bloody Ground of Reconstruction Historiography," *Journal of Southern History* 25 (November 1959).

Harold D. Woodman, "Sequel to Slavery: The New History Views the Postbellum South," *Journal of Southern History* 43 (November 1977).

Index

Page numbers in *italics* indicate illustrations.

About the Author

Photo courtesy of the author

Jere Nash is a native of Greenville, Mississippi, served as a political consultant for forty-five years, and is coauthor of three books of Mississippi history. His first book, *Mississippi Politics: The Struggle for Power, 1976–2006*, written with Andy Taggart, won awards from the Mississippi Historical Society and the Mississippi Institute of Arts and Letters.